BALL FOUR

JIM BOUTON
Edited by
Leonard Shecter

BALL FOUR

My Life and
Hard Times
Throwing
the Knuckleball
in the Big Leagues

 THE WORLD PUBLISHING COMPANY
NEW YORK AND CLEVELAND

Published by The World Publishing Company
2231 West 110th Street, Cleveland, Ohio 44102
Published simultaneously in Canada by
Nelson, Foster & Scott Ltd.

FIFTH PRINTING— JULY, 1970

Library of Congress Catalog Card Number: 78–120125
DESIGNED BY BOB ANTTA
Printed in the United States of America

WORLD PUBLISHING
TIMES MIRROR

FOR BOBBIE
Thanks, coach

CONTENTS

EDITOR'S FOREWORD

I can't even say this book was my idea. I'd known Jim Bouton since he first came up with the Yankees, was familiar with his iconoclastic views and his enthusiastic, imaginative way of expressing them, and it occurred to me that a diary of his season—even if he spent it with a minor-league team as he had the season before—might prove of great general interest. As usual, he was ahead of me. "Funny you should mention that," he said when I first brought it up. "I've been keeping notes."

Bouton talked into his tape recorder for more than seven months. Our typist, Miss Elisabeth Rehm of Jamaica, N.Y., did herculean work to keep up with the flood. There is nothing inarticulate about Jim Bouton. Before the season ended Miss Rehm had typed the equivalent of 1,500 pages (about 450,000 words) of double-spaced Bouton. From the beginning there was, fortunately, great rapport between us. I quickly found I did not need to spend a lot of time with Bouton pulling truth and anecdotes out of him. They were there, in abundance, starting with the very first tape from Arizona. We spent no more than five days together all season.

It may seem odd in an effort of this sort, but there were no disagreements. From the first we shared the opinion that the only purpose to adding to the huge volume of printed material that had been produced about baseball, was to illuminate the game as it had never been before. We resolved to reveal baseball as it is viewed by the men who play it, the frustrations and the meanness as well as the joy and the extraordinary fun. The difficulty is that to tell the truth is often, unfortunately, to offend. Bouton never flinched. It was not our purpose to offend, of course, but if in the process of telling the truth we did, so be it.

We had to make a decision, too, about the use of language. There is earthiness in baseball clubhouse language. To censor it, we felt, would be to put editorial omniscience between the reader and reality. Besides, we were not aiming this book at juveniles. Rate it X. The only thing we left out was repetitiveness.

The hardest part of editing Bouton's 1,500 pages was deciding what to leave out. There was so much that was so good, so incisive, so funny, that the choices were most difficult. In the end I managed to take it down to about 650 pages. The final cut, to about 520 manuscript pages, was made by both of us at the very last. We spent eighteen hours a day together for a week, cutting, editing, correcting, polishing. There were disagreements sometimes and frayed nerves, and we came to know each other in that special, complicated way that people who have worked very hard, very closely on a project they consider important come to know each other. I'm not sure how Bouton feels about it, but I believe I came away a better man.

LEONARD SHECTER
New York City, January 1970

INTRODUCTION

FALL, 1968

I'm 30 years old and I have these dreams.

I dream my knuckleball is jumping around like a Ping-Pong ball in the wind and I pitch a two-hit shutout against my old team, the New York Yankees, single home the winning run in the ninth inning and, when the game is over, take a big bow on the mound in Yankee Stadium with 60,000 people cheering wildly. After the game reporters crowd around my locker asking me to explain exactly how I did it. I don't mind telling them.

I dream I have pitched four consecutive shutouts for the Seattle Pilots and the Detroit Tigers decide to buy me in August for their stretch drive. It's a natural: the Tigers give away a couple of minor-league pheenoms, and the Pilots, looking to the future, discard an aging right-handed knuckleballer. I go over to Detroit and help them win the pennant with five saves and a couple of spot starts. I see myself in the back of a shiny new convertible riding down Woodward Avenue with ticker-tape and confetti covering me like snow. I see myself waving to the crowd and I can see the people waving back, smiling, shouting my name.

I dream my picture is on the cover of *Sports Illustrated* in October and they do a special "Comeback of the Year" feature on me, and all winter long I'm going to dinners and accepting trophies as the Comeback Player of the Year.

I dream all these things. I really do. So there's no use asking me why I'm here, why a reasonably intelligent thirty-year-old man who has lost his fastball is still struggling to play baseball, holding on—literally —with his fingertips. The dreams are the answer. They're why I wanted to be a big-league ballplayer and why I still want to get back on top again. I *enjoy* the fame of being a big-league ballplayer. I get a tremendous kick out of people wanting my autograph. In fact, I feel hurt if I go someplace where I think I should be recognized and no one asks me for it. I enjoy signing them and posing for pictures and answering reporters' questions and having people recognize me on the street. A lot of my friends are baseball fans, as well as my family and the kids I went to school with, and I get a kick out of knowing that they're enjoying having a connection with a guy in the big leagues. Maybe I shouldn't, but I do.

Like someone once asked Al Ferrara of the Dodgers why *he* wanted to be a baseball player. He said because he always wanted to see his picture on a bubblegum card. Well, me too. It's an ego trip.

I've heard all the arguments against it. That there are better, more important things for a man to do than spend his time trying to throw a ball past other men who are trying to hit it with a stick. There are things like being a doctor or a teacher or working in the Peace Corps. More likely I should be devoting myself full-time to finding a way to end the war. I admit that sometimes I'm troubled by the way I make my living. I *would* like to change the world. I *would* like to have an influence on other people's lives. And the last time I was sent down to the minor leagues a man I consider my friend said, only half-kidding, I guess, "Why don't you quit and go out and earn a living like everybody else, ya bum ya?"

I was piqued for a moment. But then I thought, what the hell, there are a lot of professions that rank even with baseball, or a lot below, in terms of nobility. I don't think there's anything so great about selling real estate or life insurance or mutual funds, or a lot of other unimportant things that people do with their lives and never give it a thought. Okay, so I'll save the world when I get a little older. I believe a man is entitled to devote a certain number of years to plain enjoyment and driving for some sort of financial security.

You can always be a teacher or a social worker when you've reached thirty-five. That gives me five more years and I'm going to use them all. You can't always be a major-league baseball player. There are only a certain number of years—and I know how few they are—in which you can play baseball. And I think you can be a better teacher if you *have* played baseball, if only for the fact that the kids will listen to you more. I think I'll have more value at *anything* I do later on for having been a baseball player. I believe that, foolish as it is, Stan Musial has more influence with American kids than any geography teacher. Ted Williams is better known than any of our poets, Mickey Mantle more admired than our scientists. Perhaps I can put my own small fame to work later on.

Right now, the fact is that I love the game, love to play it, I mean. Actually, with the thousands of games I've seen, baseball bores me. I have no trouble falling asleep in the bullpen, and I don't think I'd ever pay my way into a ballpark to watch a game. But there's a lot to being *in* the game, a lot to having those dreams.

A lot of it is foolishness too, grown men being serious about a boy's game. There's pettiness in baseball, and meanness and stupidity beyond belief, and everything else bad that you'll find outside of baseball. I haven't enjoyed every single minute of it and when I've refused to conform to some of the more Neanderthal aspects of baseball thinking I've been an outcast. Yet there's been a tremendous lot of good in it for me and I wouldn't trade my years in it for anything I can think of. If you doubt me, take a look at my fingertips; I'm growing calluses on them.

So what follows, then, is not so much a book about Jim Bouton as it is about what I've seen and felt playing baseball, for a season, up and down with an expansion team, and for what has been for me so far, a lifetime.

Part 1 They Made Me What I Am Today

NOVEMBER
15

I signed my contract today to play for the Seattle Pilots at a salary of $22,000 and it was a letdown because I didn't have to bargain. There was no struggle, none of the give and take that I look forward to every year. Most players don't like to haggle. They just want to get it over with. Not me. With me signing a contract has been a yearly adventure.

The reason for no adventure this year is the way I pitched last year. It ranged from awful to terrible to pretty good. When it was terrible, and I had a record of 0 and 7, or 2 and 7 maybe, I had to do some serious thinking about whether it was all over for me. I was pitching for the Seattle Angels of the Pacific Coast League. The next year, 1969, under expansion, the club would become the Seattle Pilots of the American League. The New York Yankees had sold me to Seattle for $20,000 and were so eager to get rid of me they paid $8,000 of my $22,000 salary. This means I was actually sold for $12,000, less than half the waiver price. Makes a man think.

In the middle of August I went to see Marvin Milkes, the general manager of the Seattle Angels. I told him that I wanted some kind of guarantee from him about next year. There were some businesses with long-range potential I could go into over the winter and I would if I was certain I wasn't going to be playing ball.

"What I would like," I told him, "is an understanding that no matter what kind of contract you give me, major league or minor league, that it will be for a certain minimum amount. Now, I realize you don't know how much value I will be for you since you haven't gone through the expansion draft and don't know the kind of players you'll have. So I'm not asking for a major-league contract, but just a certain minimum amount of money."

"How much money are you talking about?" Milkes said shrewdly.

"I talked it over with my wife and we arrived at a figure of $15 or $16,000. That's the minimum I could afford to play for, majors or minors. Otherwise I got to go to work."

To this Milkes said simply, "No."

I couldn't say I blamed him.

It was right about then, though, that the knuckleball I'd been experimenting with for a couple of months began to do things. I won two games in five days, going all the way, giving up only two or three hits. I was really doing a good job and everyone was kind of shocked. As the season drew to a close I did better and better. The last five days of the season I finished with a flurry, and my earned-run average throwing the knuckleball was 1.90, which is very good.

The last day of the season I was in the clubhouse and Milkes said he wanted to see me for a minute. I went up to his office and he said, "We're going to give you the same contract for next year. We'll guarantee you $22,000." This means if I didn't get released I'd be getting it even if I was sent down to the minors. I felt like kissing him on both cheeks. I also felt like I had a new lease on life. A knuckleball had to be pretty impressive to impress a general manager $7,000 worth. Don't ever think $7,000 isn't a lot of money in baseball. I've had huge arguments over a lot less.

3

When I started out in 1959 I was ready to love the baseball establishment. In fact I thought big business had all the answers to any question I could ask. As far as I was concerned clubowners were benevolent old men who wanted to hang around the locker room and were willing to pay a price for it, so there would never be any problem about getting paid decently. I suppose I got that way reading Arthur Daley in *The New York Times*. And reading about those big salaries. I read that Ted Williams was making $125,000 and figured that Billy Goodman made $60,000. That was, of course, a mistake.

I signed my first major-league contract at Yankee Stadium fifteen minutes before they played "The Star-Spangled Banner" on opening day, 1962. That's because my making the team was a surprise. But I'd had a hell of a spring. Just before the game was about to start Roy Hamey, the general manager, came into the clubhouse and shoved a contract under my nose. "Here's your contract," he said. "Sign it. Everybody gets $7,000 their first year."

Hamey had a voice like B. S. Pully's, only louder. I signed. It wasn't a bad contract. I'd gotten $3,000 for playing all summer in Amarillo, Texas, the year before.

I finished the season with a 7–7 record and we won the pennant and the World Series, so I collected another $10,000, which was nice. I was much better toward the end of the season than at the beginning. Like I was 4–7 early but then won three in a row, and Ralph Houk, the manager, listed me as one of his six pitchers for the stretch pennant race and the Series.

All winter I thought about what I should ask for and finally decided to demand $12,000 and settle for $11,000. This seemed to me an eminently reasonable figure. When I reported to spring training in Ft. Lauderdale—a bit late because I'd spent six months in the army—Dan Topping, Jr., son of the owner, and the guy who was supposed to sign all the lower-echelon players like me, handed me a contract and said, "Just sign here, on the bottom line."

I unfolded the contract and it was for $9,000—if I made the team. I'd get $7,000 if I didn't.

If I made the team?

"Don't forget you get a World Series share," Topping said. He had a boarding-school accent that always made me feel like my fly was open or something. "You can always count on that."

"Fine," I said. "I'll sign a contract that guarantees me $10,000 more at the end of the season if we don't win the pennant."

He was shocked. "Oh, we can't do that."

"Then what advantage is it to me to take less money?"

"That's what we're offering."

"I can't sign it."

"Then you'll have to go home."

"All right, I'll go home."

"Well, give me a call in the morning, before you leave."

I called him the next morning and he said to come over and see him. "I'll tell you what we're going to do," he said. "We don't usually do this, but we'll make a big concession. I talked with my dad, with Hamey, and we've decided to eliminate the contingency clause—you get $9,000 whether you make the club or not."

"Wow!" I said. Then I said no.

"That's our final offer, take it or leave it. You know, people don't usually do this. You're the first holdout we've had in I don't know how many years."

I said I was sorry. I hated to mess up Yankee tradition, but I wasn't going to sign for a $2,000 raise. And I got up to go.

"Before you go, let me call Hamey," Topping said. He told Hamey I was going home and Hamey said he wanted to talk to me. I held the phone four inches from my ear. If you were within a mile of him, Hamey really didn't need a telephone. "Lookit, son," he yelled. "You better sign that contract, that's all there's gonna be. That's it. You don't sign that contract you're making the biggest mistake of your life."

I was twenty-four years old. And scared. Also stubborn. I said I wouldn't sign and hung up.

"All right," Topping said, "how much do you want?"

"I was thinking about $12,000," I said, but not with much conviction.

"Out of the question," Topping said. "Tell you what. We'll give you $10,000."

My heart jumped. "Make it ten-five," I said.

"All right," he said. "Ten-five."

The bastards really fight you.

For my ten-five that year I won 21 games and lost only 7. I had a 2.53 earned-run average. I couldn't wait to see my next contract.

By contract time Yogi Berra was the manager and Houk had been promoted to general manager. I decided to let Houk off easy. I'd ask for $25,000 and settle for $20,000, and I'd be worth every nickel of it. Houk offered me $15,500. Houk can look as sincere as hell with those

5

big blue eyes of his and when he calls you "podner" it's hard to argue with him. He said the reason he was willing to give me such a big raise right off was that he didn't want to haggle, he just wanted to give me a top salary, more than any second-year pitcher had ever made with the Yankees, and forget about it.

"How many guys have you had who won 21 games in their second year?" I asked him.

He said he didn't know. And, despite all the "podners," I didn't sign.

This was around January 15. I didn't hear from Houk again until two weeks before spring training, when he came up another thousand, to $16,500. This was definitely final. He'd talked to Topping, called him on his boat, ship to shore. Very definitely final.

I said it wasn't final for me, I wanted $20,000.

"Well, you can't make twenty," Houk said. "We never double contracts. It's a rule."

It's a rule he made up right there, I'd bet. And a silly one anyway, because it wouldn't mean anything to a guy making $40,000, only to somebody like me, who was making very little to start with.

The day before spring training began he went up another two thousand to $18,500. After all-night consultations with Topping, of course. "Ralph," I said, real friendly, "under ordinary circumstances I might have signed this contract. If you had come with it sooner, and if I hadn't had the problem I had last year trying to get $3,000 out of Dan Topping, Jr. But I can't, because it's become a matter of principle."

He has his rules, I have my principles.

Now I'm a holdout again. Two weeks into spring training and I was enjoying every minute of it. The phone never stopped ringing and I was having a good time. Of course, the Yankees weren't too happy. One reason is that they knew they were being unfair and they didn't want anybody to know it. But I was giving out straight figures, telling everybody exactly what I'd made and what they were offering and the trouble I'd had with Dan Topping, Jr.

One time Houk called and said, "Why are you telling everybody what you're making?"

"If I don't tell them, Ralph," I said, "maybe they'll think I'm asking for ridiculous figures. They might even think I asked for $15,000 last year and that I'm asking for thirty now. I just want them to know I'm being reasonable."

6

And Houk said something that sounded like: "*Rowrorrowrowrr.*" You ever hear a lion grumble?

You know, players are always told that they're not to discuss salaries with each other. They want to keep us dumb. Because if Joe Pepitone knows what Tom Tresh is making and Tresh knows what Phil Linz is making, then we can all bargain better, based on what we all know. If one of us makes a breakthrough, then we can all take advantage of it. But they want to keep us ignorant, and it works. Most ballplayers in the big leagues do not know what their teammates are making. And they think you're strange if you tell. (Tom Tresh, Joe Pepitone, Phil Linz and I agreed, as rookies, to always tell. After a while only Phil and I told.)

Anyway, on March 8, my birthday, Houk called me and said he was going to deduct $100 a day from his offer for every day I held out beyond March 10. It amounted to a fine for not signing, no matter what Houk said. What he said was, "Oh no, it's not a fine. I don't believe in fining people." And I'm sure it never occurred to him just how unfair a tactic this was. Baseball people are so used to having their own way and not getting any argument that they just don't think they *can* be unfair. When I called Joe Cronin, president of the league, to ask if Houk could, legally, fine me, he said, "Walk around the block, then go back in and talk some more."

After walking around the block and talking it over with my dad, I chickened out. Sorry about that. I called Houk and said "Okay, you win. I'm on my way down." I salved my wounds with the thought that if I had any kind of a year this time I'd really sock it to him.

Still, if I knew then what I know now, I wouldn't have signed. I'd have called him back and said, "Okay, Ralph, I'm having a press conference of my own to announce that for every day you don't meet my demand of $25,000 it will cost you $500 a day. Think that one over."

Maybe I wouldn't have gotten $25,000, but I bet I would've gotten more than eighteen-five. I could tell from the negative reaction Ralph got in the press. And I got a lot of letters from distinguished citizens and season-ticket holders, all of them expressing outrage at Houk. That's when I realized I should have held out. It was also when Ralph Houk, I think, started to hate me.

The real kicker came the following year. I had won eighteen games and two in the World Series. Call from Houk:

"Well, what do you want?"

7

"Ordinarily, I'd say winning eighteen and two in the Series would be worth about an $8,000 raise."

"Good, I'll send you a contract calling for twenty-six-five."

"But in view of what's happened, last year and the year before that, it will have to be more."

"How much more?"

"At least thirty."

"We couldn't do that. It's out of the question."

A couple of days later he called again. "Does $28,000 sound fair to you?"

"Yes it does, very fair. In fact there are a lot of fair figures. Twenty-eight, twenty-nine, thirty, thirty-two. I'd say thirty-three would be too high and twenty-seven on down would be unfair on your part."

"So you're prepared to sign now."

"Not yet. I haven't decided."

A week later he called again and said he'd sent me the contract I wanted—$28,000.

"Now, wait a minute. I didn't say I'd sign for that."

"But you said it was a fair figure."

"I said there were a lot of fair figures in there. I said thirty-two was fair too."

"You going back on your word? You trying to pull a fast one on me?"

"I'm not trying to pull anything on you. I just haven't decided what I'm going to sign for. I just know that twenty-eight isn't it."

By now he's shouting. "Goddammit, you're trying to renege on a deal."

So I shouted back. "Who the hell do you people think you are, trying to bully people around? You have a goddam one-way contract, and you won't let a guy negotiate. You bulldozed me into a contract my first year when I didn't know any better, you tried to fine me for not signing last year, and now you're trying to catch me in a lie. Why don't you just be decent about it? What's an extra thousand or two to the New York Yankees? You wonder why you get bad publicity. Well, here it is. As soon as the people find out the kind of numbers you're talking about they realize how mean and stupid you are."

"All right. Okay. Okay. No use getting all hot about it."

When the contract came it was like he said, $28,000. I called and told him I wouldn't sign it. I told him I wouldn't play unless I got thirty.

"No deal," he said, and hung up.

Moments later the phone rang. Houk: "Okay, you get your thirty. Under one condition. That you don't tell anybody you're getting it."

"Ralph, I can't do that. I've told everybody the numbers before. I can't stop now."

Softly. "Well, I wish you wouldn't."

Just as softly. "Well, maybe I won't."

When the newspaper guys got to me I felt like a jerk. I also felt I owed Ralph a little something. So when they said, "Did you get what you wanted?" I said, "Yeah." And when they said, "What did you want?" I said, "Thirty." But I said it very low.

Now, I think, Ralph really hated my guts. Not so much because I told about the thirty but because he thought I went back on my word.

Four years later Ralph Houk was still angry. By this time I had started up a little real-estate business in New Jersey. A few friends, relatives and I pooled our money, bought some older houses in good neighborhoods, fixed them up and rented them to executives who come to New York on temporary assignment. Houses like that are hard to find and Houk, who lives in Florida, needed one for the '69 season. After a long search he found exactly what he wanted. Then he found out I owned it. He didn't take it. Too bad, it might have been kind of fun to be his landlord.

Of course, I may misunderstand the whole thing. It's easy to misunderstand things around a baseball club. Else how do you explain my friend Elston Howard? We both live in New Jersey and during my salary fights we'd work out a bit together. And he always told me, "Stick to your guns. Don't let them push you around." Then he'd go down to spring training and he'd say to the other guys, "That Bouton is really something. Who does he think he is holding out every year? How are we gonna win a pennant if the guys don't get in shape? He should be down here helping the club."

I didn't help the club much in 1965, which was the year the Yankees stopped winning pennants. I always had a big overhand motion and people said that it looked, on every pitch, as though my arm was going to fall off with my cap. I used to laugh, because I didn't know what they meant. In 1965 I figured it out. It was my first sore arm. It was my only sore arm. And it made me what I am today, an aging knuckleballer.

My record that year was 4–15, and we finished sixth. It wasn't all my fault. I needed lots of help and got it. Nevertheless my spirits were high waiting for my contract because of something Houk had said. He'd been painted into a corner with Roger Maris. There was a story around that after Maris hit the 61 home runs he got a five-year, no-cut contract. But he'd had a series of bad years and should have been cut. So to take himself off the hook with Maris, Houk said that anybody who had a poor year because of injuries would not be cut. Fabulous, man, I thought. That's me.

When I got my contract it called for $23,000, a $7,000 cut.

"But, Ralph, I was injured and you said . . ."

"You weren't injured."

"The hell I wasn't."

"Then how come you pitched 150 innings?"

"I was trying to do what I could, build my arm up, trying to help the team."

Somehow he remained unmoved. I guessed it was my turn to be humble. "Look, Ralph, I know that people think you lost the battle with me last year and I know some of the players are upset that I got $30,000. So I know there are reasons you have to cut me. Tell you what. Even though I could stand firm on the injury thing if I wanted to, I'll make a deal with you. Cut me $3,000 and we can both be happy." He said okay.

After that, it was all downhill. Which is how come I was happy to be making $22,000 with the Seattle Pilots.

Part 2

"My Arm Isn't Sore, It's Just a Little Stiff"

FEBRUARY

26

Tempe

Reported to spring camp in Tempe, Arizona, today, six days late. I was on strike. I'm not sure anybody knew it, but I was.

I had signed my contract before I knew there was going to be a players' strike and I was obligated to report on time. I found that out at the big meeting the players had with Marvin Miller, the players' representative, at the Biltmore in New York earlier this month. I'm much in sympathy with what Miller is doing and I think, given the circumstances, he won a great victory. I think the owners understand now that we're going to stick together—even the big stars, who don't have that much at stake. Still, I was going to live up to my contract and report on time. What made me change my mind was a phone call I made to Lou Piniella, a twenty-six-year-old rookie who'd been in the Baltimore and Cleveland organizations.

Since the Pilots were not a team yet we had no player representative, so the three or four Pilots at the meeting in the Biltmore were asked to call four or five teammates each to tell them what happened. I reached Lou in Florida and he said that his impulse was to report, that he was scared it would count against him if he didn't, that he was just a rookie looking to make the big league and didn't want anybody to get angry at him. But also that he'd thought it over carefully and decided he should support the other players and the strike. So he was not reporting.

That impressed the hell out of me. Here's a kid with a lot more at stake than I, a kid risking a once-in-a-lifetime shot. And suddenly I felt a moral obligation to the players. I decided not to go down.

The reason nobody knew I was on strike, though, was that I'd asked the Pilots to find a place for me and my family in Tempe. They couldn't. So I said that as long as there were no accommodations I couldn't report. I sort of took it both ways. You take your edges where you can. I learned that playing baseball.

As soon as I got to the park I went right over to Marvin Milkes' office and we shook hands and he asked me if I had a nice flight. He also said, "There's been a lot of things said about the strike and I know you've said some things about it, but we're going to forget all that and start fresh. We have a new team and everybody starts with a clean slate. I'm giving some people a new opportunity. I've got a man in the organization who is a former alcoholic. I've even got a moral degenerate that I know of. But as far as I'm concerned we're going to let bygones be bygones and whatever has been said in the past—and I know you've said a lot of things—we'll forget all about it and start fresh."

I said thanks. I also wondered where, on a scale of one to ten, a guy who talks too much falls between a former alcoholic and a moral degenerate.

I know a lot of guys on the club. Greg Goossen is one. He's a catcher, a New York Met castoff, and is up out of Triple-A. Two years ago I was playing against Goose in the International League. There was a bunt back toward the pitcher and Goose came running out from behind the plate yelling "First base! First base!" at the top of his lungs. Everyone in the ballpark heard him. The pitcher picked up the ball and threw it to second. Everybody safe. And as Goose walked back behind the plate, looking disgusted, I shouted at him from the dugout, "Goose, he had to consider the source."

I guess I got to him, because the first time he saw me—two years later—he said, "Consider the source, huh?"

The only thing separating my locker from the boiler in the clubhouse is Roland Sheldon's. Rollie said it had only exploded once this spring, fortunately while the clubhouse was empty. Reminded me of my first Yankee spring training in St. Petersburg. I was just there for a look and shared a broom closet with Jim Pisoni, an outfielder. I think my number was 129½. The higher the number, the worse chance they think you have of making the club.

The year I was given 56 was the year I made the club. Toward the end of spring training Big Pete, the No. 1 Yankee clubhouse man, Pete Sheehy, said, "Listen, I got a better number for you. I can give you 27." I told him I'd keep 56 because I wanted it to remind me of how close I was to not making the club. I still wear 56. I'm still close to not making the club.

Sal Maglie is the pitching coach—Sal the Barber of the New York Giants, my boyhood hero. He still looks like he'd knock down his grandmother. He's got those big evil-looking black eyes. Looks something like Snoopy doing the vulture bit. He told me I'd be pitching five minutes of batting practice today and that I'd be the last pitcher.

That might mean something. It's one of the tiny things you look for all during spring training. You watch who you follow in batting practice, try to find out how many minutes you've pitched compared with other pitchers, decide whether you're with the good squad or the bad squad, whether the morning workout is more important than the afternoon workout. The Yankees would divide the squad into morning and afternoon groups and they'd always say it didn't mean a thing, just two groups for convenience. Except that the morning group always had Mickey Mantle, Roger Maris, Elston Howard, Whitey Ford and guys like that. The afternoon group would have a bunch of guys named Dick Berardino. I never saw a guy hit or pitch himself off the afternoon list.

I'm not sure it's going to be that way here, though. They seem to

14

have strung us all out pretty well. I can't really read anything into the way it's broken up. And that makes me nervous.

Before the first workout, Joe Schultz, the manager (he's out of the old school, I think, because he *looks* like he's out of the old school, short, portly, bald, ruddy-faced, twinkly-eyed), stopped by while I was having a catch. "How you feeling, Jim?" he asked. I wonder what he meant by that?

FEBRUARY
27

This is the first time I've trained in Arizona. I think I'm going to like it. The park is in a beautiful setting—the center of a desolate area, flat, empty, plowed fields in all directions. And then, suddenly, a tremendous rocky crag rises abruptly to look down over the park. At any moment you expect to see a row of Indians on horseback charging around the mountain and into the park shooting flaming arrows. I'd always heard you couldn't work up a sweat in Arizona. Not true. I ran fifteen or twenty windsprints and I can testify that anyone who can't sweat in Arizona hasn't tried.

The clubhouse here is kind of cramped and the Yankees would probably sneer at it, but there's a soda fountain—Coca-Cola, root beer, 7-Up, cold, on tap, freebie. If Pete Previte saw this he'd go crazy. Little Pete's the No. 2 Yankee clubhouse man and he had this mark-up sheet. Everytime you took a soft drink you were supposed to make a mark next to your name so he'd know how much to charge you. He spent the whole day going around saying, "Hey, mark 'em up. Don't forget to mark 'em up. Hey, Bouton, you're not marking 'em up." And he'd never have enough orange juice, although that's what everybody wanted most. One time I asked him, "Pete, how come you're always out of orange juice?" And he said, "If I get it, you guys just drink it up."

We were running short sprints and I guess a couple of tongues were beginning to hang out because somebody yelled, "Marvin Miller, where are you now that we need you?"

But don't let baseball players kid you. All we did today was run about fifteen short sprints and Jim Ryun probably runs that much before he brushes his teeth in the morning. Baseball players are far from being the best-conditioned athletes in the world.

I think I detect a bit of Drill Instructor in Ron Plaza. He's the coach who gives us our daily calisthenics. He's got those California-tan good looks, All-American, and he says, "Gentlemen, today we're going to do some jumping-jacks." I don't mind the calisthenics, I think they're good for us. I just don't like the idea of Plaza looking as if he's enjoying himself. He reminds me of the DI I had who always called us "people." "All right, you people, today we are going to do fifty pushups, people." He looked like *he* was enjoying himself too.

And then there's always the coach who hollers, "Good day, good day to work." It could be raining a hurricane out there with mud up to your ass and some coach is sure to say, "Good day, good day to work."

Bob Lasko is in camp. I was glad to see him. He's a pitcher, right-handed, and we broke in together in the Rookie League in Kearny, Nebraska, in 1959. He's thirty years old, too, and he's never pitched a game in the major leagues. He's a real big guy and I remember he had a tremendous fastball and a great overhand curve. I used to try to model my motion after his. I always seemed to be better when he was around. We roomed together in Amarillo in 1961 and became close friends. His trouble was that the Yankees tried to hide him. He pitched in about sixty innings all season at Kearny. One time he got in a ball-game, struck out the side for three innings and they took him out of the game and put another pitcher in. The rule at the time was that if you didn't get drafted your first year the organization could keep you for three years without moving you up to a major-league roster. Since he pitched so few innings, no one drafted him.

Bob told me today that he'd once complained about it. "I talked to one of the Yankee coaches," he said. "I told him I didn't think the Yankees had been fair to me and his neck started to get all red and he started to holler and damn, we almost had a fight, right there."

I asked him who the coach was.

"Ralph Houk," he said.

Still, some of it is probably Lasko's fault. He led a couple of leagues in ERA (earned-run average), but he seemed to have built up a sort of minor-league psychology. He was always an easy-going guy and as a result got pushed around. I know that in the big leagues, if you come to spring training real cocky it will antagonize a lot of the players but it will help your chances with management. They notice you and they say, "Look at that son of a bitch, boy he's really brazen. Let's stick him in there and see what he looks like." And a quiet guy like Lasko might never get a good look.

So why does he go on? For one thing, he's like me. He likes baseball. And there is still the hope that he can get just a few years in the big leagues. That would make getting a job in the future that much easier. Plus, it says here, you can't beat the hours.

FEBRUARY
28

Decided to get a haircut today. My hair was quite long and the sideburns were thick and heavy. I didn't want to have a long-hair image, so I got a really short haircut and look like a stormtrooper. It's terrible, but it won't hurt me. You never can tell how spring training is going to go. I could be one of those borderline cases and the difference between making the club and not making it might be the length of my hair.

I wore a mustache all winter and thought I looked pretty good. Cut it off before I came down. Richie Allen can wear those porkchop sideburns of his if he wants because he hits all those home runs. What's standing between me and *my* mustache is about twenty wins.

When I walked into the clubhouse with my new haircut, Sheldon said, "Now you look like the old Bulldog." Bulldog! That's what they called me when I was a big winner with the Yankees. Bulldog. *Gruff!* This is the impression I wanted to create all along. Maybe they'll think because my hair is short I got my fastball back. You got to use all your weapons.

One thing you *don't* do is what Steve Hovley did. He's an outfielder I played with in Seattle last year, twenty-four years old, intellectual type. He told Milkes that he wouldn't report until March 22 because he wanted to finish up some college classes. Milkes told him he'd never make the team if he waited that long and Steve said, well, he'd looked at the roster and didn't think he could make it anyway. Besides, he thought he could use another year or two in Triple-A.

That's a big mistake. No matter what the truth of it is, Milkes will now always think that Steve doesn't have enough desire to be a major leaguer. There are times you have to show hustle, even if it's false.

Lots of holler out there in the infield. "Fire it in there, baby." "C'mon, Joey." "Chuck it in there." And the word for *that,* friends, is false chatter. You don't hear it as much during the season because nobody's nervous and nobody has to impress a coach who thinks you're trying harder if you holler "Hey, whaddaya say?" You only hear it in spring training—and in high-school baseball. I remember when I was in high school, even if we lost the game, the coach would say, "I liked your chatter out there, a lot of holler. That's what I like to see." So if you couldn't hit, you hollered.

Another thing you need in spring training is a knack for looking busy. There really isn't much to do in spring training, and it's a lot like being in the army, where the sergeant will never say anything to you if you *look* like you're doing something. I mean just stopping to tie your shoelace, or walking along briskly as if you have someplace to go. That's what pepper games are, really: looking busy without actually doing anything.

Sheldon was talking about that today. He says what he does is walk around policing up the area and no one ever hollers at him for that. He also walks back and forth to the dugout as if he's on an important mission. "Do something," Shellie said. "Walk, bend, throw a ball into your glove, swing a bat, but don't be standing there with your legs crossed and your arms folded."

Also in camp is Steve Barber, pitcher, lefthanded, who was with the Yankees last year. Naturally we got to talking about Jim Turner, The Colonel, Southern Fried Chicken variety. Turner's the pitching coach over there and has been voted the champion frontrunner of the civilized world. In case you forgot, you could always tell how you were doing by the way The Colonel said good morning. If he said, "Well now, good morning, Jimsie boy," that meant you'd won your last two or three games and were in the starting rotation. If he nodded his head to you and said, "Jimbo, how you doin', how you doin'?" you were still in the starting rotation, but your record probably wasn't much over .500. If he just said, "Mornin'," that meant you were on the way down, that you'd probably lost four out of five and it was doubtful if you would be getting any more starts. If he simply looked at you and gave a solemn nod, that meant you might get some mop-up relief work, or you might not, but you definitely weren't starting anymore and would never get into a close game again. And if he looked past you, over your shoulder, as if you didn't exist, it was all over and you might as well pack your bag because you could be traded or sent down at any moment.

MARCH

1

Joe Schultz stopped by again today to say a kind word. I noticed he was making it his business to say something each day to most of the guys. He may look like Nikita Khrushchev, but it means a lot anyway. I'm sure most of us here feel like leftovers and outcasts and marginal players and it doesn't hurt when the manager massages your ego a bit.

I was moved up from last to next-to-last, and then to second, for my five minutes of batting practice, and I've decided there's no significance to the position. My arm feels good; no pain, no problems. Every once in a while I let a fastball fly and it comes out of my hand real easy and seems like it took no effort. I can almost hear a voice in the back of my mind whispering, "You can go back to it, you can find it, you can find your old fastball and you'll be great again." Of course, I've heard that siren song in my head before and I've won a total of fourteen games in the last four years. So I'm going to stick with my knuckleball. I'll probably throw it 90 percent of the time, and if my other stuff comes around for me, I'll probably cut it down to about 40 or 50 percent. But I've got to remember that if it wasn't for my knuckleball I'd probably be back in New Jersey, raising chickens or something. Remember, stupid, remember!

19

One of the problems is that the hitters hate to hit against my knuckleball in batting practice. They don't like pitchers to work on anything out there. They want you to lay it in there and let them smash it over the fence. So I compromise. For each seven swings they get I give them two or three knuckleballs.

Gerry McNertney (now, there's one of the great names in baseball) was catching me today, and when I threw a knuckler that didn't do much I hollered in to him, "Is it better than Wilhelm's? Is it? Huh?"

Nert caught Hoyt Wilhelm when they were with the White Sox and he tried to be kind. He laughed and said, "Not bad, not bad." I asked Nert about Wilhelm's knuckleball and he said one of his problems was that he was throwing it about three-quarters because he didn't have the strength to come with it straight overhand anymore. He is, after all, at least forty-six by his own admission. Nert said it was only effective when he came straight over. "You seem to be throwing straight overhand all the time," he said, "and you should have success with it."

Things are looking up. Right now I'm thinking that I can do anything—start, relieve, be a long man or a short man. Or all of them together, every day, because the knuckleball doesn't take anything out of your arm. It's like having a catch with your sister. I'm starting to get that old fire in my stomach again.

There are some things I ought to explain about the knuckleball. I was about thirteen years old the first time I threw it. I was very little at the time, the littlest and skinniest kid in the neighborhood, but I could play ball. At least I could hit and run. Although I had a good arm, I couldn't throw very hard. So when I saw a picture on the back of a cereal package explaining how to throw the knuckleball, I thought I'd try it.

There was a picture of Dutch Leonard and a picture of how he held the ball, and about a paragraph explaining it. The knuckleball isn't thrown with the knuckles, of course. It's thrown with the fingertips, and the principle is to release the ball so that it leaves all the fingertips at the same time without any spin on the ball. The air currents and humidity take over and cause the ball to turn erratically and thus move erratically.

Wilhelm was doing pretty good with the Giants at the time, and that was another reason to try it—except that my hand was so small I couldn't hold the ball with three fingers like everybody else did. I had to hold it with all five. I still do. It's kind of freaky, I guess, but as a

20

result I throw it harder than anybody else. Anyway, it took about a week before I could get it to knuckle at all. I remember once I threw one to my brother and hit him right in the knee. From then on I was totally entranced.

I used the knuckleball all the way through high school and college, about 50 percent of the time. I might have been the youngest junkball pitcher in America. After a couple of years in the minors, however, I started to get bigger and stronger and started to overpower people with my fastball. So I phased the knuckleball out.

I never really used it again until 1967. My arm was very sore and I was getting my head beat in. Houk put me into a game against Baltimore and I didn't have a thing, except pain. I got two out and then, with my arm hurting like hell, I threw four knuckleballs to Frank Robinson and struck him out. The next day I got sent to Syracuse. Even so, it wasn't until the last part of the next season that I began throwing it again. The idea that you've lost your regular stuff is very slow in coming.

Sal the Barber came over to me today and said, "You're looking smoother than I remember seeing you in the last few years. You're getting your body into it now. I remember thinking that you were using up your force before you even released the ball and looked as though you never released it the same way twice."

That made me feel pretty good. Then Bob Lemon, manager of the Pilots' Triple-A Vancouver club, came over and said "Hello, Bill," and Mike Ferraro, an infielder, hollered while I was pitching. "Fire it in there, Bob." Thanks a lot, Hank, thanks a lot, Sam.

MARCH
2

Tommy Harper, who's an infielder listed as an outfielder on the roster, reported today. He's certain to make this team, along with guys like Barber, McNertney, Gary Bell, Mike Hegan, Ray Oyler, Don Mincher, Rich Rollins and Tommy Davis. Harper just got out of the

Air Force and they asked him if he wanted to re-up, as they call it. They told him he could come back for two years and they'd make him a staff sergeant. And he told them, "I wouldn't re-up for two years if you made me a general."

We had sliding and pick-off drills today and I noticed a lot of the guys having trouble. Lasko was standing next to me during one of them and said, "Hey, I thought this was a simple game."

It's tough in these drills to perform like you should perform because you're much better off in athletics if you do things instinctively. I suppose that's what they mean when they say baseball isn't a thinking man's game. If you have to think about it, you tend to do things mechanically rather than naturally.

I've always felt there were three kinds of athletes. First, there's the guy who does everything instinctively and does it right in the first place. I think Willie Mays is that kind of guy, and so was Mickey Mantle. I don't think these guys can articulate what they're doing, they just know what to do and they go out and do it. I put Yogi Berra in this class too. I remember Yogi standing around the batting cage trying to explain hitting to some of the guys and he started to talk about his hands and his legs and he couldn't make himself clear. Then he said, "Ah, just watch me do it."

Second, there's the athlete who's intelligent. If they're pitchers they try to figure out the mechanics of rotation and the aerodynamics of the curve ball. If they're hitters they try to figure out force and velocity in relation to weight. Jay Hook comes to mind. He was a pitcher with an engineering degree from Northwestern University. He had all the tools: big, strong, good stuff. But he was always too involved with the mechanics of pitching. Ballplayers often say, "Quit thinking, you're hurting the club." I really believe you can think too much in this game, and Hook always did.

The third kind is the one who is intelligent enough to know that baseball is basically an instinctive game. I like to think that's me. So what *I* do, kiddies, is work hard, stay in shape, practice—then, once I'm on the field I let my instincts take over. Also I don't smoke.

Euphoria: Bob Lemon called me by my right name.

Now a few hundred words about Frank Crosetti, coach. Cro, as we fondly call him, is fifty-eight years old, bald as an egg and, we all assume, rich as Croesus. We assume he's rich because he's always checking the stock tables and because between 1932, when he began to play for the Yankees, and 1968, when he left as a coach, he had pulled down some 23 World Series shares in addition to his considerable salary. And no one has noticed him spending very much of it. In addition, starting at age fifty, he elected—possibly through foolishness, more likely through greed—to collect his player pension. When the pension was raised by a considerable amount—only for those who had not yet started to draw on it—Cro sued to get the higher rate. He lost, but I haven't noticed any holes in his shoes.

I have to give him credit, though. He's out there every day, his beady little eyes shining, not an ounce of fat on him, taking calisthenics with all us kids and never missing a beat; jumping-jacks, pushups and everything. Another thing he does is get up every morning at six-forty-five and take a long, pre-breakfast stroll. When he was with the Yankees, once in a while he'd run into some of us coming back from a night on the town. We'd try to get by with a "Good morning, Cro, nice day." I doubt he was fooled. There was even some suspicion that Cro was turning in reports on the hours some players kept, although it has never been confirmed and must be considered a rumor.

Cro's a coach like every other coach, except his twin fortes are saving baseballs (he's a strong company man) to the point of jumping into the stands after them, and chasing photographers off the field. He's the self-appointed photographer-chaser of the Western world. If a photographer should just happen to step into fair territory during practice here's Cro, screaming from the other side of the field, "Hey, what're you doing? Get off the field!" He's got this high, squeaky voice, and when he was with the Yankees half the club was able to imitate it. So at night, when we'd be getting on a bus and you couldn't see individual players, Cro would get aboard and somebody would yell in his voice, "Hey, for crissakes, get the hell off the bus. What're you photographers doing on the bus?"

Don't get the idea that I consider Cro a lovable old man, butt of little jokes but a heart of gold. Like most coaches he's a bit of a washerwoman and sometimes a pain in the ass. I had an odd run-in with him when I was with the Yankees. The unwritten rule on the club was that if a pitcher was knocked out of a game early he could dress and watch it from the stands if he wished, just so long as he was back in the clubhouse after the game—in case the manager had a few nasty words to say to him. On this day we were playing a doubleheader and my wife,

23

Bobbie, was up in the stands with the kids—I have three now, Michael, five, Kyong Jo, four, and Laurie three. I got knocked out early and decided to dress and watch the rest of the game in the stands with my wife. After the game I'd get back into uniform for the second game.

Crosetti, who was coaching at third, spotted me in the stands and told The Colonel that I was in my streetclothes and looked like I was about to go home. So The Colonel, who loved to get this kind of information, told Big Pete to go up into the stands and get me. At first I thought Big Pete was kidding, but when I found out he wasn't I was burned up.

I got into my uniform and, when the game was over and Cro came into the clubhouse, I went over and told him to keep his big nose out of my business, that he was a goddam busybody and should have been watching the game instead of me. So he yelled back at me and I yelled back at him—bright, clever things that little boys yell at each other, and all of a sudden he jumped up and started punching me.

Now, *there's* a dilemma. I don't want to get hit, even by the skinny old Cro. At the same time I don't want to hit *Frank Crosetti,* for crissakes. So I sort of covered up and started backing off. Besides, I couldn't help it, I was laughing. At that point my friend Elston Howard, quickly sizing up the great dangers involved, came running over, threw a body block at me and knocked me down. I picked myself up, went over to my locker and sat down. I should have let it go at that. Instead I hollered over to Cro again to keep his nose out of my business and this was when Houk came over and said if I said one more word he'd knock me right off my goddam stool.

I didn't say another word. And that was the end of it, except you may be certain it was all recorded in my file, in red ink.

Hectic day for personal affairs. We moved out of the motel we'd been staying in where it cost us about $135 an hour and into a two-bedroom apartment. Nice place, heated swimming pool and all. Packing, loading, unloading, unpacking—the life of a ballplayer. It's one of the pains in the neck. On the other hand it's exciting, in a way, moving around, seeing new places.

The family loves it in Arizona. We've taken a few rides out into the desert and looked at the cactus and the beautiful rock formations, and the kids are excited about the weather getting warm enough so they can use the pool. Kyong Jo, the Korean boy we adopted, is doing great with his English. Every once in a while he'll burp and say, "Thank you." But he's getting the idea.

Got a big day tomorrow. Ten minutes of batting practice. I think I'll use the Johnny James (former Yankee pitcher) theory of batting practice. Under this theory you imagine you're in a game and you move your pitches around on the hitter, dust him off, throw sliders, the works. The hitters hate it. But it helped Johnny James make the team, at least for a while.

MARCH
3

When I was a kid I loved to go to Giant games in the Polo Grounds. And a little thing that happened there when I was about ten years old popped into my mind today. There was a ball hit into the stands and a whole bunch of kids ran after it. I spotted it first, under a seat, and grabbed for it. Just as I did, a Negro kid also snatched at it. My hand reached it a split second before his, though, and I got a pretty good grip on it. But he grabbed the ball real hard and pulled it right out of my hand. No complaint, he took it fair and square. I thought about it afterward, about what made him able to grab that ball out of my hand. I decided it had to do with the way we were brought up—me in a comfortable suburb, him probably in a ghetto. I decided that while I *wanted* the baseball, he *had to have it.*

Batting practice today. Arm felt fine after throwing, which is more than I can say for Steve Barber's. Two seconds after he threw he was in the trainer's room with an icepack on his elbow. And I haven't even had a twinge. It's kind of scary. Maybe I'm not throwing right.

Most pitchers are paranoid about their arms. You live in terror that you're going to wake up in the morning and not be able to pitch anymore. You wake up in the middle of the night and you make a throwing motion to see if it's going to hurt. In the morning the first thing you do is circle your arm just to see how it feels. In fact one of the reasons it takes injured arms so long to heal is that pitchers are constantly testing the aggravated part and making it worse. Trainers always tell you to give it a chance to get better, but what do trainers know about temptation? You got to *test*. I know sometimes I'll be out with my family, eating in a restaurant maybe, and all of a sudden I'll circle my arm over my head and I'm sure everybody thinks I'm calling the waiter or that I'm crazy. I'm just testing.

It's understandable. All a pitcher has is his arm. Pitching is a precise skill that requires a coordinated effort among many parts of the body. One small hurt and it's all gone. Like a tiddly-winks champion with a hangnail.

The guy pitching batting practice before me, fellow name of Paul Click, who won't make the team, got hit with a line drive. Instead of ducking behind the screen in front of the mound he turned his back. I guess he thought that if he turned his back and closed his eyes the ball couldn't find him. He got it in the back of the head and it opened up a lot of skin. It reminded me of the time when I was pitching in Baltimore, three, four years ago. I threw a low outside fastball to Jackie Brandt. He held back on it and at the last instant reached out and hit a line drive right back at me. I never saw the damn thing. It smacked me on the jaw and opened me up for about twelve stitches. Those were the days when I gutsed it, so I jumped right up and said I wanted to pitch. "Ralph, I'm ready, I'm ready," I said. "I can pitch." Johnny Blanchard was the catcher. "Not with two mouths you ain't, Meat," he said.

They wanted to carry me off on a stretcher but I knew if my wife heard I was carried off the field she'd have a miscarriage. So I went off under my own power, bloody towel and all, and listened carefully for the ovation. I got it.

Ovations are nice and some guys sort of milk them. Like Joe Pepitone. If he had just the touch of an injury he'd squirm on the ground for a while and then stand up, gamely. And he'd get his ovation. After a while the fans got on to him, though, and he needed at least a broken leg to move them.

There was an intrasquad game today after the workout, and although I didn't have to stay to watch it I did. That's what you call showing desire. Jim O'Toole was pitching when I got there, and his curve wasn't sharp and he was walking a lot of guys. He's got about eight kids and spring training means more to him than a lot of other guys, but he was really laboring. I felt sort of sorry for him, but not very.

Let me explain. It was rather early to be playing an intrasquad game and I thought, "I hope nobody gets hurt." Then I had to amend that in my mind. I meant "I hope *I* don't get hurt." I've always wanted everyone to do well. If I'm not playing I root for my teammates. But I don't want them to do well at my expense. Even when I was in junior high school, I'd sit there hollering encouragement and all the time I'd be saying, "Gee whiz, if he'd break his leg I could get in there and play." It's not exactly the perfect attitude, but it's the way I feel.

Last spring Fred Talbot said to me, "When I'm out there pitching, are you rooting for me, Bouton?"

"Yeah, Fred."

"Do you really hope I do well?"

"Yeah, Fred. But not at my expense."

What I should have said was, "Yeah, Fred, I hope you do well. I hope you have a helluva year down there in Triple-A." It ended up I landed in Triple-A and he stayed in the big leagues. When I was sent down I had a record of 1–0. Talbot was 1–8. I still think about that.

The mindless grind of spring training produces, as you might guess, a sort of mindlessness. This morning Mike Hegan and I were partners in calisthenics and were locked in something that looked like the Twist. And I said to Mike, "Hey, this gives me an idea for a dance."

"Hey, that's right," he said. "We'll call it the Twist."

"Right, and we'll open a string of dance halls."

"Yeah, and we can call them the Peppermint Twist."

"Right."

"But we need a front man with a great name. How about Chubby?"

"Great. We'll call him Chubby Checker."

This conversation actually took place, Doctor.

Then some guy farted and everybody laughed, and about five minutes later, in a sudden burst of quiet, he farted again and somebody hollered, "Will somebody answer the phone! Some ass keeps calling."

Uniform-measuring day. This is always a waste. They measure everybody carefully and the uniforms arrive three sizes too big. Part of the reason is that everybody is wearing tight-fitting uniforms these days. Pepitone refuses to take the field if his uniform isn't skintight. Phil Linz used to say that he didn't know why, but he could run faster in tight pants. And I understand that Dick Stuart, old Dr. Strangeglove, would smooth his uniform carefully, adjust his cap, tighten his belt and say, "I add 20 points to my average if I know I look bitchin' out there."

Mike Marshall is a righthanded pitcher who was 15–9 in the Tiger organization last season. He's got a master's degree from Michigan State. He majored in phys. ed., with a minor in mathematics. He's a cocky kid with a subtle sense of humor. He's been telling everybody that the new lower mound, which was supposed to help the hitters, actually shortens the distance the pitcher has to throw the ball. Has to do with the hypotenuse of a right triangle decreasing as either side of the triangle decreases. Therefore, says Marshall, any psychological advantage the hitters gain if the pitcher doesn't stand tall out there will be offset by the pitchers knowing that they are now closer to the plate.

Clever fellow, Marshall. He has even perfected a pick-off motion to second base that's as deadly as it is difficult to execute. He says one reason it's effective is that he leans backward as he throws the ball. I asked why, and he said, "Newton's Third Law, of course." Of course. Except the last time I tried his pick-off motion I heard grinding noises in my shoulder.

Steve Hovley sidled over to me in the outfield today and whispered into my ear, "Billy Graham is a cracker."

Although I've enjoyed being in Arizona, there are things about training in Florida I'll miss. Every spring Phil Linz and I would have dinner at Las Novedádes in Tampa and we'd order Cuban black-bean soup and *Pompano en papillót* and we'd have a bottle of wine and talk about our old days in the minor leagues (and the time Joe Pepitone stole an elevator). Even when Phil was with the Mets we'd make it a point to meet in Tampa and go to Las Novedádes.

I had the same kind of relationship with Roger Repoz and Fritz Peterson, two others guys I roomed with on the Yankees. Roger and I had this one spot in Detroit, the Italian Gardens. We'd go there for linguine with white clam sauce and we'd have a bottle of wine, and then some more linguine and another bottle of wine, then maybe another bottle of wine, and we'd stagger back to our room. When Roger was sold we made a pact that any time we got to Detroit we'd go alone to the Italian Gardens and order linguine and drink wine and stagger back to the hotel in memory of the good times we'd had.

I know when I'm in Anaheim next I'll do what Fritz Peterson and I used to think was a lot of fun. We'd rent a little car and speed along the freeways playing Spanish music as loud as the radio would go and we'd go down to the beach or into the mountains. In San Francisco Fritz and I made an inspection trip to Haight-Ashbury where the hippies offered to turn us on with LSD. We were too chicken to try.

The first roommate I had in pro ball was named Arturo Polanco and he couldn't speak a word of English. So he taught me Spanish and I taught him English. The first words he learned were "Son of a bleach." I think something was lost in translation.

MARCH
4

Mickey Mantle announced his retirement the other day and I got to thinking about the mixed feelings I've always had about him. On the one hand I really liked his sense of humor and his boy-ishness, the way he'd spend all that time in the clubhouse making up involved games of chance and the pools he got up on golf matches and the Derby and things like that.

I once invested a dollar when Mantle raffled off a ham. I won, only there was no ham. That was one of the hazards of entering a game of chance, Mickey explained.

I got back by entering a fishing tournament he organized and winning the weight division with a ten-pounder I'd purchased in a store the day before. Two years later Mantle was still wondering why I'd only caught that one big fish and why all the other fish that were caught were green and lively while mine was gray and just lay there, staring.

I also remember the time I won my first major-league game. It was a shutout against the Washington Senators in which I walked seven guys and gave up seven hits and had to pitch from a stretch position all game. They were hitting line drives all over the place and Hector (What a Pair of Hands) Lopez bailed me out with about four leaping catches in left field. When the game was over I walked back into the clubhouse and there was a path of white towels from the door to my locker, and all the guys were standing there, and just as I opened the door Mickey was putting the last towel down in place. I'll never forget him for that.

And I won't forget the time—1962, I guess it was—in Kansas City. I was sitting alone in a restaurant, eating, when Mickey and Whitey Ford came in and Mickey invited me to eat with them and picked up the tab and it made me feel good all over and like a big shot besides.

On the other hand there were all those times when he'd push little kids aside when they wanted his autograph, and the times when he was snotty to reporters, just about making them crawl and beg for a minute of his time. I've seen him close a bus window on kids trying to get his autograph. And I hated that *look* of his, when he'd get angry at somebody and cut him down with a glare. Bill Gilbert of *Sports Illustrated* once described that look as flickering across his face "like the nictitating membrane in the eye of a bird." And I don't like the Mantle that refused to sign baseballs in the clubhouse before the games. Everybody else had to sign, but Little Pete forged Mantle's signature. So there are thousands of baseballs around the country that have been signed not by Mickey Mantle, but by Pete Previte.

Like everybody else on the club I ached with Mantle when he had one of his numerous and extremely painful injuries. I often wondered, though, if he might have healed quicker if he'd been sleeping more and loosening up with the boys at the bar less. I guess we'll never know.

What we do know, though, is that the face he showed in the clubhouse, as opposed to the one he reserved for the outside world, was often one of great merriment.

I remember one time he'd been injured and didn't expect to play, and I guess he got himself smashed. The next day he looked hung over out of his mind and was sent up to pinch-hit. He could hardly see. So he staggered up to the plate and hit a tremendous drive to left field for a home run. When he came back into the dugout everybody shook his hand and leaped all over him, and all the time he was getting a standing ovation from the crowd. He squinted out at the stands and said, "Those people don't know how tough that really was."

Another thing about Mantle. He was a pretty good practical joker. One time he and Ford told Pepitone and Linz that they'd finally arrived, they were ready to go out with the big boys. Mantle told them to get dressed up, tie and all—this was in Detroit—and meet them in a place called The Flame. Mickey gave them the address and said to be sure to ask for Mickey Mantle's table.

Pepitone and Linz were like a couple of kids at Christmas. They couldn't stop talking about what a great time they were going to have with Mickey Mantle and Whitey Ford. They got all fancied up, hopped into a cab and told the driver to take them to The Flame. After about a half-hour the cab pulled up in front of a place that was in the heart of the slum section, a hole in the wall with a broken plate-glass window in front and a little broken-down sign over the door: THE FLAME. No Mantle. No Ford. No table.

Tommy Davis was in the training room having the ankle he broke in 1965 taped. I asked him if he thought it would ever be the same again and he said he doubted it, because it's supposed to take two years for a fracture and dislocation to heal and he was back playing after one. I'm sure that's true of a lot of injuries that athletes suffer. They come back too soon and the injury keeps recurring. Like I say, you can't beat the hours.

Freddy Velazquez was in the trainer's room too. He caught a foul ball on his big toe and it looked like a ripe tomato. The toenail was peeling off. He never made a sound while it was bandaged. Then he went out and played on it. Later Velazquez was talking Spanish to some of the other players and someone—I don't know who—yelled, "Talk English! You're in America now."

It was 55 degrees and blowing out there today, so I only watched a couple of innings of the intrasquad game. I was there long enough to see Marshall get hit pretty hard. Evidently the shorter hypotenuse didn't help him much. He just ran into Doubleday's First Law, which states that if you throw a fastball with insufficient speed, someone will smack it out of the park with a stick.

As penance for going home early I spent some time considering the possible fortunes of this ballclub. It's early, but it doesn't look bad at all. Except we're going to be hurting for starting pitchers. Gary Bell is probably the only legitimate starter we have. Which isn't bad for number 56.

In the back of my mind I see myself as a starter for this team. I think a knuckleball pitcher is better off starting. One reason is that there are usually men on base when a relief pitcher comes in. If his knuckle-ball is working well you might get a passed ball and a run. If it's not working well—and often it's not—you get hit. With no one on base, though, this isn't too important. The argument is simple and crystal clear. If only somebody would listen.

I asked one of the sportswriters if Joe Schultz had said anything about the way I threw today and he said, "Yeah."

"Well, what?"

"He said, 'It's too early to tell.' "

My reporting late has made this the first spring I've ever been behind anybody getting into shape. Usually I'm ready to pitch in the early games, but it looks like I'm not going to be ready here. It's quite different from my last spring with the Yankees in 1967. I was really impressive, right from the beginning. I led the club in innings pitched with thirty, and I gave up the fewest hits, fifteen, and no homers and only two or three extra-base hits. My ERA was .092, which means less than one run per game, and in one stretch I went nine innings without giving up a hit. At the end of spring training a newspaper guy said to Houk, "Wow, didn't Bouton have a great spring?" and Houk said, "You can't go by that too much. He always has a good spring." (The spring before I was 1–3 and had a 5.10 ERA.)

Another thing about that spring. This was after I'd pitched about 25 marvelous innings. Houk sat next to me in the dugout and told me, very confidentially, "You know, you're having a helluva spring, a better spring than Dooley Womack, and I think you're just the man we need in the bullpen."

What I wanted to say was: "I'm having a better spring than *who? Dooley Womack? The* Dooley Womack? I'm having a better spring than Mel Stottlemyre or Sam McDowell or Bob Gibson." That's what I *should* have said. Instead I just sat there shaking my head. He could've knocked me off my seat.

Instead he sold me to Seattle. Okay, so I had a lousy year there. That still doesn't mean Houk knew it all the time. You can make a lousy pitcher out of anybody by not pitching him. I'll always believe that's what Houk did to me. Besides, there's no way the Yankees can justify getting rid of a twenty-nine-year-old body for $12,000, and before the season is over I'm going to remind a lot of people that they did.

Steve Hovley and I had a discussion about Norman Vincent Peale's power of positive thinking. We agree it's a crock. Steve said it was like feeding false data into a computer. There comes a day when you realize you've been building a false sense of confidence and then it all breaks down and the dream is smashed.

I think that kind of thing happened with the Yankees. Houk used to tell us we were going to win the pennant, *we were going to win the pennant*. Then June rolled around and we knew we *couldn't* win the pennant, but instead of trying for second or third everybody threw in the towel and we finished ninth.

We might be building ourselves up to that kind of fall with this club. Everybody is saying we're going to be great. There's a difference between optimism and wishful thinking.

Not only did I have some tenderness in my elbow today but Sal told me I'll be pitching in the exhibition game Sunday. The tenderness will go away, but how am I going to pitch Sunday? I'm not ready. I haven't thrown to spots yet. I haven't thrown any curve balls at all. My fingers aren't strong enough to throw the knuckleball right. I've gone back to taking two baseballs and squeezing them in my hand to try to strengthen my fingers and increase the grip. I used to do that with the Yankees, and naturally it bugged The Colonel. The reason it bugged The Colonel is that he never saw anybody do it before. Besides, it wasn't his idea. "What are you doing?" The Colonel would sputter. "Put those baseballs back in the bag."

Immediately Fritz Peterson would pick up two baseballs and start doing the same thing. One day Fritz got Steve Hamilton and Joe Verbanic and about three or four other pitchers to carry two balls around with them wherever they went. It drove The Colonel out of his mind.

The following spring Fritz was removed as my roommate. The Colonel kept telling Fritz not to worry, that pretty soon he wouldn't have to room with "that Communist" anymore. And Fritz would say, "No, no, that's all right. I *want* to room with him. I *like* him. We get along great."

And The Colonel would say, "Fine, fine. We'll get it straightened out."

So one day Houk called me into his office and said, "Jim, we're switching around roommates this year. I think it will be good for everybody to have pitchers with pitchers, catchers with catchers."

"That's fine," I said. "I'm already rooming with a pitcher."

"Well, we want young pitchers to room with young pitchers, and since you've been with the club so long, we feel you deserve a single room. It's a status thing. Whitey and Mickey have single rooms, and we thought you should too."

I said that was fine with me and if he wanted Fritz to room with a young pitcher I'd take a single room.

Then Houk called Fritz in and said, "Bouton deserves a single room and you wouldn't want to stand in his way, would you?" Fritz said he wouldn't, so they put him in with Dooley Womack, young pitcher. He was three months younger than I.

They thought I was a bad influence on Fritz. The Yankees had some funny ideas about bad influence. What I did bad was talk to newspapermen and talk around the clubhouse about things that were on my mind, politics sometimes, and religion. That's breaking the rules. The word was around: don't talk to the newspapermen. Hell, baseball *needs* the newspapermen. So I broke a rule. But suppose you break the rules about staying up late and getting drunk. That's okay. It may hurt the team, but it's better than talking to newspapermen. You figure it.

As for teaching Peterson to do the wrong things, the only thing I ever taught him was how to throw that change-up he uses so effectively. And he still enjoys giving me the credit.

We were sitting around the clubhouse and I asked Sal the Barber about the days when he pitched for the Giants against the Dodgers. He said yeah, he'd never forget those days. "You know, it's a funny thing," he said. "When I pitched against the Dodgers I didn't care if it was the last game I ever pitched. I really hated that club. If I could've gotten that feeling everytime I pitched I'd have been a lot better pitcher."

I'll have that feeling at least a couple of times this year. When I pitch against the Yankees.

MARCH

6

Steve Hovley sidled over to me in the outfield and said, "To a pitcher a base hit is the perfect example of negative feedback."

Sal Maglie said he hadn't seen me working on my breaking ball, and he's right, because I haven't. So tomorrow I'll have to work on that too. Damn, I can't believe the games are starting so fast. Tomorrow's the first game and I don't even know who's pitching. Still, it will be kind of exciting to see how we do. I guess starting out with a new team is sort of like setting out to discover America. Sort of.

Gary Bell is nicknamed Ding Dong. Of course. What's interesting about it is that "Ding Dong" is what the guys holler when somebody gets hit in the cup. The cups are metal inserts that fit inside the jock strap, and when a baseball hits one it's called ringing the bell, which rhymes with hell, which is what it hurts like. It's funny, even if you're in the outfield, or in the dugout, no matter how far away, when a guy gets it in the cup you can hear it. Ding Dong.

At a pre-workout meeting Joe Schultz told us to learn the signs or it would cost us money. This is a lot different from Houk's theory. Houk's method was to be as nice to us as possible and if you missed a sign he would alibi for you. You could miss them all year and he would never get angry. I guess he figured that someday you'd come to like him enough to start paying attention to the signs. But the Yankees sure missed a lot of signs. Even when we were winning.

MARCH

7

Okay, boys and girls, tomorrow is my birthday and I'll be thirty years old. I don't feel like thirty. I look like I'm in my early twenties and I feel like I'm in my early twenties. My arm, however, is over a hundred years old.

Had our first spring-training game, the first real test for the shiny new Seattle Pilots. Today was the day. This was it. For keeps. The big one. Against Cleveland. Greg Goossen was the designated pinch-hitter under the experimental rule which allows one player to come to bat all during the game without playing in the field. "Are they trying to tell me something about my hands?" Goossen went around saying. "Are they trying to tell me something about my glove?" And after that he became the first Seattle Pilot to say "Play me or trade me."

I was watching the game today for some signs of what kind of team we're going to have this year. There were lots of them, but I'm still not sure. Like we gave up two runs in the first inning on the first four pitches and I thought, "Oh, oh. Move over, Mets." But in our half of the first we scored five runs and we went on to get nineteen in the game. I couldn't believe it. I think the people in Seattle will now start believing we have a good team. And, my God, maybe we do. We scored all those runs without Tommy Davis, or Don Mincher or Rich Rollins. Or Jim Bouton, for that matter.

I've started slowly tossing the real big overhand curve ball that once made me famous. I also threw the knuckleball to Freddy Velazquez and was gratified when McNertney came over with the big knuckleball glove and asked Velazquez if he could catch me for a while. Still can't believe I'm pitching day after tomorrow, although mentally I've started getting ready—I mean I'm getting scared. I love to pitch when I'm scared. Of all the big games I've had to pitch in my life—and I'm including high-school games, which were just as big to me as any major-league game—I always did my best work when I was scared stiff. In fact, if I'm not scared for a game I'll create some critical situations in my mind. Like, I'll pretend it's a World Series game and that it really counts big. I told Fritz Peterson about how I felt about being scared and one day before I was going to start a game he came over and whispered in my ear: "If you want to see your baby again you'll win today."

After the game Bobbie and I were at a party with Gary Bell and his wife and Steve Barber and his. Gary's wife, Nan, said she'd been anxious to meet me since she'd read in the Pilot spring guidebook that some of my hobbies were water coloring, mimicry and jewelry-making. "Everyone else has hunting and fishing, so I figured you must be a real beauty. I mean, jewelry-making?" said Nan. "Make me some earrings, you sweet thing."

Then we got to talking about some of the crazy things ballplayers do. Nan told a story of the time she called him on the road to check on a flight she was supposed to catch. She called Gary at 4:30 A.M., his time, and his roommate, Woody Held, answered the phone and said, without batting an eyelash, that Gary was out playing golf. And Gary's wife shrugged and said, "Maybe he was."

My wife and I burst out laughing when Gary asked me if I'd ever been on the roof of the Shoreham Hotel in Washington. The Shoreham is the beaver-shooting capital of the world, and I once told Bobbie that you could win a pennant with the guys who've been on that roof. "Pennant, hell," Bell said. "You could stock a whole league."

I better explain about beaver-shooting. A beaver-shooter is, at bottom, a Peeping Tom. It can be anything from peering over the top of the dugout to look up dresses to hanging from the fire escape on the twentieth floor of some hotel to look into a window. I've seen guys chin themselves on transoms, drill holes in doors, even shove a mirror under a door.

One of the all-time legendary beaver-shooters was a pretty good little lefthanded pitcher who looked like a pretty good little bald-headed ribbon clerk. He used to carry a beaver-shooting kit with him on the road. In the kit there was a fine steel awl and several needle files. What he would do is drill little holes into connecting doors and see what was going on. Sometimes he was lucky enough to draw a young airline stewardess, or better yet, a young airline stewardess and friend.

37

One of his roommates, a straight-arrow type—Fellowship of Christian Athletes and all that—told this story: the pitcher drilled a hole through the connecting door and tried to get him to look through it. He wouldn't. It was against his religion or something. But the pitcher kept nagging him. "You've *got* to see this. *Boyohboyohboy!* Just take one quick look." Straight-arrow finally succumbed. He put his eye to the hole and was treated to the sight of a man sitting on the bed tying his shoelaces.

One of the great beaver-shooting places in the minor leagues was Tulsa, Oklahoma. While "The Star-Spangled Banner" was played you could run under the stands and look up at all kinds of beaver. And anytime anyone was getting a good shot, the word would go out— "*Psst!* Section 27." So to the tune of "The Star-Spangled Banner" an entire baseball club of clean-cut American boys would be looking up the skirt of some female.

Beaver shooting can get fairly scientific. I was still in the minor leagues when we discovered that if you stuck a small hand mirror under a hotel-room door—especially in the older hotels, where there were large spaces between the door and the floor—you could see the whole room just by looking at the mirror. This was a two-man operation: one guy on his hands and knees looking at the mirror, the other at the end of the hall laying chicky, as they say. We usually sprinkled some change around on the floor so you'd have a reason being down on it if anybody caught you.

Spot a good beaver and you could draw an instant crowd. One time in Ft. Lauderdale we spotted this babe getting out of her bathing suit. The louvered windows of her room weren't properly shut and we could see right into the room. Pretty soon there were twenty-five of us jostling for position.

Now, some people might look down on this sort of activity. But in baseball if you shoot a particularly good beaver you are a highly respected person, one might even say a folk hero of sorts. Indeed, if you are caught out late at night and tell the manager you've had a good run of beaver shooting he'd probably let you off with a light fine.

The roof of the Shoreham is important beaver-shooting country because of the way the hotel is shaped—a series of L-shaped wings that make the windows particularly vulnerable from certain spots on the roof. The Yankees would go up there in squads of fifteen or so, often led by Mickey Mantle himself. You needed a lot of guys to do the spotting. Then someone would whistle from two or three wings away,

"*Psst!* Hey! Beaver shot. Section D. Five o'clock." And there'd be a mad scramble of guys climbing over skylights, tripping over each other and trying not to fall off the roof. One of the first big thrills I had with the Yankees was joining about half the club on the roof of the Shoreham at two-thirty in the morning. I remember saying to myself, "So this is the big leagues."

MARCH
8

Mesa

Today Joe Schultz said, "Men, you got to remember to touch all the bases." The occasion was a meeting after our glorious 19–4 victory in which one of the guys on the Cleveland club missed third base and was called out. So the lesson for today was "Touch those bases. Especially first."

A couple of things about spring training. Mike Ferraro, an infielder, was with the Yankees last spring. Bobby Cox got a big winter buildup and was supposed to have the third-base job there, but Ferraro had such a hot spring (sportswriters voted him the Yankees' outstanding rookie; he hit .351, Cox hit .186) they had to start the season with him at third. They let him play eleven games and when he didn't burn down any buildings they benched him and sent him to Syracuse. He feels that they never intended to use him at all but were embarrassed into it and were not unhappy when he didn't do well. Then there was Duke Carmel. He was supposed to be the second coming of Joe DiMaggio, and they really gave him a good shot. But he didn't hit in Ft. Lauderdale, and I remember Whitey Ford saying to him, "Well, Duke, it looks like you just can't hit in southern Florida." We made a trip to Tampa and he didn't hit there either. "Well, Duke, it looks like you're just not a Florida hitter," Whitey Ford said. Then we played a few exhibition games in the South and Carmel didn't get a hit. "Well, Duke," Ford said, "it looks like you just can't hit south of the Mason-Dixon line."

When the season started it turned out Duke couldn't hit north of the Mason-Dixon line either, and finally he was sent down when he was about 0-for-57. If they hadn't wanted him to make it so bad they never would have held on to him that long. But they'd spent all winter building him up. And they'd built up Bobby Cox the same way. They wanted Cox to make it, not Ferraro.

The other thing is a story Johnny Sain once told me. Sain is not only the greatest pitching coach who ever lived, he's a man who tells the truth. And what he says, believe it or not, is that sportswriters actually play a part in deciding who's going to make the team. Sain said he sat in on many meetings where the performance of the individual player hadn't changed, but there had been two or three articles written about him and immediately the coaches and management tended to look at him in a new light. Sain says if there's not a lot of difference between players the job will go to the guy who seems to be getting the most attention in the newspapers. Power of the press.

Tomorrow I'll be pitching three innings or less against Oakland, and I'm a little worried. My fast ball isn't ready yet and my knuckleball is just marginal. Yet, as several people have pointed out to me, I need to accumulate some good statistics to throw at them when spring training is over. I can't say, well, I've been working on my knuckleball all spring and that's why I got clobbered.

My wife reminds me that I never got clobbered in Seattle when I was first working on my knuckleball and she suggests I go with it all the way. I'll give her opinion a lot of weight. We were both freshmen at Western Michigan when we met and all she would talk about was baseball. When I told her I was going out for the freshman team, she said, "You don't have to do that because of me."

I didn't tell her it wasn't because of her. And then, when she first saw me pitch she said, "That's a big-league pitcher if I ever saw one." So she's a hell of a scout. Knuckleballs. Hmm.

I've had some pretty good advice from my family. My dad especially. He helped pick the college I went to and got me into it. My services as a pitcher were not exactly in great demand. I pitched a no-hitter in my senior year in high school but I was only 5-10 and 150 pounds. My dad got a look at the Western Michigan campus, fell in love with the beauty of it, thought I'd love the baseball stadium and had me apply. I didn't hear anything for a long while, but my dad was

40

real cool. He took a bunch of my clippings—all six of them—had copies made and sent them to the baseball coach there, Charley Maher. He wrote, "Here's a fellow that may help our Broncos in the future," and signed it "A Western Michigan baseball fan." A week later I was accepted.

It was my dad's cool that got me the bonus from the Yankees too. I'd been playing with an amateur team in Chicago in the summer of 1958 and nobody noticed me much until I pitched two good games in the tournament at the end of the season. I mean, scouts would walk up to me and ask where they could find a player, but it was always somebody else. After those two games, though, the scouts were buzzing around me, wanting to take me to dinner, and there were a lot of rendezvous in cars and a lot of cloak-and-dagger stuff, and it was all a big thrill to me.

When I got home at about nine o'clock my mom and dad were playing bridge with some friends, and when I walked in the door I said, "Dad, you're not going to believe it, but I pitched the best game of the tournament and the scouts want to sign me. Dad, they're talking about real big money."

My dad looked at his cards. "Two no trump," he said.

He didn't really believe me. Then the phone rang and I said, "Dad, that's a scout on the phone. I know it is. What should I tell him?"

"Tell him $50,000," he said. "Three spades."

He still didn't believe me. I went over to the phone, and sure enough it was a scout from Philadelphia. "My dad says $50,000," I said. The scout said, "Fine. We want you to fly to Philadelphia and work out with the team."

That ended the card game.

I flew to Philadelphia, and it was great. I met Robin Roberts and Puddin' Head Jones and a lot of the other players. And they put me up at the Hotel Warwick, which had these leather-padded elevators that impressed me tremendously. I ordered a $10 meal including three or four appetizers and a giant filet mignon. But I felt kind of guilty because all the time I was in Philadelphia it rained and I didn't get a chance to throw a single pitch. I went home and never heard from them again. For a long time I worried that it was because I spent so much on that meal.

I also went to Detroit, and I remember meeting Al Kaline and seeing Ted Williams smack five in a row into the upper deck in batting practice. I threw on the sidelines for the Tigers and all they would offer

41

me was $10,000. I went home and talked it over with my dad and we decided the money the scouts had been talking was all a lot of baloney. Hardly any of the other clubs were interested anymore. I was discouraged, disappointed.

So my dad went to work on a form letter. "My son Jim is prepared to sign a major-league contract by Thanksgiving. If you are interested, please have your bid in by then." He sent the letter to about half the major-league clubs. The only club we fooled was the Yankees.

Jerry Coleman came out to talk to us, and my dad was careful to have baseball-team letterheads strewn around as if we were up to our ears in offers. Coleman authorized the local scout, Art Stewart, to go up to $30,000, and it was laid out this way: I'd get three payments of $5,000 over the next three years. I would also get $9,000 total salary for the next three years, and I'd get the remaining $6,000 only if I made it to the major leagues. It came to $10,000 a year—if I made it. A lot of bonuses weren't as big as they sounded.

But I was happy and my dad and I threw our arms around each other and congratulated each other on how smart we were to pull such a fast one on the New York Yankees. As it turned out I spent those three years in the minors and did make the Yankees, which means they made a pretty cheap investment. In recent years I've been kidding my dad about having sold me short in the first place and how a really astute father would have been able to get me at least $50 or $60,000.

MARCH
9

Tempe

Before the game today Rollie Sheldon was talking about old-timers. It's a funny thing, but athletes have improved tremendously through the years in every sports where performance can be objectively measured—track and field, swimming, etc. Yet in other sports, especially boxing and baseball, there are always people who say the old-timers were better—even unmatched. I don't believe that, and I was very interested when Sheldon pointed out some figures in the Hall of Fame book. Like, old "Hoss" Radbourne, who played before the turn of the century. He pitched the last 27 games of the season for his team and won 26 of them. Old Hoss was 5 feet 9 inches tall and weighed 168. Some hoss! Pony is more like it.

Some of the other heights and weights in the book were great. Wilbert Robinson was 5-9 and 215 pounds. Can you imagine what he looked like? Which reminds me of what Johnny Sain used to say on Old-Timers' days: "There sure is a lot of bullshit going on in here today. The older they get the better they were when they were younger."

Pitched my three innings today and gave up two runs. I consider it a good outing, however. I struck out the first hitter I faced on four pitches, all knuckleballs. (Don't ask me who he was; hitters are just meat to me. When you throw a knuckleball you don't have to worry about strengths and weaknesses. I'm not sure they mean anything, anyway.) I noticed again that I throw a better knuckleball in a game than I do on the sidelines. Maybe because the juices start flowing.

I gave up only one hit, a line-drive single after I got behind on the count to Danny Cater—2 and 0 on knuckleballs. I had to come in with a fastball and he hit it pretty good. The only other well-hit ball was off a knuckler, but it was on the ground and went for an out.

In the three innings I walked two, committed an error (hit Bert Campaneris in the head trying to throw him out at first), was hurt by a passed ball (a real good knuckler that broke in on a righthanded hitter, went off McNertney's glove and back to the backstop) and a couple of sacrifice flies. Two unearned runs. So the old ERA starts off at zero.

In the shower room Maglie told me he felt I needed my other pitches to set up my knuckleball. He also said he didn't want me to become strictly a knuckleball pitcher and that I should work on my curve, fastball and change-up. "Even if you don't throw it for a strike, just show it to them and let them know you have it," he said. I was glad to hear that from Sal. No matter what Bobbie says, I don't want to abandon myself completely to the knuckleball. I can still hear that lost chord.

MARCH
10

Mesa

Game called on account of rain. So we sat around the clubhouse and shot the shit. We're still in the process of feeling each other out. Because we're all sort of strangers there are no old, smoldering problems. Mostly we know each other only from playing against each other. Ray Oyler was saying that here Gary Bell is lockering next to him and for the last eight years Ray'd been screaming across the field at him, "Hey, sweetheart. Where's your purse, you big pussy?" Ray says it's all very strange.

The only guy I ever hollered at on another team was Jim Gosger. He was always just a marginal player with the Kansas City A's but he would hit me like he was Ted Williams. I used to scream at him, "What the hell are you doing hitting me? You're not good enough." And he'd say what hitters always say, even if you get them out. "Can't understand how you get anybody out with that shit you throw!"

There are days, I suppose, when we are both right.

Little Mike asked me today when I would be pitching for the Seattle Angels and I had to tell him it wouldn't be the Angels, it would be the Pilots. He got used to Angels last year when Seattle was a minor-league affiliate of the California Angels. It's been rough on Mike. First it was the New York Yankees and then the Syracuse Chiefs, and just when he was getting used to Syracuse it was the Yankees again, and then the Seattle Angels, and now the Seattle Pilots. And let's hope it won't be the Vancouver Mounties. I've got to make this club and stay here all year if only so my son will know where his dad's working.

Saw a diagram of Sicks' Stadium (named after beer baron Emile Sicks) in Seattle today, and the power alleys—where the sluggers put away knuckleballs that don't knuckle—are 345 feet. Yankee Stadium is over 100 feet deeper in left-center and over 60 feet deeper in right-center. No doubt about it, I'm going to be a threat in old Sicks'.

MARCH
11

Tempe

Knuckleball to the rescue today. I pitched batting practice, and when I was warming up my elbow hurt on every pitch—except the knuckleball. It was impossible for me to get loose. So I gave each hitter three nothing fastballs and two knuckleballs, and the knucklers were really jumping. Afterward Sal came over and said, "It was really moving today." That's the first comment he's had on the knuckleball. Maybe I can make him a believer.

I guess it wasn't too good for my elbow, though. When I got through pitching it felt like somebody had set fire to it. I'll treat it with aspirin, a couple every four hours or so.

I've tried a lot of other things through the years—like butazolidin, which is what they give to horses. And D.M.S.O.—dimethylsulfoxide. Whitey Ford used that for a while. You rub it on with a plastic glove and as soon as it gets on your arm you can taste it in your mouth. It's not available anymore, though. Word is it can blind you. I've also taken shots—novocaine, cortisone and xylocaine. Baseball players will take anything. If you had a pill that would guarantee a pitcher 20 wins but might take five years off his life, he'd take it.

Reminds me of the dumb things I used to do when I was in high school. The idea in those days was that when your arm was overworked and inflamed you put heat on it. It is exactly the wrong thing to do. We did it anyway. First Atomic Balm, which is just about what you'd expect from the name. You wore that stuff in the shower and let the hot water run on it, as hot as you could stand it. Then there was this stuff called

45

Heet! I'd paint that all over my arm and I'd lie on my bed in agony. Sometimes I actually burned off a layer of skin. Now *that's* dedication.

A couple of things about sore arms. When I was throwing the kind of fast ball that made my hat fall off people would ask me, "Jesus, doesn't it hurt? It looks like your arm's going to come off." I thought it was a silly question because it felt just fine. But now when I try to throw that way it feels like all those people told me it should feel. It feels like my arm's going to come off at the shoulder.

The most painful thing about it is that you know you're damaging something. It's pain, but it's fear, too. Sometimes the pain is like you get when you bang your funnybone. It hurts like hell. Only when it's your funnybone you know it's a passing thing. When it's your shoulder you think you might be snapping a muscle or ligament and you'll never be able to throw again. Pain and fear are a tough combination.

I try to stay away from the club doctor. This is something I learned in my first season. I was at Auburn, N.Y., and I got hit with a line drive that broke the thumb on my pitching hand. The Yankees flew me to New York to see Dr. Sidney Gaynor. I walked into his office with my dad and he said, "Who are you?"

I told him my name and said the Yankees had told me to see him.

He pointed at my dad. "And who are you?"

"I'm Jim's dad."

"Anything wrong with you?"

"No."

"Then what are you doing here?"

"Well, I just came along with Jim."

"We don't need you. Stay out here."

He took me into another office, took the cast off my thumb and bent it every which way. Then he told me it was broken and that it should have a bandage instead of a cast and that I shouldn't bump it into anything.

My dad couldn't believe the way Dr. Gaynor had spoken to him and I said he must just have had a bad day. I was sure he wasn't that way all the time. But I found out later he *was* that way all the time.

When I had my arm trouble in 1965 I went to him and he put me through some stretching exercises and said. "You got a sore arm."

"Yeah, I know," I said. "It hurts when I throw."

He was offended. It was like I had told him he had gravy on his tie. "If it's sore, don't throw," he said.

"For how long? A day, a week?"

"I don't know," he said. He was growling by now. "When it starts feeling better then you can start throwing again." Real scientific.

I believe Dr. Gaynor was actually offended when you came to him with an injury. You were imposing on his time. I'm sure there were a lot of guys who chose not to go to him with injuries because they didn't want to take his guff. I know I did. Mickey Mantle and Whitey Ford would go to other doctors sometimes and once Mantle got a vitamin shot from a quack who used an unsterile needle and almost missed a World Series with a bleeding abscess on his hip.

MARCH

12

I overheard Lou Piniella having a heated discussion with Joe Schultz and, nosy as I am, I asked him what it was about. Piniella said that a couple of players had heard Joe tell a sportswriter yesterday that if Piniella couldn't throw any better than he was throwing he wouldn't make the club. Lou said his arm had bothered him last year and he just wanted to nurse it this spring. I can understand why he was upset. He's only been here two weeks and that's not enough time to get your arm ready or for them to decide that someone could make the club or not make it. It's ridiculous, particularly since Lou hit .300 last year with a Triple-A club and he was one of their $175,000 draftees. Sounds like somebody up there wants to unload Lou Piniella.

Either that, or Joe Schultz is pushing the panic button. It's a managerial disease Johnny Keane fell victim to when he managed the Yankees. John was a good, decent man, and no doubt there was lot of pressure on him. He seemed to feel that each day was the most important day of the season and it started right with the opening game of spring training. John always seemed willing to sacrifice a season to win a game. And this caused a lot of long-range problems. Guys played when they were hurt and then were out longer than they would have been if they hadn't been pushed back too soon. Mantle used to love to tell about his conversations with Keane. He said they'd go like this:

"How do your legs feel today, Mick?"

"Not too good."

"Yes, but how do they feel?"

"It hurts when I run, the right one especially. I can't stride on it or anything."

"Well, do you think you can play?"

"I don't know. I *guess* I can play. Yeah, hell, what the hell. Sure I can play."

"Good. Great. We need you out there. Unless you're hurt—unless it really hurts you. I don't want you to play if you're hurt."

"No, it's okay. I hurt, but it's okay. I'll watch it."

"Good, good. We sure need you."

After a while we used to joke in the outfield. I'd go over to Mick and say, "Mick, how does your leg feel?"

"Well, it's severed at the knee."

"Yes, but does it hurt?"

"No, I scotch-taped it back into place."

"And how's your back?"

"My back is broken in seven places."

"Can you swing the bat?"

"Yeah, I can swing. If I can find some more Scotch tape."

"Great. Well, get in there then. We need you."

Poor Steve Barber was in the training room today getting some diathermy on his shoulder. He says his arm doesn't hurt. Ballplayers learn after a while that you don't tell anybody you have an injury if you can possibly avoid it, even a teammate. It might get back to the coaches, get spread around and be blown up out of all proportion. More important, it's because you don't want to admit it to yourself.

48

MARCH
13

Pitched three innings, gave up five hits, one of them a tremendous home run over the left-field fence by a guy who caught me in Seattle last year, Tom Egan. Tommy Davis said he could follow the flight of the ball pretty good, until he lost it in a cloud. A very bad day for the knuckleball. It just didn't knuckle. The overhand curve was working pretty good and some of the fastballs hopped pretty good. Who knows, maybe my old motion is coming back. The sirens are still singing.

Steve Barber went three innings and pitched pretty well. Maybe his arm doesn't hurt him after all—except that he was in the diathermy machine again this morning. Steve reminds me of a guy who was with the Yankees for a while, Billy Short. He was a little lefthander with a face on him like a kewpie doll. He was constantly getting diathermy and ultrasound on his arm. He even wanted to use a machine between innings, and once he asked the trainer if he could bring the ultrasound out to the bullpen so he could get it on his arm during the game in case he had to warm up.

I know exactly how he felt. I've wanted ultrasound on my arm between pitches sometimes. Or novocaine.

I was judge in an age contest today. Bill Stafford, Ray Oyler, Don Mincher and Tommy Davis. I said Oyler looked oldest. They laughed, because that made Oyler a four-time winner. In the book Tommy is twenty-nine, the rest thirty, Oyler included, which made me glance into the mirror myself. I still look to be in my mid-twenties. I'm glad the mirror doesn't reflect what's in my arm.

Mike Marshall was in the Tiger organization for a while and he says that, like the Yankees, they frown on players telling reporters the truth. A reporter asked Mike what he was being paid and he said he didn't feel he could say, but it was less than the minimum. The reporter printed it and asked how the hell the Tigers could be paying their No. 1 reliever less than the minimum. So Mike got called in by Jim Campbell, the general manager. Campbell wasn't angry that Mike was making less than the minimum, but that he told.

I asked Mike if he'd ever talked to Johnny Sain about contracts and he said he hadn't. Sain gives you good advice on how to get money out of a ballclub. John's a quiet guy and follows most of the baseball rules about keeping your mouth shut, but he's not afraid to ask for money if he thinks he deserves it. He was with the Boston Braves in 1948, the year they won the pennant. It was Spahn and Sain and then, dear Lord, two days of rain. Warren Spahn and Sain were the staff and Sain really put it to John Quinn, who was the general manager. Sain had had a big argument in the spring about his contract and signed for less than he wanted. Now they were just home from a western trip and fighting for the pennant and Sain went to Quinn and said, "I'd like to talk about my contract."

"We'll talk about your contract next winter, when it comes up," Quinn said.

"No, I'd like to talk about it now," John said.

"What the hell," Quinn said. "You signed a contract and we're going to stick by it. We can't renegotiate a contract during the season."

"Well, you're going to renegotiate this one," John said.

"What the hell do you mean by *that?*" Quinn said.

"I'm supposed to pitch Thursday," Sain said. "But unless you pay me what I wanted in the beginning I'm not pitching."

That meant it would be Spahn and rain and pray for a hurricane, and then maybe a flood. So Quinn tore up his contract and gave him a new one, and John won 24 games. He used to say to me, "Now, don't be afraid to climb those golden stairs. Go in there and get what you're worth."

Those golden stairs.

Ruben Amaro is here with the Angels and I was happy to see him. We were good friends in New York. He's the kind of guy, well, there's a dignity to him and everybody likes and respects him. He's outspoken and has very strong opinions but he never antagonizes people with his positions the way I sometimes do. I wish I could be more like him.

Roger Repoz is with the Angels too, and I asked him if he had linguine last year in our restaurant in Detroit. He said he was keeping the faith.

More conversation about positive thinking today. When I pitched in the World Series in '63 and '64 I won two out of three games and the only thought that went through my mind before and during the game was, "Please don't let me embarrass myself out there." No thought of winning or losing. If you told me beforehand that I would lose the game but it would be close and I wouldn't be embarrassed, I might well have settled for that. I was terrified of being humiliated on national television and in front of all my friends. Now, that's certainly not positive thinking, and yet I was able to win ballgames. Maybe there is a power to negative thinking.

MARCH
14

Arm felt pretty good today after pitching yesterday and I don't know whether to attribute it to the aspirin or the bottle of beaujolais I polished off at dinner. Or maybe it was the ice I put on my elbow.

Marty Pattin pitched today and looked good. He reminded me of when I was a young pheenom. Straight overhand pitcher, good rising fastball, hard overhand curve. He's a little guy but cocky, with lots of guts. When I saw him throwing free and easy like that it really made me want to find my old stuff.

I looked over Maglie's record today and noticed that he had his best years after coming back from the Mexican League and was thirty-three years old. So I'm wondering if I'm not going to end up being a fastball, curve-ball pitcher again this year. But then I remember what it was like last year: how frustrating it was to find my motion and get my rhythm and how I'd get hit and then not get any regular work. All of which tells me I better stick to the knuckleball.

I guess you could say I'm torn.

Ding Dong Bell gets his first start against Arizona State U. tomorrow and he says he's not ready. I told him it's no sweat because if anybody makes this team it's going to be old Ding Dong, no matter what happens this spring. He said he realized that, and he's going to go out there and just keep from getting hurt.

Pitching against a college team, you can't look good no matter what. If you do well, they're just college kids. If you don't, you're a bum. Yet the kids are in better shape than we are and can be a pain in the ass.

Batting practice is the time to stand around in the outfield and tell each other stories. At first we all sort of felt each other out, standing fifteen feet apart and doing the job the way it's supposed to be done. By now, though, we're standing in clumps of five or ten and take turns catching whatever fly balls happen to come our way.

It was Dick Stuart-story day today, and this one was about the time Johnny Pesky was managing the Red Sox and Stuart was playing for him and showing up late for a lot of things. For some reason this upset Pesky, so he called a meeting to talk about MORALE. Stuart was late for it. In fact he didn't show up until about half an hour before the game (three is considered about right) and he walked right into the middle of the meeting. All eyes were on him as he opened the door to the clubhouse and, without missing a beat, opened his double-breasted jacket, paraded to the center of the room with his hips swinging, did a pirouette and said, "And here he is nattily attired in a black suede jacket by Stanley Blacker, with blue velvetine pants and shoes by Florsheim. The handkerchief is by Christian Dior." Everybody went nuts. Even Pesky had to laugh.

Stuart's a beauty. I remember a game we played against him in Boston with Earl Wilson (then with the Red Sox) pitching. On the first pitch of the game somebody hit a foul pop fly between the catcher and first base and Earl ran over to call who was supposed to catch the ball, and he made a tragic mistake. He called Stuart. The ball dropped to the ground in front of him with a sickening thud.

Earl picked up the ball and stormed back to the mound. The next pitch was another pop fly, this one in fair territory. Earl ran over screaming at the top of his lungs, "I got it! I got it!" He wasn't taking any chances. At the last second guess who ran into him and spiked him. Dick Stuart. The ball went flying and the runner got two bases.

Now Wilson's got a spiked left foot and a man on second and he's steaming mad. The next pitch is a ground ball on the first-base line and Earl runs over, picks it up, whirls to throw to first and Stuart isn't on the bag. First and third.

Wilson slammed his glove down and walked toward the dugout like he was quitting right there, but he thought better of it and came back to the game. And Stuart? Stuart was his usual jovial self. He knew he had bad hands and there was nothing he could do about it.

Curt Blefary is another guy with classically bad hands. When he was with Baltimore Frank Robinson nicknamed him "Clank," after the robot. Once the team bus was riding by a junkyard and Robinson yelled for the driver to stop so Blefary could pick out a new glove. (If you're going to shake hands with a guy who has bad hands you are supposed to say, "Give me some steel, baby.")

Speaking of hands, there's the story of the player who was sound asleep on an airplane when suddenly it ran into some turbulence. He woke up and promptly threw up. But just before he messed all over himself he managed to reach up and catch most of it in his hands. The guy sitting next to him, with perfect aplomb, turned to him and said, "Good hands."

MARCH
15

I'm not sure I'm going to like Don Mincher. I keep hearing that big southern accent of his. It's prejudice, I know, but everytime I hear a southern accent I think: stupid. A picture of George Wallace pops into my mind. It's like Lenny Bruce saying he could never associate a nuclear scientist with a southern accent. I suppose there are people in baseball who are as turned off by my northern accent, and I've often thought that the best way to get through professional baseball is never to let on you have an education.

Well, Mincher was talking about going to see a Johnny Cash show, and I imagine when he talks about Johnny Cash it's like the Negro players talking about James Brown. Lots of times in the clubhouse you'll have a radio on and every once in a while it gets switched back and forth between a soul-music station and a country-western station. If you're going good you get to hear your kind of music. In the Yankee clubhouse western music dominated. In the Horace Clark Memorial Lounge you heard the music from the Virgin Islands and soul music. In the trainer's room, where Mickey Mantle was king, you'd hear the Buck Owenses and Conway Twittys.

Went to the rodeo with the family, and when they played "The Star-Spangled Banner" Mike said, as he does every time he hears it, "Dad, they're playing the baseball song again."

We were toasting marshmallows in the backyard and I was sharpening a stick to put through the marshmallows when I sliced off most of the end of my left thumb. I went to the clubhouse to have it repaired. Someone saw the ugly slice and immediately a crowd formed, as it always does when something gory is on exhibit. We like to say about ourselves—we baseball players—that we're ghouls. I remember one time it was standing room only in Ft. Lauderdale when Jake Gibbs got hit on the thumb and they had to drill a hole through his nail to relieve the pressure. I had a front-row seat myself. The drill boring through the nail started to smoke and when it hit paydirt Jake jerked his hand and the drill was ripped out of the trainer's hand and here's Jake's hand waving in the air with the drill still hanging from the hole in his nail. One of the great thrills of the spring.

Looking at Steve Barber doing his jumping-jacks during calisthenics I realized that his pitching arm is all bent and much shorter than his right arm. That's from throwing curve balls. It's almost as deformed as Bud Daley's arm. Bud, who had polio as a boy, pitched for the Yankees for a while. The polio left him with a crook in his right arm. It didn't bother him, even when the players would make fun of it. Sometimes there would be twenty-five guys in front of the dugout, all of them catching the ball with a crooked arm.

When I told Barber he looked like Bud Daley he laughed and said, "Yes, but Daley didn't have to pitch with that arm, only catch."

Barber was in the diathermy machine again today and then looked pretty good in batting practice. I've been taking aspirin. My arm hurts and I didn't do as well pitching BP as Barber. Maybe there's something to that diathermy machine.

The only thing I think of these days when I go out to pitch is how my arm feels. My concern used to be about how my curve ball was breaking and whether I could get the fastball over. Now I think about my arm. Hell, once the hitter gets up there I can always make adjustments and find something to throw him. But if your arm hurts, that's it.

I've had a lot of conversations with my arm. I ask what the hell I ever did to it. I ask why won't it do for me what it used to do in the old days. I whisper lovingly to it. Remember '64? Remember '63? Wasn't it fun? Things could be like that again. Just one more time, one more season. It never listens.

When I was shaving today a rookie beside me reminded me of how old I am for this game. His name is Dick Baney; he's a young kid and has a great fastball. I hate him. "Hey, I wrote you a fan letter that you never answered," he said.

I thought, hell, he's so young, it might be true. "When did you write it?" I asked.

"When I was about six," he said.

If there's one thing I hate it's a smart-ass rookie. I know a lot about smart-ass rookies. I was one myself. The guy I got on when I came to the Yankees was Jim Coates. Actually he got on me first. He'd say, "Get a few years in the big leagues before you pop off." Or he'd get on me about my number being too high. And I'd get on him about being so skinny. One time in the trainer's room I asked him if those were really his ribs or was he wearing a herringbone suit. That one drove him up the wall.

He'd lisp at me when I was going in to pitch. "Is she going out and try it again today? Is she really going to try today?"

And I'd say, "Yeah, Coates, I'm going out there and hammer another nail into your coffin."

Another time I said, "Hey, Coates, you endorsing iodine?"

And he said, cautiously, "Why?"

"Because I saw your picture on the bottle."

MARCH
16

We had a visit from Commissioner Bowie Kuhn today. The visit was preceded by the usual announcement from the manager: "All right, let's get this thing over with as quickly as we can." What it really means is: "Okay you guys, you can listen. But don't ask any questions."

The Commissioner said that baseball is a tremendous, stupendous game and that it didn't need any drastic changes, that we simply needed to improve our methods of promotion. One of the things that none of us should do, he said, is knock the game. He said if we were selling Pontiacs we wouldn't go around saying what a bad transmission it has. In other words, don't say anything bad about baseball.

He said he was pleased with the settlement that had been made with the players but he felt there was too much bitterness in the dispute. I felt there was an unspoken warning there to be careful of things we said that could be interpreted as bitterness toward the owners. Imagine being bitter toward the owner of a baseball club.

Kuhn also talked about the integrity of the game and how he felt it's one of the only sports that the average fan knows in his heart is completely honest. (I wonder what the football, basketball and hockey people would say to *that*.) I'm not sure all fans feel that way, but I really don't think there is any gambling at all inside baseball. I may be naïve, but I don't think there's any gambling, or any intentional passing along of information.

Kuhn got a nice round of applause and nobody asked any questions. Then he left with Joe Reichler, the Commissioner's personal caddy. Commissioners come and go, but Joe will always be with us. Some guys were made to be permanent caddies.

All of which for some reason reminds me of one of our bullpen occupations: choosing an all-ugly nine. Baseball players are, of course,

56

very gentle people. If we happen to see some fellow who is blessed with a bad complexion we immediately call him something nice, like "pizza face." Or other sweet little things like:

"His face looks like a bag of melted caramels."

"He looks like he lost an acid fight."

"He looks like his face caught on fire and somebody put it out with a track shoe."

Some famous all-uglies are Danny Napoleon ("He'd be ugly even if he was white," Curt Flood once said of him); Don Mossi, the big-eared relief ace on the all-ugly nine (he looked like a cab going down the street with its doors open); and Andy Etchebarren, who took over as catcher from Yogi Berra when the famed Yankee receiver was retired to the all-ugly hall of fame.

Lost to Arizona State 5–4 yesterday, and would you believe that Joe Schultz and Marvin Milkes are steaming? In fact one of the pitchers who was taken out of the game got cut today—Bill Edgerton. He figured to get cut because he was one of the five or six guys who were asked to move their lockers to the visiting-team locker room. Of course, they were told it had nothing to do with their ability or status, just that some guys had to move. By coincidence, most of them were cut today. The only one I was really interested in was Greg Goossen, whom I'd come to like, mainly because he had the ability to laugh at himself.

That's what Milkes and Schultz should have done about losing to Arizona State—laugh. Or at least not take it so damn seriously. Except they probably think that the fans and writers are going to draw a lot of conclusions about a game like this and, alas, they're probably right. You can't educate everybody about baseball in two weeks.

Lou Piniella has the red ass. He doesn't think he's been playing enough. He's a good-looking ballplayer, 6-2, handsome, speaks fluent Spanish and unaccented English. He's from Tampa. He says he knows they don't want him and that he's going to quit baseball rather than go back to Triple-A. He says that once you get labeled Triple-A, that's it. I suggested to him that this wasn't the year to quit because the Seattle people were bound to make mistakes in their early decisions and I thought there would be a shuttle system between Vancouver and Seattle and that guys who didn't stay with the club the first month might be called up real quick. But he said he was going to quit anyway and force them to do something. And since he cost $175,000 in the expansion draft he figures they'd rather make a deal for him than lose him altogether. He's probably right. A lot of decisions in baseball are based upon cost rather than ability. Cost is easier to judge.

Now that the cut-down season is here we'll soon be talking of deaths in the family. At least that's what we did with the Yankees. When a guy got cut we'd say he died. Fritz Peterson would come over to me and say, "Guess who died today." And he'd look very downcast and in the tones of an undertaker read the roll of the dead.

A player who wasn't going well was said to be sick, very sick, in a coma or on his deathbed, depending on how bad he was going. Last year when I was sent to Seattle, Fritz asked me what happened and I said I died.

"You can't die," Fritz said. "You're too good to die."

Like Mae West once said, goodness has nothing to do with it.

On the Yankees the Grim Reaper was Big Pete. Once he whispered in your ear that the manager wanted to see you, you were clinically dead. I remember toward the end of one spring training Don Lock, an outfielder with a pretty good sense of humor (he needed it, having spent a lot of years in the Yankee chain trying to break into an outfield of Tom Tresh, Mantle and Maris), barricaded his locker. He hung sweatshirts across the top, crossed out his name, piled up his gloves and shoes in front to form a barrier, then snuggled inside the locker holding a bat like it was a rifle, and fired it at anybody who came near. It was good for a few laughs, but in the end the Grim Reaper got him anyway.

Another way Big Pete would let you know you had died was by not packing your equipment bag for a road trip. There would be a packed bag in front of every locker except yours. Rest in peace. It's kind of like, "All those who are going to New York City, please step forward. Not so fast, Johnson."

When I warm up tomorrow I'll be trying to re-create in my mind an abstract feeling I get when I'm throwing well. It can't be explained. It's a *feeling,* the feeling you get when you're doing something right, a sort of muscular memory. I find the best way to arrive at this feeling is to eliminate all other thoughts and let my mind go blank. Sometimes, when you can't find this feeling while you're warming up, panic sets in. It's one of the reasons I like to use a double warm-up. The interval between the two warm-ups gives me a chance to think about what I did and to see if I can't make some correction.

If this sounds insane, it may be.

MARCH
17

Scottsdale

Had a long chat with Steve Hovley in the outfield. He's being called "Tennis Ball Head" because of his haircut, but his real nickname is Orbit, or Orbie, because he's supposed to be way out.

Hovley is anti-war and I asked him if he ever does any out-and-out protesting in the trenches. He said only in little things. For instance, when he takes his hat off for the anthem he doesn't hold it over his heart. I feel rather the same way. The whole anthem-flag ritual makes me uncomfortable, and when I was a starting pitcher I'd usually be in dugout toweling sweat off during the playing of the anthem.

We agreed we're both troubled by the stiff-minded emphasis on the flag that grips much of the country these days. A flag, after all, is still only a cloth symbol. You don't show patriotism by showing blank-eyed love for a bit of cloth. And you can be deeply patriotic without covering your car with flag decals.

Hovley said he didn't mind being called Orbit. "In fact I get reinforcement from it," he said. "It reminds me that I'm different from them and I'm gratified."

What's different about Hovley is that he'll sit around reading Nietzsche in the clubhouse, and sometimes he'll wonder why a guy behaves a certain way. In baseball, that's a revolutionary.

I must say, though, that things are changing. When I first came up with the Yankees there was intolerance of anybody who didn't conform right down the line—including haircut and cut of suit. But as the old-timers disappear, there seems to be more freedom, more tolerance.

Hovley and I got to talking about the strange relationship between

59

baseball managers and players, and the fact that players seldom talk to managers about anything. "I ran into Joe Schultz in the shower the other day," Hovley said, "and suddenly we were all alone. I really didn't know what to say to him. The only thing I could think to say was, 'Who's going to play third this year?' or 'How many pitchers are you going to take north?' So when he said, 'Hi, Steve, how are you?' I said, 'Fine,' and immediately started lathering up my face so I wouldn't have to talk to him anymore."

I was shocked when I got to the ballpark today—figuring I was going to be the starting pitcher and go five innings or so—to be told by Sal that I was the third pitcher and that I'd only go one or two innings. Immediately my mind started churning. Does this mean I'm being put on the shelf? I've heard that last-two-innings talk before in my career and it always means, "See you later."

But it was needless worry. Dick Baney, who started and was told to go as far as he could, got nailed early. Four runs in four innings. Stafford came in for two innings and looked terrible. So I was in there in the seventh.

I started off great. I gave the first guy all knuckleballs and got him on a grounder. To the next guy I threw five beautiful knuckleballs. He missed the first two for strikes. Then he fouled three of them off and I figured now I've got him. He must be expecting another knuckleball, because every knuckler I threw him was knuckling better than the one before. Surely he isn't looking for a fastball.

I looked in for the sign and the catcher was thinking the same thing. So I cranked up and gave him a fastball, hoping to sneak it by him, and he snuck it over the left-field fence. Tommy Davis, my friend, once again lost sight of the ball when it went behind a cloud. I hate to think how far he might have hit it had we not fooled him so badly.

After the game Sal said I'll probably pitch again tomorrow, which means they now must be thinking of me as a short-relief man. I'd like to pitch an inning or so the day after tomorrow because that's when we play the Giants. I was always a Giant fan when I was a kid and I'd like to pitch against Willie Mays so I can tell my brother what it feels like. Whenever we played stickball as kids we'd take turns being the Giants and Dodgers. I pitched to Willie Mays hundreds of times, only it was my brother, batting righthanded even though he was lefthanded so he'd look as much like Willie as possible. Now I'd like a shot at the real thing, with a baseball instead of a rubber ball. I think it will be a fair match. Both of us are near the end of our careers. He's had a few more lucky years than I have, but we're both over thirty and that's a great equalizer.

Whitey Ford always said that the way to make coaches think you're in shape in the spring is to get a tan. It makes you look healthier and at least five pounds lighter. Following Ford's postulate I was sitting on the bench in the sun while Baney was pitching. This gave me an opportunity to listen in on the pearls of Sal Maglie and Joe Schultz, who were also getting some sun. These pearls are of a special kind, absolutely valueless at best, annoying enough to upset your concentration at worst. For instance, a big hitter was up with two men on base and as Baney looked in for the sign Joe Schultz hollered, "Now get ahead of this guy." And Sal hollered, "Get something on this pitch. He's a first-ball hitter."

And just as he cranked up to throw, somebody (I couldn't tell who) yelled, "High-ball hitter. Keep the ball down."

If he takes all this advice Baney has to throw a strike at the knees with Chinese mustard on it. What the hell, if you could throw that kind of pitch every time you wanted to you wouldn't need any coaching. Christ, you'd have it made.

But Baney isn't Superman. He got behind. Ball one, low in the dirt.

The next piece of advice was, "Got to get ahead now. Nothing too good."

"Nothing too good" means don't throw it down the middle and "got to get ahead" means don't throw him a ball. In other words, hit a corner.

Of course, he still has the other advice ringing in his ears. So now he's supposed to hit a corner, low on the knees, with a hard fastball. This is wonderful advice. Ball two. Ball three.

"Got to come in there now, but not too good."

That's really beautiful advice. Especially with a good hitter up there who may well be swinging at 3 and 0. Sure enough, Baney threw a good fastball—belt high. It got hit into center for a double and two runs. And as the ball went out there Sal shook his head and said, sadly, "Too high, too high."

How many inches are there between the belt and the knee? How many pitches can you control to that tolerance? How many pitching coaches are second-guessers? Answers: Eighteen inches. Very few. Most.

And this kind of bullshit goes on during most ballgames. The same things are said over and over in the same situations. They all come to the same thing. They're asking you to obey good pitching principles; keep the ball down (most hitters are high-ball hitters), don't make the pitch too good (don't pitch it over the heart of the plate), move the ball around inside the strike zone and change speeds (keeps the hitter off balance), and get ahead of the hitter (when you have two strikes on a hitter and two balls or fewer, you may then throw your best pitch as a borderline strike and the hitter will have to swing to protect himself).

This is the essence of the battle between the pitcher and the hitter, and it doesn't do any good to yell this kind of advice to a pitcher in a crisis situation. He knows it as well as he knows his name. But pitching coaches use shouted advice as protection. If they shout enough advice they can't be wrong.

Old Chicken Colonel Turner was a master at this. He'd sit in the dugout and shout to Stan Bahnsen, "Now, keep the ball down, Bahnsen," and Stan would throw a letter-high fastball that would get popped up into the infield and The Colonel would look down the bench and say, "The boy's fastball is moving. The boy's fastball is rising." Two innings later, same situation, the very same pitch, home run into the left-field seats. The Colonel looks up and down the bench and says very wisely, "Got the ball up. You see what happens when you get the ball up?"

Then you'd get a weak lefthanded hitter up in Yankee Stadium and somebody would throw him a change-up and he'd hit it for a home run into the short porch and The Colonel would say, "You can't throw a change-up to a lefthanded hitter, boys. Not in this ballpark." A week later a guy would throw the same pitch to the same kind of hitter and the guy would be way out in front and The Colonel would say, "Change-up. One of the best pitches in baseball. You can really fool the hitter with it."

Whatever the result, The Colonel always knew the cause. And in the little world of baseball, he is not alone.

Merritt Ranew hit a pinch-hit home run that tied the game up in the ninth inning. He got a very cold reception in the dugout. The reason is that nobody wants to play extra innings in a spring game. It happened that we scored two more runs in the inning and won it, but it was a narrow escape and nobody was very happy with Ranew. By coincidence I have a soft spot in my heart for extra-inning games in the spring and believe that every player—at least every player who doesn't have the team made—should feel this way. I made the Yankee ballclub in an extra-inning spring game.

This was in 1962, and I wasn't even on the roster. They asked me to pitch the ninth inning of a game against St. Louis when we were behind by a run. We tied it up in the bottom of the ninth, so I wound up pitching five scoreless innings and lost it on an unearned run. But four days later I got to pitch in another game, and then two more, and I made the club. If I'd pitched only one inning in that first game they might never have taken another look. In fact, all the scrubeenies pray for extra innings in the spring. Or at least they should.

MARCH
18

Tempe

We lost an 8–5 ballgame today and I did my part, giving up two runs in a single inning. There was a triple on an ankle-high knuckleball (I hate triples off ankle-high knuckleballs), and then Tommy Davis lost a fly ball in the sun and it fell for a double.

When I was a kid I might have run out there and kicked him in the shin. I actually used to do that. I would stop the game and scream at a kid if he made an error, and everybody hated me for it. In recent years, though, I've turned full circle. I may say to myself, "Ah, Tommy, you should have had that," but I go out of my way to show absolutely no reaction. I don't pick up the resin bag and slam it down, and I don't kick dirt, and I don't stare out at the player.

The reasons are selfish. First of all, people think terrible thoughts about you when you do that kind of thing, and I don't like people to think terrible thoughts about me. Secondly, you get on a player that way and he may miss the next play too. So I say nothing.

While warming up to come into the game I was wondering if my wife was in the park. I enjoy playing baseball better when I know there are friends or family watching. It's a bit of hot dog in me. I got a special kick when my parents and my brothers used to come to a ballgame because it seemed like I was putting on a special performance just for them. I've pitched some of my best games when I knew I had left a lot of tickets for my countless admirers. The longest game in the American League was played in Detroit a few years ago. I pitched the last seven innings for the Yankees in a 22-inning game and there were 15 Bouton passes sitting up there behind the dugout, all relatives of my wife. I really think I did better because I knew they were there. Sometimes, when I know there are no friends or family present, I pretend they're home watching on television, thousands of them. You take your ego trips, I take mine.

Lost the game today, so we had a chance to prove we could be more silent than thou. After a loss the clubhouse has to be completely quiet, as though losing strikes a baseball player dumb. The radio was blaring when we came into the clubhouse and Joe Schultz strode the length of the room, switched it off and went back to his office. After that you could cut the silence with a bologna sandwich. The rule is that you're not supposed to say anything even if it's a meaningless spring-training loss. Feeling remorse has nothing to do with it. Those who did poorly in the game and those who did well, even those who didn't play, all are supposed to behave as if at a funeral.

The important thing is to let the manager and coaches know you feel bad about losing. I'm sure they believe that if you look like you feel bad about losing then you're the type who wants to win. So you go along with the little game. And they played this game real hard with the Yankees when I got there, but every once in a while Phil Linz, Joe Pepitone and I would giggle about something after a losing game and we got some pretty nasty stares from the old guard.

This was what was behind the famous Phil Linz harmonica incident. It was in 1964, when Yogi Berra was manager, on a bus ride from Comiskey Park to O'Hare airport in Chicago. It was hot, we were tied up in Sunday traffic, we'd blown a doubleheader, we'd lost four or five in a row, we were struggling for a pennant and tempers were short. Linz was sitting beside me, stewing because he hadn't played, and all of a sudden he whipped out a harmonica he'd bought that morning and started playing "Mary Had a Little Lamb." The reason he played "Mary Had a Little Lamb" was that it was the only song he knew how to play. He really played very respectfully and quietly, and if "Mary Had a Little Lamb" can sound like a dirge, it did.

64

Yogi, who was in the front of the bus, stood up and said, "Knock it off."

Legend has it that Linz wasn't sure what Berra said, so he turned to Mickey Mantle and asked, "What'd he say?"

"He said play it louder," Mantle explained.

Linz didn't believe that. On the other hand he didn't stop. In a minute Yogi was in the back of the bus, breathing heavily and demanding that Linz shove that thing up his ass.

"You do it," Linz said, flipping the harmonica at him. Yogi swatted at it with his hand and it hit Pepitone in the knee. Immediately he was up doing his act called, "*Oooooh,* you hurt my little knee." Pretty soon everybody was laughing, even if you're not supposed to laugh after losing, especially a doubleheader.

And that was really all of it, except that I should point out that in the middle of it all Crosetti stood up and in his squeaky voice screamed that this was the worst thing he'd ever seen in all his years with the Yankees.

Ray Oyler was racked up at second base by Glenn Beckert of the Cubs, and when he came back to earth he was heard to call Beckert a son of a bitch. This is not on the same order as motherfucker, but he didn't have a lot of time to think.

It has become the custom in baseball to slide into second base with a courteous how do you do, so when somebody does slide in hard everybody gets outraged and vows vengeance. A few years ago Frank Robinson slid into Bobby Richardson with murderous aplomb and the Yankees were visibly shocked. *How could he do that to our Bobby? We'll get him for that.* Actually this was a National League play and the Yankees simply weren't used to it.

Before the game Joe Schultz asked me how the old knuckleball was coming along and I said fine. I was ready to pitch. Indeed, I added, it was my opinion that if a knuckleball pitcher got himself into proper shape he could probably pitch every day because the knuckleball takes almost nothing out of your arm. I was about halfway through this little speech when I noticed that Schultz was staring over my shoulder into the blue, blue sky. If I had said I just cut my grandmother's throat from ear to ear, he would no doubt have said, "Fine, fine."

Managers don't like to be told who should play and who shouldn't, and who should be a starting pitcher and who shouldn't, and when Joe started feeling I was telling him I should be a starter he turned me off. I shouldn't have said anything. I should have just lathered my face.

MARCH

19

Phoenix

Two talks today from my main men, Schultz and Maglie; one okay, the other terrible.

Schultz said we weren't in shape and that we were making physical mistakes that we wouldn't if we were—in shape, I mean. (I'm not sure I understood that.) But then he obviously felt he'd hurt our feelings and tried to take it all back. "Shitfuck," he said, using one of his favorite words ("fuckshit" is the other). "Shitfuck. We've got a damned good ballclub here. We're going to win some games."

I agree. I don't see how we can avoid it.

What Schultz is afraid of, I guess, is that we might get down on ourselves and then, well, the losing might never stop. Baseball players are a special breed for getting down on themselves. When they do, it's look out below.

The meeting with Maglie was disappointing, largely, I guess, because he was my hero when I was a kid and I expected a lot out of him. Also because he didn't get along with Dick Williams, the Boston manager. I count that as a good sign because managers, being what they are, often don't get along with coaches who have something on the ball. I thought Sal Maglie might turn out to be another Johnny Sain. Afraid not.

Maglie started out saying, "Look, you guys got to concentrate out there. You're not concentrating."

Now what the hell does that mean? There are about thirty pitchers here, young and old, and not one of them isn't concentrating when he's pitching. I mean I *know* nobody is out there thinking about going out to play golf or about how the beer is going to taste after the game. If

66

anything, most of us are concentrating too much, getting too tense, trying to do too much. Johnny Sain always told guys who had control problems that they were trying too hard to throw the ball to a specific spot, not that they weren't concentrating. Sain would compare pitching to a golfer chipping to a green and say that if you tried for the cup you might miss the green. The thing to do was just hit the green, pitch to a general area.

Control was our big problem, Sal said. We've walked eighty and struck out only forty and the ratio should be the other way around. He's absolutely right. But he's got the wrong reason.

Then he surprised me by mentioning my name. "Some of you guys think you can get by on only one pitch," he said. "You can't do it. Nobody is a one-pitch pitcher." He added: "Bouton, they're just waiting for your knuckleball. You got to throw something else."

In the immortal words of Casey Stengel, "Now, wait a minute." Are we trying to win ballgames down here or are we trying to get ready for the season? What I have to learn is control of the knuckleball. And I'm not going to learn it by throwing fastballs. I tried to explain that to Sal after the meeting and he said, well, yes, but I should have some other pitches to set up the knuckleball.

I said I agreed with him 100 percent. I said it because I'm in a shaky position here and the first thing you got to do is make the ballclub, and you don't make ballclubs arguing with pitching coaches.

Afterward in the outfield we talked about one-pitch pitchers. Ryne Duren was a one-pitch pitcher. His one pitch was a wild warm-up. Ryne wore glasses that looked like the bottoms of Coke bottles, and he'd be sort of steered out to the mound and he'd peer in at the catcher and let fly his first warm-up pitch over the screen and the intimidation was complete. All he needed was his fastball and hitters ducking away.

And just for the hell of it I got into a conversation with Maglie about when he was a great pitcher, and I asked him what he used to get the Dodgers out with in his glory with the Giants. "Ninety-seven snappers," Sal Maglie said.

So much for one-pitch pitchers.

Anyway, Gary Bell said not to worry about Maglie. "Last year in Boston he told one of the newspaper guys I'd never last throwing across my body," Gary said. "Chrissakes, I've been here fourteen years. You think he meant I'd never last past fifty?"

MARCH
20

Day off, so I'll take the opportunity to discuss the bean-ball. Everybody asks.

When I used to throw very hard I was always concerned that I would let a fastball go and hit somebody in the head. Occasionally I would dump somebody by accident and I'd run right up to the plate to see if he was all right. I fractured Wayne Causey's arm with a fastball and I felt terrible about it for days.

The beanball (it's sometimes called "chin music") is a weapon. Hitters don't like pitchers throwing at them, and there are guys in the league who have a reputation for not hitting as well after they've been thrown at a few times. Nor do I look down on pitchers who use it as a weapon. They're probably shrewder than I am. I'm just not a crafty person, I guess, especially when it comes to pitching. I probably should have cheated more. I should have thrown a spitter. I should have used a mudball. I didn't, and I'm not sure why, except that when I was successful throwing real hard, I didn't need to. And when I was going bad, I was so bad nothing would help.

Only once in the years I've been pitching has anybody ever ordered me to throw a duster. It was last year at Seattle and Joe Adcock, a man I like, was the manager. I came into a game in relief and John Olerud, the catcher, came out and said, "Joe wants you to knock this guy on his ass."

I couldn't believe it. So I said something clever. "What?"

"Joe wants you to knock this guy on his ass."

"I just got in the game. I got nothing against this guy."

"Well, he says to knock him on his ass."

"Bullshit," I said. "I haven't thrown that much. I'm not sharp enough to know where the hell I'm throwing the ball. I'm not going to do it. You go back there and tell him that you told me to knock him down and that I refused and if he wants to say something afterward let him say it to me."

Adcock never said a word.

I mean, what if I screw up a man's career? I'm going to have that on my conscience for . . . well, for weeks maybe.

The fact is, though, that I once did throw at a guy. I mean to maim him. His name was Fred Loesekam. He was in the White Sox organization and he was a bad guy. He liked to slide into guys spikes high and draw blood. During warm-ups he liked to scale baseballs into the dugout to see if he could catch somebody in the back of the head. He even used our manager for target practice. So I took my shots at him. We all did. Once I threw a ball at him so hard behind his head that he didn't even move. The ball hit his bat and rolled out to me, and I threw him out before he got the bat off his shoulder.

When you throw a ball behind a hitter's head you're being serious. His impulse is to duck into the ball. If you're not so serious and all you want to do is put a guy out for a piece of the season, you aim for the knee. An umpire will give you two or three shots at a guy's knee before he warns you. Mostly, though, I just brush guys back from time to time. Considering my control, I've brushed lots of guys back accidentally.

And don't believe it when you hear that a pitcher can throw the ball to a two-inch slot. A foot and a half is more like it, I mean with any consistency. When I first came up I thought major-league pitchers had pinpoint control, and I felt terrible that the best I could do was hit an area about a foot square. Then I found out that's what everybody meant by pinpoint control, and that I had it.

Of course, hitters hear things from the bench: "Stick it in his ear!" That's almost as good as throwing at a hitter because now he thinks you're going to, and that's half the battle. I know not what course others may take, but for me, my most precious possession is the three balls I'm allowed to throw before I walk somebody. If I give up one of them merely to frighten the hitter, I'm giving up half my attack. I decided long ago I couldn't afford that.

MARCH
21

Death came calling today. Joe Schultz gathered a bunch of guys in his office and told them that because of space requirements they'd have to work out on our other field with the Vancouver squad. "You're not cut," Joe said. "Your stuff is still in your locker and you're still on the team. Don't draw any conclusions from this."

It wasn't really death. It was just the priest coming to your bedside to say a few choice Latin words. Among the casualties were Steve Hovley, Rollie Sheldon, Skip Lockwood and Jim O'Toole. One of the guys who got the call, Lou Piniella, didn't go into Joe's office, but sort of sulked outside. "Come on in, Lou," Joe said. "It's not going to be anything bad." Lou knew better.

Piniella is a case. He hits the hell out of the ball. He hit a three-run homer today and he's got a .400 average, but they're easing him out. He complains a lot about the coaches and ignores them when he feels like it, and to top it off he's sensitive as hell to things like Joe Schultz not saying good morning to him. None of this is supposed to count when you judge a ballplayer's talents. But it does.

Besides, Schultz has his problems. They're named Tommy Davis, Wayne Comer, Jose Vidal and Jim Gosger, and somebody has to go. I'm sure that whoever is sent down will be the best of them.

The fellow I feel rather sorry for is Rollie Sheldon. His record is about the same as mine, except he's got fewer walks, and I'll wager he's wondering why I'm still here and he's getting the message. All I can think is that my knuckleball made me a better bet, a stickout among the mediocrities. Of course, a couple of poor performances by me and Joe Schultz will be telling me I don't have to worry either.

I was also rather sad about Claude (Skip) Lockwood. Hate to lose a funny man. The other day we were talking about pitching grips in the outfield (it was the day after I'd been mildly racked up by a couple of doubles) and Lockwood asked me, "Say Jim, how do you hold your doubles?"

About a week ago Lockwood said, "Hey, the coaches are calling me Fred. You think it means anything?"

"Don't worry about it, Charley," I told him.

And today he came over and said he was a little confused, that he didn't know which field he was supposed to be working on. He said he guessed things were getting better for him. "Last week I didn't know who I was. Now all I don't know is where."

I should point out that the Lockwood case is a perfect example of what happens to a guy who reports an injury. He was scheduled to pitch in one of the first two exhibitions but came up with a sore arm. Four days later he went to Sal and said he felt fine. This was almost two weeks ago. He still hasn't pitched. When he asked Schultz about it the dandy manager said, "I didn't want to take a chance with your arm."

That's a crock of crap. What it amounts to is having a reason to cut a young guy. If you can cut him for some reason other than his pitching it's just that much easier on your psyche. Decisions, decisions.

It's also why, when you ask Steve Barber, while he's sitting in the diathermy machine, if he's having trouble with his arm, he says, "No, no. I'm just taking this as a precautionary measure."

Sure enough, after the two workouts today on the two fields, the Grim Reaper struck. Five or six of the guys who were told not to worry this morning were cut this afternoon. Sheldon, Goossen, Lockwood, Bill Stafford and a couple of guys I don't know.

As I drove home after the game I passed the Vancouver practice field and saw Goossen working out at first base. He's hard to miss, with his blocky build and blond, curly hair, working without a hat. I was already missing him and the nutty things he does and I thought here's a field that's only about fifty yards away and yet it's really hundreds of miles away, the distance between the big leagues and Vancouver. Those guys all work out at different times, change in different locker rooms, listen to different coaches. They moved into a different world when they got cut from the big club. There were no tears, no sympathy, no farewells and no handshakes. And no one goes down to that field to tell Goose to hang in there. One day he's here and the next he's gone. It happens every day and it's a reality to all of us, yet I can't help thinking how strange it is. There should be more fanfare when a guy leaves, more goodbys, more hang-in-theres. And once in a while maybe we should stop when we drive by the practice field and give Goose a wave and let him know we still like him and that he's still alive.

MARCH
22

There was a notice on the bulletin board asking guys to sign up to have their cars driven to Seattle. Price $150. The drivers are college kids. I think I'd prefer Bonnie and Clyde. I say this because I remember college and how I drove an automobile in those days and I would not have hired me to drive my car. Still, a lot of guys put their names on the list—very tentatively.

Baseball players' words to a beautifully tender song (Actually Overheard in the Clubhouse Division): "Summertime, and your mother is easy."

Steve Hovley was dancing to a tune on the radio and somebody yelled, "Hove, dancing is just not your thing."
"Do you mind if I decide what my thing is?" Hovley said.
So I asked him what his thing was. "I like sensual things," he said. "Eating, sleeping. I like showers and I like flowers and I like riding my bike."
"You have a bike with you?"
"Certainly. I rent one. And I ride past a field of sheep on the way to the park every day and a field of alfalfa, and sometimes I get off my bike and lie down in it. A field of alfalfa is a great place to lie down and look up at the sky."
I sure wish Hovley would make the team.

When I got to the ballpark this morning I ran into Frank Kimball, one of the young catchers. He was standing under the eaves in order to keep out of the pelting rain, his soggy equipment bag beside him. I knew, but I asked anyway. "What's up?"

"I just got sent down."

"Too bad. When did you find out?"

"They did it chickenshit. They told me in the office when I went to get my paycheck."

"You mean Joe didn't tell you?"

"No. And when I went back to him to ask him what the story was he said he was sorry, he forgot to tell me."

Eccch.

I haven't been pitching very well and I think that as a result my sideburns are getting shorter. Also, instead of calling Joe Schultz Joe I'm calling him Skip, which is what I called Ralph Houk when I first came up. Managers like to be called Skip.

I'm scheduled to pitch in the doubleheader they have scheduled tomorrow. I'll be at Scottsdale to pitch against the Cubs and a good outing by me could clinch a spot on the staff—maybe. What I've got to concentrate on this time is control and throwing other pitches beside the knuckleball. Whatever Sal Maglie says, Jim Bouton does. I'll impress the hell out of him with my curve and fastball and I'll just use the knuckler to get them out.

MARCH
23

Scottsdale

We lost a heartbreaker in the tenth, 7–6, but my heart wasn't broken. Indeed, I counted it as a pretty good day. Sorry about that, folks. I pitched three innings, gave up two hits and no runs and was ahead of most of the hitters. I used a good mixture of fastballs, overhand curves, change-ups and knuckleballs. Take that, Sal Maglie.

Going in to pitch those three innings I told myself that it was life or death, that everything depended on the way I pitched, that my dad was extremely interested in how I did and I would be calling him after the game. It was a good psyche job. Not only did I give up no runs, I popped up Ernie Banks and I popped up Ron Santo, both on knuckleballs. After each inning I looked up at my wife in the stands and we exchanged smiles, and in the last inning I pounded my hand into my glove in triumph and when I looked up at her she was as happy as, in the immortal words of Harry Golden, a mouse in a cookie jar.

My wife actually believes that it's possible, through concentration, to transfer strength from one person to another. She believes that during the game she transferred her strength to me and I pitched well. She is, of course, a nut.

A revelation about Joe Schultz. Mike Hegan has been hitting hell out of the ball and at this point is to the Seattle Pilots what Mickey Mantle was to the Yankees. Today he was hit on the arm by a fastball, and when Joe got to him and said, "Where'd you get it, on the elbow?" Hegan said, "No. On the meat of the arm, the biceps."

"Oh, you'll be okay," Joe said. "Just spit on it and rub some dirt on it."

Hegan couldn't move three of his fingers for an hour. But it didn't hurt Joe at all.

Riding back to Tempe I had a beautifully serene feeling about the whole day, which shows how you go up and down an emotional escalator in this business. It was my first really serene day of the spring and I felt, well, I didn't care where the bus was going or if it ever got there, and I was content to watch the countryside roll by. It was desert, of course, with cactus and odd rock formations that threw back the flames of the setting sun. The sun was a golden globe, half-hidden, and as we drove along it appeared to be some giant golden elephant running along the horizon and I felt so good I remembered something Johnny Sain used to talk about.

He used to say a pitcher had a kind of special feeling after he did really well in a ballgame. John called it the cool of the evening, when you could sit and relax and not worry about being in there for three or four more days; the job done, a good job, and now it was up to somebody else to go out there the next day and do the slogging. The cool of the evening.

Of course, there's the converse. If a pitcher doesn't do well, he has

74

three or four days to contemplate his sins. A hitter is back in there the next day, grinding his teeth and his bat. Still, I was feeling so good that I began to think about pitching against the Yankees, and what it would be like going back to Yankee Stadium and facing them. I had all four of my pitches working today, and I had good control, and I thought how much fun it's going to be to get back to the Stadium and toy, really *toy* with them. They haven't even seen my knuckleball. It could really be a picnic.

I think coach Eddie O'Brien is going to prove a gold-plated pain in the ass. He must think he's Frank Crosetti or something, because when I reached into his ballbag he said, "What are you going to do with it?"

"I'm going to count the laces," I told him. "And then I'm going to juggle it."

Later on O'Brien noticed some of the guys were eating sunflower seeds in the bullpen. "Hey, none of that," he said. "No eating in the bullpen."

"Not even sunflower seeds, Eddie?"

"Nothing. Not even sunflower seeds."

Eddie O'Brien will have to be clued in on what happens in the bullpen. Maybe the way to cure him is to make him head of the refreshment committee.

Ran my long foul-line-to-foul-line sprints in the outfield and kept myself going by imagining I was Jim Ryun running in the Olympics: I'm in the last fifty yards and I'm going into my finishing kick and thousands cheer. If I'm just Jim Bouton running long laps very little happens. Let's see. Here's the World War I flying ace . . .

Bill Stafford and Jimmy O'Toole got their releases today. Stafford hopes to hook on with the Giants (I don't see how) and O'Toole is shopping around. I've had some big discussions with O'Toole. His father is a cop in Chicago and was in on the Democratic Convention troubles. I'd been popping off, as usual, about what a dum-dum Mayor Daley was and O'Toole said hell, none of those kids take baths and they threw bags of shit at the cops, and that's how I found out his father was a cop. Even so, I feel sort of sorry for him because he's got about eleven kids (I should feel more sorry for his wife) and he seemed a forlorn figure as he packed his stuff. I told him good luck but somehow I didn't get to shake his hand, and I feel bad about that.

75

It's funny what happens to a guy when he's released. As soon as he gets it he's a different person, not a part of the team anymore. Not even a person. He almost ceases to exist.

It's difficult to form close relationships in baseball. Players are friendly during the season and they pal around on the road. But they're not really friends. Part of the reason is that there's little point in forming a close relationship. Next week one of you could be gone. Hell, both of you could be gone. So no matter how you try, you find yourself holding back a little, keeping people at arm's length. It must be like that in war too.

MARCH
24

Tucson

On my way to the park today I passed the Vancouver practice field and spotted Sheldon over there playing pepper. It gave me a sinking feeling. There but for the grace of the knuckleball go I. Not that it still can't happen. I still may not fit in with Schultz's plans. What we need is a lefthanded pitcher, starter or reliever, and I can see a trade for one. But where does an aging righthanded knuckleballer fit in? Vancouver?

I know I felt differently after those good three innings yesterday, but I'm already tossing around in my mind how I'll react if I'm sent down. I'll take it calmly, see, and say to Joe, "Skip, I know you've got a lot of things on your mind and you didn't really have the chance to give everybody the amount of work that would have helped them the most. But I don't want to be a problem. I'll go to Vancouver and do a good job there and expect to be called up after a month of the season goes by."

On the other hand, would that be the best approach? Maybe I could talk him out of it. Maybe I could get a couple of more chances to pitch and then he'd wind up cutting somebody else.

There's a third possibility. Maybe right now, at this very moment, I've got the team cinched. Dream city.

Jake Gibbs of the Yankees once ordered pie à la mode in a restaurant and then asked the waitress to put a little ice cream on it.

A sportswriter came up to Darrell Brandon today and asked him where he thought the club would finish. "Where did Joe Schultz say?" Brandon asked.

"Third," the reporter said.

"Put me down for third too," Brandon said.

Obviously I'm not the only worried guy in this camp.

We had dinner with Gary and Nan Bell and he said that if he could pick a place to play it would be Boston. He said he didn't like Cleveland because Gabe Paul would interfere in his personal life. (Nobody interferes in Gary Bell's personal life, not even his wife.) But Boston was money paradise. He said guys with 12–12 seasons there automatically got a $5,000 raise.

I'd heard that about Boston. The year Dick Radatz had his big year was the year I won 21. We both had two years in the big league and we were both young pheenoms. While I was trying to get $20,000, a $9,000 raise, Radatz was going to $41,000. Radatz told me that at a banquet and said that if he'd really battled them he could have gotten $45 or $50,000. I absolutely refused to believe him. But Bell said it was true. Good grief, $41,000! The bastards were *stealing* my money.

MARCH
25

Marvin Miller is coming around tomorrow to hand out some checks for promotions the Players' Association was paid for. So everybody was busy reminding everybody else not to tell the wives. We get little checks for a lot of things, like signing baseballs, which are then sold. In our peak years with the Yankees we were getting around $150 for signing baseballs. It's all pocketed as walking-around money. The wives don't know about it. Hell, there are baseball wives who don't know about the money we get for being in spring training, or that we get paid every two weeks during the season. John Kennedy, infielder, says that when his wife found out about the spring money she said, "Gee whiz, all that money you guys get each week. How come you've never been able to save anything?" And John said, "We just started getting it, dear. It's a brand-new thing."

Joe Schultz asked Wayne Comer, outfielder, how his arm felt. Comer said he wasn't sure, but that every time he looked up there were buzzards circling it.

Tommy Davis has been having trouble with his arm too, which was why he was playing first base when I came into the game against the Indians with runners on first and third and none out. Second and third, really, since before I drew a breath the guy stole second. Rich Sheinblum, outfielder, rookie, was up and I threw two curve balls to him for a 1-and-1 count. He missed a knuckleball and then hit a one-hopper hard and deep to first. I covered and got Sheinblum, and when the guy tried to score from third I nailed him with a strike to home plate. Two thirds of an inning. Another perfect Bouton day.

One of the dumb things I do sometimes is form judgments about people I don't really know. Case history: Jack Hamilton, pitcher, Cleveland Indians. He was with the Angel organization last year and played with me in Seattle, which is where I got to know him. Before that I played against him in the minors and considered him stupid, a hard-throwing guy who didn't care whether or not he hit the batter. In the majors I figured him for a troublemaker because he used to get into fights with Phil Linz. Nobody fights with Phil Linz.

Then, when Hamilton hit Tony Conigliaro in the eye a couple of years ago and put him out for the season, I thought, boy, this guy is some kind of super rat. But when I played with him in Seattle I found he was just a guy like everybody else, honestly sorry he'd hit Conigliaro, a good team player, a friendly fellow who liked to come out early to the park and pitch batting practice to his kids. All of which made me feel like an ass.

*　　*　　*

The Unsinkable Molly Brown almost was sunk tonight. Unsinkable is what we call Laurie, our youngest. She's only three, but a tough little broad. This spring alone, for example, she's been bitten by a dog, hit in the head by a flying can of peas and had nine stitches sewed into her pretty little head. Nothing puts her down. Tonight, though, the kids were playing in the bedroom and suddenly we heard shattering glass followed by Laurie crying. Seems her head had made contact with a jalousie, resulting in broken glass and a bit of blood. The reason she had made such violent contact is that Kyong Jo had pushed her, and the reason he had pushed her is that I had told him to. I told him to push her because little girls are very often pests to little boys and the best way to get rid of little girl pests is to give them a push. Only it's not supposed to result in blood, and poor Kyong Jo was severely chastened. He had this look of terrible shame on his face. Fortunately little Laurie wasn't hurt much. No stitches were required and we were able to reassure both her and Kyong Jo. After all, she *is* the Unsinkable Molly Brown.

MARCH
26

Tempe

Six cuts today. You walk into the clubhouse and you see a guy packing his bag and you both try not to look at each other. Most guys won't pack until they know everybody is busy on the field, but sometimes you surprise somebody in there and it's always awkward.

Steve Hovley was one of the six. He was able to smile and say it came as no surprise to him and that Vancouver is a very nice town.

I was surprised to see Merritt Ranew get cut. He's been hitting well and we're short of lefthanded hitters. Very strange.

Got another flash from Eddie O'Brien today. I had a minor eye infection and was wearing dark glasses in the bullpen and O'Brien said, "What's with the shades?"

"I'm having trouble with my eyes."

"Well, I don't think you should be wearing shades down here."

"But, Eddie baby, the doctor says I have to. Do you want I should get a note from him?"

"Well, if the doctor says so . . ."

MARCH
27

Yuma

Our first big road trip today to Yuma, Arizona, and we did what ballplayers do at the start of every trip—stand around the airport, inspect the threads and make funny comments: like, if a guy is wearing a turtleneck that's too big for him, "Who gave you that turtleneck, Bronco Nagurski?"

You can start fights if you get on a guy about something meaningful, like race or religion. But you can kid a guy about his clothes, or about the way he looks. We couldn't decide, for example, whether Sal Maglie looked more like an Indian chief or Mafia enforcer. But we didn't tell him.

Me: "If you're a customs official would you check Maglie's bag?"

Bell: "I'd strip him to his shorts."

Then there was Gabe Paul, Jr.'s, haircut. Worst haircut I ever saw. It was military all around, except on top, where it was kind of new left. Ugh. Ray Oyler's comment was, "Hey, Gabe, where'd you get that nice razor cut?"

Today Joe Schultz said, "Many are called, few are chosen." He said it out of the clear blue, several times, once to Lou Piniella. Said Lou: "Is that a bad sign?" I said I didn't know. But I did. And it was.

Would you believe that we were playing a ballgame in Yuma, the winter home, as they say, of the San Diego Padres, which is a place you pass through on the way to someplace else, a place that doesn't even have a visiting clubhouse, so that we had to dress on the back of an equipment truck, and in the middle of a game before about twelve people, one of them yelled at us, "Ya bums, ya!" I mean, would you believe it?

Although we won the game Joe Schultz wasn't impressed. There were a couple of minor dumb plays, so Joe had a meeting on the bus. One of the things he was upset about was that one of the guys asked, "Who do we play tomorrow?"

Said Joe: "Boys, if you don't know who you're going to play you don't have your head in the game."

The guy who asked the question was Lou Piniella, and now he knows what Joe meant by "Many are called, few are chosen." Goodby Lou.

Still, at the end of the meeting I wanted very much to say, "By the way Joe, who *do* we play tomorrow?" But I'm not pitching all *that* well.

Today Joe Schultz also said, "Put your hat on."
He said it to me.

Five minutes later Eddie O'Brien came over and said, "See, what'd I tell you? Put your hat on."

You would think that managers have too much on their minds to notice things like that. But they don't. I know, for one example, that Al Lopez hated Bob Shaw because he was blond and handsome and used to keep his hat off as much as possible so the girls in the stands could get a good look. And one day Lopez called out of the dugout to him, "Shaw, I see you with a different broad every night. You must be a lousy lay."

We were doing windsprints and Gary Bell was having a terrible time because of certain local poisonous fluids he'd encountered the night before. We decided that Eddie O'Brien would let him off if he got a note from his bartender.

Bell is a funny man and, along with Tommy Davis, is emerging as one of the leaders of the club. He's got an odd way of talking. Instead of saying, "Boy, that's funny," he'll wrinkle up his face and say, "How funny is that?"

Or he'll say, "How fabulous are greenies?" (The answer is very. Greenies are pep pills—dextroamphetamine sulfate—and a lot of baseball players couldn't function without them.)

There is an odd sort of sexual liberation among baseball players—

a verbal one. It's considered perfectly all right to make sexual remarks about your wife and other players' wives. It's a nothing-sacred game, and Bell is one of the leading practitioners. "When I get home I'm going to knock my old lady's eyebrows off," he'll say. Or he'll go up to Ray Oyler and say, "Ray, when you come to the ballpark tomorrow will you bring my socks? I left them under your bed."

Sometimes you'll get this kind of conversation:

"Gee, your wife was great last night."

"Oh, she wasn't all that great."

"You should have been there earlier. She was terrific."

After the game today many of us repaired to the local pub and spent the fading hours of the afternoon drinking beer. Johnny Podres, the old Dodger who seems to be making it with the San Diego Padres (that's sort of nice, Podres of the Padres), was there, feeling little pain, and took it upon himself to straighten me out as a pitcher. "Listen, Jim, let me show you what you used to do and what you're doing now."

Pretty soon there was a beer glass where my right leg was supposed to be, an ash tray for my left foot and martini glasses for the length of my stride, and he was going through all my motions, two ways. Of course, I had to do it too, and after a while we drew a pretty good crowd. What he was saying was that I had to get my body into the ball and that I should hold my weight back and let it go all at once. It was sound advice and it embarrassed the hell out of me.

Still, it was a good afternoon. I was pleased that Podres should care and that he remembered my old motion and there was that little stirring in my belly that maybe he was right, maybe I could still find the old magic. But then I remembered baseballs disappearing into clouds and I smiled and tried to sit down. "One more time," Podres said. And all the guys said, "Yeah, one more time, Bouton, and this time get it right." So I did it one more time, wishing I could drink beer faster and get drunker.

On the airplane, Darrell Brandon, sitting next to me, said, "You like to read a lot, don't you?"

"Yeah," I said cleverly.

"Does it make you smart?"

He wasn't being sarcastic. I think he really wanted to know. "Not really," I said. "But it makes people think I am."

Actually I was somewhat embarrassed by the question. In fact

I *do* like to read on airplanes, but when I do I'm not in on the kidding and the small talk, so as a result I'm an outsider. I've resolved not to be an outsider this year. I'm not reading so much and no one can accuse me of playing the intellectual. And here I get caught up in a magazine article and Darrell Brandon is asking if reading makes you smart.

A little more about the new Bouton image. If the guys go out to a bar after a game for a few drinks, I'm going too. I'm going to get into card games on airplanes. I don't like bars much, and card games bore me, but I'm going to do it. If you want to be one of the gang, that's one way to do it.

It's odd, but you can be seven kinds of idiot and as long as you hang around with the boys you're accepted as an ace. Johnny Blanchard of the Yankees was an ace. He was just another jocko, but he was an ace because he was always out with Mickey Mantle and the boys, drinking, partying, playing cards. Every once in a while, just to enhance his image, he'd smack some poor guy off a bar stool and that was great. Johnny Blanchard was one of the boys.

Why should I be one of the boys? Why should I yield to the jockos? Oh, I'm not going to hold back if something comes up I feel strongly about, but I'm going to soft-pedal it a bit, at least at the beginning, until I'm sure I can make this club. I really believe that if you're a marginal player and the manager thinks you're not getting along with the guys it can make the difference.

I'm positive that the one reason Houk got rid of me was that I'd made a lot of enemies on the club (including Houk, I guess) simply because I refused to go along with the rules they set up.

Here's an example. I always felt that players should cooperate with the press, and when the Yankees got angry at me for talking too much to reporters I was quoted as saying, "Well, I don't get angry at them for *not* talking to reporters, why should they get angry at me because I do?" And that made it even worse.

Or they'd make a rule, because of some story or other, that nobody should talk with this or that reporter. So when he came into the clubhouse I'd give him a big smile and talk with him and be seen having lunch with him, just to let them know I wasn't going to buy that nonsense.

In September 1966 when the Yankees were in ninth place 26½ games out of first place, Murray Olderman of Newspaper Enterprises Association, asked me what I thought was wrong with the Yankees. After carefully examining our statistics and lofty place in the standings I said,

83

"I guess we just stink." The headline in the papers the next day said "Bouton: Yankees Stink." The distortion was only minute.

Houk called me into his office. "Olderman made you look bad," he said. "The players are all upset. I'm sure he misquoted you. You've got to be careful when you talk to these guys."

"Well, he didn't really misquote me," I said.

Houk didn't think that was enough. He thought I should say more. I asked him like what. And he said I should apologize to the players. I said I would. And I did. I'm not sure what for, though. I mean, boy, did we stink.

Then there was the matter of talking too much, not to reporters, to the guys. You see, you *could* talk about the war in Vietnam, only you had to say, "Look at those crazy kids marching in the street. Why don't they take a bath?" Or you could say, "What right does Rev. Groppi have to go out in the streets like that? He should be in the pulpit where he belongs." If you said these things, no one would accuse you of talking politics, because you were *right*.

On the other hand, if you said things like, "We've got no right to be in Vietnam," or that, "Rev. Groppi is certainly making his religion relevant up there in Milwaukee," then you shouldn't be talking about things like that, because you were *wrong*.

And it could cost you too. When Joe Garagiola was running "The Match Game" on television, a lot of the Yankees, almost all of them, were getting on the show. I mean even Steve Whitaker. And me, the articulate Jim Bouton, spontaneously witty, always at ease in front of the camera, never got a call.

This year, though, it's a new Bouton. At least until I win some ballgames.

MARCH
28

Holtville

Mike Hegan has been hitting like fury. He does that from time to time. His history is streaks. He's either hitting .450 or .150.

I wondered if he ever got any help from his father, who has been in baseball twenty years and is now a Yankee coach. Mike said he never did. In fact, when he was growing up he hardly saw his father at all, and to this day they seldom talk about baseball.

The help he gets is from his mother. He said that he believed it was she who put him into his current hot streak. She knows a lot about hitting and she sends him little reminders all the time of what to do and think about while he's hitting. She's a big reader of golf manuals and applies them to baseball, sending him helpful hints for the duffer that actually help.

We don't have a hitting instructor here. So I've been thinking that maybe Mike Hegan's mom, since she has such a good record . . . ah, I don't think Eddie O'Brien would go for it.

When Lou Piniella said he'd been to a palm reader the other day the guys wanted to know what she'd told him.

"She told me I was hitting in bad luck," Piniella said.

Today, while we were sitting in the bullpen, Eddie O'Brien, the All-American coach, said, just after one of our pitchers walked somebody in the ballgame: "The secret to pitching, boys, is throwing strikes."

Gee, Eddie! Thanks.

I came in to relieve in the ninth and got the last out. After the game, Joe Schultz had the whole team run around the bases and then said, "Okay, everybody in—except Bouton and Baney. I want to see you two."

Baney got this horrified look on his face and said, "Oh, my God!"

I couldn't resist, so giving him my sincere look, I said, "This is it."

He turned pale and moped over to Joe, slowly, as if attached to a large rubber band. But all Joe wanted was to tell us to run some extra laps since we were in the bullpen and weren't able to run when everybody else did.

I never saw anybody run laps looking so happy as Dick Baney. Unless it was Jim Bouton.

Wayne Comer got into an argument with an umpire, and they were jawing back and forth. The last thing said was, "All right, Comer. You'll be sorry you said that."

And he probably will. Umpires do get even with people, even good umpires. I remember when George Scott first came up to Boston. He must have irritated Ed Runge somehow because the word came out from Elston Howard that when Runge was behind the plate and Scott was hitting the strikes wouldn't have to be too good.

The first pitch I threw to Scott was about six inches off the plate. Strike one. The second pitch was eight inches outside. Strike two. The third pitch was a curve in the dirt. Scott swung and missed. He never had a chance.

Runge is one of the more powerful umpires in the league, mostly, I suppose, because he's a real good one. He's been wearing these long, gray sideburns that look just great against his tan. He is a striking figure out there. I asked him if he thought he could get by wearing the burns during the season and he said he didn't know, that Joe Cronin, the league president, hadn't seen them yet. But I'm betting on Runge. He's got power.

There was the time, for example, when Steve Whitaker was with the Yankees and bitched to him on a couple of calls and Runge told Mickey Mantle, "You better straighten that boy out."

That night Mantle and Whitaker ran into Runge at a restaurant and Mantle told Whitaker he'd better go over and apologize. Whitaker said the hell he would. But after Mantle explained to him what it might mean he succumbed. Just call him *Mr.* Runge.

One would have thought Comer was through arguing with umpires, but I guess he's a slow learner. The other day he got himself in trouble with another umpire by getting on his son, who is trying to be an umpire. The son told the father and the father told Tommy Davis that

Comer better come up swinging. He meant he wasn't likely to get any balls called.

Sure enough the first pitch to Comer was a high curve and he called it strike one. Comer didn't even look back. He swung at the next pitch and hit a line drive off the fence for a triple. The ump looked over to our bench and said, "See, it makes him a better hitter."

Rich Rollins has a good story he tells in the same vein. It goes back to when we were playing against each other in the Class-B Carolina League. Rich had hit two home runs in the first game of a doubleheader and the club had some deal that anybody who hit three home runs in one day would get $300. So the other players on Rollins' team told him to go to our catcher, Norm Kampshor, and get him to tell him what was coming by offering him half the money.

Rollins: "I didn't want to do it at first. I said I didn't think it was right, but they said hell, it was common practice, and there I was just out of school and didn't know a damn thing. So I told Kampy I needed another home run and that he'd get $150 if he told me what was coming. He didn't even hesitate. Just said sure.

"And not only did he tell me what was coming, but after a while he started asking me what I'd like to have thrown. And I'd say fastball, or change, and I'd get it."

The big joke, of course, was that I was the pitcher at the time.

"You know, I really felt sorry for you," Rollins said. "There you were sweating your guts out trying to make the big leagues and not only did I know what was coming, but I was calling your game for you."

In the end, though, the joke was on Rollins. Calling my game for me, he managed only one double in four times at bat. And if he had come to *me,* I probably would have grooved one for him. Not for money, just for the hell of it.

Sorry kids, things like that happen. Phil Linz was batting .299 going into the last game of the season at Modesto and asked the other catcher to help him get to .300. "When you come up I'll have the third baseman play real deep," the catcher said. "All you have to do is lay down a bunt and beat it out."

That's exactly what happened. Phil got the hit for his .300 average and got the manager to take him out of the game. Now it's in the record books forever that Phil Linz hit .300.

The same thing happened with Tommy Davis. He was hitting .299 for the Mets and playing against his old teammates, the Dodgers. Johnny

Roseboro was catching. "Hey, baby, you're my main man," Davis said. "How about a little help?" Roseboro said sure and told him what was coming. Davis got his hit and had his .300 batting average.

MARCH
29

Palm Springs

Tommy Davis is loose and funny and a lot of guys look to him, not only Negroes. Everybody sort of gravitates toward him and his tape machine, and he's asked his opinion about things. Like, "Hey Tommy, what kind of town is Palm Springs?"

So far I haven't heard any of the white guys say, "Tommy, what are you doing for dinner tonight?" Maybe it will come. Maybe.

At least Tommy is no Elston Howard. The best way I can explain Howard is to recall the day Jimmy Cannon, the elderly columnist, Howard, his wife Arlene and I got involved in an argument about civil rights; Arlene and I on one side, Cannon and Howard on the other. Arlene and I were the militants.

The guys are grumbling about Joe Schultz. I'm not sure if it's serious or just the normal baseball grumbling. Joe has been insisting that the guys do more running and more pick-ups, and nobody likes that, so they're calling him things like "Step-and-a-Half" because he walks with a slight limp and sniggering behind his back.

I hope it doesn't get to be the kind of thing the Yankees had with Johnny Keane. None of the guys were happy when Houk moved up to general manager in 1964, and they didn't like Yogi Berra as a manager, and they hated Keane. They constantly grumbled about Keane, and when he'd, say, flash the bunt sign, they'd say to themselves, "What the hell does Keane know about our style?" They never respected anything he did. So they'd make a half-hearted attempt to bunt and pop it up or hit into a double play. Then the newspaper guys would ask them what was the matter and they'd say they didn't know, they were trying just as hard as they always did. The hell they were.

I mean if Houk flashed the bunt sign they'd think, "Oh boy, what a genius." And they'd lay down the bunt. It's a mental thing. If you're going to give physically 100 percent you have to be giving mentally 100 percent. Except how can you give 100 percent for a guy you call Squeaky or Midget or other rotten things?

MARCH

30

Holtville

Now about Roger Maris. Roger fought a lot with the people in the stands, especially in Detroit, where he used to give them the finger. He and the fans would get to calling each other names and then Maris would roll out his heavy artillery.

"Yeah? How much money are *you* making?"

Roger was making $70,000 a year.

After a while every time Maris got into an argument the guys in the dugout would say, "C'mon Rodg, hit him with your wallet."

Thinking about the great Rodg reminded me of a brief encounter. One day there appeared a clipping on the bulletin board in the Yankee clubhouse. It was a quote from me after Mel Stottlemyre had hit an inside-the-park home run, which is very hard for a pitcher to do. One of the writers came to me after it and said, "What were you thinking when Stottlemyre was going around the bases?" It was a nice, silly question, so I gave him a nice, silly answer. I said I was hoping that Stottlemyre would fall down because if he hit an inside-the-park home run it would put pressure on all us other pitchers to hit inside-the-park home runs, and who needed that? And now it's on the bulletin board like I was serious.

I asked around to find out who put it up, but I couldn't, although I eventually decided it must have been either Clete Boyer, another one of my boosters, or Maris. So one day when they were standing together in the outfield I went over and said, "I wish you guys would tell me who put that clipping up on the board, because I'd like to get my hands on the gutless son of a bitch who did it."

And although Maris had already denied to me that he put up the clipping, he said, "Don't call me gutless."

Somehow I managed not to get into a fight with him. But I felt I'd won the battle of wits. Which is probably why he didn't own up posting it the first time I asked him. He didn't want to contend with my rapier-like mind.

Maris' friend Clete Boyer was the kind of guy who would always tell me to be careful who I brought into the clubhouse. Yet he led the league in hosting the obnoxious offspring of clothing manufacturers. The way it worked, he'd get free sweaters and in return he'd have to bring the sons of the manufacturer into the clubhouse where they could run around, ask for autographs and make pests of themselves. He and Maris got the sweaters, and we got the kids.

And a final word about my favorite baseball writer, Jim Ogle, of the Newhouse papers. Ogle was a Yankee fan and he reacted to players purely on how much they were helping the Yankees to win. Charm, personality, intelligence—nothing counted. Only winning. Ogle didn't have even the pretense of objectivity. He was the only writer in the pressbox who would take the seventh-inning stretch in the Yankee half.

Once at a winter press conference, when the Yankees were announcing the signing of three or four guys, Stan Isaacs, who writes a really good column for *Newsday,* on Long Island, passed a note to Houk. It said: "Has Ogle signed his contract yet?"

Isaacs may not have known how ironic he was being. In fact Ogle's ambition was to work for the Yankees. But they would never give him a job.

Not that this prevented him from doing little jobs for them. Like when I was sent down he was on television with Yankee broadcasters and said that it wasn't so much that I was pitching poorly, but because of the kind of person I was. He said that none of the players liked me and there were some terrible things about me he couldn't even talk about. This left it up to the public imagination. What was I? Rapist, murderer, dope peddler? Jim Ogle wouldn't say.

MARCH
31

Tempe

It's getting to be, as the boys say, nut-cutting time. And it was not good news to hear that we're going to start the season with only nine pitchers. Besides that, we traded Chico Salmon to Baltimore for Gene Brabender, "a hard-throwing righthanded country boy," said Steve Barber. I look at the pitching staff and I see six guys who have it made: Diego Segui, Marty Pattin, Jack Aker, Gary Bell, Steve Barber (including sore arm) and, because he had such a good year in Triple-A, Mike Marshall. Add Brabender and we have seven. So all spring there have been maybe thirty pitchers fighting for two spots on the staff.

I like to think I'm in pretty good shape. I haven't been scored on my last three or four times out and I've looked pretty good. But if they decide to keep, say, two lefthanders, where am I? Or suppose I get bombed tomorrow? Now I know what life on a tenterhook is like.

I thought the Salmon trade was pretty good for us because we didn't really have a spot for him. But he was very disappointed. He slammed the door when he left Joe's office. I know he counted on going to Seattle. He spent the winter up there and went to a lot of promotional dinners and leased an apartment and rented furniture, the works. Now it's Baltimore instead. Life in the big leagues.

Jack Aker, who's been our acting player representative, called a meeting today to elect a permanent player rep and alternate. Aker has quite a bit of experience in that area. He was the player rep in Kansas City when the players had all that trouble with Charley Finley and he's the most qualified guy on the team. He was elected with no opposition.

Tommy Davis nominated me for alternate, which both surprised and pleased me. Don Mincher seconded. Then someone nominated Gary Bell and the two of us left the room. Gary won it by one vote, and

91

Tommy Davis kidded that Mincher had switched and voted for Bell. Don was embarrassed, but I don't blame him. He doesn't know me that well and Gary's been around a lot longer.

Actually it felt rather good to lose by only one vote. When I was with the Yankees I once campaigned for player rep and didn't come that close.

Understand that *nobody* campaigns for player rep. Mostly you get the job the way Aker did. "All right, who wants to be player rep? Aker? Okay, Aker, you're the player rep."

But I campaigned with the Yankees because I wanted to dump Clete Boyer, and I guess that worked because when we had nominations he stood up and said, "I want to quit this fucking job." Also I actually thought I had a chance of winning and that I was probably the best man for the job.

So I mimeographed a two-page statement on why I felt I would be a good player rep and what qualities I thought we should look for and why I felt I met those requirements. I added some silly things in order to keep it all rather light, like I wanted to be a player rep so I could get to ride in a big airplane and write player rep on my underwear.

I got three votes. One of them was on an absentee ballot by Fritz Peterson. He had to leave, but left it for me in case I needed it. I never embarrassed Fritz by casting it. So everyone thinks I got only two votes. Let history record it was three.

APRIL

1

Four pitchers were cut before the game—Dick Baney, Chuck Bates, Buzz Stephen and Bob Lasko. I walked in on Lasko in the clubhouse and he was sipping coffee and had a smile on his face.

"What are you so happy about?" I said.

"The pressure is off," he said. "The pressure is off and I'm going to Vancouver, which means I'll be with my family."

I don't think I'd have taken it quite that well.

I got into the game, pitched two innings and looked good. I gave up a run, unearned. The catcher dropped a foul pop and then the hitter walked. He scored on a double, which was the only well-hit ball off me. I had a good assortment of stuff and was able to throw fewer knuckleballs, which must have pleased Sal Maglie.

After the game John Morris and Darrell Brandon got it. So one lefthander, Bill Henry, and I had made it. It's a good feeling, but if I had known all along what the odds were I'd have been less optimistic and more nervous.

Brandon has taken being sent down pretty hard, although he did have a poor spring. He took a long time packing his bag and after we were through with our workout he was still in the clubhouse, just sitting there in front of his locker, looking as though he hoped Schultz might change his mind and tell him it was all a mistake. No one went over to talk to him. It was sad and strange.

When I came to the park and saw Baney, Bates and Stephens packing, I started to smile. I was so relieved it wasn't me. And knowing that with them gone it would be that much easier for me, I felt this silly grin pop out on my face, so I bit my lip to get it off and turned into my locker. I didn't want anybody to see me smiling. I didn't want to *be* smiling. But I was, I was.

Anyway, we're down to twenty-five players now with a nine-man pitching staff, which means if we do anything, we'll *add* a pitcher, so I feel fat, safe and secure. Also I know that if I don't make it, or if I don't get to pitch, it'll be because I wasn't good enough. It won't be on my mind that someone is trying to sabotage me the way I felt when I was with the Yankees. Even if it isn't true, even if Houk wasn't out to get me, even if all the times I had to go into ballgames without having enough time to warm up properly, and if all the times I would go ten days without so much as throwing a ball in batting practice, were all accidental, it seemed to me I was being set up to be canned.

Like we all knew Piniella would be canned and it happened today. He was traded to Kansas City for Steve Whitaker and John Gelnar, a pitcher. It was a giveaway. Bound to happen, though. Lou wasn't their style.

We were talking about what we ought to call Brabender when he gets here. He looks rather like Lurch of the "Addams Family," so we thought we might call him that, or Monster, or Animal, which is what they called him in Baltimore last year. Then Larry Haney told us how Brabender used to take those thick metal spikes that are used to hold the bases down and bend them in his bare hands. "In that case," said Gary Bell, "we better call him Sir."

Hey, funny thing. This isn't a real bad ballclub. It hits like hell. We have six guys hitting over .300 and Hegan is hitting over .400. We're scoring a lot of runs. We've won five in a row this spring and we're nearly back to .500. And the Angels have yet to beat us. Maybe we really *can* finish third.

APRIL
2

John Kennedy says he knows the reason he's been hitting so poorly this spring. The low mound has screwed up his swing.

We had a meeting on catchers' signs today and I was glad that it was decided to use the pump system rather than the finger system. I have trouble with the finger system because I can't see the fingers. But the pump system is fine. It's not how many fingers are involved, but how many times they are flashed.

You use the pump with an indicator, which can be changed if you're worried about somebody reading you. Let's say you number your pitches this way: 1-curveball, 2-fastball, 3-change, 4-knuckleball or slider or screwball or whatever odd pitch you happen to have. The fifth pump starts the cycle again. Now, say the indicator is three. That means the first pump is for the change, second pump the knuckleball, third back to number one, the curve. And so forth.

It's simple, and I wish I'd worked something like that out with the Yankees. I used to make Jake Gibbs wear adhesive tape on his fingers so I could count them.

The other signs will work on a similar principle, with an indicator that can be changed. Some sample signs: touching the left side of the chest is the take, right side of the chest is the bunt, touching the left leg is the steal and right hand to the right leg is hit-and-run. The principle here is that hitting signals are above the belt and running signs are below. The takeoff is wiping the hand across the letters and the indicator will be touching the right arm. That is, no sign is valid until after the right arm is touched. As a variation you can make the sign the *second* one after the indicator is flashed. Or the third. That way even if somebody knows all your signs he can't tell what you're putting on.

Speaking of signs, I'm reminded that when I came to the Yankees and Yogi Berra was catching, if there was a man on first he'd call nothing but fastballs. That was so he would have a better chance if the guy was trying to steal. In fact Yogi liked to call mostly fastballs because they're the easiest to catch. I understand that part of the difficulty between Berra and Sain goes back to the days when Sain pitched to him and he couldn't get him to call anything but fastballs.

I am, of course, an optimist. Each year I'm certain I'm going to be great again. Every winter I get a questionnaire from *Sport* magazine on picking the pennant races and I always pick myself as Comeback of the Year. Each year I believe it. Each winter I pay a college kid $5 three nights a week to catch me in a gym. Each year I'm certain.

And here I go again. I'm more positive than ever. My arm feels great. I've made the ballclub. I'm starting to throw like I used to throw, and I'm thinking I'll be a reliever for a while and then I'll do well in long relief and get a spot start now and then. Then I'll complete a ballgame and along around June they're going to stick me into the rotation and I'm going to wind up winning a flock of games, just like I did when I first came up to the Yankees. I see the team doing real well and I see me as one of the keys to our success. I see myself as one of the reasons we might finish third or fourth, I see myself as a goddam hero. That's what an optimist is, isn't it? A goddam hero.

The bench was treated to a lovely Sal Maglie second-guess today. Steve Barber was pitching and he had men on second and third with Jim Fregosi up. On 3 and 2 Barber threw a change and Fregosi lunged, hit it to left and knocked in both runs. As soon as the ball was hit Maglie, who was standing next to Schultz, snapped his fingers and said, "Son of a bitch—3-and-2 change. That goddam 3-and-2 change."

Whenever something goes wrong Maglie is quick to show disgust,

95

especially if Schultz is around. I guess he wants the manager to know he's in the ballgame and that he doesn't take adversity calmly. But I was surprised about him fussing over a 3-and-2 change, because I think it's a helluva pitch. In a spot like that the hitter is looking for something the pitcher throws often, like the fastball, or if he's got good control of his curve he might throw that. So the off-speed pitch in that situation really throws the hitter off.

Later on I asked Sal about it. "Sal," I said sweetly, "I saw you get mad at the change-up Steve threw Fregosi. What's your feeling about the change on 3 and 2?"

"It depends on the situation," says Sal.

"I've had pretty good success with the 3-and-2 change."

"Well I did too," says Sal. "I remember once I threw one to Stan Musial with the bases loaded and he was so surprised he just stood there with the bat on his shoulder. Strike three."

We kicked that around for a while and Sal wound up saying that the 3-and-2 change was a helluva pitch, if you threw it to the right guy.

But not to Jim Fregosi. By Barber. Today.

APRIL
3

Bill Henry retired today, just like that. First he makes the team, then he walks in on Joe Schultz and announces his retirement. Joe told us about it and said that he admired the man, that he had a lot of guts to walk out.

John Morris, who was brought up from the Vancouver squad to replace Henry, was pretty frisky, like he'd just gotten a reprieve from the governor. He said he had some long talks with Henry—which is something, because when you say hello to Henry he is stuck for an answer—and thinks he quit because he was holding back a young player. "What am I doing keeping younger guys from a chance to earn a living?" he said to Morris. "I'm forty-two years old. I've had thirteen years in the big league. I don't really belong here."

During the meeting Joe Schultz said, "It takes a lot of courage for a guy to quit when he thinks he can't do the job anymore."

So I opened my big yap and said, "If that's the case a lot of us ought to quit."

Which gave Sal Maglie the chance to say, very coolly, "Well, use your own judgment on that."

I'm not sure Sal likes me.

Today Joe Schultz said, "Well, boys, it's a round ball and a round bat and you got to hit it square."

APRIL
4

Packing day. Baseball players and their wives are very good packers. I can pack for a two-week trip in less than an hour and my wife has moving the whole family down to a science. I'm sure this will prove very valuable to us later in life. Especially if I become a big-game hunter. Or an astronaut. Of course it helped that Mike Marshall arranged, on a split-second timetable, to have our cars shipped to Seattle by rail. Maybe *he* should be running the Long Island Rail Road.

APRIL

5

San Diego

Gary Bell is my roommate. Good roommate. Good beaver-shooter. He tells a story about a guy who climbed a palm tree to shoot some beaver and got stranded when the tide came in. I wonder where the hell that palm tree was.

I think it should be known that when Whitey Ford was pitching for the Yankees he set up a table with a checkered tablecloth in the bullpen. On the table there was an empty wine bottle with a candle in it. Also hero sandwiches. Whitey Ford had style.

Bruce Henry, the Yankee road secretary, is one of my main men. He hated to buy bats for me. He always claimed I didn't need them. When he finally did, he had them inscribed not with my name, but my batting average—.092. And once when I complained that the people I'd given passes to were upset about getting poor seats, he said, "How'd they like the price?"

Wayne Comer says that Mayo Smith, the Tiger manager, once said to him, "Wayne, I think you're going to hit .290 this year—but you're going to be doing it in Montgomery, Alabama."

I am reminded that not long ago I ran into Bob Smith of the old "Howdy Doody" show at a Rexall in Ft. Lauderdale, and was able to sing to him the Howdy Doody theme song at the toothpaste counter:

> *It's Howdy Doody time,*
> *It's Howdy Doody time,*
> *Bob Smith and Howdy Doody say Howdy to you.*
>
> *Let's give a rousing cheer,*
> *'Cause Howdy Doody's here.*

It's time to start the show,
So kids, let's go.

Bob Smith went out of his gourd.

I also count myself as having a rather large store of answers to trivia questions.
Q. Who was the dog and who was the villain in Rooty Kazootie?
A. Galapoochie Pup and Poison Sumac.
The end of spring training always brings out the best in me.

APRIL
6

We played Vancouver before coming here to play San Diego a doubleheader for our last two exhibition games. I pitched two innings in the first game and gave up two runs. My arm felt good but I had poor control of my knuckleball. I asked Maglie if there was a chance I could get some more work in the second game. He said no. His reason was that they still had a couple of minor-league pitchers to look at. I said hell, I thought the team was set, and why didn't he ask Joe if he could squeeze me in. But he wouldn't. So I went to Joe. At the precise moment I started to explain why I thought I needed more work, Joe Schultz took a huge bite out of the liverwurst sandwich he was eating, got up off his stool, went to the Coke machine and mumbled something to me through his full mouth and over his shoulder. I didn't pitch. That's how I know what he said.

Part **3** And Then I Died

APRIL

7

Today, the day before opening day, Joe Schultz said, "Well, it's back to the old salt mine, boys."

Later he encountered Tommy Davis and asked if that was "an old Budweiser" he was pouring down. "No, a Coke," Davis said.

And Joe Schultz said, "That's not too good for the old sto*macho*."

Joe Schultz calls Jose Vidal "Chico," which is Spanish for "boy."

APRIL

8

Anaheim

Opening day—or Opening Day. Depending on how you feel about it.

I got a wire from Toots Shor in Anaheim before the game. It said "Good luck, Jim. I hope you pitch often and win many games." Who says Toots never talks to has-beens?

Actually I don't know Toots that well. I've been in his place a few times and once when I was going bad he told me my whole problem was that I was striding three inches too far and if I just shortened up on the stride by those three inches everything would be fine. I was so desperate I actually tried it. It didn't help.

Everyone works out pregame nervousness in his own way. Tommy Davis was standing in the middle of the clubhouse taking a hitting stance with no bat in his hands, anticipating the pitch, striding into it, checking his swing and then going back and doing it all over again. It reminded me of a guy going over his notes just before a final exam, knowing all the time it wasn't going to do any good. If you don't have it by now, Tom, you're not going to.

There was a lot of grousing about the uniforms. It isn't only that they don't fit (no baseball uniforms fit, possibly because you are carefully measured for them). It's that they're so gaudy. I guess because we're the Pilots we have to have captain's uniforms. They have stripes on the sleeves, scrambled eggs on the peak of the cap and blue socks with yellow stripes. Also there are blue and yellow stripes down the sides of the pants. We look like goddam clowns. The only worse-looking uniforms are the ones they wear in Vancouver.

Naturally we won the first game. Beat the Angels 4–3. Mike Hegan hit the first home run for the Pilots and Joe Schultz, jumping up and down in the dugout, clapped his hands and actually yelled, "Hurray for our team."

When we came into the clubhouse, all of us yelling and screaming like a bunch of high-school kids, Joe Schultz said, "Stomp on 'em. Thataway to stomp on 'em. Kick 'em when they're down. Shitfuck. Stomp them. Stomp them good."

Already we're better than the Mets.

APRIL
9

Made my pitching debut today. Threw two fastballs to Hoyt Wilhelm, the elderly knuckleball pitcher who may one day be my idol. Got him out.

It took about a day into the season for us to be like every other ballclub, not just an expansion team full of strangers. I'm going out after the ballgame and have a few beers with the guys, maybe six or seven, which makes me blind. There is unquestionably a close feeling among the guys who go out and drink because they hash over the ballgame and it gives us all a feeling of common purpose. Slogan: The team that drinks together stays together.

Other things that draw a team together:

You're riding down the street in the team bus and you see a guy walking along with a big beer belly and his pants hanging below it and you say, "Mincher in ten years."

Or a guy is hanging on to a lamppost, a wino in a drunken stupor, severely defeated by life. "That's what happens when you can't hit the curve ball."

Marty Pattin does a pretty good Donald Duck. Before he pitched the opener he was going around the clubhouse saying in Donald Duck that you got to be loose, *quack,* you got to be loose. He was whistling in the dark. Later I found out he'd gone to bed at seven the night before and stayed in bed until noon. That's seventeen hours. I wonder if he got any sleep.

Today Joe Schultz said to the clean-shaven Rocky Bridges, Los Angeles coach,"Hey Rocky, how's your old mustache?"

Joe Schultz also said to Lou Johnson of the Angels, a man whom disaster has robbed of a piece of his left ear, "Hey, what's new, Half-Ear?"

Add to the saga of Mike Marshall: The other day he had a blister on his hand and the trainer told him the best way to help it was to keep it soaked in a cup of strong tea. A lot of guys would have told the trainer to shove the tea up his bippy, but Mike took the advice. Now he was walking around with his hand in a cup of tea—on the bus, in the clubhouse, sitting on the bench during the game and in his hotel room. So his roommate, John Kennedy, told everybody he had a nut for a roommate. Tea all over the goddam room. Even in his bed.

That's the way you become a nut. You have guts enough to walk around all day with your hand in a cup of tea.

APRIL
10

Seattle

A few more words about Eddie O'Brien and Ron Plaza. O'Brien is one of the fairly famous basketball O'Brien twins who played with Seattle from '49 to '53. Actually his job is athletic director at Seattle U. but he had four years in the big leagues with the Pirates— as infielder and pitcher—and now he's here as a friend of management (or because his brother is in city government) to get his fifth year in on the pension plan. You only need four now, but Eddie's after five and no one's going to stop him.

Plaza was a coach under Schultz in Atlanta when it was still a minor-league city, and that's one of the ways you get to be a coach in the big leagues.

Coaches have little real responsibility, so it seems to me they should, at the very least, try to help club morale—cheer guys onward and upward, make jokes and smooth out little problems before they become big ones.

O'Brien and Plaza are officious types, though, and cause more trouble than they smooth over. And because they try to find things to do they become nothing but annoyances. Like O'Brien will say to Jack Aker, "Jack, you're in the bullpen tonight." Jack has been in the bullpen for eight years.

Another example: It is customary for players to pair off and throw easily on the sidelines before a workout or a game. So as I reached into the ballbag to grab some baseballs for the guys Plaza said, "What are you going to do with those baseballs, Bouton?"

"I'm just going to take three or four out to the field because a few guys asked me to."

"Just take one."

"Yes, sir."

Steve Barber was in the diathermy machine again, all day, and I asked him again how it felt. "Better," he said, "fine, great. It just bothers me a little until I get loose and then there's no sweat." It's killing him. He hasn't been able to pick up a baseball and he was supposed to start today and didn't.

Standing around the outfield the conversation turned to religion. Don Mincher said he came from a very religious home and used to go to church every Sunday where people did things like roll in the aisles. He said there was a big circle of numbers on the church wall and when your number came up with somebody else's number you had to visit them and have a prayer meeting. As he got older Minch would say, "Well, let's have a few beers first." They didn't think that was very religious of him.

This afternoon Gary Bell and I went to Pershing Square (in Los Angeles) to listen to some of the old ladies in sneakers tell us to be prepared to meet our maker. I confess I enjoy rapping with them and usually wind up assured that eternal salvation is beyond my reach.

106

Later on we came across a group that was into the Indian thing and they were chanting *Hari Krishna Rama Rama,* etc., and I got to talking to one of them, who said that their religion simply was to reaffirm love of God regardless of the particular religion and I thought that was fair enough and we hung around enjoying the chanting and sitar music.

Then a priest, probably about fifty-five years old, happened by and got into conversation with one of the group. When he left I asked what it was about. "He said this was a religion that didn't belong in this country," the young man said. "He said we already had enough religions in this country and that we should go back to India or wherever it was we came from."

Going over the hitters is something you do before each series, and before we went against the mighty Angels Sal Maglie had a great hint for one of their weaker hitters, Vic Davalillo. "Knock him down, then put the next three pitches knee-high on the outside corner, boom, boom, boom, and you've got him."

Everybody laughed. If you could throw three pitches, boom, boom, boom, knee-high on the outside corner, you wouldn't have to knock anybody down. It's rather like telling somebody if he'd just slam home those ninety-foot putts he'd win the tournament easily.

APRIL
11

Home in Seattle at Sicks' Stadium, graveyard for pitchers, home-run heaven, the major leagues. The clubhouse is small and crowded and there's no rug, just rubber runners, and the lockers are small and close together, and there was a lot of grousing about it, and Joe Schultz said, "It's just like the old winter league. You've got to follow the crowd."

Gary Bell pitched and beat the White Sox, 7–0. Mincher hit two home runs. Tomorrow the world.

APRIL
12

Before today's game Joe Schultz said, "Okay men, up and at 'em. Get that old Budweiser."

APRIL
13

Pitched against the Chicago White Sox today and got bombed. Three runs in an inning-and-a-third. My knuckleball just doesn't seem to be ready yet. I can't get it over the plate consistently, and when I get behind I have to come in with my fastball, which somehow isn't too fast. So I got ripped for long hits, including one Don Pavletich hit over the left-field wall.

There were other problems. Pete Ward's a lefthanded hitter and I threw him a knuckler that was about a foot off the ground, outside. This is the kind of pitch he should have missed by a foot if he swung, but he followed it all the way and belted it deep to center. It was caught against the wall, but it scored a run from third and I was damn relieved it didn't go out. That he was able to hit it at all is an indication that I wasn't throwing the knuckleball hard enough, probably because I was so worried about getting it over.

Pavletich hit a fastball, the first pitch I threw, and I thought, "Jesus, I didn't even get a chance to throw him a knuckler." It was supposed to set him up. So much for setting people up with my fastball, Sal Maglie, you fink. As soon as he hit it I said to myself, "Oh Christ, what a way to start. It's going to be a long time before I'm in there again." And I wondered how many innings I'd have to pitch in order to redeem myself and whether I'd be coming to bat in the next inning (sure enough) and subject to being pulled for a pinch-hitter (and I was).

We were behind like 4–0 when I came in and 7–0 when I left, and I have to admit I didn't cry when the other guys got clobbered too. You stand out less in a crowd.

After five games our record is 3 won and 2 lost, and we've scored a lot of runs. The team looks good. Tommy Harper is doing a helluva job at second base and I thought he'd be one of our weak spots. Ray Oyler's been fine at short and we've had some outstanding catches in the outfield. Third place doesn't look impossible. And if you don't count me, our pitching looks pretty good. Except for Steve Barber. Joe Schultz is upset with Barber because he has a sore arm. It's not as unusual as it sounds. Managers get angry at injuries. An injury is beyond a manager's control and he doesn't like anything he can't control. So if you're out too long with an injury he gets angry at you. The logic is almost perfect.

Johnny Keane was particularly prone to this kind of thinking. I remember going to Joe Soares, the Yankee trainer, and telling him my arm was bothering me and that I probably shouldn't throw and suggesting that he tell Keane.

"You tell him," Joe said. "The last time I told him anything he chewed my head off."

A kid named Tom Byrd, who belongs to the Seattle organization and goes to school here, came over to work out with the club. And before the workout he was in the clubhouse shaving off his nice long sideburns. He got the word that Dewey Soriano, who is the president of the club, thought he would look better with shorter sideburns. Well, I think Dewey Soriano would look better if he lost weight.

I'm not getting enough pitching in, even as a short man, which is what I guess they've decided I am (although why they would want to bring in a knuckleballer with men on base, I can't understand). I need lots of work on my knuckleball and I'm not getting it. My other pitches aren't that bad, except they don't get anybody out, so I'm going to concentrate on the knuckleball. Last summer I threw to a catcher for about fifteen minutes every day, just knuckleballs, and if I was needed at night, I could still pitch. But Sal is not very enthusiastic. A couple of times I've asked him if I could warm up and he said, "You've been throwing the whole damn day." He was referring to the fact that I had played catch in the outfield before the game. The man's got big eyes.

The trouble is that coaches and managers have a thing about being strong for the ballgame. They don't realize that sometimes you can be too strong—sacrifice sharpness for strength. With a knuckleball, this can be particularly costly. I've tried to talk to Sal about this. I say, "Sal, I'd like to talk about my knuckleball."

And he snaps, "What?" and he's already looking at something over my shoulder. My impulse is to say that my Aunt Francis has a great knuckleball and would he like to give her a look. But when Sal snaps, "What?" he gives you the impression he doesn't want such a long answer.

If he had a liverwurst sandwich I'd expect him to take a big bite.

With Hovley gone, Mike Marshall is probably the most articulate guy on the club, so I asked him if he had as much trouble communicating as I've had and he said, "Of course. The minute I approach a coach or a manager I can see the terror in his eyes. Lights go on, bells start clanging. What's it going to be? What's this guy want from me? Why can't he be like everybody else and not bother me? It's almost impossible to carry on a conversation or get a direct answer to a direct question."

In baseball they say, "He's a great guy. Never says a word."

Like a lot of players, Jack Aker chews tobacco. But he's only been at it for two years and doesn't do it well. Hasn't learned to spit properly. As a result his uniform is always covered with brown spots.

All people who chew tobacco should have happen to them what happened to Steve Hamilton of the Yankees. Steve is an ace with chewing tobacco. Most players chew only on the field, Hamilton even chews at home and has a spittoon in the middle of his living-room floor. He says he also has a wife, which I don't altogether believe. Anyway he got careless once while pitching in Kansas City. He swallowed his chaw. So he turned around and gave it up, along with his cookies, on the back of the mound. In front of all those people.

I've felt like that on the mound too, and I don't even chew tobacco.

APRIL
14

I died tonight.

I got sent to Vancouver.

My first reaction: outrage.

Second reaction: Omigod! How am I going to tell Bobbie? The *problems*. Where to live? How to get rid of the place we'd already signed a lease on in Seattle? What would happen to the $650 deposit? Moving again. *Again*. And we just got here.

But mostly outrage.

We'd lost a 2–1 game to Kansas City when Sal came over and said "Joe wants to see you in his office."

My heart started racing. I mean Joe never wants to see me anywhere. So I knew. At the same time I thought, "Nah. It's too early. I've really only pitched the once. How can they tell anything from that? Maybe it's a trade? Or maybe he's just sore at something I've done. Let's see, what have I done lately?"

It takes a lot longer to tell it than to think it. As soon as I got into his office Joe Schultz said, "I hate to tell you a thing like this after such a close loss."

I almost laughed in his face. As though I'd be so brokenhearted over losing a lousy ballgame that I couldn't bear anything more, even a small thing like being sent to the minors.

Then Joe said he had to send me to Vancouver, and I thought, "What the hell, I'll go out with some class." I told him I would have done anything to help the club and that I really felt bad about having to leave it.

"I know," Joe Schultz said. "You work hard and you do all your running and you did everything we asked of you. We just didn't think your knuckleball did that much in Arizona and we wanted to see what it looked like when it got out of the light air, and it didn't look like it was coming around like we thought it should. We need pitching bad."

So I said, "Well, if I do real good down there, I'd like to come back."

I expected him to say, "Of course. You do good down there and we'll yank you right back here, stick you in and you'll win the goddam pennant for us." Or something reassuring like that. Instead Joe Schultz said, "Well, if you do good down there, there's a lot of teams that need pitchers."

Good grief. If I ever heard a see you later, that was it.

So I said thanks a lot and left.

I went back to my locker and there was a Coke sitting there that I'd opened. I gave it to Mike Marshall and opened a beer. This was not a night for Cokes. I threw my half-eaten corned-beef sandwich in the wastebasket and went over and told Gary Bell what had happened. He was kind of shocked, but as I started throwing stuff into my bag I could feel a wall, invisible but real, forming around me. I was suddenly an outsider, a different person, someone to be shunned, a leper.

Jose Vidal was the first guy to come over and say he was sorry to see me go. Velazquez was the second. And at that point I really felt close to them. Don Mincher came over and told me to hang in there—and, you know, I really was wrong about him. He's a good fellow.

I stopped by to shake hands with Gene Brabender and Tommy Davis, but I missed Tommy Harper and Jack Aker and some of the other guys. I realized I didn't have any money with me to pay the clubhouse men, so I told them I'd send a check. Then I picked up my bag and walked out. It felt lousy.

I suppose the man I'm most outraged at is Sal Maglie. The Screaming Skull, as he is being called (because he looks like a character in a movie of the same name), said the second really lucid thing to me that he has all spring. The first was, "Don't talk to the fans." And the second: "Joe wants to see you in his office."

That was all. No goodby, no suggestions about what I should work on, or what I needed to improve, or what I had done wrong this spring, or what pitch I should work on. Not even a hang in there. Silence. I can't believe this is Sal the Barber, my idol.

I stopped by to see Marvin Milkes, and he wasn't any help either. I told him I was running into some big and sudden expenses and could he do anything about it, and he said—and this was beautiful—"Well, you didn't show us much all spring" (10 games, 19 innings, 16 hits, 11 walks, 5 strikeouts, 3.25 ERA). If I *had* shown much more I wouldn't be getting sent down. I felt like kicking him in the shins, but I said,

"Hell, I had a better spring than four or five guys. In fact, I'm healthy, which is more than you can say for at least two of the guys." What I didn't say, but what I thought, was: "What about Steve Barber? He hasn't been able to pick up a baseball. He had a brutal spring. What's this love affair with Barber? Why can't he go on the disabled list?" Ah, the hell with it.

One of the worst things about getting sent down is the feeling you get that you've broken faith with so many people. I know my mother and father were rooting real hard for me, and all my friends back home, and they'll all feel bad—not for themselves, but for me.

Quitting altogether crosses my mind. But I won't. I *can't*. I'm convinced I can still get out big-league hitters with my knuckleball. I *know* I can. I know this is crazy, but I can see the end of the season and I've just won a pennant for some team, just won the final game, and everybody is clamoring around and I tell them, "Everybody have a seat. It's a long story."

I could be kidding myself. Maybe I'm so close to the situation that I can't make an objective judgment of whatever ability I have left. Maybe I just *think* I can do it. Maybe everybody who doesn't make it and who gets shunted to the minors feels exactly the way I do. Maybe too, the great cross of man is to repeat the mistakes of all men.

Part **4** I Always Wanted
to See Hawaii

APRIL
16

Yesterday Bobbie and I drove up to Vancouver with the kids to look for a place to live. We found a nice home about twenty minutes from the ballpark, near the beach. We had to put down $480, which represented the first and last month's rent, May and August, and we had to give postdated checks for June and July. The owner is concerned that there might be another shift. He's not taking any chances.

In the meantime I still have that $650 deposit in Seattle and don't know if I'll be able to get that back. And we haven't received the $100 deposit we left in Arizona. That's $1,230. I lead the league in deposits. Fortunately there's a baseball rule that says when a player is transferred he's not responsible for the remainder of his rent, so we won't be liable for any more money, but we might not be able to get the $650 back if we can't rent to somebody else.

A lot of players don't have the problems we do because they leave their families at home and live in hotels. That's for one of two reasons. They're just starting out and don't make enough money. Or their kids are old enough to be in school and they don't want to take them out. These guys have their families with them only two months of the season. I don't know if I'll last long enough to have to make that kind of decision.

The Vancouver Mounties (little Mike is going to have a terrible time with that one) are still in Phoenix and I won't join them until they come home. They play in Tulsa first, so I called Bob Lemon, who's the manager, and asked if he intended to use me as a starter right away and he said no, he planned to use me in relief and that I might as well wait for them to get home.

So I got permission to work out with the Pilots. I felt terribly awkward in the clubhouse and I saw that the guys also felt funny about me being there. They had these funny looks on their faces, and I felt I had a rare and communicable disease.

Driving over to the park I thought about what I would say to them. "They made a mistake, realized it and asked me to come back." But nobody would believe that. Or if I was going to pitch batting practice, I could have told them that Sal and Joe decided that I hadn't been mean enough and I was going to show them how many guys I could knock down. But it was raining and there was no batting practice. So I ran in the outfield and threw to McNertney for about twenty minutes and to Larry Haney for fifteen. I threw strictly knuckleballs, which is what I'm going to be now, a knuckleball pitcher and nothing else. My wife was right. No more kidding myself, no more trying to bring along four or five mediocre pitches. I'm all through listening to managers and coaches about how much or how little I should be throwing. *I'm in business for myself.* As long as there's going to be no special protection for me, I've got to make all my own decisions. Sal always wanted me rested in case I had to pitch eight innings of relief, which I never did. So now I'm going to throw as much as I think I have to.

There was a meeting before the game with Minnesota, which I did not, of course, attend. Gary Bell filled me in. They were going over

117

the Twins' lineup—it's a tough one—and the conversation went about like this:

"Pitch him high and tight."

"Hell, he'll hit that one over the left-field wall. You got to pitch him low and away."

"Pitch him away and he'll go to right field on you."

"I don't know about all of that. I do know you got to curve him."

"Oh no, he's a hell of a breaking-ball hitter."

Finally, Sal Maglie: "Well, pitch around him."

When the meeting was over, Gary added up the pitch-around-hims and there were five, right in the beginning of the batting order. So according to Sal Maglie you start off with two runs in and the bases loaded.

It's like the scouting reports we used to get on the Yankees about National League teams. We'd get the word that this guy couldn't hit the good overhand curve. Well, *nobody* hits the good overhand curve. In fact, hardly anybody throws the good overhand curve. It's a hard pitch to control and it takes too much out of your arm.

And the word on Tim McCarver of the Cards was that Sandy Koufax struck him out on letter-high fastballs. Which is great advice if you can throw letter-high fastballs like Koufax could.

Anyway, I guess Gary didn't pitch around enough of the Minnesota hitters because they bombed him out in the first inning with three runs. We lost it, 6–4—I mean *they* lost it. There were several relief pitchers in the game and I could have sworn I saw Joe Schultz waving for his knuckleballer, but he was already gone to Vancouver.

One of the reasons I'll probably be playing baseball for the next few years is that I really don't have a career waiting for me outside. I'd find it hard to work for some big company. I'm not a nine-to-five type. I have a vague hope I might be able to work into television or politics somehow, and my friend Jim Jacobs and I have talked about making films. Jim, who once was the world's greatest handball player, has done great things with old fight films and we've talked about working up a baseball film and possibly films on other sports. But I'm not ready for that yet.

The only thing I'm involved in now is that real-estate venture. My brother Pete handles the business during the season, but there's really not much more than bookkeeping to it, since we do all the buying and selling when I'm home. Even so, it doesn't seem to be the kind of thing that would ever keep me occupied full time. So I'm a baseball player. A Seattle Pilot—pardon, a Vancouver Mountie. A Vancouver goddam Mountie.

I listened to the Pilots game over the radio and wouldn't you know it, I found myself rooting for them. When the Yankees sent me down all I wanted was for them to get mashed. Even now I hope they finish lower in their division than the Pilots do in theirs. I can't explain it, but that's what I feel. The only bad thing I wish for the Pilots is that they get into a lot of high-scoring games; win them, but need pitching help.

APRIL
17

Got a letter today from two girls who were members of my fan club. They'd read the article in *Signature* about us adopting Kyong Jo and wanted to congratulate us and wish me luck with my new team. I really liked that fan club. I enjoyed being a big-league player and having people recognize me and having little kids get a charge out of meeting me. I remember what it was like when I was a kid and what a thrill I got just watching Willie Mays climb out of a taxicab. So the fact that I had my own personal fan club (would you believe an annual dinner and a newspaper called *All About Bouton*?) always pleased me. Of course I realized how old I'm getting and how quickly time passes when I heard that one of the fan-club members was in Vietnam. It just doesn't seem right that a member of my fan club should be fighting in Vietnam. Or that anybody should be.

The fan club started in 1962 when these two kids—George Saviano and Al Gornie—came to me and asked if they could start one. I told them to cool it until I did something. I didn't want them to waste a lot of time and energy on someone who might not be around too long. Of course I talked to them. I figure that's part of the game. Besides, I enjoyed it.

Not everybody agrees. I was a big New York Giant fan when I lived in New Jersey as a kid and then we moved to Chicago. I used to go to all the Cub-Giant games out there. And I remember once leaning over the dugout trying to tell Al Dark how great he was and how much I was for him and, well, maybe get his autograph too, when he looked over at me and said, "Take a hike, son. Take a hike."

Take a hike, son. Has a ring to it, doesn't it? Anyway, it's become a deflating putdown line around the Bouton family. Take a hike, son.

Having made the move to Syracuse a couple of times and then to Seattle and now to Vancouver makes me a member of a not very exclusive club. Us battered bastards of baseball are the biggest customers of the U.S. Post Office, forwarding-address department. I've seen letters chasing guys for months, years even. Sometimes you walk into a clubhouse and there's a letter on the table for a guy who was released two years ago. A guy like Rollie Sheldon still has mail coming to him in Yankee Stadium, and once they start forwarding, it can be a year before it catches up.

One of Gary Bell's parting lines about me was, "Here comes the guy who opened and closed a checking account in three days." True. We have taken the money out of our Seattle account and will deposit it in Vancouver. But we're optimistic. We're leaving a few dollars in the Seattle account in case I get called up later this summer. I should say *when* I get called up.

APRIL
18

Tacoma

There's nothing like walking into a minor-league clubhouse to remind you what the minors are like. You have a tendency to block it. It was cold and rainy in Tacoma when I went there to meet the Vancouver club and the locker room was shudderingly damp, small and smelly. There's no tarpaulin on the field, so everything is wet and muddy and the dirt crunches underfoot on the cement. The locker stalls are made of chicken wire and you hang your stuff on rusty nails. There's no rubbing table in the tiny trainer's room, just a wooden bench, and there are no magazines to read and no carpet on the floor and no boxes of candy bars. The head is filthy and the toilet paper is institutional-thin. There's no batrack, so the bats, symbolically enough, are stored in a garbage can. There's no air-conditioning and no heat, and the paint on the walls is peeling off in flaky chunks and you look at all of that and you realize that the biggest jump in baseball is between the majors and Triple-A. The minor leagues are all very minor.

There's no end to the humiliation. The kid in the clubhouse asked me what position I played.

The Vancouver team never got to the clubhouse because the game was called off before they left the hotel. So the uniforms never got there and I sat around in my underwear feeling sorry for myself. Whitey Lockman, the Tacoma manager, passed through and I told him I had just seen his most famous double, the one he hit before Bobby Thomson's home run in 1951, on television again. He enjoyed being reminded.

I went out to work in my long underwear with a warm-up jacket over the top and I thought to myself, "Damn, I wish somebody could see me out here being this conscientious—Whitey Lockman maybe, or a scout." If they only knew how hard I was willing to work and how much I was willing to sacrifice they'd know I'll make it back and that they ought to buy my contract now, at a bargain price. If I have a good year I'm not going to forgive these other ballclubs who passed me up. Even the Mets had a shot. They didn't even nibble.

APRIL
19

Tonight I told Bob Lemon that I'd made a tactical mistake this spring in trying to do too much and that what I wanted to do from now on is what I did at the end of last summer—throw knuckleballs. I told him I also wanted to work out a program of throwing on the sidelines before the game for about ten minutes even if I'd be pitch-ing a lot in the games. The idea is to maintain the feeling you need to throw the knuckleball and at the same time prevent the arm from get-ting too strong. If it's strong you have a tendency to bring it through too fast and you impart spin to the ball.

And Lemon said, "You throw any pitch you want and you throw it as often as you want and set up any working program you want. It's all up to you."

Gee, how am I going to handle all that responsibility?

For me, one of the savers of being in the minors is that it makes me an underdog. I like to be an underdog. I've always been the guy that never was the big pheenom but that came out on top unexpectedly. When I was a kid we used to—my brother and I and a couple of other kids—challenge eight guys to basketball games, two against one. Often we'd win and the other guys just couldn't believe that four could beat eight. The answer is that the underdog role is fun to play, and easy, because there's no pressure. You've got nothing to lose.

I enjoy the fact that my high school (Bloom Township HS, Chicago Heights) has decided to award a trophy that is given every year not to the guy who is the best, but to the one who shows the most desire and works the hardest. The trophy is called the "Jim Bouton 110 Percent Award."

Not that you can't carry that sort of thing too far. In 1959, I guess it was, I weighed 150 pounds and decided I should put on a lot of weight in order to throw a better fastball. So I ate. I ate a lot. I ate five meals a day, all very rich. In six weeks I put on thirty pounds and wrecked my stomach permanently. I don't have an ulcer, but there's an inflammation that won't quiet down, and I have to take Maalox every day. The fastball went, the stomach stayed.

How much running should a pitcher do? The idea, of course, is to be in good physical shape. However, it's quite possible to be both out of shape and a good pitcher. As Johnny Sain says, "You don't run the damn ball across the plate. If running did it, they'd look for pitchers on track teams." It's one of the reasons he's such a popular pitching coach.

There are pitchers who tell you that they've played for men who made them run miles a day and some who made them run hardly at all and that it never made any difference in their pitching. Personally, I've never been out of shape, so I wouldn't know.

The problem for a long-relief man is that he doesn't want to tire himself out before a game in which he may pitch eight innings. But if he doesn't run and then he doesn't pitch, he very quickly is out of shape. A short man can stay in shape just pitching. And then there's Mickey Lolich, who doesn't look like he's in shape to do anything but pitch. One of the nice things about baseball is that there are no rules you can't break.

Had a talk with Bob Tiefenauer about his knuckleball and he said he'd recently gotten a good tip from Ed Fisher. He says that when you're pitching with the wind at your back (which is very bad for the knuckler) you throw the ball harder. This seems to keep it out ahead of the wind and it knuckles pretty good. Tief says it sounds crazy, but there's logic to it and it seems to work. I'll have to remember that.

I've been thinking about my options in life these days. There aren't many. If I do poorly here I could easily be dropped. I don't think they want to pay $22,000 to some guy to pitch Triple-A. On the other hand I could be sold or traded, or brought back to Seattle. I don't think they want me back there, though, or Schultz wouldn't have said that about a lot of clubs needing pitchers. I see by the boxscores that a lot of pitching staffs are getting bombed. It's a lot different than last year.

Washington lost 6–0, and I wonder if they can use some pitching help. I sure would like to be with a club in the East, because if there's anything I want to do before I'm through it's win a few games in Yankee Stadium, and being with Washington would give me some extra shots at them. If this sounds like a grudge, it's only because it is.

APRIL
19

Got my first inning of pitching in for the Vancouver Mounties and I was only super. We were leading 15–3 when Bob Lemon asked me if I wanted to pitch an inning. I said sure and went in to pitch the ninth. I struck out the first hitter on four knuckleballs. I struck out the second hitter on five knuckleballs. And I really wanted to strike out that third guy because striking out the side is the kind of thing that gets back to the big club. But the third hitter grounded out on a 1-and-2 knuckler. Still, it was almost too easy.

Corky Evans was the catcher. He's a good, enthusiastic kid. He caught me in the bullpen when I warmed up and he'll be catching me on the sidelines before the games. He's so enthusiastic he actually jumps around and says happy things when one of our guys gets a hit. In fact the first time he jumped up and started cheering I looked around to find out what had happened. All that happened was we got another one of about twenty hits. So at least he won't be grumbling about having to catch my knuckler.

Meal money in Triple-A is $7.50 a day. In the big league it's $15. I don't know if they mean to have you eat half as much or half as well.

Most baseball people have two ages, real and baseball. The older they get, the greater the discrepancy between their numbers. Some of the players were clever enough to cheat by two or three years as soon as they signed and thus were more valuable throughout their careers. I made the mistake of telling my real age right along and now it's too late to start lying. All this explains why Bill Monbouquette was able to say a couple of years ago that he was thirty-one. I was twenty-nine at the time, and I remember him pitching for the Red Sox while I was still in school.

The greatest all-time age put-on was engineered by Rollie Sheldon. When he signed he told scouts that he was nineteen. The Yankees brought him into spring training as a twenty-year-old pheenom and he won the James P. Dawson award as outstanding rookie of the spring, and just before the team went north it was discovered that he'd spent three years in the Air Force and three years in college and that he was actually twenty-six. By now, though, there was nothing anybody could do. And if he'd told them his real age he never would have had a chance.

I've also been reflecting on Joe Schultz. I'm afraid I'm giving the impression I don't like him or that he's bad for the ballclub. Neither is true. I think Joe Schultz knows the guys get a kick out of the funny and nonsensical things he says, so he says them deliberately. If there's a threat to harmony on the club I think it comes from the coaching staff.

On the other hand, it has been said that harmony is shit. The only thing that counts is winning.

Dick Baney is a fashion plate—I mean in a baseball uniform. There is a right way to wear a baseball uniform and a wrong way, and in order to do it right you have to break some rules. Like you're not allowed to cut your baseball socks. But if you don't cut your socks you're nothing.

I'm referring to the outside socks, the colored ones. Underneath you wear long white socks that are called sanitaries. Over those go the colored socks with the stirrups under the feet. This leaves narrow half-moons of white showing. It has become the fashion—I don't know how it started, possibly with Frank Robinson—to have long, *long* stirrups with a lot of white showing. The higher your stirrups the cooler you are. Your legs look long and cool instead of dumpy and hot.

The way to make stirrups longest, or what are called high-cuts, is to slice the stirrup and sew in some extra material. It's against the rules, but Baney ignored them. Not only that, he took his uniform to a tailor and had it made so form-fitting the whole thing looks like it was painted on. He says this is important and the reason he did poorly his first time out was that "I looked down at myself and I looked like a clown. I figured if I look like a clown I must be pitching like a clown, and so I did."

Do you know that ethyl chloride can be fun? This is a freezing agent kept around to cut the pain of cuts, bruises, sprains and broken bones. It comes in a spray can and it literally freezes anything it touches; hair, skin, blood. Also ants, spiders and other animals.

The way you have fun with ethyl chloride is spray it on a guy who isn't looking. First thing he knows there's a frozen spot on his leg and the hair is so solid it can be broken off.

Or you spray it on crawling creatures. They're frozen, they thaw and they resume their appointed rounds. Once we froze and thawed one bug thirty times just to see if it could be done. It could.

Hot-feet, or hot-foots, depending on your attitude toward the language, can also be fun if your life is drab and empty and puerile and full of Phil Rizzuto. I once gave Phil my famous atomic bomb hot-foot, which consists of four match heads stuck inside another match. It was such a lovely hot-foot his shoelaces caught fire and the flames were licking at his pants cuff.

125

One of the great hot-foots (hot-feets?) of all time was administered to Joe Pepitone by Phil Linz. The beauty part was that Pepitone was giving a hot-foot to somebody else at the time and just as he started to turn around and grin at the havoc he had wrought, a look of horror crossed his face and he began to do an Indian dance. The hot-footer had been hot-footed (feeted?) himself. Joe Pepitone is a gas.

APRIL
20

Vancouver

Today I got hung with a loss I didn't deserve, but possibly merited. It happened because a perfectly lovely knuckler got by the catcher. In the ensuing confusion, during which I personally covered home plate on a close play, the run scored amidst great argument. The man was out, but the umpire disagreed.

Merritt Ranew was the catcher, and although he's a fine fellow he had a lot of trouble with the knuckleball. Lemon suggested I stop off at the ballpark in Seattle on my way home (we haven't moved yet) and pick up McNertney's big glove. When I got to the stadium I spent a half-hour wandering around yelling to get somebody's attention. I couldn't, so I finally climbed over the fence in left field and went all the way to second base and screamed at the top of my lungs, "Is there anybody here?" No answer. "Christ," I thought, "anybody who wants to could come into this place, dismantle it and take it away by morning. I found the glove in the clubhouse and after I climbed back over the fence I noticed a sign that said: WARNING, GUARD DOG PATROLLING AREA. I could just see the papers the next morning: "Former Seattle Player Ripped to Shreds at Second Base."

APRIL
21

Honolulu

There are compensations to being in the minors. Like Hawaii. Arrived here today and it's beautiful. On the airplane, if you're Leo Marentette you play gin rummy. Leo used to be in the Tiger organization and the first thing he asked me was "How's Moon Man?" which is what the Tigers called Mike Marshall, the way the Pilots called Steve Hovley "Orbit." Leo took $70 meal money from Darrell Brandon and the word is that he bought rights to Jerry Stephenson, a gin-rummy mark, for the five-hour plane ride.

On the plane I discovered that Greg Goossen is afraid to fly. On the takeoff he wrapped himself around his seatbelt in the fetal position, his hands over his eyes. Then, as we were landing, he went into frenzied activity, switching the overhead light on and off, turning the air blower on and off, right and left, opening and closing his ashtray and giving instructions into a paper cup: "A little more flap, give me some more stick, all right, just a little bit, okay now, level out."

I asked him, "What's the routine?"

"I always feel better when I land them myself," Goose explained.

Hawaii is not exactly like the rest of the minors. The first thing they did at the ballpark was line us up on the foul line, where two Hawaiian girls presented each of us with a lei and a kiss on the cheek. When the girl got to me I bent her back over my knee and kissed her like they do in the movies. Nailed her a hell of a kiss, if I say so myself. For another there's a topless nightclub in the Polynesian Hotel, where we're staying, and the girls who work there live in the hotel. There's nothing minor league about that at all, at all. I mean, Kearney, Nebraska, was never like this.

Having been sent to the minors for at least parts of the last three seasons now, I've become somewhat defensive about it. It's disturbing to be considered a failure, to have a stigma attached to you just because you're sent down. For the fact is that by any sane comparative standard I'm much better at my job, even in Triple-A, than most successful professional people are in theirs.

As a Triple-A player I'm one of the top thousand baseball players in the country, and when it's considered how few actually make it out of the hundreds of thousands who try, it's really a fantastic accomplishment. So I don't feel like a failure, and anybody who is guilty of thinking I am will be sentenced to a long conversation with Joe Schultz's liverwurst sandwich.

Not that there aren't little annoyances to being in the minors. Players have to do things that coaches do for them in the big leagues—like shag balls. Baseballs are thrown in from the outfield during batting practice and someone has to gather them up and give them to the batting-practice pitcher. In the minors the job is done by the pitcher who pitched the night before. I had forgotten this little duty when I was sold to the Seattle Angels, and when I was reminded I said—facetiously, of course—"But I'm a name player." And I had another nickname: Name Player.

Name Player got off the bus today and went off to inspect the Honolulu playing field where some of the Angel players I had played with last year were working out. I could see the surprised looks on their faces when they saw me. Jimmy Reese, the coach, hollered over at me, "Hey, Bouton, what are you doing down here?"

"That's what happens when you have a bad inning," I said.

Pitched again today and did not have another bad inning. It was my third appearance in three days, and the dear knuckler has been jumping. One pop-up, one groundout, one strikeout. I know this is the kind of work I need, but I'm wondering why they're pitching me so often. They have fourteen pitchers on the staff. Could it be that somebody in Seattle thinks I need the work? Or maybe they want a last look before they release me? *Release me?* Good grief.

Things are going so well I'm thinking of how much the family will enjoy Vancouver. It's a beautiful town, with the mountains coming right down to the edge of it. We've taken a place near the beach and it should be lovely indeed.

I'm really riding that emotional rollercoaster these days. In spring training I was going good and getting to pitch a lot. I led the club in

128

appearances and I was excited about making the team. And then I didn't. All of a sudden I'm at a new low, like some crazy Dow Jones chart, and I have to start all over. Now I've pitched well in four games and I feel like the rollercoaster is on the way up, and that if I have three or four more good appearances I might even get called back to Seattle. In baseball you're only as good and as happy as your last appearance.

I read in the paper that Hoyt Wilhelm says there are only four guys throwing the knuckleball consistently in the major leagues—Wilbur Wood, Eddie Fisher, Phil Niekro and himself—and the reason is that you don't learn to throw the knuckleball, you have to be born with it. I wonder if I was born to throw the knuckleball and have been wasting myself all these years.

Jim Coates pitched against us tonight and beat us 4–1. Coates, as has been noted, could pose as the illustration for an undertaker's sign. He has a personality to match. He was the kind of guy who used to get on Jimmy Piersall by calling him "Crazy." Like, "Hey, Crazy, they coming after you with a net today?"

Piersall used to get mad as hell and call Coates a lot of names, the most gentle of which was thermometer, but it didn't seem to hurt the way he played. I remember a game in Washington. Piersall was playing center field and Coates was giving him hell from the Yankee bullpen. Piersall was turning away from the game to give it back when somebody hit a long fly ball to left-center and Piersall had to tear after it. All the time he was running he was screaming at Coates, and when he got up to the fence he climbed halfway up it, caught the ball, robbing somebody of a home run, and threw it in. But not for a second did he stop yelling at Coates.

Coates was famous for throwing at people and then not getting into the fights that resulted. There'd be a big pile of guys fighting about a Coates duster and you'd see him crawling out of the pile and making for the nearest exit. So we decided that if there was a fight while Coates was pitching, instead of heading for the mound, where he was not likely to be, we'd block the exits.

There was, of course, no fight. We'd all rather talk than fight.

APRIL
22

My great roomie, Bob Lasko, has led me down the trail of sin and perdition and gotten me smashed on *mai tais* (pronounced "my ties"). This is a Hawaiian drink brewed by the evil gods of the volcanoes and no fit potion for a clean-cut American boy like me. I could barely make it back to my room and turn on the tape recorder. (Can you sing a book?)

I almost can't believe it, but I was in another ballgame tonight. Pitched two-and-a-third innings, gave up one hit, a double by Bob Rodgers, one walk and no runs. I'm throwing the knuckleball for strikes. I'm almost feeling sorry for the hitters. And I *am* feeling guilty about the amount of work I'm getting when a guy like Lasko is getting almost none. But not very.

One of the natural beauties of Hawaii is the bullpen refreshment. There is a terrific soup sold in the ballpark called *siamin* (pronounced "sigh-a-*min*"), which contains native goodies, noodles, pork and herbs. Beats Cracker Jack every time.

APRIL
24

I've been poisoned by *mai tais* twice more and sun-burned once in the past two days. I also pitched in two more games, coming in both times in the ninth inning with a one-run lead and giving up no hits and no sweat. After the game tonight I walked by Jimmy Reese and he said, "What are you doing in this league?"—which made me feel very nice indeed. Could all this be due to the sun and the *mai tais?* Is it all just an illusion?

I've pitched six days in a row and everybody thinks I'll soon be called up. Hey, up there, you listening?

I called my wife during the seventh inning tonight because I didn't think I'd be used again, and just as the operator was asking her if she'd take a collect call, Sheldon came back to tell me there was a call for me to warm up. In fact, when Lemon gave the signal the guys in the bullpen pretended they didn't understand in order to give Sheldon time to come get me. I thought he was kidding until I saw the terrorized look on his face. So I hung up, went in and saved another. Another day, another save.

APRIL
25

It's great to be young and in Hawaii. Not only did I pitch in my seventh-straight game and get my third save, but I had a smashing bowl of siamin, corn on the cob and teriyaki out in the bullpen. Major league bullpen.

We get up around ten in the morning, put on our bathing suits, go down to the beach for three or four hours, come back to have a nice home-cooked meal (we all have kitchenettes and share the cooking), do some shopping and get out to the ballpark at around five. Sheldon brings a radio down to the bullpen and always asks if we want to listen to a ballgame or music. Sheldon, you must be kidding.

Talk in the bullpen turned to Joe Schultz, and I recounted what he'd told me when he sent me down. Everybody was surprised that I didn't get the recording: "This is a recording. Pitch two or three good games and you'll be right back up here again. This is a recording."

Sheldon recalled the moment the Grim Reaper cut him down. He was in the outfield shagging and Sal Maglie stood at third base and hollered at the top of his voice, "Hey, Sheldon, Joe wants to see you in his office." Everybody in the outfield heard.

"I was so embarrassed, I turned red," Sheldon said. "I had the impulse to holler, 'Find out what he wants.' I'm still sorry I didn't."

Also a beaver-shooting story was told. It seems that the Detroit bullpen carried a pair of binoculars and a telescope. The binoculars were used to spot an interesting beaver in the stands and then the telescope was used to zero in. So when the guy using the binoculars spotted a likely subject he'd say, "Scope me."

Strange bullpen incident tonight. Some dum-dum fan came by with his girl, who was wearing tight slacks, bare midriff and revealing top. Naturally we all looked pretty hard. "What the hell you guys looking at?" he said. Since we figured he could guess, we didn't say. So he started yelling and giving us the finger and like that until somebody said, "You don't like it, big boy, come on over and we'll talk about it." (It's not unusual for players to get into shouting matches with fans and yell things like "Go check your wife, there's a ballplayer missing.")

The girl pulled him away, but he must have complained to a cop or somebody because pretty soon it got back to Lemon that there had been an incident in the bullpen. Between innings he ran out and chewed us all out, not only for getting into a fight with a fan but for not paying attention to the game. "You guys are having enough trouble getting anybody out," he said. He really knows how to hurt a guy.

When he left there was much consternation over him talking like that to our man Bill Ferrell, who happens to be nineteen years old and has a perfect pitching record, 1–0—and in his only time at bat he got a base hit. We call him "1 and 0" and "A Thousand," and what he should have told Lemon is that *he's* not having any trouble getting anybody out.

The reason I suffer from *mai tai* poisoning so often is that the other guys can drink them with no effect at all while I get drunk. They insist I come along so that they can, as they say, put the hurt on my body. Then in the morning they invite me for breakfast so they can observe the havoc they have wrought. While they gorge themselves on the veranda I bathe my eyes with Murine.

All of which decided us on two things about playing baseball in Hawaii: that in addition to the $7.50 meal money there ought to be a beverage allowance; and that if a guy's home team was Hawaii and he was called up to the big leagues he might well decide he didn't want to go.

APRIL
26

After seven-straight appearances I didn't get into the game tonight. We lost 5–1, and after the game Lemon called me into his office and said, "You mad at me?"

"No, why?" I said.

"Because I wasn't able to get you into the game tonight."

We laughed. A winner's laugh.

Dick Bates got called up today. Not me, not Darrell Brandon. Dick Bates. We were sitting around the hotel pool when Sheldon arrived and asked us if we'd heard about Bates. We said no. When he told us, at first I thought he was kidding. Then I got pissed off. I was sure I'd be next. You just can't tell what goes through their minds up there, though. Like Lemon was telling me that after last night's game he was talking to Milkes on the phone, giving him the statistics of the ballgame, and when he got to where I came into the game he said, "And guess who relieved?" And Milkes said, "Him again?"

"Yep," Lemon said, "and he got a save. And do you know he's thrown 80 strikes and 47 balls so far?" (This is good even if you're *not* throwing the knuckleball.) Milkes was impressed. The point I started to make is that Milkes told Lemon that Edgerton had looked pretty good but that "they're beginning to get to him." When Lemon asked how many games Edgerton had pitched in, Milkes said two. *Beginning to get to him!* For crying out loud.

At the end of our talk I was going to ask Lemon about the possibility of getting a start or two while I was down here. Just then Bob

Lasko came along and asked when he was going to pitch next and I didn't have the heart to say anything. I was afraid Lemon would give me a start and cut into Lasko's time. Really.

A note here about motivation. Marv Staehle has been talking about quitting after this season. He's been bouncing up and down between Triple-A and the majors for nine years now without getting close to his four years in. Now he says he just wants to have a good year, not because he expects to go anywhere, but for pride.

My own reaction is that pride counts.

When I called my wife after my third save there was a gathering of Vancouver Mounties outside the phone booth. So on the bus today I was asked if I always call home after a save or a win and I said yes, I did. And Greg Goossen said, "Big deal. It means about three phone calls a year."

Corky Evans, my catcher, doesn't drink, smoke or swear. He spends his spare time reading *Field and Stream* and writing three letters to his girl every day and reading the three letters he gets from her in return. Corky doesn't even go out for a milkshake. So tonight Bob Lemon said to him, "Hey, Corky, if you go out looking for broads tonight, make sure you take that big glove."

I was glad to hear the score of the Seattle game tonight—sort of glad. They lost 14–2. I would rather they won 15–14.

APRIL
27

I was on a radio show after the ballgame last night and today the guys were kidding me about the gift. In the majors it's usually something worth $25 or $50, but in the minors it's a choice: you can have a "best wishes for the rest of the year" or an "everybody's rooting for your comeback."

Although I gave up my first earned run tonight, I got my fourth save. Right after the game we catch a midnight flight back to the mainland. I feel like a conquering hero returning.

APRIL

28

Seattle

I bummed a ride to Vancouver with Lemon rather than fly up with the team so I could have an afternoon at home. Lemon had to stop off for a conference with Milkes and Schultz. At three in the afternoon he called me. "You don't have to come back with me," he said. "Enjoy the day with your family and call Milkes tomorrow."

"What does that mean, Bob?"

"I don't know, Meat. Just call Marvin tomorrow."

My wife and I spent the rest of the day trying to figure the percentages. First, of course, it could mean I was being called up by the Pilots, and since they're home, I could join them tomorrow. It could also be that the Pilots are trying to make a trade and if it goes through there'll be an opening on the staff. If the trade doesn't go through, I'll be heading back to Vancouver. On the other hand, they may be trying to get a pitcher in a trade and if they do, it's also back to Vancouver for me. But if they *don't* get the pitcher, then I'll be called up. Finally, it could be that *I* may be involved in a trade.

We're covered for houses here and in Vancouver. But suppose I'm traded. I don't think I can afford any more deposits. And another thing. My wife just got through buying a bunch of beach toys for the kids. And this afternoon, before the phone call from Lemon, the kids ran around the neighborhood saying goodby to their friends of two weeks. Tomorrow morning they may be saying hello again.

135

Part **5** The Yanks Are Coming,
The Yanks Are Coming

APRIL

29

Hello again.

The news came this morning. *"Hrrrmph,"* Marvin Milkes said, or words to that effect. I was back with the Seattle Pilots. Not only that, but I had an hour-and-a-half to get my ass to the clubhouse and into uniform. Not only that, right after the game we're going on a road trip, first stop Minneapolis. Not only that, my suitcase has gone on ahead to Vancouver. Not only that, my hang-up suit bag is up there too and doesn't even have my name on it. Not only that, I'm inordinately happy.

I'm so happy I wasn't able to sleep last night, just thinking about being happy. So I got out of bed at four in the morning and spent two hours writing notes for a speech I'd like to deliver to Sal Maglie and/or Joe Schultz.

This is what I decided to say:

"I've given a lot of thought to this. In fact it's all I've thought about for weeks. Number one, the knuckleball. I'd like you to understand it takes a feel to throw it, not strength. So I think I have to throw fifteen minutes on the sidelines to a catcher every single day, no matter how many days in a row I've pitched, or how many innings I might be expected to go that night.

"Number two, we have to adjust our thinking on walks. Walks are inevitable with a pitch that jumps around so much. What's more important, when you're a knuckleball pitcher, is the total number of walks and hits. For instance, for Vancouver I pitched eleven innings and gave up four hits and seven walks, a total of eleven baserunners. If this were three walks and eight hits it wouldn't be as good because runners move faster and farther on base hits than they do on walks. Also I think it's wrong to throw a fastball to a good hitter with a 3-and-2 count unless I've got a big lead, and I think it's wrong to throw a fastball 3 and 1 in a close game, and it's wrong to throw a fastball 3 and 0 when a home run or hit would beat me. In every case I'd rather walk the guy with my best pitch than let him beat me with one swing at my worst.

"I'd also like to say that I don't mind talking about the mistakes I've made in certain situations. Some people call it second-guessing, but I don't. It's good to go over mistakes—after the game. What I want to eliminate is too many hollered instructions during the game. For example, if somebody hollers out to me, "Make him hit the ball," I think he means I should throw a fastball or slider, since I'm always trying to throw every knuckleball right down the middle anyway. I have to choose my own pitch, and chances are it's the knuckleball.

"Now, about that start. I think it's possible that someday I could pitch every three days with only two days of rest, or every four days, and relieve in between. I know I did it last year and Marvin Milkes can be a witness to that. The only other knuckleballer who is as young and strong as I am is Niekro, and he's starting every four days now. It's taken the Braves a long time to come around to the idea that a knuckleball pitcher can be a starter, but they have and the results are great. I'm so convinced this could be done that I'd be willing to go to the minors and prove it. In fact, the very nature of the pitch is such that it's more adaptable to starting than relieving. A starting pitcher doesn't have to worry about coming in with men on base.

"Finally, I don't think it's fair to compare me right away with guys like Niekro, Wood, Fisher and Wilhelm. They're top pitchers and I think I should be allowed to be only fair or even mediocre for a while—say, a month or six weeks. After all, the other guys have had years."

That's my speech. Now I wonder if I can pry anybody away from his liverwurst sandwich long enough to hear it.

When I got to the clubhouse today it was as though I'd never left. It was fun being back with all the guys again, and I really laid my week in Hawaii on them.

Sal and I had our big conversation.
Sal: "Hi, what time'd you get in?"
Me: "Eight yesterday morning. From Hawaii."
Sal: "Humglmpf."
That was it.

Marty Pattin won the game for us tonight with a two-hitter. He had a no-hitter going into the eighth and I thought, how could anybody not know he's pitching a no-hitter. The fans were cheering while Pattin was picking up the resin bag. We won 2–0, and I walked into the clubhouse feeling happy with myself for having given the ballclub such a tremendous lift that Pattin went out and pitched a two-hitter.

I was also gratified that Joe Schultz had me warming up, along with Jack Aker, in the ninth. This was a close game and he had me warming up. L'il old me.

MAY
1

Minneapolis

I started warming up before the game today in Minnesota and it was so damn cold—and the American League ball is definitely bigger than the Pacific Coast League ball—that I couldn't get the damn thing to break at all. Every single knuckleball I threw was rolling over, or spinning sideways, and I started to panic. I could feel the sweat break out on me, and I was cold and sweaty at the same time. Here was Lemon sending in good reports on me, I thought, and here I was letting him down. Not only that. When they get a look at this junk they're going to think all I have is a minor-league knuckleball. Baseball people think like that. And I thought if I didn't have a good knuckleball *right now* they'd send me down again and I'd *never* come back up.

Of course, when I got in the game my knuckleball was great. I came in with the bases loaded and promptly went to 3 and 1 on the hitter. What do I do now? Fastball or knuckleball? Before I was sent down it probably would have been the fastball. I threw the knuckleball and got a grounder to first base for the out at the plate. Then I struck out the next hitter to end the inning. I saved all three runs from being charged to my roomie.

I pitched two more innings, throwing only one fastball. Not a ball was hit out of the infield. We lost, 4–1.

Dick Bates was sent back down to make room for Darrell Brandon. I'm not sure of what they think they're doing, but at a guess front offices are more interested in players who are far than those who are near. They were more interested in Bates than Brandon and Bouton, but only until they saw Bates up close.

We also just bought John O'Donoghue and when Gary Bell and I walked into the coffee shop this morning he was sitting there. Gary said that when ballplayers get up in the morning and go into the coffee shop and see a player from a different organization sitting there, "Everybody starts stepping lightly."

Gary has come up with a good nickname for Freddy Valazquez. Freddy just sits there in the bullpen, warming up pitchers, and he never gets into a game and just looks sad. So Gary calls him Poor Devil.

Last night Gary and I stayed up late talking about real estate and what future there might be in it for him as investor or salesman or broker and I suggested he might get involved by reading some real-estate books. Gary is a typical ballplayer in some ways in that he doesn't seem to have any plan for himself, nothing to fall back on. The day he's out of baseball is the day he'll start thinking about earning a living. And then it could be too late.

We stayed up so late talking that I needed a nap in the bullpen. Fortunately the Minnesota bullpen is out of sight. So I slept four solid innings before going into the game. There may be better ways to earn a living, but I can't think of one.

Gary wasn't very happy, of course, after being knocked out in the fifth. He had a couple of beers and said, "Maybe we ought to break out those real-estate books pretty soon." Then he had a better idea. He suggested that tonight the two of us go out and see what we could do about restructuring parts of San Francisco (we were to leave for Oakland after the game).

"San Francisco," Gary said, "is absolutely going to catch hell."

I was sitting in front of my locker this afternoon and suddenly someone walked over to me and there was a shadow on the newspaper I was reading. My heart started thumping. I could almost hear Sal Maglie say, "Joe wants to see you in his office." That's what insecurity is.

Today Joe Schultz said, "Hey, I want to see some el strikos thrown around here."

I'm always fascinated by what people say during infield practice. It's a true nonlanguage, specifically created not to say anything. This one today from Frank Crosetti as he hit grounders: "Hey, the old shillelagh!"

Had a big talk with Sal Maglie today. Not *the* big talk, with note cards and all that, which I carry around waiting for the right, quintessentially right, moment. It went about like this.

Me: "Sal, I've made some decisions about my knuckleball and I'd like to talk them over with you."

Sal: "*Mblvckd?*"

Me: "Yes. Well, I think I've got to throw the knuckleball all the time and forget about my other pitches."

Sal: "Of course. Christ, if you don't do that you won't get anybody out. That's your bread and butter."

Me: "Another thing. I've got to throw the ball for about fifteen minutes before the game to get the feel of it. I don't worry about tiring my arm. Strength means nothing to me."

Sal: "Certainly. Absolutely. Otherwise you can't stay sharp with it."

So I went back to my locker and tore up my index cards. Well, the truth of it is I tried to talk to Joe Schultz on the airplane, but every time I checked he was asleep. When he was awake, I had some second thoughts. Translation: I didn't have the nerve. I decided he would take it as me, Jim Bouton, trying to give orders to him, Joe Schultz. So I, Jim Bouton, said "Aw, the hell with it."

Now I've got permission to do it my way anyway. Sal Maglie. Love that man.

The man I love had quite an adventure tonight. Darrell Brandon pitching, and with Rod Carew on third base he goes into a full wind-up. At the last moment he decides to take a look over at Carew, who's taking a pretty good lead. So he backs off the rubber and Sal yells at him, "For crissakes, get the hitter. The runner isn't going anyplace."

So Darrell winds up and lets fly. *And Carew steals home.*

When Darrell comes into the dugout at the end of the inning, Maglie lets him have it. "Dammit," he says. "You *know* you've got to pitch from the stretch in that situation."

Eddie O'Brien has finally been nicknamed. Mr. Small Stuff. It's because of his attention to detail. Says Mr. Small Stuff: "Put your hat on." He said that to me today. Also to Mike Hegan. We were both running laps at the time.

Another thing Eddie O'Brien does is stand next to you when you're warming up. I think he does it so he can be near the phone when it rings. He has to answer it. One of these days I'll beat him to it

143

and when Schultz asks for O'Brien I'll say, "He ain't here," and hang up. Add dreams of glory.

Oh yes. As I went out to pitch he said, "Throw strikes."

I don't think Eddie O'Brien understands this game.

Maybe nobody does. Like when I went out to do some throwing on the sidelines before the game Sal Maglie said, "Do your running before you throw."

"Gee, Sal," I said agreeably, "I don't like to throw when I'm plumb tuckered out from running. I'd rather throw first, then run."

So Sal said, triumphantly, "What if it rains?"

"If it rains, then I'd rather have had my throwing in than my running."

At which point Ron Plaza said, to no one in particular, "Aw, c'mon, let's go."

I went. But first I did my throwing. And it didn't rain.

MAY
2

Oakland

Talked to my wife and she said there were some interesting things in the Seattle paper about my knuckleball. The quotes from Joe and Sal were that, well, it was better than it was before. Then there was a quote from Billy Martin, the bold and brash (as they say) manager of the Twins, which said it was a "helluva" knuckleball. The thought naturally occurred that Sal and Joe are not yet willing to make that kind of commitment to my knuckleball.

The knuckleball was fine tonight against Oakland—when it knuckled. When it didn't, it got hit for two home runs. That was in the first of three innings I pitched. One ball was completely still. It must have looked like a watermelon floating up there. Float like a watermelon, fly like a rocket. The other rolled a bit and was hit just as hard. On the other hand, I threw only four pitches in the whole three innings that didn't do what they were supposed to do. It's aggravating, of course, that two of them were hit out of the park, but the others jumped so much that I struck out Reggie Jackson and Rick Monday, and the rest were tapped for pop flies and grounders.

After the game McNertney told me that Sal Bando thought it was a better knuckler than Wilhelm's because it breaks more sharply and it's thrown harder. I'm not sure how to take that, since it was Bando who hit one of the homers off me.

Meanwhile, in the dugout, I found out from Darrell Brandon that Sal had thrown a fit when the home run was hit. He had a toothpick in his mouth at the time and he threw it hard on the ground (so hard a tree may yet grow on the spot) and said, "Jesus, he's got to start throwing something else. They're just waiting on that knuckleball."

I think McNertney understands the situation better. "Keep throwing it," he said. "It's getting better. Had a real good one tonight that was really jumping down. So a couple of them spun and they hit them out. But you got to go with it. Even 3 and 0."

It was a weird game. We were behind 4–0 and 6–1 and tied it at 6–6. They went ahead 8–6, and we damn near came back again but lost it 8–7. Now we're six games under .500 and in last place, and something is going to happen around here. Marvin Milkes is not a guy who will sit around in a situation that calls for panic.

This afternoon Gary Bell and I hired a car and drove up to the Berkeley campus and walked around and listened to speeches—Arab kids arguing about the Arab-Israeli war, Black Panthers talking about Huey Newton and the usual little old ladies in tennis shoes talking about God. Compared with the way everybody was dressed Gary and I must have looked like a couple of narcs.

So some of these people look odd, but you have to think that anybody who goes through life thinking only of himself with the kinds of things that are going on in this country and Vietnam, well, he's the odd one. Gary and I are really the crazy ones. I mean, we're concerned about getting the Oakland Athletics out. We're concerned about making money in real estate, and about ourselves and our families. These kids, though, are genuinely concerned about what's going on around them. They're concerned about Vietnam, poor people, black people. They're concerned about the way things are and they're trying to change them. What are Gary and I doing beside watching?

145

So they wear long hair and sandals and have dirty feet. I can understand why. It's a badge, a sign they are different from people who don't care.

So I wanted to tell everybody, "Look, I'm with you, baby. I understand. Underneath my haircut I really understand that you're doing the right thing."

Emmett Ashford was behind the plate tonight and did an especially good job calling the knuckleball. A couple of times I threw it knee-high and the ball seemed to drop into the dirt. But it was only after it had crossed the plate, so he called both of them strikes. Some umpires call the pitch where the catcher catches it, not where it crosses the plate. If he catches it as a ball, it's a ball. But Ashford was great.

He missed one pitch. It was when a guy was stealing second and McNertney came out of his crouch to get the ball. This blocked Ashford's view and he called it a ball. I yelled at him. "But Emmett, it was a perfect strike." That's all I said, and it was true, but I felt guilty about having said anything at all. I try to be especially nice to Ashford because everybody else harasses hell out of him. He's not exactly the best umpire, but he is far from being terrible. He doesn't miss that many calls, and when he does he misses them on both sides, like any good umpire. But other umpires talk behind his back. Sometimes they'll let him run out on the field himself and the other three who are holding back in the dugout will snigger. I hate that kind of stuff. I mean, I don't mind it when it's pulled on a ballplayer. But Ashford, for goodness sakes.

And, of course, the players pick it right up. As soon as he makes a bad call they start yelling, "Oh, that hot dog son of a bitch." Sure he's a flashy umpire and sure he does a lot of showboating. That's what got him into the big league in the first place. It's his bread and butter. Instead of bitching the players ought to give him credit for hustling. He hustles every minute he's out there, which is more than you can say for some other umpires.

It's not hard to understand why he's resented, though. They feel he doesn't belong in the big league with his way of umpiring. Besides, he's a Negro and they believe he's here just *because* of that.

It must be terrible for Ashford. When you're an umpire and travel around the big leagues in a group of four and three of them are white and the kind of guys who let you run on the field yourself—well, it can make for a very lonely summer.

I know about lonely summers. In my last years with the Yankees I had a few of them. You stand in a hotel lobby talking with guys at dinnertime and they drift away, and some other guys come along and pretty soon they're gone and you're all alone and no one has asked you what you're doing about dinner. So you eat alone. It must happen to Ashford a lot. And it's one of the reasons I can't bring myself to argue with him.

Encountered Marvin Milkes sitting in the lobby tonight, and whether he knows it or not that's fairly nerve-racking. Anytime a general manager is on the road with his club there's a feeling that a trade is in the works. From the way things are going here, I get the feeling that the front office watches the game, and when you throw a strike you're immediately in their plans for the near future, and when you throw a ball you're on the trading block. The players go up and down like some crazy yo-yo, and what that looks like most is a panic operation.

Brought a copy of the Berkeley *Barb* back to the clubhouse and several of the guys were crowding around to read it when John Kennedy said, "Bouton, I bet you bought that paper." I told him I had. "Now, how did I know it was you bought that paper?" he said. Dunno, John. Extrasensory perception?

MAY
3

Steve Barber pitched a pretty good game while I was down on the farm, but he was in trouble again yesterday, loading up the bases with none out in the first. He said he couldn't get loose on the sidelines, and the only time his arm bothers him is when he's loosening up. He says once he gets into the game he's fine.

Oh.

Another thing Sal Maglie looks like is the friendly neighborhood undertaker. You can just see him standing in the mortuary doorway saying, "Oh yes, we have something very nice for you in mahogany." And Gary Bell recalled the old Digger O'Dell line, "Well, I'll be shoveling off now."

The friendly undertaker really put it to Marshall the other day. He told him that if he didn't use better judgment on the selection of his pitches, they'd be called from the bench by S. Maglie, pitching coach. Mike was furious. Any pitcher would be. As Johnny Sain has pointed out, a pitcher will in the course of his career throw to thirty or forty catchers, work for ten or fifteen managers and pitching coaches. If he let all those people tell him what to throw he'd never amount to anything but a confused pitcher.

Anyway, the discussion with Sal seemed to do something for Marshall because he went out today and pitched a fine game. He lost 3–2, but in his heart a pitcher counts that as a victory, just as the hitter counts as a hit the sharp line drive that somebody makes a leaping catch on. Marshall went all the way and gave up only four singles, probably the only four mistakes he made in the game. Well, five. The other one was not getting enough runs.

I was warming up late in the game in case Marshall's sturdy arm should falter, which, considering the closeness of the game, was rather encouraging. After I gave up those two home runs I naturally went to the bottom of the pile. But I think two good innings after that redeemed me.

The other man warming up was John O'Donoghue. He's pitched one scoreless inning for the club so far and that puts him right on top. Indeed, the way things are, any new man is No. 1 until he gets hit, which is soon enough.

Today's Marvin Milkes' stories concern Gene Brabender and Merritt Ranew. The Bender's been having a tough time—thirteen runs in seven innings, or terrible enough to receive serious notice. So Milkes told him he has three more starts to straighten out, and if he doesn't do well in them he could just mosey down the road.

Ranew was called up to fill in for Larry Haney, who had to put in some service time. Ranew had been hitting like .400 at Vancouver and in his first game here he got two hits. Today he got another and he's hitting the ball good every time up. So Marvin Milkes told him, "You keep hitting the ball like that and you'll be back up here again sometime."

And never is heard a discouraging word.

MAY
4

Darrell Brandon wanted a start and got it, just by asking for it. He also got shelled, lasting an inning and a third. He thinks he knows what happened. "I was good last night," he said. "I stayed in my room. Called my wife. Drank nothing stronger than orange juice. Then I read from the Gideon Bible and went to sleep. Then I last an inning and a third and I got two greenies in me I got to work out in San Francisco. Never again."

As for me, I was only as good as I had to be last night and I also lasted an inning-and-a-third and three earned runs. That puts me on the bottom of the heap again and depresses the hell out of me. I figure two like that and my ass is back in Vancouver.

We were playing trivia on the back of the bus the other day, and among the questions was:

What was the name of Roy Rogers' dog?

What was the name of the cat in the Buster Brown Show?

What three pitchers were sent down to the minor leagues with less than five innings of work among them?

The answers are Bullet, Midnight, Dick Bates, Bill Edgerton and Jim Bouton.

Brandon and I felt so badly about the whole thing we dragged Gary Bell off to a Chinese restaurant and I ate bird's nest soup, which disgusted them both.

Gary Bell and I have become the Falstaffs of the back of the bus. Gary entertains with quotes, anecdotes and insults, and when he goes back to his real-estate book I do my routines. In a trivia game recently I asked who the moderator of "You Asked For It" was. The answer was Art Baker, which led me into my "You Asked For It" routine. "We have a letter from a listener, Mrs. Sadie Thompson of Jablib, Wisconsin.

Mrs. Thompson writes: 'Dear Art, I've always wanted to see a cobra strike an eighty-year-old lady. I wonder if you can arrange this on your show.' Yes, Sadie Thompson out there in Jablib, we went all the way to India for you and not only did we get a cobra, we got a bushmaster, the most deadly snake in the world. And right before your eyes the snake will be placed into a glass cage with sweet little white-haired Mrs. Irma Smedley. Here comes the snake into the cage, and just look at that sweet little old lady tremble. The snake strikes and that's it, ladies and gentlemen, the end of Mrs. Irma Smedley. Remember now, it's all because *you asked for it.*"

The boys ate it up. Sick humor is very big in the back of baseball buses and "You Asked For It" is almost as good as "Obituaries You Would Like To Read." Tune in next week, folks.

Some of the mores and manners of the back of the bus crew. Others who usually sit in the back are Oyler, Mincher, Kennedy, Hegan, Rich Rollins (The Listener), Gene Brabender (Lurch), Pattin (who does the Donald Duck) and Gosger (who does a splendid Porky Pig). The middle of the bus is dominated by Tommy Davis and his groovy tape machine, and the quiet guys sit in front, guys like Gus Gil and Freddy (Poor Devil) Velazquez. Mike Marshall also sits in front looking for somebody to play chess with him. I've played with him a few times and notice that he thumps me real bad a couple of times and that when he notices I'm losing interest he lets me come close to beating him. That turns me on again for a while. He makes me feel like the rabbit chasing the carrot on the stick.

One of the favorite back-of-the-bus games is insulting each other's wives, sisters, mothers and girlfriends. Some of the guys, among them Brabender and Marshall, refuse to participate in this game, but sometimes they're in it anyway. That's because any man who laughs when another man's wife or mother is insulted is automatically chosen as the next victim. Back-of-the-bus is a very rough business.

MAY

6

Seattle

The worst part of playing baseball is that you become a part-time father. I feel as though I've been on the road for a month—first with the Pilots, then with Vancouver, now back with the Pilots again. It's not terribly tough on a man and his wife, in fact absence often makes them appreciate each other more. But it's unsettling to the kids. They don't have a man around, and then when they do, well, you don't feel like disciplining them. You just want to enjoy them.

Before the game with the Red Sox tonight, we terrified pitchers huddled together and whispered about the power that club has. We decided that if Fenway Park in Boston is called "friendly," then the stadium here would have to be considered downright chummy. After the pitchers took batting practice we were wondering if we should stay in the dugout and watch the Red Sox hit. We decided it would not be a good thing for us to see.

We saw enough in the game. They beat us 12–2. Brabender started and went four innings, having thrown nearly 100 pitches. It was not all his fault. There were about four errors behind him and we wound up emptying the bullpen. I came in with two runners on and stranded them and had a perfect inning-and-a-third. Then Brandon, Aker and Segui were stomped. So I should be back on the top of the heap again. Baseball isn't such a funny game.

I was asked if I'd go to a women's club dinner and say a few thousand well-chosen words and I said sure. I sort of like that kind of thing. Besides, it shouldn't hurt my standing with the front office, knowing I'm a guy who does that well. My only condition was that I be allowed to bring my family along. I'm away enough without leaving them to make a speech.

MAY

7

I caught Joe Schultz without a liverwurst sandwich today, backed him into a corner and asked him, gently, about my chances of starting a game. I talked fast. I told him that I felt strong enough to go nine innings with the knuckleball and that I could relieve besides if he needed me.

So Joe said, "We got four starters now."

I told him I knew that and that I didn't want to bump anybody. I just wanted him to keep in mind that I was available and could step in at any time. I pointed out that a knuckleball pitcher *should* be a starter, like Niekro in Atlanta.

So Joe said, "He doesn't throw all knuckleballs."

I told him he throws 90 percent knuckleballs, sometimes more.

So Joe said, "He throws only about 80 percent knucklers. The rest of the time he throws curveballs and fastballs and change-ups."

I wanted to tell him, well, maybe, but if I were a starter I'd have time to warm up properly and work in all those other pitches. I decided to let it ride. Because even if I do get a start I'm going to throw 95 percent knucklers. I've been through that war. So I said, "I think I can do the job. Give it some consideration."

He said he would, which is better than nothing. Somewhat.

Warming up in the bullpen tonight I got back the good knuckler, the one I had last year. They moved like a bee after honey, and I was throwing them real hard. Haney was catching and he said, rubbing a knee, that he'd never seen anything like it. "If you can just get someone to catch you," Haney said, "you'll be all right."

MAY
8

Another day off. Took the family on a ferry ride to the Olympic Peninsula. Stayed at a cabin on a lake and hired a little motorboat, and I don't know who had more fun, me or the kids. Pitching seemed very far away.

MAY
9

Mike Marshall pitched a helluva game tonight, shutting out Washington 2–0. A two-hitter, one of them by Frank Howard, called Capital Punishment. McNertney and I had a talk about the game when it was over. He said Mike called about 30 percent of his pitches, less than the usual 50 or so. Mike has some interesting ideas on what kinds of pitches should be thrown. He thinks a completely random pattern is best, that the hitter should never have an inkling of what's coming next. As a result, if a guy gets a hit off a curve ball he may get a curve the very next time up. On the other hand, McNertney believes that if you get a guy out on fastballs you keep throwing him fastballs until he proves to you he can hit them. As for me, I throw the knuckleball.

Incidentally, the pitching staff was happy to learn tonight that Marvin Milkes had stationed a man outside the ballpark to measure the home runs that the Senators hit out of sight. Instead Marshall threw his two-hitter. Take that, Marvin Milkes.

The meeting before the game was marvelous. When we went over the hitters, Gary Bell had the same comment on each one: "Smoke him inside" (fastball inside). Frank Howard, McMullen, Brinkman, Epstein—every hitter. "Smoke him inside," said Gary Bell.

It got to be funny as hell after a while, because not only did he get no opposition, but he was taken seriously. According to the gospel of Gary Bell you pitch to the entire Washington team by smoking them inside.

I guess Marshall smoked them on the inside.

Chatted with Brant Alyea, the outfielder, about what was happening with the Washington club. He said Ted Williams was doing a fantastic job. "I'm just beginning to realize that baseball is at least 65 percent psychological," he said. "Williams has these guys so psyched they actually think they're great ballplayers. Brinkman's starting to think he's a hitter for crissakes and he's hit .200 all his life. Now he's up to .280. The team is up, the guys are emotionally high and Williams actually has them believing they're winners."

I wonder how he is with the pitchers.

The big confrontation is coming closer. The Yankees will be in town in a couple of days and I've been invited to appear at the sportswriters and sportscasters dinner on Monday afternoon. The idea is us against them. Mel Stottlemyre for the Yankees, me for the Pilots. I hope I can pitch against the Senators before the Yankees get here so I can show Joe Schultz how ready I am. I'm scared stiff the Yankees will get away without me pitching against them. At the same time I'd hate to get into one of those lost-cause games against them. I want them when they can feel the game in their guts.

MAY
10

Big meeting today. The way it happened, Marvin Milkes has been reading in the papers that some of the players aren't happy. So he suggested to Jack Aker that a meeting be called so the players could air their gripes. At the meeting, which lasted about twenty minutes, there were complaints about the beds in some of the hotels, the lack of a roof over the bench in the bullpen, the bare cement floor in the clubhouse and the absence of a watercooler in the clubhouse. Imagine having to take our greenies with beer. Big things like that.

It was also pointed out that when an exhibition game is scheduled for a Monday at the end of a road trip (as several are), the players should be permitted to go home Sunday night for at least a half-day at home. (This led to a certain amount of hilarity. The suggestions were that a half-day at home is just enough, or too much, and that a better place to spend the half-day was Las Vegas.) My gripe was that I thought that any ball hit into the yellow seats in left field should be a ground-rule double instead of a home run.

My own belief about the whole thing is that the players have only one serious gripe—the behavior of the coaches. But since they were all sitting right there no one complained.

When the meeting was over Aker asked Gary Bell what he thought about it all and he said, "Smoke him inside." Gary Bell is a beautiful man.

The sad truth about baseball, I'm afraid, is that there is not enough in it to occupy a man's mind. In desperation they turn to insignificant things and blow them up. Example: It was cold in the bullpen tonight, so I ran into the clubhouse and picked up three parkas. While I was at it I asked Curt Rayer, the trainer, if he could get some handwarmers going for us. Later, Larry Haney came out of the clubhouse and gave me a hot-water bottle he'd hidden under his jacket.

"Thanks," I said. "How come you had to smuggle it?"

"Curt didn't want any of the coaches seeing a hot-water bottle come out here," Haney said.

After the game Curt said I had bugged out at least half the coaching staff. Ron Plaza had overheard me asking for handwarmers and he told Curt it wasn't cold enough for them, and then somebody, maybe Joe Schultz, had said, "The hell with it, no handwarmers." Curt said everybody was very upset that I should ask for them, so he'd sent out a quiet hot-water bottle. It had been a warm day, so I guess the idea of handwarmers in May boggled the little minds.

This reminded me of something that happened the other day. Joe Schultz called me over and I thought he wanted to talk about my knuckleball, or pitching in general, or perhaps the state of the nation. Instead, with a straight face, he asked me whether I had any light-colored sweatshirts or did I have only the dark kind I was wearing. I told him I had about fifteen dark sweatshirts since the other clubs I had been with all had dark blue sweatshirts. I said I used the dark ones in practice before the game, then changed to the Pilots' light blue for the game.

He considered that for a while, then finally nodded and said, "I guess that's okay."

Joe Schultz has yet to say a word to me about my knuckleball. Not even, "I guess that's okay."

I don't suppose I should care about any of this, except it *is* important to me to have a warm hand when I throw the knuckler. But even if I didn't need it, why should anybody care that I wanted it? And I would like to think that Joe Schultz has more important things to think about than the color of my sweatshirt.

At the meeting before the ballgame Sal Maglie said, "Okay, let's get some runs." He was kidding. We've been scoring a fantastic number of runs, which is either a tribute to our hitters or the size of this ballpark. Tonight, for example, we were losing to the Senators 11–3 in the sixth inning. First we came back to tie it, then we won 16–13. We ran through the whole pitching staff and only Gary Bell and I came out with any glory. I had a wicked knuckleball.

At one point, with the man on first, as I was about to release the ball, Ron Plaza yelled, "Throw it to first!" It disconcerted me enough so that the pitch was way off the plate. My impulse was to warn Plaza not to yell at me once I had released the resin bag and to shove those handwarmers up his bippy. But I managed to contain it.

156

Bell pitched the ninth inning and got them out. It was a minor miracle because he's supposed to pitch tomorrow and ran fifteen wind-sprints before the game and ate three sandwiches in the fourth inning. When he came into the clubhouse in the seventh to put on his supporter he asked no one in particular if it was too late to take a greenie.

Are greenies fabulous? Probably. Some of the guys have to take one just to get their hearts to start beating. I've taken greenies but I think Darrell Brandon is right when he says that the trouble with them is that they make you feel so great that you think you're really smoking the ball even when you're not. They give you a false sense of security. The result is that you get gay, throw it down the middle and get clobbered.

During the game the public-address announcer explained where to pick up the ballots to vote for "your favorite Pilot." I thought it necessary to remind the people sitting near the bullpen that your favorite Pilot did not necessarily have to be good.

The Yankees have lost thirteen out of fourteen now and I feel so bad about it I walk around laughing. Actually I just say that. In fact I'm beginning to feel sorry for some of the guys. The guy I care most about is Fritz Peterson, and he's doing well. He won the only game they won in the last ten days.

I'm still not sure about the Pilots. Sometimes I think the pitching staff can develop enough to help. Other times it looks like a bad staff. I sometimes think that a Marty Pattin should be able to win twenty and then I realize he's going to have all the ups and downs new pitchers in the big league are prone to. The same with Mike Marshall. He pitches a good game and they expect a lot of him. But what the hell, if he wins ten games he'll be doing great.

The other starters don't look so good. Gary is not really ready yet, and neither is Brabender. Barber has been taking cortisone shots in that elbow that hasn't bothered him all spring and he can't lift a baseball, much less comb his hair. Maybe Joe Schultz will consider *me* as a starter. If he started me in two or three games I might surprise him. But I think Sal has drummed it into his head that I can't be any good throwing the knuckleball all the time. My only chance is if they get desperate.

More baseball-player paranoia. First guy up in the bullpen today was Jack Aker. Second guy to go in was O'Donoghue. Then me. When O'Donoghue was called in, Darrell Brandon said, "That does it. I'll never go into that trainer's room again."

"Why not?" I asked.

"Because I was getting diathermy on this stiff neck I got and Joe Schultz spotted me and asked if I was all right. I said yeah, I was okay, but he probably thinks there's something seriously wrong with me. That's what I get for going into that goddam room."

MAY
11

With the Yankees coming in I'm beginning to feel like it's World Series time, my own personal World Series. I started out thinking that I was going to come in in the ninth inning and strike out the side, or start a game and pitch nine, but right now I don't care about winning or losing. I just don't want to embarrass myself.

Frank Howard drove in five runs with two home runs and a single against us and we beat the Senators anyway, 6–5. It was three straight over them, but all I got out of the evening was a marvelous nickname given to Frank Bertaina, a pitcher, by Moe Drabowski, also a pitcher, when they were with Baltimore. Bertaina, Drabowski decided, was not too smart, and was flaky besides. So Drabowski called him "Toys in the Attic."

This is the kind of nickname that could be turned around into an offensive weapon. There is no bigger flake in organized baseball than Drabowski. Once, out in the bullpen in Anaheim, he picked up the phone, called a number in Hong Kong and ordered a Chinese dinner. To go.

Brabender was the pitcher tonight and he looked pretty good giving up two runs before tiring in the fifth. He was throwing the ball good and I think he's coming around. On the other hand, there's the continuing sad saga of Steve Barber. The only thing he's done lately is pull a hamstring while running in the outfield. So now, as he gets diathermy on his shoulder, he gets icepacks on his leg. He says he feels fine, except for a little tightness in his shoulder.

The story on him, I understand through the grapevine, is that he was asked to go to the minors until he's ready to pitch. As an eight-year man, however, he had the right to refuse, and did. He can be sold or traded to another major league team or given his release. That's all. And since they paid $175,000 for him in the expansion draft Barber will no doubt be around until he's able to pitch enough batting practice to get his arm in shape enough to pitch. I'm not sure I'd do the same in Barber's place. On the other hand, I'm not sure I wouldn't.

My taste in clothing is, I'm afraid, conservative. Tonight, though, I did show up in a rather mod outfit and John Kennedy said, "Hey, look at Bouton. He's getting there."

Maybe so. But I told him it's taking me so long to get there that by the time I do, everybody will be someplace else.

MAY
12

The first thing I felt when the Yankees showed up at the park today was embarrassment. That's because our uniforms look so silly with that technicolor gingerbread all over them. The Yankee uniforms, even their gray traveling uniforms, are beautiful in their simplicity. John O'Donoghue said that when Johnny Blanchard was traded to Kansas City he refused to come out of the dugout wearing that green and gold uniform. I would guess it's the only feeling I've ever had in common with Blanchard. At any rate, Blanchard never came out except to play the game, but I steeled myself and ran over to chat with the guys. There were a lot of visitors—Crosetti, Hegan, Kennedy, me. There was a lot of kidding and a lot of laughing, and this was one time Crosetti didn't feel it necessary to enforce the rule against fraternization.

Then the game. It was fantastic, unbelievable and altogether splendid. We scored seven runs in the first inning and made them look like a high-school team. They threw to the wrong bases. Their uniforms looked great; they looked terrible.

It reached the point where we were going nuts in the bullpen, jumping up and down and screaming and hollering. And suddenly I wasn't embarrassed by my uniform, I was embarrassed for the Yankees. They looked so terrible. Cheez, I wanted to beat them bad, but this was ridiculous. Seven runs. I wound up telling the guys to sit down and cool it.

It was not a cool night, though. A big fight, two benches and two bullpens emptying, fifty guys milling around on the field. What a lovely war. It started when Marty Pattin threw one over Murcer's head. In his previous at-bat Murcer had hit a home run, and that sort of thing will sometimes result. So Murcer got on base and then came in high on Oyler, head first and fists flying.

The rule is that you're not allowed to just sit there when your teammates are in a fight, so everybody came off the bench and out of the bullpen and the only guy who sat there was Crosetti. I guess he was paralyzed by the choices involved. Too bad. I was hoping he might mix it with The Chicken Colonel and maybe they'd both get spiked or something.

I was very careful to keep a big smile on my face when I reached the scene of action. I didn't want anybody to think I was angry or serious. By and large nobody is serious about these baseball fights except the two guys who start them. Everyone else tries to pull them apart and before long you've got twenty or thirty guys mostly just pulling and shoving each other. The two guys who started it have so many guys piled on top of them they couldn't reach for a subway token, much less fight.

At the bottom of the pile Murcer and Oyler found themselves pinned motionless, nose to nose. "Ray, I'm sorry," Murcer said. "I lost my head."

"That's okay," Oyler said. "Now how about getting off me, you're crushin' my leg."

"I would," Murcer said, "but I can't move."

There are a few guys on the Yankees I knew would love to have a shot at me, especially Fred Talbot, who I don't think would know the meaning of quit if he ever got into a fight with me. So I kept one eye out for Fred and the other for my friend Fritz Peterson.

I sort of circled the perimeter of action with both arms out to fend off any blind-siders and here came Fritz running toward me. He was laughing his head off and we grabbed each other and started waltzing like a couple of bears. He tried to throw me off balance and I tried to wrestle him down and all the time we were kidding each other.

"How's your wife?" I said. "Give me a fake punch to the ribs."

"She's fine," he said. "You can punch me in the stomach. Not too hard."

Finally he got me down and we started rolling around. Two umpires came running over and told us to break it up. "But we're only kidding," I said, protesting. "We're old roommates."

"Break it up anyway," the umpire said. Which made me think that here are two of four umpires breaking up a playful little wrestling match while there's a war going on nearby with forty guys piled on each other. I guess they both recognized that they were in a very safe place.

After the game Fritz and I went out to dinner and I asked him what he would have done if Talbot or somebody else from the Yankees came over to help him out.

"I'd have had to tackle the guy," Peterson said.

The most interesting thing about the fight was Houk's reaction to the police, who came on the field to break it up. When he saw them he went out of his skull. "What the hell are cops doing on the field?" he shouted. "I've never seen cops on the field before. They ought to be at the university where they belong."

What he didn't understand, of course, is that the very thing that made *him* angry at the sight of cops is the same thing that puts kids uptight seeing them on campus.

It's not altogether surprising that the Yankees got into a fight. When I was with the club and we lost a few games Houk would have a meeting and he'd say something like, "Now, don't anyone be afraid to start something. If you get into a fight we'll all be with you."

Houk believed that fights woke teams up and made them play better. He also used the clubhouse meeting for effect. Like before the game with us he asked Len Boehmer, the catcher, how to throw to Hegan. "When Hegan was in our organization," Boehmer said, "they used to get him out with fast balls down the middle."

"Good," Houk said. "Meeting's over."

I think somewhere about the middle of the first inning they wished they'd had one.

One of my favorite Houk meetings took place before a game with the Red Sox during a losing streak in 1963.

"I just got to looking at these two lineups," he said, "and I thought I ought to compare them for you. Take the leadoff man. They got Mike Andrews. We got Bobby Richardson. Any comparison there? No. Number two we got Tom Tresh and they got Rico Petrocelli. [This was when Petrocelli was just coming up and Tresh was just off rookie of the year.] Could you imagine trading Tresh for Petrocelli? Third is Carl Yastrzemski and Roger Maris. Well, Yastrzemski is not a bad player, so maybe there's a standoff there. Now look who's batting fourth. Jim Pagliaroni and Mickey Mantle. Now who the hell is Pagliaroni?" It broke up the whole clubhouse and really made his point.

The Yankees know I've been throwing the knuckleball and they all asked me how it was coming. I told them great. I think Chicken Colonel Turner is worried about it, concerned that I might have come up with a good one. This wouldn't show him in a very good light since he never even talked to me at the end, much less encouraged me to experiment. But get this. While I was warming up in our bullpen he told a couple of Yankee players, "You know, when we sent Bouton to Syracuse, the year before last, I told him to start throwing that knuckleball, but he wouldn't listen to me."

MAY
13

I think I should have a chance to pitch against the Yankees tonight. It's Stottlemyre against Gary Bell, and my roomie has been giving up runs. Against Stottlemyre we could easily be down a couple of runs by the fourth or fifth inning and then pinch-hit for Bell. At least I'm hoping I'll be first up. It hasn't been happening that way. I've been pitching better than Aker, and although Segui has won our last two games, he's been hit both times. Last night Schultz had O'Donoghue and Aker warming up and then O'Donoghue and Segui in a short situation. So why do I think it will be me tonight? Because I'm an optimist, that's why.

If I do get in, and if I should win, I'll send for Jim Ogle and insist he interview me. I wonder if he talks to rapists.

Hot flash! Whitey Ford's Italian restaurant in the bullpen has a real rival in the Baltimore bullpen: wienie roasts.

The pitchers' game is in full operation, and it's been costing me a few bob. The reason is that a system of bets and fines has been set up, and one of the fines is for fraternizing with the opposition. With the Yankees in town this has already cost me $2. On the other hand, I have had some satisfactions. One of the games is splitting the pitching staff into two teams during batting practice, with the losing team having to drop 50¢ into the kitty. I'm a terrible hitter in batting practice, possibly because I'm a terrible hitter in games. I'm so bad they call me Cancer Bat, and when they made up the teams I was, naturally, thrown in at the end. When one of the guys on the other team complained that Bell's team had all the good hitters, he said, "Whaddayamean? We got Bouton." That seemed to mollify the opposition. So the first night of competition I got four line-drive singles and led my team to victory. That'll teach them to fool around with the Bulldog.

Another fund-raiser is electing the leading "fly" at the end of each road trip, the guy who had the worst trip for bugging people, being a pest, just flying them. The man elected is charged a dollar. Also, if you get caught eating at the table after a game with Charley uncovered, that costs a dollar. (On the Yankees this would have kept both Elston Howard and Yogi Berra broke. They were famous for dragging Charley over the coldcuts.)

The money goes into a kitty and at the end of the season it will be spent on a lavish party, for pitchers only. Gene Brabender is commissioner of the kitty and sergeant-at-arms because he's so big, and I'm secretary-treasurer, I'm not sure why. Perhaps because I look so honest.

An outfield game is making up singer-and-actor baseball teams purely on the sound of their names. Example—Panamanian. Good speed, great arm, temperamental: shortstop Jose Greco. Or big, hard-hitting first baseman; strong, silent type: Vaughn Monroe. And centerfielder, showboat, spends all his money on cars, big ladies man, flashy dresser, drives in 75 runs a year, none of them in the clutch: Duke Ellington. Finally—great pitcher, twenty-game winner five years in a row, class guy, friendly with writers and fans alike. Stuff is good, not overpowering, but he's smart, has great control and curve ball, moves the ball around: Nat King Cole.

If you think this is a silly game, you haven't stood around in the outfield much.

Another one about passing time. Larry Haney says that in the Baltimore bullpen Dave Leonhard, who went through Johns Hopkins with a 3.9 average (that's out of a possible 4.0, kids) prepares quizzes on various subjects for the fellows: history, current events, literature, personal idiosyncrasies of players on the club. Sounds almost as good as singer-and-actor baseball teams.

And then we played a game of baseball. We knocked Stottlemyre out and won 5–3. I warmed up in the bullpen, not to pitch but just to keep my knuckleball sharp. It's been four days since I've been in a game. And I don't see much chance of getting in tomorrow either. Mike Marshall is pitching and he's been throwing real good. Bill Burbach is pitching for them and we should rack him up. He's a high-ball pitcher, and this is the wrong park to pitch high in. And I haven't been getting into games we win at all.

MAY
14

Shows what I know. We lost. We should have won. We were losing 3–2 going into the eighth and they brought Aker in. Jack's been getting bombed while I've had two good appearances in a row, and I thought I was ahead of him. But that's not what Joe Schultz thought. So he brought Aker in and he got ripped for a triple and a homer and now it's 5–2 and the game is about gone. So guess who got called in? Jim Bouton, or Lost Cause, as they say around the French Foreign Legion. I had a good inning. Call it pretty good. Roy White got to a mediocre knuckleball for a double down the first-base line. Then Pepitone connected solidly for a weak little roller down the first-base line and I personally tagged him out. They got zero runs.

In the bottom of the ninth, though, Gus Gil hit a double with two on and suddenly it's 5–4 and I wonder if Joe Schultz is sorry he brought in Aker instead of me. Better relief and we'd have won the game. Even so, it's one run and a man on second with none out and inside I'm jumping up and down because if we win it's seven-straight losses for them and a victory for me, my first win of the season and against the New York Yankees. Just like in my dreams. Except that we don't score and lose.

I wonder if their general manager, Lee MacPhail, noticed my knuckleball.

MAY
15

Boston

Off day for travel to Boston. As dusk fell Gary Bell and I went out to celebrate the fact that we've won five of our last six. We chose Sonny's as the ideal place, and it was, because when we returned to our hotel it was three-thirty in the morning and we were still able to have a long discussion about the world, the ghettos and civil rights (all of which we disagree about). We also decided that it would be a good idea, at each baseball game, to allow a fan to suit up and play in the game. Just announce on the public address that if there are any fans in the stands who think they could do a good job at any position, to come down and draw lots for the privilege. We could designate him as our wild-card fan.

And so to bed, after deciding that we are both promotional geniuses.

MAY

16

I knew I was going to enjoy this day. I just didn't know how much. It was going to be a good day because my brother Bob was coming up from Fairfield, Connecticut, to see the game and also Bill Morehead III of Harvard and Pittsburgh would be there. Morehead once sent me a long involved questionnaire about the knuckleball. He said he wanted to be a pitcher for Harvard and since he had hurt his arm he thought his only chance was to learn to throw the knuckleball. I called him on the phone and told him that answering the questionnaire would take too long and wouldn't teach him that much anyway and suggested he come down to Connecticut when I worked out there in a gym with my brother. He came down twice and I think now he understands the principle of it. It's just a matter now of him working on it. In any case, I was looking forward to seeing him.

So with friends in the stands I had my greatest night of the season. I pitched three innings against the Red Sox—the eighth, ninth and tenth—and shut them out with no hits. In the eleventh we scored six runs, and although the Red Sox came back with five in their half, while I paced up and down in the clubhouse cursing the other relief pitchers, we won 10–9 and I ended up with my first big W, as we baseball players call it. It was my first major-league win earned with the knuckleball. I don't think I threw more than a couple of fastballs during the three innings. The knuckleball was just great. So was the company after the game.

MAY
17

I thought it would be a good time to talk to Maglie. He was shagging balls thrown in to second base from the outfield, and I got him between shags. I told him about my conversation with Schultz and his thought that I couldn't be a starter because I had only one pitch. I told him that Niekro said after his last game that he'd thrown 95 knucklers out of 104 pitches.

"Well, you can do that if it's breaking," Sal said.

"Fine," I said. "Then I can throw it all the time."

"But they start looking for the damn thing," Sal said. "And if it doesn't break you got nothing else."

"What about Wilhelm?" I said. "They wait for *his* knuckleball."

"He throws that slider of his once in a while."

"Sure, but they don't look for his slider. They look for his knuckleball. And what about when you threw the curve ball?"

"When I was pitching they always looked for the curve," he said, not without a certain pride.

"But you threw other pitches, didn't you?"

"Oh yeah."

"But they always looked for your curve, right?"

"Yeah, but they just couldn't hit it. They tried, but they couldn't."

Even after all that he wouldn't admit that it didn't matter if the hitter was looking for it as long as the pitch was good enough.

What I think is going on here is something in Sal Maglie's head. He said in spring training, in front of everybody, that you can't get by with one pitch. Now he doesn't want to admit he might have been wrong.

Then we played the game and it was lousy. Gary got beat real bad. It was especially tough because he wanted so much to do well in his old ballpark and when they announced his name before the game he got a standing O, which is an ovation. There were 30,000 people in the park and it was exactly the kind of day in which you want to look good against your old club and in honor of the occasion Gary put down at least three greenies. They didn't do a bit of good.

I sat down next to him in the clubhouse afterward and said, "Hang in there, Rooms. Tonight we'll go out and celebrate until we forget what happened. Besides, you got nothing to worry about. We've both done our jobs and we both have some good years behind us and a game like this doesn't really matter."

"Yeah, you're right, Rooms," he said. "But when we're all through celebrating my loss tonight and when we get back to our room, we're going to start working on that knuckleball."

MAY

18

Today I've been thinking about God and baseball, or is it baseball and God? In any case, this rumination was caused by the sight of Lindy McDaniel of the Yankees. Although I've never met him, I feel I know him pretty well because of this newsletter he sends out from Baytown, Texas, called "Pitching for the Master." One of the first I got from him—and all the players receive them—was a complete four-page explanation of why the Church of Christ was the only true church. The dogmatism of this leads to the kind of thinking you find in the Fellowship of Christian Athletes and in *Guideposts* and *The Reader's Digest*. The philosophy here is that religion is the reason an athlete is good at what he does. "My faith in God is what made me come back." Or "I knew Jesus was in my corner." Since no one ever has an article saying, "God didn't help me" or "It's my muscles, not Jesus," kids pretty soon get the idea that Jesus helps *all* athletes and the ones who don't speak up are just shy or embarrassed.

So I've been tempted sometimes to say into a microphone that I feel I won tonight because I don't believe in God. I mean, just for the sake of balance, to let the kids know that belief in a deity or "Pitching for the Master" is not one of the criteria for major-league success. But I guess I never will.

Tonight I was making some notes in the bullpen and Eddie O'Brien was slowly going out of his mind with curiosity. Finally he sneaked over and snatched the paper out of my hand. I snatched it right back. That's all Mr. Small has to find out—that I'm writing a book. It'll be all over for the kid.

MAY
19

Front running is not limited to coaches. Here's what I mean. I've had about three appearances lately in which I haven't given up any runs. But no one bothered to talk to me. As soon as I win my first game, though, I'm on an interview show back to Seattle and they want to know the whole Jim Bouton story. "Give it to us from the beginning, Jim. Tell us all about it."

Hell, I could write a book.

It's like what happened to Diego Segui. About a week ago Segui won two games. He pitched about two innings and gave up two runs and then about four innings and gave up two more runs. He was pitching lousy, but he was in there when our team was scoring runs, so he got credit for two wins. And so the reporters started coming around. "Gee, Diego, you're starting to win ballgames. Tell us what you're doing different."

He wasn't doing anything different, except maybe pitching worse. All they care about is results. "The world doesn't want to hear about labor pains," Johnny Sain used to say. "It only wants to see the baby."

MAY
20

It's been four days since I had my great night in Boston and I still haven't appeared in a ballgame. It's goddam depressing. I haven't even been the first or second man warming up. Hell, I'm going backward. One more good outing, I guess, and they'll ship me out.

Two trades today. We sent outfielder Jose Vidal to the Yankees for outfielder Dick Simpson. We also traded Aker for my old friend Fred Talbot. This is a little disturbing because Talbot and I didn't care too much for each other over there in New York. We're exact opposites. He's country and I'm city, and I always felt uncomfortable around him.

It's interesting, though, to see the Yankees trade Talbot, the guy they decided to keep instead of me two years ago. And they traded him for a guy who is, or at least should be, below me on the pitching totem pole over here. I believe Seattle would have wanted more than Talbot for me in a trade.

Marty Pattin, Donald Duck (his great routine is where he has Donald reaching orgasm), pitched a strong game tonight. In the eighth he gave up a home run to Mike Epstein after walking Frank Howard and we lost 6–5. Marty did not do Donald Duck tonight.

I mistakenly thought there would be a meeting tonight to elect a new player rep. I was sure Gary Bell, who was assistant rep, would get it. I also thought I'd like to be Gary's assistant, so I asked Larry Haney, who was sitting next to me, if he would nominate me, and the minute I asked him I realized I'd made a mistake. Larry got a big grin on his face and immediately got up to tell the guys that I'd asked to be nominated. One the spot it was decided to add this to the list of fines our pitchers pay into the party kitty for various infractions, so I was assessed an *ex post facto* dollar fine for campaigning.

170

MAY
21

Today Mr. Small came out to the outfield where the pitchers were running and said, "Gentlemen, from now on we can all run with our hats off. It's really silly for us to run with our hats on, because the band gets all sweaty and ruins the hat."

"How come you weren't able to think of that a few weeks ago?" I asked him.

"Well, it wasn't as warm then and we weren't sweating at the same rate we are now."

Oh.

We've been running short of greenies. We don't get them from the trainer, because greenies are against club policy. So we get them from players on other teams who have friends who are doctors, or friends who know where to get greenies. One of our lads is going to have a bunch of greenies mailed to him by some of the guys on the Red Sox. And to think you can spend five years in jail for giving your friend a marijuana cigarette.

There's a zany quality to Joe Schultz that we all enjoy and that contributes, I believe, to keeping the club loose. Last night he got thrown out of a ballgame for the first time after disputing a home run that everybody knew was foul except the umpires. But that's not what he got thrown out for. He got thumbed out for offering the plate umpire his glasses, a very obvious gesture, which I enjoyed all the way out in the bullpen.

On the bench he's always saying all kinds of silly things. Like the other night when we scored six runs in the eleventh and the Red Sox scored five in the bottom half, he said, "Had them all the way." He gives a countdown on the outs when we're ahead. "Only eight outs to go—oops, only seven." And he's running up and down the dugout and

171

jumping around like a little kid. At the same time he's letting Harper run on his own and letting the guys hit and run, and he doesn't get angry when they get thrown out stealing. It makes for a comfortable ballclub.

The knuckleball is groovy and still I can't get into a game. Tonight they could have put me in early with a 4–0 lead and Brabender pitching in a lot of trouble. They warmed me up, which means they're now thinking of me as a long man, which isn't a very good sign because there aren't many chances for a long man to get into a game when it matters. When they need short relief both Segui and O'Donoghue get into the game.

Intellectually, I can understand Schultz's thinking. He has a lot of confidence in Segui, who was a top reliever last year, and O'Donoghue is his lefthanded relief man and does pretty well against lefthanders. Still, it gets me angry when the phone rings and it's not for me. After a while I cool off and think how I would have felt about the position I'm in now while I was with Vancouver, or in spring training, when I wasn't sure I was going to make the team. Also, the team is managing very well without me. We're playing heads-up ball. The guys on the bench are alive, and when the other team makes a mental error we take advantage of it right away. We're hitting the hell out of the ball, and we're even getting the breaks, which is part of it too. Besides, California is losing a lot of games, and what I see again in the crystal ball is third place.

What I also see in my crystal ball is that I'm the only guy in the big leagues who may finish behind his team. I was so embarrassed tonight I wanted to go off and join a monastery. We had the voting for player rep. Bell handled the meeting so well that it was impossible not to vote for him. Good for him. He'll enjoy driving the free car this summer, at least until he's traded.

The team doesn't take voting for player rep seriously. If it did Mike Marshall would have been elected. He's the most qualified guy on the club; bright, well read, knows a lot about the pension plan and is just the man for persistence and the paperwork. (Like he handled the shipping of our cars without a hitch and no fuss.) Except that he wasn't even nominated, because the vote for player rep is more of a popularity contest.

Which doesn't say much for me. Don Mincher, Tommy Harper and

I were nominated for assistant. Tommy got six votes, Mincher got seventeen. I got one. I couldn't even break my Yankee record. I shudder to think what would happen if I wasn't trying to be one of the boys. I seem to be bearing up well under all of this. Inside, though, I'm a mess.

MAY

22

On the way to the ballpark tonight Ray Oyler, sitting in the back of the bus during a bumpy ride, discovered an erection. He promptly offered to buy the bus from the driver.

My pal Sal told me tonight that I was throwing too damn many pitches in the bullpen. He clocked me last night, he said, and I threw 180, which is like a game-and-a-half and I never even got into the game.

When I tried to explain again that the knuckleball is not like other pitches he looked over my shoulder into the setting sun and said, "Yeah, no more throwing in the bullpen unless I tell you to warm up."

"Look, Sal, can't we talk this over?"

"No," he said striding off. "If you want to talk it over, talk to Joe."

Fuck you, Sal Maglie.

I walked directly into Joe's office and told him I needed to throw a lot in the bullpen and that if he needed me for five or six innings early in the game that was fine, because I wasn't throwing until late in the game.

So Joe said, "All right."

"All right, I can throw on my own out there?"

"All right, I'll talk to Sal about it."

I saw Sal and Joe talking on the field a few minutes later, then Sal came over to me in the outfield and said, "It's exactly what I said to you before. You just got to cut down on your throwing in the bullpen."

I could feel my neck getting red. "When I talked to Joe he seemed to think I could throw on my own whenever I felt I needed it."

"Oh yeah, you can throw on your own," Sal said. "But just watch it and make sure you're ready to pitch if we need you."

Here's how Mike Marshall got into his most recent trouble. He was taken out of the ballgame in Boston the other night after giving up a grand-slam home run to Carl Yastrzemski. He told the writers that he should have finished the game. What he meant, of course, was that he should have been good enough not to give up the home run and good enough to hang in there. His remarks were interpreted as criticism of Joe Schultz for taking him out of the game. So pretty soon it got around the clubhouse that Mike was on the manager for something that was his own goddam fault and I ended up explaining that Mike had been misinterpreted. But the players were not anxious to give Mike the benefit of the doubt. Now Mike's in trouble with the newspapermen, the guys and probably Joe Schultz. Can't anybody around here understand English?

In the bullpen Talbot revealed an awful truth about Joe Pepitone. He has two different hairpieces. He's got a massive piece, which he wears when he's going out, and a smaller one to wear under his baseball cap. He calls it his game piece. On opening day he was wearing his game piece and hadn't put it on very well. So when he was forced to take his cap off, there it was, sitting on his head all askew. He was so embarrassed he tried to hide his head in the shoulder of the guy standing next to him. Kiss me, Joe baby.

Pepitone took to wearing the hairpieces when his hair started to get thin on top. And the hair he still has is all curly and frizzy when he lets it grow long. So he carries around all kinds of equipment in a little blue Pan Am bag. Things like a hot comb, various greases and salves, glue for the hairpiece, hair-straightener—and even a hair-dryer. He carries it wherever he goes, on the buses to the park, on airplanes. You never see him without that little blue bag. At any rate, one day Fritz Peterson and I, a bit bored during a game we were winning about 6–2, went into the clubhouse and filled his hair-dryer with talcum powder. Then we cleaned it up, left it where he had and went back to watch the game. By this time it was 6–3, and then they tied it up and we lost it, 7–6, in extra innings. And one of the reasons we lost is that Pepitone struck out in a clutch situation.

So everyone was tired and angry and upset and you could hear a pin drop in the clubhouse, because after a loss that's the way it's supposed to be. After a while Pepitone came out of the shower and turned his hair-dryer on. *Whooooosh!* Instant white. He looked like an Italian George Washington wearing a powdered wig. There was talcum powder over everything, his hair, his eyebrows, his nose, the hair on his chest. Of course, everybody went crazy. Loss or no, they all laughed like hell. To this moment, Pepitone never knew who turned on the powder. He always thought it was Big Pete Sheehy. Wrong again.

Gary Bell was hit again tonight, four runs in less than five innings. I relieved him with two on and two out and got Paul Casanova to pop up. They pinch-hit for me in the next inning so I had a total outing of one-third of an inning.

In the clubhouse Gary was sitting in front of his locker sucking up a beer and I told him to hang in there.

"Rooms, my career is over," he said. "The Big C has got my arm."

"Besides that, how're you feeling?" I said.

"I feel fine," he said. "This is my fifth beer."

Ranew tells me that Vancouver sent Bob Lasko to Toledo, which is another Triple-A team in the International League. It burned me up because here's Lasko, a guy with ten or eleven years in professional baseball, most of it in Triple-A, bouncing around all over the country, playing for three, four, five different organizations in thirty or forty different towns, all without his family, and now, in the twilight of his career he gets a chance to play in his own home town and he gets sent to Toledo.

There's no justification for this. No one can tell me there wasn't another pitcher they could have sent to Toledo instead. I bet no one even realized Vancouver is home to Lasko. So one day, if Lasko ever makes it in the big leagues and has a good year, the owner will scream bloody murder if he tries to get an extra thousand in salary.

Don Mincher goes up to people, and asks for a cigarette. When they give him one he pulls out a pack, puts the cigarette into it and puts it back into his pocket. Then he walks off.

There is often homosexual kidding among the players. Tonight Ray Oyler combed his hair forward and started mincing around the clubhouse, lisping, "Hello, sweetheart," or "C'mere, you sweet bitch." Then Gary Bell said, "Ray, you convinced me. You really are queer."

And Ray said, "Well, it doesn't make me a bad person."

MAY
23

Cleveland

Flying in to Cleveland last night I thought about life in this great American city and decided that if you were going to crash on a Cleveland flight it would be better if it was an inbound flight.

Jose Cardenal was in center field fixing the legs of his tight pants and Talbot recalled the time in winter ball when Cardenal refused to play for three days because his uniform wasn't tight enough.

Joe Schultz had a short meeting before the game and said that we have enough ability to win a lot of games if we just used our common sense out there, just used our heads. So I went out and played like I had left my head back in the hotel room. You wouldn't think it was possible for me to play dumb baseball, considering my charm, intelligence and good looks. But I played dumb baseball.

The first inning was fine. I came in with the bases loaded and one out and got Cardenal to hit a one-hopper right back to me for the DP, pitcher to catcher to first base. That's good. What I did in the next inning was bad.

With one out (Alvis struck out on a knuckleball), Hawk Harrelson doubled down the left-field line. No complaint, he hit a pretty good knuckleball. Then there was a little bouncer in front of the plate. Instead of settling for an out at first, I tried to get Harrelson going into third. I didn't have much chance of getting him and made a bad throw besides. So instead of two out and a man on third, I've got runners on first and third, one out. Larry Brown then hit one into right for a

176

single, Harrelson scoring. The other runner was headed for third and the throw from right field was wild, over third and into the dugout. It shouldn't have mattered, because I should have been over there backing up the play. Instead I stood on the mound watching, like it was a John Wayne movie, while the second run scored and Brown went all the way to third.

I got the next two hitters and was unscathed in the next inning. I rate the performance fair because I got away with no runs in a bases-loaded situation. But there is no excuse for playing such dumb baseball.

MAY
24

Fred Talbot invited me out to dinner with his roommate, Merritt Ranew, after the game. It's a sign that we're living through a reincarnation with the Seattle Pilots. I found myself enjoying their company. Could I have been wrong about Talbot? Me, Jim Bouton, wrong?

I had planned to ask Joe—or my pal Sal—if I could start the exhibition game Monday against Spokane, but today I noticed that Gary Timberlake is around. He said he'd been called up to pitch the exhibition game. He was with our Double-A team. He's going to fly from Cleveland to Seattle, pitch against Spokane and then go back to the minors. I guess they want to look at him. I mean they *know* what I can do. Or do they?

Steve Barber started the game tonight and pitched four innings, giving up two runs. He was taken out when his arm stiffened up. The situation was discussed in the bullpen.

Bell: "His next start will probably come next July."

O'Donoghue: "Or later."

Me: "Depending on how his arm feels."

MAY

25

At the pregame meeting the discussion was about how to pitch to Alvis. Ron Plaza pointed out to Mike Marshall that the way we play him will depend on how he's pitched. And Marshall said he didn't know yet. "I have to wait until I get out there," he said.

If no one else understood what he meant, I did. The way he pitches to any given hitter depends on how he feels at the moment, what his instincts tell him.

This was just one more reason to count him as a weirdo. And yet there's nothing weird about it at all.

Take something that happened in the 1964 World Series (when young fireballer Jim Bouton won two games). Bill White, lefthanded hitter, good power, is the subject. I usually throw lefthanders a lot of change-ups, but his first three times up I threw him none. I don't know why, I just didn't. Fourth time up I struck him out—on a change. The next day the quote from White in the papers was: "I waited all day for that change-up and he never threw it. Then I gave up looking for the damn thing and started looking for the fastball and here it came."

If I'd been required to come up with a pregame plan on how to pitch White, I'd have committed myself to throwing him the change and I would have thrown one early in the game and he'd have clobbered it. But nobody was asking me to stick to a plan and, I think instinctively, I did the right thing.

It may have been the last time.

MAY
26

I'm trying so hard to be one of the boys I'm even listening to country music. And enjoying it. The back of the bus is the country-music enclave, and most of the players are part of it. So far, though, we've not been able to swing over city boys like Tommy Davis, Tommy Harper and John Kennedy. I think we'll get them in the end, though. Maybe with a bull fiddle.

Back at the hotel, Gary and I talked about the relationship between country and city guys on a ballclub, which is intertwined with the relationship between whites and blacks. There are lots of walls built up between people, and I pointed out that if I'd never roomed with Gary I would still think, "Oh, he's just a dumb Southerner." So probably the solution is to have people live together. I mean we still disagree about a lot of things—religion, politics, how children should be raised—but because we've been able to talk about these differences, spend so many hours together, we've been able to at least understand them. How's that for a solution? Put people together in a hotel room in Cleveland.

Getting on the airplane in Cleveland we ran into the Kansas City Royals. There was a lot of conversation because we're both expansion teams and a lot of us have been rescued from the same junkpile. The funniest line was about Moe Drabowski. They said he was sick on the bus the other night and puked up a panty girdle.

MAY
27

It's been a great trip for the Seattle Pilots. We took two out of three in Boston, Washington and Cleveland, and since we won three straight before we left home we're now only two games under .500 and I'm beginning to think we might have a shot at the divisional title. Of course, we'd need a little help. Maybe a small air crash involving the Minnesota and Oakland clubs. Nothing serious. Just a few broken arms and legs.

We'll know better after this next series. The Baltimore Orioles are in town. Which reminds me of a cartoon I once saw. It showed a little boy forlornly carrying a glove and a bat over his shoulder. "How'd you do, son?" his father asks. "I had a no-hitter going until the big kids got out of school," the kid says.

Another round of musical lockers today. John Gelnar was called up from Vancouver and Darrell Brandon was outrighted to Tucson. Brandon didn't take it very well. I was sitting next to him when Eddie O'Brien said, "Joe wants to see you."

"Oh, oh," Brandon said.

"Can't be that, Bucky," I said. "It's the wrong time."

When he came out of Joe's office he said, "Tucson. They outrighted me to Tucson. Boy, this just kills me. What am I going to tell Liz? She just got up here and we just got settled in and now we've got to move again."

At that moment I happened to look across the room—and there was Steve Barber getting his road uniform refitted. I guess he wants to look good while sitting in the diathermy machine. "You son of a bitch," I said to myself. "You're the guy who won't go down in order to help the club. Instead you hang around here, can't pitch and other guys are

180

sent down because of you." I got tremendously pissed off just thinking about it.

Talbot and I got to talking about Houk in the bullpen and we agreed that sometimes the man is 99 percent pure bullshit. "I was 0 and 8 last year," Talbot said, "and he came around to tell me he was taking me out of the rotation, not because I was pitching bad but because he thought the club was pressing too much behind me." That's called having smoke blown up your ass.

I tried to let Joe know that I haven't been pitching much lately. "I sure could use a workout," I said.

And Joe Schultz said, "If you need a workout go down to a whore-house."

Second best suggestion of the day. Going over the hitters it was decided that we should pitch Frank Robinson underground.

Ray Oyler (dubbed Oil Can Harry because he always looks as though he had just changed a set of rings) hit a home run into the left-field corner that must have traveled all of 305¼ feet. "As soon as I hit it, I knew it was out," he said. They have named the spot after Greenberg Gardens. They're calling it Oil Can's Corner.

Sitting in the bullpen it suddenly occurred to me that no one had said anything about Brandon being sent down. Not a word. It didn't seem right to me. A guy shouldn't be forgotten that quickly. At the very least we should have burned a candle.

MAY

28

Bobbie and I were talking about our plans for this fall and discussed the possibility of buying a trailer and taking a slow trip cross-country. On the other hand, we might ship the car, fly home and spend some time up at Cape Cod. Or we might wait until December and go sit on a warm island someplace. And why shouldn't we go to Europe?

What it all boils down to is money. If I get a raise next season we could afford to do any of these things. But if I have a bad season and they don't like this book, I may not even get a contract. So we decided that what I probably should do is get them to give me a contract at the end of this season, before they know about the book. Of course, the kind of contract I get will depend on what kind of season I have, and so all of it—plans, trips, contract—boils down to my knuckleball.

I had another Crosetti pulled on me tonight. When I was with Vancouver the baseball coach at the University of Oregon called me and asked if I would talk to one of his kids about the knuckleball. I said sure and arranged to see the kid in Tacoma. As it happened I got called back by the Pilots and he had to come down to Seattle. Now this is a rainy night, the tarpaulin is on the field, there's nobody in the stands and it's an hour-and-a-half before game time. I've got this kid standing behind me while I'm throwing on the sidelines and here comes an usher to tell me I can't have an unauthorized person on the field. I explained what I was doing, but the usher said that Mr. Crosetti had sent him out and that the kid would have to leave. I gritted my teeth and told him that the kid was staying and if Cro didn't like it he could come over and tell me himself. He never did.

Jim Pagliaroni joined the club tonight and is going to be a welcome addition. He was describing a girl that one of the ballplayers had been out with and said, "It's hard to say exactly what she looked like. She was kind of a Joe Torre with tits." This joke can only be explained with a picture of Joe Torre. But I'm not sure any exist. He dissolves camera lenses.

Joe Schultz was put away by Earl Weaver of the Orioles tonight. We had a two-run rally going when Weaver came out of the dugout and pointed out that we were hitting out of order. Seems that Joe had made out two lineup cards and given the umpires the wrong one. Weaver, who spotted it right away, let us hit until we got something going and then we had to call it all back. Since we lost the game 9–5, and since there was no telling how many runs we might have scored that inning, Joe's

182

face was very red indeed. I don't think he'll be telling us to keep our heads in the game again very soon.

Pitched one inning tonight and the greatest hitters in the American League were at my mercy. I struck Frank Robinson out on four absolutely hellacious knuckleballs; Boog Powell swung at two and missed for another strikeout, and Brooks Robinson popped up. The way that ball was moving, it's almost impossible for anyone to hit it solidly. They're at my mercy, I tell you.

Of course, since we were behind I was taken out for a pinch-hitter after my inning. Which means I'm still just a mop-up man. Maybe when the doubleheaders start piling up they'll give me a start. I can't wait.

MAY
30

I almost missed a ballgame today. It was Friday and I assumed we were playing our usual night game. I planned to spend the afternoon with the family at an art museum and I was lying around in my pajamas reading stories to the kids at one-thirty when the phone rang. It was Gary Bell.

"Where the hell are you?" he said.

"Where the hell are *you?*" I countered cleverly.

He told me. I flew in eight different directions, and the kids were scurrying around looking for my shoes and socks, and my wife was running after a shirt, and I felt like Dagwood Bumstead going to the office in the morning. I arrived at the ballpark at one-forty-five, fifteen minutes before game time, only two hours and forty-five minutes late, having missed running, batting practice and infield practice.

Almost to a man the guys were nice about it. I had a big grin on my face when I walked into the clubhouse and got a round of applause, and a lot of the guys told me they were glad I could make it today. Except Fred Talbot, who waved a little Yankee at me. "Jesus Christ, eleven years in baseball and you don't know whether it's a day game or night game."

I was absolutely not prepared to say I gave the umpire the wrong schedule card if Joe Schultz said anything to me, but he never said a word. Nobody was mad, including Maglie, who said it was a good thing I'd run the day before in my backyard. He was kidding about the fact that it rained yesterday and I called and asked whether I should come in or whether I could just run in my backyard. All the whole thing cost me was $10 to the pitcher's kitty for being late and $1 for missing infield.

I once came late to a game when I was with the Yankees—a World Series game. I wasn't pitching or anything, and it had rained all morning and I assumed, correctly, that there would be no batting practice, so I came in time for infield. But they'd called a pregame meeting and I missed it, so when I walked into that clubhouse there wasn't a single smile. Everyone was highly offended that I should take the Yankees and baseball and the World Series so lightly as to show up forty-five minutes before game time. I could have stayed out all night and come to the game with a hangover and I would have been forgiven. But I couldn't come late.

We split two games with the Orioles and lost our first today to the Tigers. So we've lost two out of three to the big kids and who knows where it will all end.

Fred Talbot had a marvelous story about Mel McGaha, who had a short run as manager of the Kansas City A's. McGaha called a meeting during spring training for eight o'clock on a Friday night, an unforgiveable sin. Guys had to leave their families and dinner parties and come in from all over the place. When they got there, McGaha said, "Boys, I'm glad you all got here tonight. We're not really having a meeting. I just wanted to see how quick we could all group up if we had to."

With the Tigers in town I've tried to call Johnny Sain and talk with him about my knuckleball and tell him how well I've been doing since I came back from Vancouver. I've missed him at the hotel a couple of times, but I'll keep trying.

I know Detroit needs relief help and they could get me cheap. If he looks in the newspaper he'll see a 4.2 ERA, although since I've returned from the minors it's only a bit over 3.0. In my last ten appearances I've given up one earned run, walked three and struck out eight. I've given up only five hits in eight innings. Of course, my own club doesn't seem very impressed, but that's another story.

I get the feeling that Sal and Joe just don't trust me. I think they're convinced that I need more than just the knuckleball to get by for more than an inning or two. One of these days they're going to need me for five or six innings and I'll show them. I'll show them. I'll show them. I think I'll show them.

Now they're talking about using Talbot as a starter, and this reduces *my* chances, except that the seer my wife went to this winter told her that our fortunes wouldn't rise until June. So I guess I won't get a start until then.

Do I really believe all of that? No, I don't.

Before we left the park today we were told that tomorrow's game would start at twelve-fifteen because of national television and that we'd have to take batting practice at ten-thirty. "Ten-thirty?" said Pagliaroni. "I'm not even done throwing up at that hour."

MAY
31

Tony Kubek and Mickey Mantle were here to do the TV broadcast and before the game Mickey was down in the clubhouse. With me standing right there, Joe Schultz says, "Mickey, what do you think of a guy who comes to the ballpark fifteen minutes before the game starts?"

Mickey shook his head sadly. "I know he's got some strange ideas," he said.

Don Mincher was worried about appearing on national television. "My mother's going to watch this ballgame in Alabama," he said, "and she's going to notice first thing that I'm not using the batting helmet with the earflap on it. And tonight she's going to be on the telephone, guaranteed, asking me why I'm not wearing my earflap."

Between innings of the game I got up in the bullpen and worked with the iron ball Mike Marshall keeps out there. Talbot was certain I was only doing it so I would get on television, and maybe I was, partly. After the third time up Talbot said, "Jesus Christ, Bouton, why don't you just run across the field and slide into second base and get it over with?"

The people who watched this game on television saw some of the dumbest baseball ever played this side of a sandlot. I hope Kubek and Mantle pointed it out to all the Little League, high-school and college players who were watching, but somehow I doubt it. So I'll do it here. It started in the first inning when Joe Sparma walked Tommy Harper, leading off, on four-straight pitches. Hegan was the next batter. Ball one. On ball two, way over Hegan's head, Harper tries to steal second and is thrown out. Sparma *still* hasn't thrown a strike. Two more balls and Hegan's on first base. Sparma has thrown eight balls in a row and he's got one out.

Tommy Davis up. First pitch, ball one. Second pitch is shoulder high, a ball, but he swings at it and tops it down the third-base line. He had no business swinging, of course. By now he should have been wondering if Sparma would *ever* throw a strike. Instead of wondering, he's thrown out at first. In the meantime, with two out and second base all his very own, Hegan decides to try for third. It's very important that he go to third base because he can score from there on a base hit. He can also score from second on a base hit. So he needs to go to third base like Frank Howard needs more muscles. Of course, he's out from here to there and Sparma is out of an inning in which all he threw was ten pitches—all balls.

A couple of innings later Al Kaline, of all people, steals third with two out. Can't imagine what he was thinking of.

To cap it all off, we lost the game 3–2, and I didn't get into it. Diego Segui did. Since my win in Boston two weeks ago I've made just four appearances and pitched a total of four-and-a-third innings. We got starters around here who get knocked out in the second and third inning and this relief ace can't get any pitching in. I'm getting psycho about it, starting to feel the way I did in New York: that there's some kind of conspiracy to keep me out of ballgames just when I'm starting

186

to throw good. I even have this morbid fear that someone in the front office has discovered I'm writing a book and is trying to work me out of the system. Then there's this weird one. It occurs to me that the Yankees may have prevailed upon Milkes, or the Pilot organization, to soft-pedal me so that I won't embarrass them. These two clubs have made quite a few trades and I know it embarrasses the Yankees to have Hegan doing so well here. So maybe they said, "Do us a favor, don't let Bouton look good." My wife says that soon the voices will be after me.

Maybe my problem is that I'm not merchandising my product properly. Knuckleball. It's got no pizzaz. How about Super Knuck? Or maybe I can borrow one of Satchel Paige's names for a pitch: Bat Dodger. Why not Super-Knuckling Bat Dodger? Or High-Velocity Super-Knuckling Bat Dodger? Nah. It's got to be short and snappy. Maybe tomorrow I'll ask Sal to think of a name for my pitch. He'll probably say how about working on that pitch they call The Curve?

Got a letter congratulating me on my great victory in Boston from Fritz Peterson today. It's an indication of how far down I've fallen when one miserable win calls for congratulations. Fritz said a lot of guys on the Yankees agreed that I had a real good knuckleball. Then he wrote: "It's a good thing Jim Turner taught you that pitch before you left New York."

There was also something about Fred Talbot. Fritz said that Talbot seemed to have changed a lot in the last year and that I'd probably like him now. I showed Talbot the letter and he said, "That son of a bitch. I thought he always liked me." I guess Fred *is* changing. The other day, after he won in Cleveland, I reminded him that he'd already matched last year's output of wins (one). A couple of years ago he'd have gotten angry. Now he just laughed.

Of course, he was damn lucky to get that win. We had an 8–2 lead in the fifth, and when he went in to pitch I told him all he had to do to get the win was to keep from getting a heart attack. I admit he pitched well. He gave up only three hits in five innings. But I couldn't help a feeling of jealousy stealing over me like green slime. Here I'd been scraping and scuffling, pitching in mop-up situations all year long, and I end up scratching together just one win, against Boston no less, in extra innings, and here comes Fred, he's with the club just two days, and he absolutely waltzes to a win. Oh well, it'll make my comeback speech at the Americana Hotel that much more interesting.

The latest adventure of Mike Marshall has him feuding with Sal Maglie about his screwball. A screwball is a curve ball that breaks in the opposite direction of a curve ball: when thrown by a righthanded pitcher it breaks in on a righthanded hitter. Mike wants to throw screwballs and Sal wants him to throw curve balls, so they're at each other all the time.

"Why don't you just throw screwballs and tell Sal they were curve balls?" I suggested.

"I would," Marshall said. "But the catchers tell Sal what I'm throwing."

See, the catchers are angry at him for trying to call his own game. So they go back to the bench and commiserate with Sal when he complains about the way Marshall is pitching. Mike won fifteen games last year and until recently he's been our most effective pitcher. They haven't disproved any of his theories. Why can't they just leave him alone?

I'm afraid Mike's problem is that he's too intelligent and has had too much education. It's like in the army. When a sergeant found out that a private had been to college he immediately assumed he couldn't be a good soldier. Right away it was "There's your college boy for you," and "I wonder what our genius has to say about that?" This is the same kind of remark Sal and Joe make about Marshall.

I think Sal and Joe put me right up there with Marshall in the weirdo department. They don't believe that my kind of guy can do the job, so when I *am* successful they're surprised. When Fred Talbot does the job, well, he's from the old school, blood and guts, spit a little tobacco juice on it.

Another thing. When I was winning a lot of ball games my double warm-up was a great idea, an innovation, maybe even a breakthrough. After I hurt my arm the double warm-up became a terrible idea. It was sapping my strength. In fact it was downright weird.

JUNE

1

We came from behind three times tonight to beat the Tigers 8–7. I pitched a third of an inning, coming in with a man on second. I got Tom Matchick on a ground ball back to me on a 3-and-2 count. After the game I told Joe Schultz that the reason I went to 3-and-2 was that I needed the work. "I figured you were doing *something* out there," Joe Schultz said.

In the clubhouse Joe delivered his usual speech: "Attaway to stomp 'em. Stomp the piss out of 'em. Stomp 'em when they're down. Kick 'em and stomp 'em." And: "Attaway to go boys. Pound that ol' Budweiser into you and go get them tomorrow."

This stuff really lays us in the aisles.

Jerry Neudecker was the umpire at third base. His position is just a few steps away from our bullpen and he stopped by, as umpires will, to pass the time between innings.

"Why is it that they boo me when I call a foul ball correctly and they applaud the starting pitcher when he gets taken out of the ball-game?" says Neudecker.

Says I: "Because, Jerry, the fans recognize the pitcher as being a basically good person."

He laughed.

Actually I think umpires can be too sensitive. They have this thing about a word. You'd think it was sticks and stones. The word is mother-fucker and it's called the Magic Word. Say it and you're out of the game. I have only one question. Why? Now think about that.

One of the things baseball players take pride in is their crudity. The day Brandon was sent down, for example, Gary Bell, who is his friend, asked if he would mind leaving his tapes so the guys could con-tinue to listen to his good music while he was gone. Which is like the guy in spring training who went up to a rookie and said, "Hey, if you get released, can I have your sweatshirts?" The crudity takes other forms. Like the fellow who rooms with the great chick-hustler. The hustler will spend all of his time pounding the streets, spending money in bars, working like hell at running down girls. His roommate just lounges around the room, watching television, taking it easy. And he does great just taking his roommate's leavings.

Then there's the tale Jim Gosger told about hiding in a closet to shoot a little beaver while his roommate made out on the bed with some local talent. Nothing sneaky about it, the roommate even provided the towel for Gosger to bite on in case he was moved to laughter. At the height of the activity on the bed, local talent, moaning, says, "Oh darling, I've never done it *that* way before." Whereupon Gosger sticks his head out, drawls "Yeah, surrre," and retreats into the closet.

After he told us the story, "Yeah surrre," became a watchword around the club.

"I only had three beers last night."

"Yeah, surrre."

And I've known ballplayers who thought it was great fun to turn on a tape-recorder under the bed while they were making it with their latest broad and play it back on the bus to the ballpark the next day.

Johnny Sain returned my call this morning and we had a long talk. I told him how my knuckleball was going and he asked me what pitch I was using for my off-pitch to go with it when I needed a strike. I said fastball. He suggested I use a slider instead. His reason is that when a hitter is looking for a knuckleball and gets something else, he thinks, "Fastball!" He may have time to adjust. But if the ball does something, has a little movement to it, he'll be fooled.

I said I'd try it, sort of cut my fastball a little and see if it would move. I asked him if he could use an elderly righthanded knuckleball pitcher in Detroit and he said, "No chance. We've got four pitchers now who've all pitched less than ten innings this year. That Mayo Smith [the manager] is not a very good man to pitch for. The last guy to pitch a good game is his man, and he overuses him and neglects everybody else. There are three or four pitchers on the club he doesn't even talk to."

He told about what had happened with a guy named Mike Kilkenny. He's a lefthanded pitcher and Sain had been teaching him to get lefthanders out by coming sidearm on them. It can be a really effective pitch. But Kilkenny pitched in an exhibition game recently and, with the bases loaded, he came sidearm on a lefthanded hitter and plunked him in the ribs. Said Smith: "When I saw you come sidearm I liked to die. You take that goddam sidearm pitch and shove it up your ass."

So here's another case where the manager is trying to make rules for his pitchers that go right over the head of the pitching coach.

Not long ago John went home for a day and Smith took the pitchers to the outfield and ran them hard, foul line to foul line. Sain was angry when he found out. So he went into Mayo's office and said, "Is this the pitching staff that led all baseball in complete games last year?"

"Yes, it is," Mayo said.

"Well, are we going to follow a formula that I used last year or one that hasn't been successful here for twenty-five years?"

"I guess we'll stick with what's been successful," Mayo said.

But he didn't like it. I'd bet right now the Tigers don't win the pennant again.

I told John about the trouble I'd been having getting enough work and how they always want to save me for the seven innings I never pitch. John laughed and said that he personally was a believer in throwing before a game, and that what he does is take a guy out of sight into the bullpen and let him work. He said if a pitcher is just throwing on the sidelines his arm can bounce back in twenty minutes. He's been able to sell pitchers on that, but it's hell selling managers.

JUNE

2

Big meeting before the game about personal appearances and autograph signing. It was proposed that we charge no less than $100 for any personal appearance and no less than $100 an hour for autograph-signing sessions. I said I didn't think it was a very good idea because it would work a hardship on the lesser-known player who could not command such a large fee. A player like Harper or Mincher or Davis might get that kind of money but a Gus Gil or a John Gelnar, guys who might be offered $25 or $50 for an appearance, might never get any shots at all. I suggested that it be left up to the individual what he wants to take for an appearance.

So Steve Barber said, "This is a big-league town and these people are going to have to learn to go big league."

And Don Mincher said: "If we go for $25 and $50 we'll never get it up there where it belongs."

And Brabender said, "If you want to dance, you've got to pay the fiddler." (This got a big laugh because it's what we say to a guy who's been out drinking the night before and has to do a lot of running with a bad body to get the alcohol out of his system.)

And O'Donoghue said: "We made that mistake in Kansas City, where the guys went for $25 or $50 and that's all we could ever get."

So I said: "Well, if a guy doesn't want to go for $50 he doesn't have to. He can pass it on to one of the lesser players. Besides, suppose it's a friend, or a good cause or something."

Then Joe Schultz said: "Well, whatever you do, I think you should all get together on it and everyone do the same thing. Hell, you guys are big-league ballplayers. Just make it a club rule and everybody will stick to it."

So much for my doctrine of laissez faire. The tyranny of the majority over the minority will always be with us. The vote was unanimous, except for my abstention. If someone offers me $25 or $50 and can't afford more, I'll take it.

The next thing we talked about was signing autographs for kids before the ballgame. Apparently there is a league rule that supposedly prohibits players from signing autographs when they're in uniform on the field. The rule is ignored. Some players were upset by this. Said Brabender: "If you don't feel like signing and you say you're not allowed to and some other guy comes up behind you and starts signing, you look like an ass."

So Joe Schultz said: "Make it my rule—no autographs once the gates open. No autographs at all."

Great. If a kid comes to the ballpark and wants an autograph, when the hell is he going to get it if not before the game starts? Of course, he can stand around outside in the dark for an hour or so after the game and hope he can stop us when we're rushing to get home. Who wants an autograph that bad? Especially from a Seattle Pilot.

At the end of the meeting Gary Bell brought up the fact that when we're in Baltimore next time we've been asked to go to Washington to attend a clinic Ted Kennedy is running for underprivileged children. Did anyone want to sign up? Mike Marshall signed, and Marty Pattin signed, and I signed. But before I did I stood up and said, "Now, wait a minute. We've got a free clinic here, right? For underprivileged kids? Well, isn't there some way we can get these kids to kick in their lunch money or something to us?"

Almost everybody laughed.

Ah, the ballgame. Steve Barber started. The last time he got a big lead but had to leave in the fifth. That's how Talbot got his quick win. The rule is that the starter can't get credit for the win unless he pitches five full innings.

Sure enough we score three in the first, two in the second and another in the third. We've got a 6–0 lead and it looks like Barber is having trouble out there. He's twitching his arm and cranking it around and doing a lot of fussing. So Talbot goes down and tells Maglie, as a joke, that he's absolutely ready, that his arm never felt better, just in case they should need him. Now every time Barber throws a ball Talbot holds up his hands in the sign of a T—for Talbot.

In the fifth, when Barber walks a couple, the call comes—for me. With two out I'm all set to go in and collect my Big W when Barber, the rat, goes ahead and gets the third out on a pop-up. Says Talbot: "Ah, sit down. No chance now. All you can get is a save or your ass kicked in." And he went down and told Sal his arm felt terrible.

I pitched the sixth, seventh, eighth and ninth, gave up three hits, one home run—Ken Harrelson took me over the left-field wall on a high knuckleball. And all I wound up with was a save.

I had a great knuckleball when I went in, but I lost it in the eighth. I got by on fastballs. In the bottom half we took an awful long time hitting so I asked Sal if I could try throwing a little to get the feel of the knuckleball back. "Nah," he said. "You're doing all right. Besides, it would look horseshit."

I was rooting for Steve Barber to look horseshit tonight and get his ass shipped out. Instead he had good stuff out there, good enough for them to keep him another month even if he can't pitch. I suppose down deep I'd like him to do well enough to make a contribution to this club. I think we have a chance to move now. We're in third place, only four out of first. And we're scoring all kinds of runs—six, seven a game. And we haven't been shut out. Not once. If we get some decent pitching, why, for goodness sakes, maybe we can win the pennant.

Talbot is in rare form these days. Like he was telling us how it used to be in the sheet-metal shop of the industrial school he went to. When they were taught how to weld, the first thing they did was weld the door shut when the teacher left the room. The next thing they did was weld every tool in the place onto a metal tractor, which was kept in the center of the room. And for kicks, they'd heat a steel bar until it was red hot, let the color cool out of it and then ask the new boy to bring over the metal bar. All it would cost was the skin off his hand.

JUNE
5

Baltimore

Arrived in Baltimore today, which is always depressing. The town puts you down, and the hotel is dingy, and they don't have bedboards, which means my back will ache tomorrow, and my roomie is supposed to pitch tomorrow and he's got a worse back than I have. It's dreary. Besides, I'm still suffering from having given up two earned runs in an inning-and-a-third the other night and losing the ballgame besides.

Even the newspaper depressed me tonight. I read where they're discussing the possibility of an integrated Davis Cup team in South Africa and a fellow named Alf Chambers, president of the South African Lawn Tennis Association said that the discussions had nothing to do with protests of other countries. And the increase in the number of swimming pools in Harlem has nothing to do with the riots and the troop withdrawals having nothing to do with the protest movement and the baseball owners broadened our pension coverage not because of any strike but out of an innate sense of fair play. Yeah, surrre.

And why is it, I ask myself, that baseball players are allowed to smoke during a game and that it's all right to sneak a smoke in the runway or even to go back into the clubhouse for a goddam cigarette, but if you take a candy bar out to the bullpen you get all kinds of static.

The bed in this hotel in Baltimore makes me think these bad thoughts. I think I'll go wash out my brain with soap.

JUNE

6

D.C. Stadium is being renamed Robert F. Kennedy Stadium and there are dedication ceremonies and those clinics that Marshall, Pattin and I signed up for. The Baseball Commissioner's office called Bell to ask if he could get guys like Sal Maglie, Joe Schultz, Tommy Davis, Tommy Harper and Don Mincher to attend. Sal said he had plans for tomorrow. Harper said he didn't want to go. Mincher said he would go, and Schultz sort of agreed. Tommy Davis said he would make the clinic if he could.

In the bullpen during the game the conversation turned to many things (Fred Talbot on the American destroyer that was cut in half by the Australian aircraft carrier: "The bastards must have been playing chicken out there"). But especially the talk was about the strike in the spring and the players who signed their contracts despite it—like Pete Richert of Baltimore. He said he had to sign his contract because he was just buying a house and the story was that he'd borrowed the money from the club and if he'd borrowed it from the bank he'd have had to pay a high interest rate. O'Donoghue thought this was justification enough. I said I didn't think so. I said that *everybody* could use the money, and that those who didn't sign were risking the owner's getting angry at them besides. And what about the marginal players? And the rookies? A lot more was at stake for them than some high interest rate on a loan.

There *was* agreement about the large number of Atlanta Braves who had signed. And we agreed *that* was all Paul Richards' fault. He put a tremendous amount of pressure on his players and I guess I blame them a helluva lot less than I do Richert.

And then Carl Yastrzemski's name came up because he'd just ignored the strike and Gary Bell said, "Didn't surprise me. Carl Yastrzemski is for himself first and second and the hell with everybody else."

Gee, Gary, Carl Yastrzemski?

Yes. Besides, during the strike Yastrzemski called several superstars in an attempt to form a separate committee and settle things without the Players' Association. Fortunately they told him to take a hike, son.

I don't think the only bad guys in this thing were the few players who caved in. Richards was particularly beautiful, calling Marvin Miller "a mustachioed fourflusher." And many others were willing to take a strike and use Triple-A players and flush the game right down the drain if necessary. These are the same guys who want us to think they're sportsmen who run the game out of civic pride. They're not in this thing for money. They're not. We know because that's what they tell us. And we believe. Like Clete Boyer once told me that Dan Topping, former Yankee owner, was all for the players and a wonderful man. I asked him how he knew. And he said, "Ralph Houk told me."

Mike Marshall was sitting against the fence in the bullpen watching the ballgame. In order to get close to the fence he turned his cap around backward and used the leather band to protect his head from the cold steel. Without saying a word, Eddie O'Brien lifted the hat off his head and put it on him peak-front. "I don't want Joe getting on me because you guys are wearing your hats backward," he said.

With that, Marshall took his hat off, slammed it on the ground and said, "How's that? I don't have it on wrong now, do I?"

All the Orioles are wearing their socks with high cuts, like Frank Robinson, and no one seems to object. I watched very closely and saw no lack of spirit on the club as a result of these high cuts. Of course, the club is winning, but I don't know whether they're winning because of their socks or because a lot of them aren't wearing hats during batting practice.

If you ever see a baseball player stick his tongue out at someone in the stands it's not because he's mad at anybody. It happens to be a form of beaver shooting. The player scouts the stands for good-looking girls, and if he catches a doll's eye he sticks out his tongue. If she looks away, it means she's not interested. If she smiles, something might come of it. It's called shooting stingers.

Roomie got shelled out of the game in four innings. The Orioles are so hot right now it could happen to anybody. But poor Gary took it pretty hard. After I pitched my third of an inning I went into the clubhouse. "Rooms, I'm diving off the hotel tonight," he said. "Something's happening to my body. I'm going to be dead in six months."

Jim Gosger came over to cheer him up. "Hey, Gary, who's going to drive to Vancouver, you or I?"

Just then Marty Pattin walked by. "Hey, Pattin," Gary said. "Your shoes are terrible. Try and get some new shoes before I'm traded, will you?"

"You better get them before tomorrow morning," I said, trying to be helpful.

I felt bad for Gary. I also felt hungry. "Tell you what," I said. "Let's go out and get something to eat. Then we'll go out and tie one on."

"Rooms, I'm not hungry," Gary said. "Just thirsty."

"You're on an empty stomach," I said. "Let's go somewhere nice. We'll have cocktails and wine with dinner, then we'll do the town up right. But you got to get something to eat."

"Don't worry about me, Rooms," he said. "You're a great roomie and I love you. You've been teaching me new things. You've told me about the stars and the planets and I don't believe in Noah's Ark anymore, and you're making a non-believer out of me. I appreciate that, Rooms, but I got to go drinking tonight."

So Gary Bell went drinking, without his roommate. I didn't hear him come in.

There was another somewhat revolting development tonight. Actually it's a continually revolting development that I haven't wanted to admit is happening. The catchers are getting tired of catching me— and scared because the little darling dances so much it not only can strike out a batter but break the catcher's finger. So they've been beefing. The other day Haney went to Sal Maglie and said he believed I was throwing too much. He said he thought it was bad for my arm.

I don't blame Haney. Or Pagliaroni, who doesn't want to catch me either. And I've told them that. I'm liable to take their living away from them. It's like Ranew told me once. "What if I've got to go up there and hit and I've got a bone bruise from your goddam knuckleball? Like you hit me on the knee tonight. It could have been my hand. Then I can't do my job."

I agreed with him, so I went over to Eddie O'Brien and said, "Eddie, old pal, how about you putting on a mask and catching me?"

"It's not my job to warm up pitchers," Eddie said.

"Why not? The bullpen coaches on other teams warm up pitchers."

"What if I get hurt?"

"That's a tough thing, Eddie," I said. "If you get hurt it's not as bad as if some other guy gets hurt and can't play when he's needed."

"Oh hell, there's not that much chance of getting hurt," he said. "I've seen guys get hurt on sliders. But if you think I ought to be catching your knuckleball, take it to the manager."

"I don't want to bother him with something so unimportant. It's so small I think it's a decision *you* can make."

"It's not my job."

And that's the way it went.

"As soon as the game is over I'll tell Joe our exact discussion," he said finally.

"Not after a loss," I said.

"If the point has to be brought up, it has to be brought up."

As it happened, I pitched to one hitter, Frank Robinson. He belted a line drive to the centerfielder. So I got out of that.

Then they pinch-hit for me and I felt empty, like a hungry man cut off after his shrimp cocktail. I told Sal I needed a pitching fix and that I was going out to the bullpen to throw. "That's your whole trouble," Sal said. "You're throwing too damn much."

Some trouble, I thought. I've only had one bad outing since I came back from Vancouver. What the hell was he talking about? Except that I knew. I was asking to do something unorthodox, and unorthodoxy does in baseball what heresy does in the priesthood.

I set my bulldog jaw. "I need to throw," I said. "And I'm going to throw."

"Oh, crissakes. If you have to throw, go ahead."

But by this time he'd made his point to everybody in the dugout. I was being a weirdo again.

Later on Mike Marshall said that while I was throwing in the bullpen Joe Schultz kept walking down to the end of the dugout to look out at me. He'd come back each time shaking his head. And in the shower after the game Sal was telling the catchers that I was throwing too much. Know something? The catchers agreed.

JUNE
7

This was the big day for the underprivileged kids of Washington, D.C. It was a pretty big day in the life of the Seattle Pilots too.

Breakfast with Mincher, Pattin and Marshall, and of all things, we got to talking about old Guess Who? Not vindictively, you understand, rather the way you talk about something funny that happened last night. Mincher said we were missing something by being out in the bullpen, that Maglie was great in the dugout—especially when Marshall was pitching. "If a guy hits a fastball when Marshall is out there," Minch said, "Sal says, 'Son of a bitch, he's throwing that fastball too much.' In the very next inning a guy will get a hit on a curve ball and Sal says, 'Son of a bitch, why doesn't he go to his fastball more?' "

"I try to sit next to him whenever I can," Mincher said.

At ten o'clock, five of us boarded the bus for Washington: Joe Schultz, Don Mincher, Mike Marshall, Marty Pattin and I. On the bus were six Orioles: the bullpen catcher Charley Lau, outfielders Dave May, Paul Blair and Don Buford, coach Billy Hunter and Jim Hardin, the pitcher.

During the one-hour ride Joe Schultz was asking around about what kind of deal we were getting into and he found out that we were going to the Sheraton-Park Hotel, where we'd be assigned a playground in which to conduct a clinic. After that we were all going to the stadium for the dedication. "Oh shitfuck," Joe Schultz said. "I didn't think it was going to be like that. Oh fuckshit." He seemed agitated.

At the hotel things seemed pretty well organized. Everybody's name was on a list and they gave out tags and the addresses of the playgrounds and assigned drivers to take us out. Naturally this all took a while and we were standing out in the corridor waiting when Joe Schultz said to Mincher, "Shitfuck, Minch, what do you say? Let's get the hell out of here."

Mincher hesitated for a moment and it was all over. Schultz had his man. "Hell, I'm getting out of here and grabbing a cab," Joe Schultz said.

"Crissakes, don't leave me behind," Mincher said. "I'm going with you."

And the two of them left the hotel and took a cab back to Baltimore.

Ah, shitfuck.

At the end of the day, after the clinics and the elimination races for the kids at the playgrounds and the meet at the Stadium, and after guys like Sam Jones and Red Auerbach and Jim Beatty and a lot of Olympic swimmers and pro-football players had made their little talks and done what they could—little as it was—for the black kids of Washington, D.C., we took the bus back to Baltimore and Mike Marshall said he thought he understood what had happened with Joe Schultz and Don Mincher.

"I could see it coming," Marshall said. "Joe couldn't cope with the situation. He wasn't in charge. He was forced to follow along. It was frustrating to him not to know what the plan was and he's neither intelligent nor competent enough to be at ease with the unknown. That's why he surrounds himself with other people, coaches, who are as narrow as he is. He wants to rule out anyone who might bring up new things to cope with. He wants to lay down some simple rules—keep your hat on straight, pull your socks up, make sure everybody has the same-color sweatshirt—and live by them."

And it was obviously true. Like on the bus going to Washington, Joe Schultz and I were sitting across the aisle from each other. I handed him the sports section of the paper and when he was through with it I asked him if he wanted to read the rest of the paper. "Nah," he said. "I don't read that."

There's no comfort for Schultz in the front of a newspaper. When he wants comfort he can get it from somebody like Mincher. I don't think Joe would have gone back to Baltimore alone, and I don't think Mincher would have either. But they gave each other just enough support to do it together. They were less afraid, both of them, of running out than they were of facing this great unknown that involved so many people.

Talking about Joe Schultz reminded Marshall of something that happened the other night. Although we had just blown a game to the Orioles, when Schultz came back into the clubhouse he was smiling. Mike thought that was kind of strange until he heard Schultz say, to nobody in particular. "Lou Brock stole his 25th base tonight. That's 25 out of 25."

And Mike Marshall thought, "My God. The man's living in a dream world. He still thinks he's with the Cardinals."

I had a long talk with Marty Pattin on the bus. He's had a tough, interesting life. He's from Charleston, Illinois, and his mother and father were separated when he was a baby and he was shipped off to live with his mother's folks. He was still a junior in high school when his grandfather died, so he moved into a rooming house and tried to work his way through the rest of high school. It was then he met a man named Walt Warmouth who helped him get through school—not only high school but college. Warmouth owned a restaurant, and Marty worked there and got his meals there, and every once in a while he'd get a call from the clothing store in town and be told he could pick out a suit and a bunch of other stuff and it was all paid for. They never would tell him who had paid, but Marty knew anyway. "The guy was like a father to me," Marty said. "And not only to me. He must have sent dozens of kids through school just the way he did me." Marty has a masters degree in industrial arts, and when he can he likes to help kids. That's why he signed up for the clinic.

What a terribly lonely life Marty must have had. Hell, it was a traumatic experience for me just going away to college and living in a dorm with a bunch of other kids. And here's Marty, still in high school, living in a rooming house. Not only that, but he goes on to become an All-American boy, complete with all the good conventional values. Like he was telling the kids at the clinic that sure it was difficult to throw a ball well or be a good basketball player. It was difficult to do a lot of things, but that they were all capable of doing a lot of difficult things if they were willing to work hard and practice. I guess he ought to know.

I also thought that what these kids need is not a half-hour of conversation with some big-name guy who's just passing through. What they

201

need is day-to-day attention from people like Marty's grandparents and Walt Warmouth and full-time workers in the ghettoes. And once again I wished I had the guts to chuck baseball and go out and do something for somebody besides myself. And getting mad at myself for *not* being able to do it, I look around for somebody else to blame and I decide, what the hell, one less goddam bomb and we could have somebody working full time in every one of those sixteen playgrounds in Washington they sent us famous athletes to.

It wasn't a half-hour after I got back from Washington that the phone rang in our room. It was Gabe Paul telling Gary Bell that Marvin Milkes wanted to see him.

"Rooms, what do you think it's going to be?" Gary said as he got dressed.

I told him it must be something about the Players' Association. I told him it might be that they found out I was writing a book and they wanted to check with him on how it was coming along. I told him that maybe Milkes was lonely and just wanted somebody to talk to. But we both knew.

Gary was gone only fifteen minutes. When he opened the door he said one word. "Chicago."

To the White Sox, for Bob Locker.

He sat on the edge of the bed and I could see the thoughts racing through his mind. How do I move? What do I do with my car? Who's on that club? Any friends? It's like, I suppose, when you're wounded. You don't know where you've been hit and you have to sit there a minute and feel around to find out just how seriously you've been hurt.

"One good thing," Gary said after a while. "Woody Held is over there. My old roommate."

He thought for a while, then he said, "We just bought a big TV. I'll have to call Nan and tell her to try to bring it back to the store. We sure as hell can't haul it clear across the country."

You worry about the damnedest things.

It didn't come as any big shock. Gary hadn't been pitching well and the papers had a lot of rumors about a trade. But I felt particularly close to Gary, because we were roommates and because we spent time together—our wives too—when we were at home. Another thing. Gary was my link to most of the other players. Despite my efforts to be one of the boys, the fact that I was Gary's roommate is what helped most. Whatever the reasons, I felt awkward, empty, not knowing what to say.

Gary took the bus to the ballpark with the team so he could pick up his equipment and say his goodbys. There was a lot of kidding, of course. That's what you're supposed to do when a guy gets traded. There was a sort of stunned tension underneath, though, because, as Mike Hegan says, "Gary's the kind of guy who's good for a club even when he's not pitching well."

It was still before game time when Gary lifted his big equipment bag and walked down that long corridor from the visiting clubhouse in Baltimore to where the cabs unload. I watched him all the way. He didn't turn back once.

I asked Eddie O'Brien to catch me for a while tonight in the bull-pen. Again he refused, and again I got pissed off. Ranew is developing a bone bruise on his hand. Also, I hit him on the knee the other night, so I hate to ask him to catch me. He had to for a while because I warmed up to go into the game. It was one of those safe games—we were behind 10–0. I pitched one inning, threw eight knuckleballs, seven of them for strikes. I struck Buford out on a beauty that went right over the plate, then broke outside. Got the next two guys on a pop-up and soft grounder. After the game no one came over and said I'd been throwing too much.

That was a lot of day today. I'm not sure I can take many like that.

JUNE
8

I grabbed myself by the seat of the pants this evening and marched myself into Joe Schultz' office. "I want to talk to you about my throwing program, Joe," I said. I didn't wait for him to say anything, but plunged ahead. I told him I knew Sal Maglie was telling him I was throwing too much, but that my arm didn't get tired throwing the knuckleball and the more I threw it the better it got.

"You mean I can use you every day?" Joe said.

I thought he knew that. "Hell yes," I said. "You can use me every day and twice on Sunday. But I'm not trying to tell you how to pitch me. All I'm saying is I need to throw."

"Listen, don't worry about Sal," Joe Schultz said. "I let a lot of the stuff Sal says go in one ear and out the other. Don't worry about it. Do whatever you have to do to get ready."

I could've kissed him. I mean there's a man who understands a lot better than I ever suspected. But then he said, "The problem with your knuckleball is that sometimes you can't get anybody out. You're not throwing it for strikes enough."

"Gee," I said boyishly, "I'm surprised to hear you say that. Since I came back from Vancouver there's only been one time I couldn't get anybody out. And that was the other day in Seattle. One bad outing, and I've had fifteen good ones. So far I've come in with fifteen runners on base and none of them have scored. And I'm not walking that many guys."

I think I convinced him.

"Well, you're doing a good job for us," Joe Schultz said. "If you weren't I'd have called you in here. You've helped the team. I'm pleased."

He wasn't going to let me off without some kind of lecture, how-ever. About a week or so ago I'd been warming up for what seemed like an hour and finally put my jacket on and sat down. "Crissakes, don't sit down out there," Sal Maglie had told me. "It looks horseshit when you come into the game."

"But I was ready to pitch," I said. "I didn't have to throw any-more."

"That doesn't matter," Sal said. "Even if you just stand there with the ball in your hand it looks better."

Well, looks count, I decided. Now I was going to get it from Schultz anyway.

"Oh yeah," he said. "For crissakes, when you're warming up in the bullpen and it's in the middle of an inning you might get called in, don't sit down. Crissakes, it looks terrible. Real horseshit."

"Sal told me that," I said. "It was real horseshit. I won't do it anymore."

If I let it go now, I thought, this whole thing will have been wasted. He'll think of it as a time when he called in that joker Bouton to tell him not to sit down in the bullpen when he's supposed to be warming up. So I shifted gears. "About Eddie O'Brien," I said, then quickly explained to him that the catchers were beginning to hurt and that O'Brien seemed like a natural solution. Only he kept saying it wasn't his job.

"Can he catch the damn thing?" Joe Schultz asked.

I said he seemed to catch it okay when we played catch in the outfield. And what the hell, if he misses it, who cares? Wouldn't we rather have him get hurt than Ranew or Pagliaroni?

"All right. I'll talk to Eddie about it," Joe Schultz said.

I can't wait.

During batting practice the Orioles sneaked into our bullpen—word is that it was Eddie Watt and Pete Richert—and deposited three goldfish and a little black fish into our water cooler. They looked very pretty swimming around in our drinking water.

This was in retaliation for Brabender and O'Donoghue going into *their* bullpen the other night and depositing their benches on the roof of their weathershed.

Everybody thought this was all very funny except Eddie O'Brien. "Guess what he said to me," Talbot said. "He said we ought to protest this game to the Commissioner because how could we use the bullpen with fish in our water cooler?"

"He wasn't *serious*," I said.

"Oh yes he was," Talbot said. "He was until he saw us all laughing. Then he tried to make out he was kidding. But he was serious as hell."

O'Donoghue told a story about the best pep talk a manager ever delivered. This was at Columbus in the International League and Don Hoak was the manager. "Boys, I'm just going to say one thing to you," he said at a clubhouse meeting. He held his thumb and forefinger about an inch apart and up where everybody could see them. "I want to remind everybody that you're just this far away from big-league pussy."

A young girl asked one of the guys in the bullpen if he was married. "Yeah," he said, "but I'm not a fanatic about it."

Mike Marshall said he learned something important tonight. He went to Curt Rayer, the trainer, and asked him to put some hot stuff on his arm. "I think it's a little tired," Marshall said.

It wasn't two minutes later that Rayer was in Schultz's office telling him that Marshall had a tired arm. It was good information. I mean, you know there's always a pipeline on a club. The trick is to find out who it is. When Johnny Keane was manager of the Yankees his spy was Vern Benson, the coach. We called him "Radar" because he always seemed to have an ear in our conversations. O'Donoghue says that in Cleveland it's George Strickland, the coach, who is called Pipeline.

And when I talked to my wife tonight she said the last time the wives got together one of the coach's wives (my wife insists we don't tell which) said some things she probably shouldn't have—namely that Curt Rayer was the guy on the club who was telling Milkes and Schultz which guys stay out late and which guys fool around and which guys spend a lot of time in the trainer's room. She also said that there were a couple of deals on the fire, one of them involving Comer and the other Ray Oyler. Now I sort of understand how Milkes and Schultz feel. It's nice to have your own pipeline.

JUNE
9

Detroit

I asked Eddie O'Brien if he'd talked to Joe Schultz recently.

"Yeah," he said. "And I'm not going to be catching knuckleballs. It's not my job."

I was dumbfounded. "Did Joe say that?" I said. In moments of tension my voice has a tendency to rise. I must have sounded like a girl with a short skirt in a high wind.

"Well, I talked it over with the coaches and they agreed that I'm not going to be able to keep my head in the game and check on what's happening in the field and be able to answer the telephone in a split second if I'm spending all my time catching that goddam knuckleball."

"You didn't talk to Joe," I said.

"Well, for a minute. He said I could do whatever I wanted as long as I didn't let it interfere with my job. And I think catching knuckleballs would interfere with my job."

"What job is that?" I said gently. "You haven't *got* a job. All you do is go over to that ballbag and hand everybody a ball and then you sit there and watch the game. When the telephone rings you jump up and tell somebody to warm up. That's your whole goddam job. A monkey could do your job." And as I talked I got angrier. There was a corner of my mind that calmly told me to shut up, but I was able to ignore it. I was having too good a time. "You know what you do on this club?" I continued. "More harm than good. You get guys pissed off at you and you don't contribute a thing."

"We've got trained, professional catchers here," O'Brien said. "They're here to catch and that's their job. I've got my own job and I'm going to do it and that's the way it's going to be for as long as *you'll* be around."

"Oh boy, a threat," I said. "But I got news for you. You're not going to be here too long yourself. You just better hope one of these catchers doesn't get hurt. Because if he does, it's going to be your ass."

After the game Sal said, "Joe wants to see you in his office." He meant me.

"Oh, oh," said Brabender, who was standing next to me. "What do you think it is, J.B.?"

"I don't know, Bender," I said.

"I bet you O'Brien went in and told him," Talbot said. Fred was there during my talk with O'Brien, and I'd felt bad about that. Some things should be said in private, but baseball isn't a very private game.

When I walked into his office, Schultz gave me a dirty look.

"What's this about you getting on O'Brien?" he said.

"Joe," I said sincerely, "I've been trying for some time now to work out an arrangement so that the two catchers don't have to catch my knuckleball as often as I have to throw it. They don't like to catch it and I don't blame them. O'Brien should be catching it and he's trying to get out of it."

"Jim, you got to learn to get along with the coaches," Joe said. "If you got any problems with them, you come to me."

"I didn't want to bother you, Joe," I said. "That's why I tried to deal through Eddie. You got enough things on your mind without being bugged about who's supposed to warm up what pitcher."

It was at about this point that Joe Schultz started to smile. I couldn't tell whether he was smiling with me or laughing at me.

"You have to understand about Eddie," Joe said, smiling. "He's been out of baseball for a long time now."

I said I tried to make allowances, but he was exasperating the hell out of me and I still felt he was absolutely wrong, although I felt bad about blowing up.

"Well, we'll see what we can do," Joe said.

For some reason I felt he'd come around to see things my way. When I came out of Joe's office Fred Talbot said, "Did O'Brien tattle on you?"

"Yes." I said. "O'Brien tattled."

And one of these days he *is* going to catch me, and if we're all lucky the worst I'll do is fracture one of his knees.

The great story in the bullpen tonight was about having this chick up in the room and she's saying, "Tell me you like me, please tell me you like me, just tell me you like one thing about me, anything, just one thing you like about me."

"Like you?" the guy says. "I love you."

A pause. And the chick says, "How can you love me? You don't even know me."

Which reminded another guy of the girl in spring training who was stood up by one player, we'll call him Joe, and went out with another instead. At the end of the evening, he finally coaxed her into bed, but not until after she said, "I'm only doing this because I'm in love with Joe."

Which reminded yet another guy about something that happened to him. "Right next to the ball park there was this little gas station," the guy said, "and after the ball game this chick and I parked there in the dark. We were at it hammer and tongs, I guess you could call it, when all of a sudden I see these lights in the rear view mirror. Here comes this big electric utility truck and it pulls up side of us. The driver looks right in on us and says, 'Nice game tonight. Go get 'em tomorrow.' Jesus, I thought he was going to ask me for my autograph."

During the game a guy came down from the stands to the dugout and said to Mike Marshall, "Hey, is Mike Marshall in the dugout? I'm a good friend of his."

"No, he's not down here," Mike Marshall said. "Maybe he's in the bullpen."

The fellow went off to look.

This was the first of three games with the Detroit Tigers and Joe Schultz said, "Let's go get 'em. We're just as good as they are." Can he really believe that?

Joe asked Mincher when he was going to have a meeting to elect a player representative and alternate, and Mincher said we'd have an election for alternate tomorrow, which means he's decided he has inherited the job. Gary didn't work it that way, although he did sort of guide the election. But Mincher isn't taking any chances. I guess he really wants the car that goes with the job. It's a nice car.

Anyway, Kennedy said, "I nominate Bouton," and everybody laughed. I declined on the spot. I refuse to give them another chance not to vote for me.

During infield drill tonight Frank Crosetti yelled, "Thataway. That's the old Rufus Goofus."

Johnny Sain was working with a couple of Tiger pitchers on the sidelines and one of the catchers was Hal Naragon, the bullpen coach. I thought it might be a funny idea to ask Naragon if he had time to catch *me* for a while. On second thought, I don't see why Naragon should think it was funny.

We beat the Tigers 3–2 with two runs in the tenth. Maybe we *are* as good as they are. What happened was that Mayo Smith left a right-hander in to pitch to Mincher with two on in the tenth and a lefthander warming up in the bullpen. Mincher knocked them both in with a single. When he got to first base Norm Cash was really boiling. "Crissakes," Cash said. "Mayo Smith has got to be the dumbest manager in baseball."

It was 3–1 when Diego Segui came in. He gave up two singles and a walk and had to be lifted. It was his third-straight bad outing. I think he might be getting a little tired. Gelnar came in with the bases loaded and one out, struck out Willie Horton on four pitches and got Tom Matchick on a grounder to end the game. It was a beautiful exhibition, especially for a guy who hasn't had that much time in the big leagues. Now he'll be the No. 1 righthanded short man while Segui rests up. It was interesting that O'Donoghue went in to face a lefthander and Gelnar came in against a righthander while at no time was I asked to warm up in a tough game. I wonder whether it's my knuckleball or arguing with coaches that counts most.

After the game Joe Schultz said, "Attaway to stomp on 'em, men. Pound that Budweiser into you and go get 'em tomorrow." Then he spotted Gelnar sucking out of a pop bottle. "For crissakes, Gelnar," Joe Schultz said. "You'll never get them out drinking Dr. Pepper."

JUNE
10

I'm pleased to note today that the New York Mets are 28–23 and in second place in their division and that the New York Yankees are 28–29 and in fifth place in their division. Perhaps justice is about to triumph.

I also note with some puzzlement that the Yankees have bought veteran righthander Ken Johnson from the Atlanta Braves. Ken Johnson is thirty-six years old (I'm thirty) and throws a knuckleball. He has pitched 29 innings this season and so have I. He's 0–1 this season and I'm 1–0. His ERA is 4.9 and mine is 3.8. And I bet they paid more than $12,000 for him.

Bob Locker, who is called "Foot," or "Wall," for obvious reasons, and "Snot" because Mickey Mantle swore he personally had that kind of locker back home, was elected alternate player rep before the game. Mincher announced that as his first move as player rep he had gotten the Pilots to agree to move to a new hotel in Baltimore, from the Belvedere to the Statler Hilton. "A hell of an idea," one of the guys said. "Now my broad is going to be wandering around the wrong hotel."

It was suggested that as Mincher's next move, he arrange to get

Marvin Milkes a room in whatever hotel we happen to be staying in. We're all convinced that Milkes never has a room, which is why he's in the lobby all the time, especially late at night.

Talking about his Chicago White Sox days, McNertney said that Eddie Stanky always insisted there was only one excuse for not being in the lineup—if there was a bone showing. Stanky was also responsible for storing the baseballs in a cool, damp place. McNertney: "You had to wipe the mildew off the balls before the game. First you'd take them out of the boxes, which were all rotted away anyway, wipe the mildew off and put them in new boxes. Then you gave them to the umpires and they never suspected a thing."

The idea, of course, is that cold, damp baseballs don't travel as far as warm, dry baseballs, and the White Sox were not exactly sluggers.

The game was lost 5–0. I could stand that. What I couldn't stand was pitching two-thirds of a miserable inning, giving up two runs and leaving the game with the bases loaded. (Fortunately, Bender got the third out without costing me any runs.) My knuckleball was so bad the only thing I could think of was suicide. This was no false sorrow. It was all I could do not to cry. Maybe I haven't been throwing it enough. Maybe I've been throwing too much. Maybe I'm going out of my mind.

I couldn't wait to get back to the hotel and call my wife so she could cheer me up. After I talked to her and the kids I felt better and agreed with her when she said that if I was going to allow myself to get this upset I wasn't getting paid enough. This did not change the nagging feeling that maybe I've lost it for good, that the knuckleball and I have gone our separate ways.

Milkes and Schultz just happened to be sitting in the lobby again around curfew time and Pagliaroni allowed as how he'd give us all the benefit of his experience. "If you're going to be late," he said, "be at least three hours late. Because if you're only an hour late they'll still be around trying to catch you."

At dinner Don Mincher, Marty Pattin and I discussed greenies. They came up because O'Donoghue had just received a season supply of 500. "They ought to last about a month," I said.

Mincher was a football player in high school and he said, "If I had greenies in those days I'd have been something else."

"Minch, how many major-league ballplayers do you think take greenies?" I asked. "Half? More?"

"Hell, a lot more than half," he said. "Just about the whole Baltimore team takes them. Most of the Tigers. Most of the guys on this club. And that's just what I know for sure."

JUNE
11

In the bullpen it was can you top this on general managers. Bob Locker told this one about a contract argument with Ed Short, general manager of the White Sox. This was after Locker had had his best season in 1967—77 games, 125 innings and a 2.09 ERA. It was a year after Phil Regan of the Dodgers had had his super year— 14–1 and a 1.62 ERA—in relief. Short had offered Locker $16,000 and he was asking for $18,000. Short said he was asking a lot and that what the hell, Regan had just signed a contract for $23,000. "If Regan is making only $23,000 then I'm asking too much," Locker said. "You check that. If he signed for $23,000 I'll sign for $16,000."

The next day Short called him and said, "I called Buzzie Bavasi (the Dodger GM) and he told me Regan was making $23,000 this year."

"All right," Locker said. "I'll take the $16,000."

After he signed he got to thinking about it and just for the hell of it he wrote Regan a letter. He asked if Regan would mind telling him about what he had signed for. And Regan wrote back saying he'd signed for $36,500.

"You know, you don't mind a guy deceiving you a little during contract negotiations," Locker said. "You get used to it. They all do it. But when a guy just outright lies right to your face, that's too much."

Brabender told about the generosity of Harry Dalton, the Baltimore general manager. When the minimum salary was raised from $7,000 to $10,000 he was making $8,000 and had a year-and-a-half in the majors. When he went to talk contract with Dalton he was told that he was getting a $4,000 raise, to $12,000. He felt pretty good about it—for about a minute. Then he realized that no matter what, his salary would *have* to go to $10,000, so he was therefore getting only a $2,000 raise. Dalton didn't think he'd see it that way.

And O'Donoghue chipped in with the one about Eddie Lopat, when he was GM of the Kansas City A's. O'Donoghue agreed to terms with Lopat over the telephone and went down to spring training. When he got there he was offered a contract for a lot less money. "But you agreed to a different figure on the telephone," O'Donoghue said. By this time, who knows, he may have been crying.

Said Lopat: "Prove it."

This kind of stunt was pulled on several players. It cost Talbot $500. He offered to throw Lopat through a closed window, but it didn't do him any good.

In the end Lopat must have been hurt by all of that. Because now no one will ever forget that when Tony Oliva first came up Lopat's pronouncement was, "The kid will never hit in the big leagues."

Jim Gosger was sent back down to Vancouver. "You know, I didn't think I was that bad a ballplayer," he said. "But they're making a believer out of me."

Probably because we're going to be in New York soon, the conversation was about Whitey Ford and what great stuff he had when he was pitching for the Yankees. Fred Talbot, who came to the Yankees when Whitey was about through and looking for all the little edges he could find, said Ford could take advantage of every little nick on a ball and make it do something, dive or sail or hop or jump. "If Cronin's name wasn't stamped on the ball straight, he could make it drop."

For a long time Whitey got away with throwing a mud ball that was positively evil. Sometimes Ellie Howard would load it up for him by pretending to lose his balance and steadying himself with his hand— while the ball was in it. Ford could make a mud ball drop, sail, break in, break out and sing "When Irish Eyes Are Smiling." Eventually the opposition, particularly Bill Rigney, the manager of the Angels, got wise to him and he had to quit using the mudder.

Then he went to his wedding ring. He gouged such sharp edges into it that we used to kid him about having lost the diamond out of it. He'd scuff up the ball with the ring and make it do all the things the mud ball did, except maybe now the song was different. He got by with the ring for a couple of months until umpire John Stevens, I think it was, or John Rice (for some reason, every time Rice came onto the field, somebody would holler, "What comes out of a Chinaman's ass?") got wise. The ump could have caused real trouble, but he went out to the mound and said, "Whitey, go into the clubhouse. Your jock strap needs fixing. And when you come back, it better be without that ring."

After that, Ellie Howard sharpened up one of the buckles on his shin guard and everytime he threw the ball back to Whitey he'd rub it against the buckle. The buckle ball sang two arias from *Aïda*.

JUNE
12

New York

Day off today and into New York for a three-game series starting tomorrow. There is always a flood of remembrances when I come back to New York. Like all the trouble I used to get into with the Yankees. One time nobody in the bullpen would talk to me for three days because I said I thought that Billy Graham was a dangerous character.

This was after he had said that Communists were behind the riots in the black ghettoes. I said that when a man of his power, a man with such a huge following, makes a statement like that, he is diverting attention from the real causes of riots in the ghettoes. As a result he delays solutions to those real problems, and this is dangerous. My heavens, you'd think I had insulted Ronald Reagan.

Another time, I recall, Crosetti and Jim Hegan were reading the paper and complaining about Father Groppi interfering in things he had no business getting involved in and I simply couldn't resist the temptation to let them know that I thought Groppi was doing a fine and courageous thing. As Mort Sahl says, you've got to fight the madness.

It's just the sort of thing I did when I went back to my old high school in Chicago Heights, Illinois, some years ago. I was invited to speak there as a returning hero. One of the things they wanted me to do was help calm some of the racial problems they were having. The principal asked me to speak from his office over the intercom that reaches the kids in all the rooms. I knew what I was expected to say; that students are here to learn and teachers are here to teach and that any feelings they might have, any grievances or problems, should be left outside the school. So let's all work together for a better education. Instead I sat down and wrote that I understood there were tensions within the school and that I recognized that they came about because of legitimate beefs that some of the kids had, and when the principal and the teachers who were there saw it they said, "No, Jim. Maybe you shouldn't, Jim. Why don't you just say hello to the kids and tell them you'll see them at the dinner tonight?" That's as far as I ever got. They told me politely and firmly that they didn't want me telling the kids any of that stuff.

And once at a father-and-son banquet, a kid with long hair got up and asked me what I thought about long hair and sideburns. The man sitting next to the kid was obviously his father and he just as obviously didn't like the long hair. So I said that the thing that disturbs me about long hair is not the fact that suddenly a whole lot of kids in this country decided to let their hair grow, but that a whole nation of adults would let it disturb them to the point where they were ready to expel otherwise excellent students from school simply because of their long hair. I got a big cheer from the kids. The parents sat there with clenched teeth resolving never to invite Jim Bouton again.

It turns out that Pagliaroni is a telescope buff. He has a 300-power telescope at home with which he not only explores the heavens but shoots a little beaver. The only problem shooting beaver with a 300-power telescope, he says, is that the image comes in upside down. He says it's very tough looking through the telescope while standing on your head.

JUNE
13

Getting on the bus to go from the Biltmore Hotel to Yankee Stadium, O'Donoghue said, "Well, boys, here we start our tour of the funny farm." He meant the streets of New York.

Ray Oyler shouted out of the bus to a long-haired guy on the street. "Don't you feel there's something itching you all over?" He got a very big laugh in the back of the bus.

Since we were in New York, the talk turned to sex (the talk also turns to sex in the eleven other American League cities). It was decided that the most interesting offbeat milieu for sex was a tubful of warm oatmeal. So Mike Hegan promptly leaned out of the bus and hollered to a girl walking by, "Hey, do you like oatmeal?"

Larry Haney read a selection from the New York *Post,* a story by Vic Ziegel. "Today Mel Stottlemyre goes after his seventh victory," Ziegel wrote, "and Gene Brabender goes after whatever the Gene Brabenders of the world go after."

Ray Oyler: "Hey Bender. That guy just shit all over you."

Brabender: "Will someone point out that fucker to me?"

Pagliaroni: "He must never have seen you in person, Rooms."

Footnote: Brabender beat Stottlemyre 2–1.

JUNE
14

Fifth inning and we're down 3–2. Bases loaded, nobody out. I'm warmed up. I get the signal. I climb into the golfcart that will take me to the mound. Yankee Stadium, and my heart is thumping under my warm-up jacket. It feels like a World Series. As the cart rolls along the clay track in left field I hear the fans saying, "Hey, that looks like Bouton." "Yeah, it *is* Bouton." My public.

They were out there before the game. When our bus pulled up there must have been twenty kids there chanting, "We want Bouton, we want Bouton." The guys on the bus said I must have been a big man in this town. I said yeah, modestly.

The infield is in as I start to pitch. The knuckleball is working. I get Ken Johnson, the pitcher, on a ground ball to Tommy Harper. But instead of going home with the ball, he goes to second and a run scores. Roy White pops up. Jerry Kenney grounds out. End threat. None out, bases loaded and they got only one run. Not bad.

In the next inning there are three fly balls, by Bobby Murcer, Joe Pepitone and Horace Clark. Two innings, no runs charged to me. I rated it an excellent performance. Almost as good, we went on to win the game 5–4. Fritz Peterson said afterward I should have been given credit for the win because when the Yankees got only one run out of that situation, the game was turned around. Fritz Peterson is a nice man.

JUNE
15

Today in the visiting dugout at Yankee Stadium, Joe Schultz said to nobody in particular: "Up and at 'em. Fuck 'em all. Let it all hang out."

I pitched against one hitter in the game, Jimmy Lyttle. Struck him out on five knuckleballs. Nothing to it.

I wonder how the Yankees feel now about picking up Johnson.

On the plane from New York to Milwaukee, where we play the White Sox a game tomorrow, the stewardesses (we call them stews) were droning about fastening seatbelts. "Fasten your seatbelt," Fred Talbot said. "Fasten your seatbelt. All the time it's fasten your goddam seatbelt. But how come every time I read about one of those plane crashes, there's 180 people on board and all 180 die? Didn't any of them have their seatbelt fastened?"

People are always asking me if it's true about stewardesses. The answer is yes. You don't have to go out hunting for a stew. They stay in the same hotels we do. Open your door and you're liable to be invited to a party down the hall. They're on the road, same as we are, and probably just as lonely. Baseball players are young, reasonably attractive and have more money than most men their age. Not only that, baseball players often marry stews—and the stews know it.

Baseball players are not, by and large, the best dates. We prefer *wham, bam,* thank-you-ma'am affairs. In fact, if we're spotted taking a girl out to dinner we're accused of "wining and dining," which is bad form. It's not bad form to wine and dine an attractive stew, however. A stew can come under the heading of class stuff, or table pussy, in comparison with some of the other creatures who are camp-followers or celebrity-fuckers, called Baseball Annies. It is permissible, in the scheme of things, to promise a Baseball Annie dinner and a show in return for certain quick services for a pair of roommates. And it is just as permissible, in the morality of the locker room, to refuse to pay off. The girls don't seem to mind very much when this happens. Indeed, they seem to expect it.

In Chicago there's Chicago Shirley who takes on every club as it gets to town. The first thing she does is call up the rookies for an orientation briefing. She asks them if there's anything she can do for them, and as the ballplayers say, "She can do it all." Chicago Shirley says that Chicago is a great place to live because teams in both leagues come through there. She doesn't like to miss anybody.

JUNE
16

Milwaukee

In the Milwaukee clubhouse there's a sign that reads: "What you say here, what you see here, what you do here and what you hear here, let it stay here." The same sign hangs in the clubhouse in Minneapolis. Also, I suppose, in the CIA offices in Washington. If I were a CIA man, could I write a book?

Steve Barber has been placed on the disabled list, although there's nothing wrong with his arm, just a little stiffness. The three weeks on the list will give him a chance to work it out.

Pitched an inning-and-two-thirds against the White Sox and gave up one hit, no runs, no walks. There was one strikeout. That's three good outings in a row since I last wanted to commit suicide. This might be a good time to ask Joe Schultz for a start again. He may not be much for the underprivileged, but I'll try anyway.

JUNE
17

Chicago

More examples of how easy it is for this veteran right-hander to get into trouble. Yesterday a clubhouse meeting interrupted a chess game Mike Marshall and I were playing and during it we both

219

stole glances at the board. Pretty soon, Ron Plaza was giving us some hard stares. Afterward I found out that when I didn't show up in the outfield quick enough for Crosetti after the meeting, he sent Plaza down to the clubhouse to see if I was still playing chess.

And today, I managed to let it slip my mind that we were playing a twi-night doubleheader. I strolled out to catch the bus at a quarter to five and no bus. Panic set in. All I could think was that we were playing another game in Milwaukee and how the hell would I get there in time. I dashed back to my room for my itinerary and that, of course, explained it all. So I got to the park at five-thirty, a half-hour before game-time, and this time they weren't quite so friendly about it all. Hegan tried to help. "Quick, dress in your locker," he said, "and maybe they won't notice you're late." It didn't work, largely because when O'Donoghue spotted me in there he said in a loud voice, "Well, look who's here." Then Talbot, trying to be funny, stood in front of my locker with his hands on his hips and said, "Where in the hell have *you* been?" I made shushing motions at him but he said, "I'm telling." And he pranced down to where the coaches were sitting and said, "Hey, Sal, was Bouton out there during infield practice?" With friends like Fred Talbot I'm not sure you need any enemies.

JUNE
18

Mike Marshall asked Merritt Ranew to catch him a while in the bullpen and in no time the phone was ringing. It was Sal Maglie telling him never, never, *never* to throw without permission. Later on Marshall heard Sal telling Ranew never to warm up any pitcher unless instructed to do so by Sal himself. Then Ranew must have said something about the way Marshall had been pitching, because Sal said, "He always looks good in the bullpen."

I'm not the only one who gets into trouble. But this business about asking permission to throw sounds ominous for the knuckleballer.

One of Marty Pattin's friends or relatives from downstate Illinois sent him a big box of cookies and he put them out on the table before the game. "Let's get to these cookies," Joe Schultz said. "They came all the way from southern Illinois."

Sitting at the table at the time was one of the young clubhouse boys, and he was reading a high-school biology book. Joe peered over his shoulder for a while and then said, "Hey, Bouton, this is something that might interest you. A book about human tissues. Real scientific. Hey, look, they even got a picture of a cunt."

As we stood there, laughing helplessly, he added, "And don't forget, boys, pound those cookies into you."

John Kennedy flew into a rage at Emmett Ashford over a called strike and was tossed out of the game. Still raging, he kicked in the water cooler in the dugout, picked it up and threw it onto the field. Afterward we asked him what had gotten into him. He really isn't that type. And he said, "Just as I got called out on strikes, my greenie kicked in."

One of the guys asked Curt Rayer if he had any greenies available and he said no, he wasn't allowed to dispense them. "But I'd like to know who's taking them." This confirmed the feeling that Curt is selling information.

John McNamara, the equipment manager, is the sort who gets along well with ballplayers, but he's been told—warned in fact—not to hang out with us. I guess they think we can be easily corrupted, although I suspect we could corrupt Mac quicker than vice versa. Anyway Mac was standing in the hotel lobby the other night and Curt said, "Where you going, Mac?"

"To bed," Mac said.

Ten minutes later the phone rang in McNamara's room. It was Rayer. "Just wanted to see if you made it to your room all right," Rayer said.

The only thing that makes any sense, Mac said, is that Curt was checking up to see if he'd sneaked out with any players.

Also checking up on us, we're certain, is Marvin Milkes personally. The other night Talbot and Oyler came in a little while after curfew and there was Marvin in the lobby. "Good evening, Marvin," one of them said, cool.

"Good evening," said Marvin, just as cool. "See you in Seattle." Which means fine city.

Had dinner with Mike Marshall in a place called Cafe Bohemia. It's one of the few restaurants in America that serves what can accurately be called exotic food—like lion, tiger, hippopotamus and elephant steaks. Also buffaloburgers, which is what Mike had. I ordered elk steak. In the next room there were the coaches. Mike and I speculated on what Eddie O'Brien would order. I said a steak—beefsteak. Marshall said fried chicken. We were both right. He ordered lambchops.

JUNE
19

We got to talking about Marvin Miller. Pag said that when he was the player rep in Pittsburgh John Galbreath, the owner of the club, had a heart-to-heart talk with him about Miller. Galbreath said Miller would be bad for baseball.

"It just shows how out of touch these guys are," Pag said. "After his long heart-to-heart talk I had to tell him it was too late. Miller had already been signed."

There had been, by the way, a concerted effort to stop the players from hiring Miller. The St. Louis players were told by the front office, for example, that of all the candidates for the job Miller would be the worst choice. They voted for him unanimously.

My own mind was made up about Miller when Joe Reichler put his arm around me and solemnly warned me to be "very, very, *very* careful about this guy Miller."

Then there's this. Soon after Miller was elected to run the Players' Association, Joe Cronin, president of the American League, put his arm around him and said, very earnestly, "Young man [Marvin was forty-nine], I've been in this game a long time now and I've learned something that I want you to think about. Players come and players go, but owners will be here forever, and don't forget it."

Locker said he understood very well why the owners get so mad at Miller. He said it was because Miller never lets up. "If he has a point he jumps on them with both feet and never gets off," Locker said.

I couldn't help saying that was fine with me. I told Locker that Miller isn't doing any more than any lawyer would do in the same situation and that the problem was not Miller, but the owners, who were so used to having things their way, getting away with technicalities, pushing things on us, that they were now affronted when all Miller was doing was his job. I'm not sure he understood.

Pag also said that he nurses a grudge against Bowie Kuhn, our new Commissioner. He remembers when Kuhn was the owners' rep and when we submitted a proposal to raise the minimum salary from $7,000 to $10,000 he waited six months before he answered. And then it was at a meeting and what he said was, "Oh yes, we've heard something about that. Just what are the details?"

Okay, so he was the owners' Marvin Miller. Now I'm glad *we* got one.

Broke bread with Gary Bell and he was feeling much down. He said he hadn't been able to find his rhythm and that he was afraid he'd lost it altogether. Gary said Ray Berres was a good pitching coach, but that nothing could help him anymore and he was terribly worried about his future. Not only that, his wife was still in Seattle and he hadn't been able to find a place in Chicago that wasn't crazy expensive, and all in all it was depressing.

Mike Marshall and I talked about the possibility of becoming roommates and he said he hesitated to because we'd probably have to take too much crap from the players and coaches—two kooks rooming together. And if there was crap, he said, he'd probably blow up. "I remember the time you were nominated for alternate player representative and got only one vote," he said. "If that happened to me I'd stand up and say, 'Fuck all you guys.' I mean, here you were obviously better qualified to do the job than anybody else and you get one vote. To me that's sheer stupidity and I couldn't let them get away with it."

All of which reminded him of a line Sal Maglie delivered tonight. Talbot was pitching and threw a slider that was nailed into the upper deck, just barely foul. So Sal hollers out, "Hey, watch the first pitch on this guy." Now, that's a classic second-guess because there can no longer be a first pitch to this guy. It's now strike one.

Joe Schultz is not like Sal with the pitchers. Gelnar was telling us about this great conversation he had with Joe on the mound. There were a couple of guys on and Tom Matchick was up. "Any particular way you want me to pitch him, Joe?" Gelnar said.

"Nah, fuck him," Joe Schultz said. "Give him some low smoke and we'll go in and pound some Budweiser."

JUNE
20

Seattle

At the meeting before the twi-nighter against Kansas City, Joe Schultz asked if anybody knew anything about John Martinez. Silence. "Well," said Joe Schultz, "we'll just zitz him. Up and at 'em men, and let's win two tonight." One of these days I'll find out how to "zitz" a guy. It sounds like a valuable pitching weapon.

Right after that I ran into Sal Maglie and, because I'd been pitching a lot lately, I felt I ought to tell him that I wasn't tired. Rather than just say I was ready to pitch, old stonehead here said, "Sal, I could pitch both ends of this doubleheader if you need me."

And Sal Maglie said, "Let's get one first."

I had broken a baseball taboo. You're not supposed to talk of winning two games. You should only be thinking of the first game, the big one, the one you play today after putting your pants on one leg at a time. If you're thinking about the second game, you can't be concentrating enough on the first game. Got it? Which is why I thought it sweet of Joe Schultz to tell us to go out there and win two—and pound some Budweiser.

Today the Seattle Pilots enjoyed one of their finest hours. We pulled off one of the great practical jokes of all time. The victim was Fred Talbot. Chief perpetrator, as the police like to say, was his roommate, Merritt Ranew. But we were all aiders and abettors.

When Talbot arrived at the ballpark a uniformed policeman

224

handed him a letter. He sat down to read it in front of his locker. We all knew what it was; a legal document written by a local lawyer friend of Ranew's that announced a paternity suit against Talbot by an anonymous girl in New York. A paternity suit is only somewhat worse than being accused of murder. No matter how innocent you are, you lose. Who wants to win a paternity suit?

Business in the clubhouse seemed to be normal, but in fact everybody was watching Talbot. He opened the letter, looked at it, put his head down, looked at the floor for a while, gazed up into the air, shook his head slowly from side to side, started to read the letter again. Then he folded it, put it back in the envelope, tossed it onto the shelf in his locker, lit a cigarette and stared around the room. The expression on his face was one of shock and disbelief.

Meanwhile everyone in the clubhouse was biting his lips, trying not to laugh. Talbot stomped out his cigarette, reached up into his locker, opened the envelope and read the letter again, as though he was hoping it would say something different this time. Finally, after he'd devoured both pages, put them back in the envelope and thrown it on the floor of his locker, Brabender felt he had to tell him it was a joke. He might have slashed his wrists. "Some joke," Talbot said. "Why didn't you just send me a telegram telling me my kids had been burned to death?" While Talbot then looked around trying to figure out who would do such a terrible thing to him, there were, among others, the following remarks:

Tommy Davis: "I didn't think you Caucasian guys could get any whiter."

Ray Oyler: "You couldn't have pulled a needle out of his ass with a tractor."

Finally Talbot decided that it was Marshall and I who had sent the letter. Of course. Fortunately we were able to convince him he was wrong. I wouldn't want to fight him. As far as he's concerned the Marquis of Queensberry is some fag hairdresser.

JUNE
21

Gene Brabender went all the way tonight and pitched a beautiful game. He had a no-hitter going for six innings. One of the nice things about it was that he gave the bullpen the rest it needed. I've pitched in four- or five-straight games now (my outings are beginning to blur together in my mind) and although I like the work, I liked the day off too. My earned-run average is down to 3.45. There are only four guys ahead of me in ERA. I wonder if anybody is thinking of giving me a start.

Another way Mike Marshall gets into trouble. He has conversations with Joe Schultz, such as:

"I went to him and said, 'Joe, what should I do in a situation like this? I started on Monday. On Tuesday I threw on my own. I pitched two innings in Wednesday's game. Then you had me warm up three times on Thursday. The first time I felt all right. The second time I felt a little tight. The third time my arm was tired and stiff and I wasn't effective.' All the time I'm talking Joe doesn't look at me, only at the floor. Suddenly he looks up and says, 'You shouldn't have thrown on your own on Tuesday.'

"So I said, 'Well, yes. But the point is that I wasn't ready to pitch on Thursday. Now, what should I do in such a situation? Should I call down from the bullpen and tell you, or should I let you put me into the game knowing I wasn't going to be effective? It doesn't matter to me. I'll go out there and pitch no matter how tired my arm is. But I don't want to hurt our chances of winning. What do you think, Joe?'

"At that point Joe turned his back and walked away."

JUNE
22

In the rain the little Seattle clubhouse takes on an aura of great intimacy. The talk flows freely and takes in everybody. It's like sitting around in somebody's living room. Tonight we got into the Pilots' yearbook and we kidded each other about what it said in there about us.

Fred Talbot read out loud that when John Kennedy was in high school he was used for late-inning defense, which is funny because most guys in the big leagues were superstars in high school. Talbot then composed a last line for Kennedy's career. "Also has been known to pop a greenie." (Which reminded Wayne Comer that rainy days were sure tough on greenie-poppers. You never know whether to pop.)

Gene Brabender's biography noted that he was an outstanding athlete at Black Earth, Wisconsin. I wondered what the school song was there. "Black Earth, we love you, hurrah for the rocks and the dirt." Someone else suggested that Brabender had probably made the Future Farmers of America All-America football team.

Mike Hegan had made the All-Catholic High School baseball team and said that Jim Bouton had probably made the All-Agnostic High School team.

"Hey, Fred, how come you never went to college?" said Ray Oyler after reading that Talbot had received several football-scholarship offers.

"You ever hear of an entrance examination?" I said and was rewarded with a dirty look from Talbot.

And Hegan said, "Here's one for Oyler. Now taking correspondence courses for his high-school diploma."

JUNE
24

For a while I was getting almost no work at all. Now I'm getting plenty. I've been in 29 games and about eight of our last ten. But I suddenly realized *I never get in at crucial times.* I'm never in there if it's close and we have a chance to win. No wonder I have 29 appearances and only one win and one save.

Today there was a perfect example of what I mean. We're playing a doubleheader against Chicago and in the first game Timberlake (even he gets a start) is taken out in the second inning, losing 4–0, bases loaded, two out. I come in and get the first hitter I face on a fly ball. I then get the next nine-straight hitters, three scoreless innings. Now we've tied it at 4–4 and I come out for a pinch-hitter. We end up losing 6–4.

In the second game we're losing 4–2 in the fifth and O'Donoghue's in there, pitching in relief of Talbot. They let O'Donoghue bat for himself in the fifth even though we're two runs down, which I don't understand at all. Anyway he's out. Somebody gets a base hit and Comer hits a home run. Now if somebody had batted for O'Donoghue, we might have gotten three runs instead of two. Instead we have a tie game and O'Donoghue is still pitching. Pretty soon they're ahead of him 5–4 and then 6–4. And when we tie it at 6–6, who goes into this critical situation? The knuckleball kid? Nah. Diego Segui. He's in trouble right away with a walk and a base hit, but he gets out of the inning. By this time I'm warming up. But do they take him out? Nope. So he gives up a home run. Do they take him out now? Nope. Not until he gives up a double in the ninth. *Then* I go in. I need one out, I get it. One third of an inning. And we lose 7–6. I never got a real chance to save either game, and if I had we might have won both. I think I'll go bite Sal Maglie on the leg.

JUNE
25

I read in the paper today that Richie Allen, who has left the Phillies, says he wants to be traded and will not play for them next year. Then I heard Van Patrick on the air complain that baseball ought to have some recourse against a player who simply walks out on a team during the season. Bullshit, I thought to myself, gently. Here's one of the few cases where a baseball player has enough courage or money or both to tell baseball to take its one-sided contract and shove it. How many times does a ballclub release a player without a thought to his future? The players have zero recourse, but Van Patrick wants to think up another weapon for baseball.

I've admired Richie Allen from afar ever since his second year in the majors when, after a great rookie season (.318, 125 runs, 13 triples, 29 home runs and 91 RBIs—I looked it up) he demanded a large salary, $50 or $60,000 and said he wouldn't play unless he got it. Philadelphia must have thought he meant it, because he got it. (I wonder if they told him there was a club rule against quadrupling salaries.)

The minute somebody refuses to work for somebody else at a particular wage, the onus, in the public mind, is on the person who chooses not to do the working. I'm not sure why this should be, but it is. Like the lady in my Wyckoff, N.J., bank who said to me during a plumbers' strike, "Well, they don't *have* to be plumbers if they don't like it." She probably thinks, well, Allen doesn't *have* to be a baseball player if he doesn't like it. Sure, he can always be vice-president of the Wyckoff, N.J., bank.

In the bullpen tonight Eddie O'Brien said he'd recommended me for a start if things get tight in the next week or so, especially with Timberlake going into the army for six months. Eddie O'Brien. How about that? Suppose he thinks that if I get a start I'll expose myself?

229

Hy Zimmerman, sportswriter, was around looking for a story and I said I had a good one for him.

"Of the 29 appearances I've made this year," I said, "how many times have I done well, and how many poorly?"

"Cheez, I don't know," Zimmerman said.

"I've done well 24 out of 29 times," I said. "I've had four bads and one fair. All the rest were either good or excellent."

"You know, cheez, I didn't realize that," Zimmerman said.

"Do you happen to know what my earned-run average is since I've come back from Vancouver?"

"No, I don't."

"I didn't think you did. It's approximately 2.6542."

"Cheez, is it that good?" he said, reaching for a notebook.

"Right. And do you know how many runners have been on base when I've come in and how many have scored?"

"No, I don't."

"There were 28 runners on when I came in and only six scored."

"Cheez, I didn't realize you were doing that good."

"I know you didn't. And as soon as I win a ballgame here you're going to come around and say, 'Hey, great. When did you put it all together?' I just want you to know that every day I'm putting it together a little bit more."

When all of that gets into the paper I hope the coaches and the manager don't think I said those things only for their benefit, although I really did.

I'm taking the family to Disneyland on our next trip to Anaheim and I asked Marvin Milkes if he minded if I stayed with them in a hotel next to Disneyland rather than the team hotel. Actually, the guys prefer that you don't bring your wife on road trips and I thought this would be less awkward.

Milkes said I couldn't. "Nothing personal," he said. "You're doing a good job for us. If you weren't you wouldn't be here. I wouldn't want you to misconscrue [*sic!* baseball fans] my meaning on this. It's just a club rule and it has to be followed."

The reason for the rule, he said, was that he remembered when he was with the Angels and the Yankees used to come into town and stay out all night at those Johnny Grant parties. (Grant is what they call a radio personality in Hollywood.)

"But Marvin," I said. "The way I remember it we would stay out all night and then beat you guys anyway. I remember having a particularly good time at a Johnny Grant party and then pitching a two-hitter against you."

In fact I remembered more than that. I remembered doing a strip to my underwear to the theme song of *Lawrence of Arabia* and then treading water in the swimming pool with a martini in each hand and *then* going out and beating the Angels the next night. In fact, every time I hear the *Lawrence of Arabia* music my mind still snaps.

"Yeah, well, maybe," Marvin said. "But I could always count on you guys keeping late hours and I want to crack down on it."

"I'm more likely to go to bed early if my family is here than if I'm with the guys in the team hotel."

"That may be true. But we're going to stick to this rule. As I said, don't misconscrue it. Nothing personal."

Having lost one argument, I brought up another. I had bought myself some Gatorade, which is supposed to restore the minerals and salts you lose through perspiration. I bought it because a lot of athletic teams use it and it's got to be better than Coca-Cola. I asked McNamara to buy some for the clubhouse. He said he didn't know where to get it so I volunteered and bought ten cases, which cost $50. When I asked McNamara for the money he suggested that since Gatorade was sort of medicinal, the club should pay for it. What do you say, Marvin old boy?

"I'll have to think about it," he said. "I'll taste it."

"Try it with vodka," I said.

In the bullpen tonight Jim Pagliaroni was telling us how Ted Williams, when he was still playing, would psyche himself up for a game during batting practice, usually early practice before the fans or reporters got there.

He'd go into the cage, wave his bat at the pitcher and start screaming at the top of his voice, "My name is Ted fucking Williams and I'm the greatest hitter in baseball."

He'd swing and hit a line drive.

"Jesus H. Christ Himself couldn't get me out."

And he'd hit another.

Then he'd say, "Here comes Jim Bunning, Jim fucking Bunning and that little shit slider of his."

Wham!

"He doesn't really think he's gonna get me out with that shit."

Blam!
"I'm Ted fucking Williams."
Sock!

Today Joe Schultz said, "Nice going out there today, Jim."
The only thing I'd done all day was warm up.
"Joe, I had a fantastic knuckleball today," I said. "Just fantastic."
"Did you?" Joe Schultz said. "Did you have the feel of it?"
"I sure did."
Whereupon Joe Schultz grabbed his crotch and said, "Well, feel this."

JUNE
26

It's true that Joe Schultz does seem to have a firmer grip on reality than other baseball men. Example: Joe got into a terrible argument with an umpire at home plate about a checked swing and when it was over he stormed back to the dugout, still muttering. Just before stepping into the dugout, though, he spied a blonde sitting in the first row behind it and said, "Hiya, blondie. How's your old tomato?"

O'Donoghue was saying in the bullpen today that he hopes he's not asked to pitch because he has this stiffness in his arm. It's not sore, just stiff. This is baseball newspeak. Nobody has a sore arm anymore, not O'Donoghue and not Steve Barber.

Another way kook Bouton convinces people he's a kook. When I come into the game in a bunt situation I like to check the turf around home plate to see how firm it is and whether I can field a bunt, stop, turn and make a throw without falling on my face. So I walk in and stomp around for a while, and a couple of times I've looked into the dugout and seen Joe and Sal giggling at each other. It's the exact same reaction Mike Marshall gets when he decides to trot in from the bullpen instead of walking in the way everybody else does. In baseball the only thing that's really changed in a hundred years is the attitude toward beards.

There was a meeting in the clubhouse on the new contract negotiations between the players and owners, which should be taking place soon but probably won't until after the season. I suggested that if you apply the standard-of-living index to the base of $7,000 that was set up eleven years ago you come up with about $14 or $15,000 as a minimum instead of the present $10,000. So somebody said, "Why not $20,000?" and everybody broke up laughing. But when you really think about it, $20,000 is not out of line at all. Consider how hard it is to make a big-league club. If only the same proportion of the population were accepted as lawyers, the going starting salary would be a lot higher. When you overcome odds of better than 10,000 to 1 you ought to collect big.

Steve Hovley has been called up. Old Tennis Ball Head hasn't had a haircut since he left. Which means Joe Schultz had four comments to him the very first day.

"Where's your barber?"

"Don't you need a haircut?"

"You're getting awfully mangy-looking."

"Are you sure you don't need a trim, Steve?"

Hovley explained to me why he had started out with such a tight crewcut and then let it grow. "In the spring I cut all my hair the same length—short," Hovley said. "After that I simply chose not to be selective against any of the hairs. Most people cut their hair around their ears and not on top. That doesn't seem fair. I want to let each hair do its own thing. Now everybody is upset—not about these hairs on top, just the ones around my ears and on the back of my neck. Those are the offending hairs. But they don't offend me."

Just before Hovley rejoined the club we were talking about him in the bullpen. I count him as one of the most intelligent men, the closest to a real intellectual, I've ever met in baseball. So I volunteered that he was a pretty bright fellow. "Yeah, but does he have any common sense?" Talbot said.

"I know just what you mean about not having any common sense," O'Donoghue said. "He doesn't."

I asked him what he meant by that.

"Well, one time we were sitting in a restaurant," O'Donoghue said, "and Hovley was walking down the street with a ski cap pulled down over his face and he came past the restaurant and stood outside on the sidewalk peering in at us."

Oh.

Another reason Hovley has no common sense is that he may wear the same shirt five days in a row and the same sportscoat and he doesn't dress the way most players do.

Sometimes I think that if people in this little world of baseball don't think you a little odd, a bit weird, you're in trouble. It would be rather like being considered normal in an insane asylum.

JUNE
27

Anaheim

During a radio interview before the game today, the manager was asked what the secret of the success of the Seattle Pilots had been so far and Joe Schultz said, "Well, we just come out and go to work and play ball. Use a little common sense, so to speak."

Going to Disneyland, I remembered going to the World's Fair in New York a few years back. Driving one of those little tour buses there was Dusty Rhodes, the guy who in 1954 helped win a pennant and a World Series pinch-hitting for the Giants. Dusty Rhodes, one of my heroes, wearing that blue uniform and driving a bus. I wondered how he'd feel if somebody hollered from in back of the bus, "Hey, bussy, there's a dog pissing on your rear wheel"—which is what we've said many times to a guy who wasn't driving the bus fast enough. Maybe Dusty said it too one day, a long time ago.

I am glad to note that Tommy Davis has become upset about our autograph rule. He has decided that to tell the kids that it's club policy not to give them is to alienate future fans. Which was my point when it first came up at a meeting. Hardly anybody listens when Bouton talks. But I hope they'll listen to Tommy Davis.

At our meeting tonight Joe Schultz said, "Now, this is for you new guys. The curfew is two-and-a-half hours after the ballgame is over at night and midnight after a day game. And watch yourself. The brass is here. They're all here this time."

"What about the night before an off-day?" I said. "Can we stay out later than twelve if we don't have a game the next day?"

Joe put his hands on his hips and smiled. "Jesus Christ, Bouton, you're always coming up with something tricky," he said.

Most of the guys laughed and I never did get an answer from Joe.

"I don't know why everyone laughed," Brabender said later. "I thought it was a good question."

"Yeah, but Jim asked it," Marshall said. "So we're all supposed to laugh. You should have asked it, Gene. Then we would have gotten an answer."

"Sorry, fellas," I said. "I didn't realize I was going to hurt our chances."

Steve Hovley got three hits tonight and nobody said a word about his hair. I suggested to him that the number of comments he gets will, from now on, vary inversely with the number of hits he gets. And if he ever stops hitting he may even have to get a haircut.

Mike was throwing in the bullpen and Eddie O'Brien asked Sal Maglie how much Mike should be throwing. Said Sal: "Tell him to throw until just before he comes."

JUNE
28

Lefty Phillips has replaced Bill Rigney as manager of the Angels. I wish Rocky Bridges, the coach, had gotten the job. He's familiar with the personnel over there and he was a great minor-league manager. He was successful, colorful, funny and the players loved him. A minor-leaguer named Ethan Allen Blackaby told me about the time Bridges gave the signs from third base while standing on his head. Blackaby promptly stood on his head in the batting box so he could get the sign properly.

I told the story to Pag. He said he'd love to see it but that baseball would consider it, well, sacrilegious. "Baseball wants color," he said. "But not that much."

"By 'color,' " I said, "they mean they want you to wear your cap at a jaunty angle."

Tonight we had a three-run lead in the fourth and the starting pitcher got into a little trouble, so Sal Maglie got on the telephone to the bullpen. "Anybody around here see a phone booth?" I said. "This looks like a job for Superknuck."

The call was for Segui. Good grief, how foolish can I be? How could it possibly have been me? We weren't behind.

I note today that the Topps Gum people have doubled their fee to players, from $125 to $250, for using their pictures on bubblegum cards. They explained that they were able to increase payments because of increased revenues. It had nothing to do with Marvin Miller and the players going to Topps and demanding the increase. Topps just happens to have a big heart. Yeah surrre.

And speaking of big hearts, a hearty mention here of Frank Scott, the player agent. During one of my big years with the Yankees, Scott called me and asked if I wanted to give a little talk before an IBM group for a fee of $300. "Delighted," I said. I made the speech and collected the fee from Scott. Then my brother Bob, who worked for IBM at the time, called me and said, "Congratulations."

"Thank you," I said. "What for?"

"Your speech to IBM."

"It was nothing."

"Well, $500 is good pay for nothing."

"Three hundred."

"Five hundred, babe. I got it from the guy who ran the dinner."

"Oh."

John McNamara is asking Don Mincher about Hovley. "Doesn't he need a haircut, Minch?" he says.

"I can't say anything about anyone's hair, needing a haircut like I do," Mincher says.

"Well, I think it looks horseshit," Marty Pattin says.

Moments later, perhaps feeling bad about his comment, or perhaps wishing to stick the needle in further, Pattin approaches Hovley and says, "I don't care how long you wear your hair, Hovley. You can wear it down to your ass as far as I'm concerned."

Nah. That would look horseshit.

JUNE
29

Today Joe Schultz said to Steve Hovley: "Don't you think you ought to at least get a *trim?*"

Hovley thought it over for a while and said, "I guess so."

Actually, Hovley said later that he hasn't made up his mind and doesn't feel he committed himself by what he said to Joe: "It's interesting," he said, "that no one really talks to me about the length of my hair. All they do is drop remarks. I guess that's because no one wants to get into a discussion."

If they do they have to listen to *your* position, consider it, come up with an answer. But by just dropping a remark they can get in and get out with no harm done.

On the other hand, there's the Plaza way, which also leads to no discussion. "You better get a haircut," Plaza said to Hovley.

JUNE
30

A note on the complicated life of a moonlighting author. I usually keep my notepaper in the back pocket of my uniform trousers and my pen in my jacket pocket. The reason is that I don't want to be separated from my notes and the jacket is often left on the bench. On the other hand, I don't want my pen with me when I'm pitching because I wouldn't want to fall on it. So today when I went out to the mound I discovered I had my pen in my pocket. I took it out and tossed it behind me on the mound. When the inning was over I went to sit on the bench and Ron Plaza, who coaches at third, handed me the pen. Without comment.

Bobbie and I went to San Francisco with Gus Gil and his wife and we got to talking about what fun it was to be on a baseball team and have the opportunity to listen to coaches and managers at work. Gus said that the other day on the bench they were looking for Mike Marshall, who was back in the clubhouse using the bathroom or something, and someone said, "Where the hell is he?" And Joe Schultz said, "He's probably setting up the chessboard."

Another time Schultz said about Marshall, "Lookit. Brains is warming up out there."

Gus also said that when I was pitching, every time I threw a fastball that wasn't hit Sal would tell Joe how much of a help the fastball was. I'm a one-pitch pitcher now, just what I said I had to be and what Sal said I couldn't be. So he covers his early tracks with Joe every chance he gets.

Would you believe the talk in the bullpen was about pitching? At least the second-guessing of coaches and managers *about* pitching. One of the questions I asked was, "Has a good pitch *ever* been hit?" What I meant was that every single time a guy hits the ball it was in the wrong place, or the wrong pitch at the wrong time. Hitters almost never

238

get credit for hitting good pitches. Every breaking ball that's hit "hung." It's a world of second-guessers.

McNertney told a story about Al Lopez when he was managing Chicago. Danny Cater of the A's was the hitter and Tommy John the pitcher. John threw a curve ball that was so low it was going to be in the dirt. He said he went down on his knees to dig it out and as he did Cater reached out with one hand and hit it into left field for a single. When he got back to the dugout McNertney was shaking his head and mumbling about Cater having hit a good pitch.

"It was a high pitch," Lopez said.

"No. If he doesn't swing it's in the dirt," McNertney said.

"It was right there," Lopez said, holding his hand out thigh-high. End argument.

(Cater, by the way, has the reputation of being able to figure out his batting average to four decimal places on his way down to first base. He's almost as quick as I am figuring out my ERA.)

The second-guess is so ingrained in baseball that you can almost call it a first-guess second-guess. First a manager will say, "For crissakes, if a guy can't hit the curve ball, keep throwing the damn thing until he proves to you he can hit it." Of course, there's a logical converse. You keep throwing the curve ball to a guy and eventually he *will* hit it. And immediately you hear, "Jesus, you can't keep throwing a guy the same thing. He's bound to hit it."

Everybody has stories about that kind of thing. Jerry Stephenson says that over at the Red Sox when Billy Herman was the manager and there was a debate about how to pitch to a hitter, Herman would say, "Fuck him. Give him good stuff."

And that's the catch. You have to have it. And if you do, pitching isn't at all complicated.

Checking out of the hotel Wayne Comer called for a bell captain to send up a bellhop to pick up his bag. There was no bellhop around, and no bell captain either. So Don Mincher, who happened to be standing there, picked up the phone. When he heard it was Comer, Mincher said, "Now wait a minute. It's about time you guys started carrying your own bags down. All you prima donna cocksuckers are alike, always wanting people to do things for you. Why the hell don't you carry them down yourself?"

Comer didn't even splutter. He slammed down the phone and carried his own bags.

JULY

2

Oakland

In the clubhouse meeting yesterday on the Oakland Athletics Sal Maglie said about Reggie Jackson, "Once in a while you can jam him."

I could just see the situation. Reggie Jackson up. Pitcher throws one high and inside, perfect jam pitch. Jackson leans back, swings and puts it into the right-field bleachers. And Sal screams from the bench, "Not now, goddammit, not now!"

Fred Talbot says that after listening to Sal in these meetings he's decided what kind of pitcher he must have been. "A mother," Talbot said. "A real mother."

Mother Maglie also said in the meeting that one way to handle Jackson was not to throw him any strikes. So Jackson hit three homers in the game, and after each one someone said, "There's one of those goddam strikes."

After Reggie Jackson's third home run O'Donoghue said, "I'd have to plunk the man."

And I said, indignantly, "John, how the hell can you throw at the guy? He's just doing his job. He has no comeback at you if you get him out. So why should he have to risk getting injured just because he's successful?"

"I wouldn't mean to hurt the guy," O'Donoghue said. "I don't mean throw at his head. Just let him know that he should have some fear up there."

"What if you hit him in the kneecap or something?" I said. "You don't know how good your control is going to be. What if you hit him in the ankle? Or how do you know you're going to hit him just hard enough in the ribs so that you don't break something?"

John's jaw got tight. And he said, "Look, I don't want to argue about it? So we'll leave it at that."

How come nobody wants to argue with me? Can it be because I'm always so right?

Today I asked Joe Schultz for a start. I sat down with him on the bus and told him that I could help the team better if I started. I said I felt that being the ninth man on the pitching staff and being used as the mop-up man didn't help the team much. I reached into my pocket to show him my statistics and Joe Schultz said, "Aw shit. I don't want to see any statistics. I know what's going on out there just by watching the games."

"All right," I said. "I just wanted to show you that I've only walked one man in the last 16 innings and only three in the last 21."

"I know you've been getting it over."

"That's all I wanted to say."

"Well, okay, Jamesy," Joe Schultz said.

Steve Hovley broke up the clubhouse today when he undressed to get into his uniform and underneath his dress shirt he was wearing a Seattle Pilots T-shirt with his name and number on the back. Almost everybody just laughed, but some guys seemed upset—like Fred Talbot and Merritt Ranew.

Out in the bullpen Ranew said to me, "You think Hovley's a pretty smart guy?"

"Yes, I do," I said.

"Do you think wearing a Seattle Pilots T-shirt has anything to do with common sense or intelligence?"

"I don't think so," I said.

"Well, do you think it's very intelligent to wear something that isn't proper?" Ranew said.

"What's wrong with wearing a Seattle Pilots T-shirt?" I said.

At this point, I couldn't hold back and started to laugh.

Ranew sort of waved at me and walked away.

Another Hovley story. He was standing by the clubhouse man's tobacco shelf opening up a can of snuff. (Just wanted to try it, he said later.) Joe Schultz walked by wearing nothing but a towel around his waist and hollered out, "Hey, men, look who's dipping into the snuff." Then he grabbed a paperback book out of Hovley's pocket. It was Dostoevski's *The Possessed*. Schultz held the book up in the air and said, "Hey, men, look at this! What the shit kind of name is this?"

By this time there was a group of guys around him looking at the book like a group of monkeys might inspect a bright red rubber ball. Schultz read off the back cover—a sentence anyway—until he got to the word "nihilism." "Hey, Hy," Schultz said to Hy Zimmerman, "what the hell does 'nihilism' mean?"

"That's when you don't believe in nothing," Zimmerman said.

Whereupon Schultz, shaking his head and laughing, flung the book back at Hovley, hitched up his towel and strode off, amid much laughter.

If Hovley weren't 9 for 20 (.450) since he was called up I'd figure him to be back in Rochester in a matter of days.

Afterward Hovley said that this was, of course, anti-intellectualism at work, but that he didn't mind since he counted himself as anti-intellectual too—that is, if by "intellectual" we meant the academic community. Academic people bore him, Hovley said, and that while he wouldn't choose to spend all his free time with Joe Schultz, he rather enjoyed the company of players.

And Mike Marshall pointed out that Joe's act might have been more a tactic than an expression of his real feelings about college types. "You have to keep in mind that Joe's goal is to keep a loose clubhouse and that he uses this as a device to make people laugh," Marshall said. "I'd be careful not to put him down as merely a buffoon."

Well, I don't know. If it *is* an act, he's finding it awfully easy to play.

JULY
4

Kansas City

What could be better than a Fourth of July doubleheader in Kansas City? Anything up to and including a kick in the ass. Kansas City gets hot like few places get hot. The temperature was in the 90's and the humidity was in the 90's and most of us were in a blue funk. Fred Talbot, one of today's starters, was complaining louder than anybody about the heat on the bus, so when we got to the clubhouse a lot of guys came by to say a few words.

My crazy Guggenheim bit. The Yankees hated it, considered it a disgrace to the uniform. In worse times I would have been drummed out of the corps. But this was 1964 and I was in the process of winning 18 games. *Scharfman*

Future big-league baseball star marries the scout who discovered him and later became his best coach; both set off on honeymoon from Allegan, Michigan. Future big-league baseball star would have been better off if he listened more closely to his best coach.   *Kalamazoo Gazette*

The Bouton family in our back yard in Seattle. That's me with the neat haircut. If the others ever want to play baseball they'll just have to conform.

Central Park in New York City, November, 1969. Moratorium. I talked, the kids listened. They *do* listen, you know.   *Martinez*

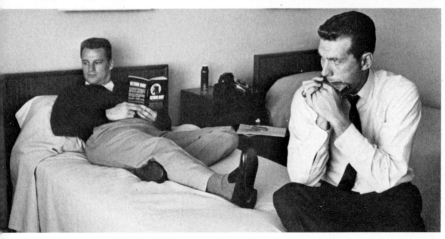

Phil Linz, the harmonica rascal, and I do our things in a hotel room somewhere in the United States. I was supposed to be reading a book about Vietnam, Linz was supposed to be playing his harmonica. Actually, we were both watching television.   *Sports Illustrated (Bath)*

Amarillo, 1961. Note the youthful complexion. Note the boyish innocence. Note that this was before I ever met any general managers. (Note also that factory in the background. Somebody once hit a ball over it off me.)

Amarillo Daily News (Warden)

The old fastball delivery. My arm refuses to believe we once did it this way.
UPI (Kuntz)

Coach Johnny Sain demonstrates his pitching-instruction invention. Trouble was, they never let me use one in a game.
Popular Science Monthly (Morris)

Pennant-clinching party, 1963, after I beat the Twins in Minnesota. That's Coach Dale Long and John Blanchard enjoying their work. *AP*

World Series, 1964, third game. I set a series record by losing my hat 37 times in a nine-inning game. The previous record was one. That's Clete Boyer overreacting at third base to what was probably a weak pop-up. *UPI*

This isn't where Ralph Houk is telling me that I was having as good a spring as Dooley Womack, but it could have been. That's not his tongue Ralph has in his cheek, either. It's chewing tobacco. *Balterman*

"Got to pace yourself today, Fred."

"Don't think about the heat, Fred. Just go out there and go as long as you can."

"Boy, it sure is a hot one today, Fred."

"Fred, why does it have to be you pitching on such a hot day?"

Finally Fred shook his head from side to side and said, "I knew I should have gone to college."

Joe Schultz announced that there were a lot of places in Kansas City that were off-limits because they were hangouts for gamblers. We expected to hear about three or four names. There must have been twenty-five. "Christ, you can save $900 just by drinking in the hotel bar," Ray Oyler said.

What he meant was that the hotel bar is forbidden to us at a penalty of $100. But if we got caught in one of those off-limit places, it would cost $1,000.

It came as no surprise today that Ron Plaza said, at least twice, "Good day to work, men."

It was a terrible day to work. With one pitch I undid all the good work I've been doing for weeks. I gave up five earned runs in a big one and one-third innings. I couldn't get my knuckleball over. I felt uncoordinated on the mound, and I threw one to Gene Oliver with the bases loaded that spun, and he knocked it over the center-field wall. On the bus some son of a bitch asked me if it was the longest home run I ever gave up.

It doesn't seem right that my ERA should have jumped back to 3.75 from 2.95 after only one and one-third innings. I felt so damn depressed after the game that I immediately forced it all out of my mind—all of it. What did you say my name was?

When Joe Schultz came to the mound to take me out of the game I was so angry with myself that all I could think to do was stand there and shout obscenities at the scoreboard. I still don't know if Joe said anything to me or not. I know he waved for a pitcher from the bullpen. The rest was all one dirty word.

Joe was cool enough not to get angry at me or think I was screaming at him. He knew I was just blowing off steam and let me go ahead and do it. There are managers who wouldn't have been so cool.

Mike Marshall and I started rooming together when we got to Kansas City, and in the room tonight we got to talking about the special pressures there are on ballplayers. We wondered what it's like for a guy when baseball is his whole life and he has nothing else, no financial security, no job or profession to fall back on, no real interests. We talked about Fred Talbot saying, "I should have gone to college," and decided that, yes, the pressures on him are worse than the pressures on us.

I know that a guy like Gary Bell felt that pressure all the time. He'd say things like, "Rooms, tomorrow we go to a bookstore and buy some of those real-estate books." Or, "Rooms, if you were in my shoes, what kind of job would you start looking for?" And then, sometimes, after a bad game, he'd sit in the back of the bus with five or six beers in him and he'd mumble to himself, "I don't give a shit. I don't give a shit."

But he did.

JULY
5

Steve Barber says he was watching me closely while I was pitching and thought I'd speeded up my motion too much and that my arm was dragging behind the rest of my body. He thought that if I slowed down I'd be able to get the proper release on the ball. As soon as I could I dashed out to the bullpen and asked Eddie O'Brien to catch a few knuckleballs. He said sure.

This is a new Eddie O'Brien. Since our big blow-up he's become a pussycat. He still doesn't warm me up during the game, but he's been great about catching me at other times and seems to be making an effort to do all the little extras. He even eats candy in the bullpen. No one has called him Mr. Small in a month.

Anyway I concentrated on a slow, easy motion—and, son of a gun, Barber was right. I threw about ten knuckleballs and every one of them jumped all over the place.

Then I got called into the game. The first thing that leaps into your head when you've been going bad is, oh Christ, here we go again. You have to lick this, get it out of your mind or you really *will* go again. Fortunately I was able to get two good innings in. At least now I won't be walking out to the mound with the taste of failure in my mouth.

Today Sal walked over to me, picked up a baseball and showed me the grip he remembered Hoyt Wilhelm using for his knuckleball when he was with the Giants. Here it is, midseason, and that was the first time Sal Maglie said anything constructive to me about pitching. In all this time he's never said anything about my grip, my motion or my release. Zero. Since he seemed interested, I suggested he keep an eye on me when I was pitching and if he thought I was speeding up my motion to let me know. He said he would.

JULY
6

Bat day in Kansas City. All the kids get free bats. Makes it very bad for beaver shooting because there are too many kids, too many bats and not enough beaver. John Gelnar brought a pair of binoculars out to the bullpen and we took turns looking into the stands. Then somebody said that we better not let the umpires catch us with binoculars in the bullpen—they're liable to think we're stealing signs. And I said, "No. If we explain we're shooting beaver, they'll understand." And they would. If there's a baseball universal, that's it.

Pagliaroni says that one of the great things about Gene Brabender as a pitcher is that he's big enough to intimidate hitters with his size. "He looks like if you got a hit off him," Pag said, "he'd crush your spleen."

Flying home from Kansas City we ran into a storm and were bouncing around in the air like a knuckleball. Pagliaroni and I started singing "The Lord's Prayer." "Our Father who art . . ." Suddenly Brabender, who was sitting in front of me, turned around, kneeled on his seat facing us, and, with neck flaming, shook a finger and said, "Now, look. No more of that. I don't go for that stuff, and I'm serious."

When Gene Brabender is serious, everybody is serious. We stopped singing.

After the storm Brabender turned around again and said, "Hey, J.B., I'm sorry I got mad. But that really scares me, especially when it's about the Big Man."

"Bender," I said, "it didn't scare you nearly as much as you scared me."

Right before the plane landed the guys were telling stories about how much we'd been getting on the road. And as we were getting ready to leave the plane and dash into the loving arms of our waiting wives, Pagliaroni said, very loud, "Okay, all you guys, act horny."

JULY
7

Seattle

Mike Marshall was sent to Vancouver today. I'm having very bad luck with roommates.

I feel a little funny about him getting it because I know his wife warned him right from spring training about getting too closely associated with me. Not that she doesn't like me, but she knew my reputation and was worried about guilt by association. Now he rooms with me three days in Kansas City and gets cut.

Mike was concerned when one of the reporters wrote that he and I play chess on airplanes and sometimes carry the board out of the plane and into the bus without dropping a single piece. He didn't think it helped our images any.

Tonight my knuckleball was so good it was getting by the catcher in the bullpen and going out onto the field.

After the game I was shaving, as it happens, right beside Joe Schultz. "Looks like your knuckleball was jumping all over the place tonight," he said.

"It was a good one," I said. "As good as it was three weeks ago. Lately I haven't been able to throw it that good."

"Why not?" Joe said.

"Well, I kind of lost the feel of it in my hand, but tonight . . ."

At that point Joe Schultz turned his back and walked away.

Jerry Stephenson, who was also shaving, took note of this and said, "Boy, he was really interested."

"Yeah, that'll teach him to start a conversation with me."

It all reminded me of Charlie Maher, my baseball coach at Western Michigan. He was upset when I signed a professional contract and had to drop off the team. When I went back to school after my first season, I ran into him on campus and he said, heartily, "How are you doing, Jim? What kind of year did you have?"

"Not too good," I said. "I broke the thumb of my pitching hand and didn't get to throw all summer long."

And he said, "Good, good. Have a nice fall here in school," and walked away.

JULY
8

By threatening to quit, Mike Marshall has blackmailed the club into sending him to Toledo rather than Vancouver (Toledo is near his home, although not nearly as pretty as Vancouver). Mike willed us his secondhand English racing bike, so we've added it to our collection, which includes a Gary Bell bedroom lamp.

One nice thing about the whole business. Marshall's basic faith in the way the game is run remains unbroken. He gives this illustration. When Joe Schultz told him he was being sent to Vancouver, Mike said,

"What about another major-league team? Isn't anybody interested in me?"

Schultz: "We asked waivers, and nobody wanted you."

So Marshall went to see Marvin Milkes and said he was quitting.

Milkes: "We just can't let you go like that. We paid $175,000 for you. We've got to get something for you. Isn't there something we can work out?"

Marshall: "Why don't you just sell me to some other club?"

Milkes: "Well, we've had feelers. But they haven't been for the right price. We couldn't let you go at the waiver price."

Now, some people would call that a contradiction. Others might call it a lie. Mike Marshall called it baseball.

One of our jocko things is to mince around like a fairy, which is pretty funny sometimes, especially while wearing baseball underwear. There is something hilarious about a lumpy, hairy guy trying to act like a queer while wearing the things we wear under a baseball uniform. Take my word.

After a while some of the guys began to walk up to each other and pretend to kiss on the lips. In fact one of them would put his hand on the other's face and kiss the back of it. If you did it fast it looked like a real kiss.

Then it began to spread. As a gag, of course. You'd be walking down the aisle of a bus and all of a sudden a guy would clamp his hand over your mouth, kiss the back of his hand and continue on down the aisle. It was quite a game. And Gary Bell was a big one for it. So were Mike Hegan and Don Mincher.

Then we got a little drunk on a bus one night and the guys started kissing without bothering to put their hands up. And then *that* became a joke. We'd kid about how many guys had kissed other guys and then there was this little club, and only guys who had kissed and been kissed could be members. At one point I was standing in the clubhouse and John Kennedy came over and said, "Hey, c'mere, Jim, I got to tell you something. A secret." And he puts his face up close to mine and the next thing I knew, kiss! I was a club member. Everybody broke up. Eventually there were, I believe, at least a dozen guys in the club.

On our flight from Oakland to Kansas City, Wayne Comer, who had had a few beers, leaned down over Don Mincher, who was playing cards, and kissed him on the cheek. Wetly. Mincher whirled around and punched him on the jaw, knocking him down and into the aisle. It struck

248

everybody as funny that Mincher, a member of the club, should suddenly get so uppity with a guy we all knew he was very friendly with.

"Wayne, I just had enough," Mincher said. "And I had to haul off and punch you."

Comer was still lying in the aisle feeling his jaw. "Well, that doesn't make you a bad person," he said.

Tonight Comer got his revenge. Mincher was on the postgame radio show because he was the hero of the game. He hit a three-run homer in the first inning, and we won 3–1. The moment Mincher came into the clubhouse, Comer, who by this time was wearing only a jock strap, dirt and no teeth, ran across the room with an insane gleam in his eye, leaped on Mincher's back and kissed him on the ear.

This time Mincher didn't punch him.

Had a spot of trouble with Ranew in the bullpen tonight. He warmed me up when Schultz ordered that I get up early in the game. But later on, when I got up to throw on my own, he let me know his heart wasn't in it. He stuck his glove up at every pitch and if the ball went into it, fine. Otherwise it bounced off and he had to go after it. And he took his time chasing it. If I have to wait a minute or more between pitches I'm not getting anything out of it, and he knows it.

Another gimmick he uses is to throw the ball back to me erratically so I have to scoop it out of the dirt or jump into the air. Or he'll steam it into me until my hand hurts.

The fact that I hurt Pagliaroni's thumb the other day, added to Ranew's obvious reluctance, makes it hard for me to ask anybody to catch me. It's part of the reason, probably, the knuckleball has been so in and out.

Studying my statistics today I note that in the last fifteen days I've pitched a grand total of six-and-a-third innings. That's an even bigger reason for being in and out. My statistics scream out that I have to work to be effective. But I'm not getting the work. Not even in the bullpen.

Not only that, but Jerry Stephenson is getting a start. Now, I like Jerry, but he was just called up from Vancouver, where he had an 0–3 record and an ERA of 4.78. Here's a guy released by the Red Sox, picked up as a free agent, does poorly in the minors, gets called up and is handed a start. Who's going to get the *next* start? Ray Oyler?

JULY
9

There's a promotion they run here in Seattle called "Home Run for the Money." If a listener has his name drawn, he is assigned a certain hitter. If that hitter hits a home run in the right inning, the listener wins the jackpot. Sometimes there are several thousand dollars in it. And if the right hitter hits a grand-slam homer at the precise moment required, there is a $25,000 bonus.

It so happened that, *mirabile dictu,* Fred Talbot hit a home run with the bases loaded tonight. And thus a man named Donald Dubois, who lives in Gladstone, Oregon, won $27,500. The applause in the stands had not yet died down when it was decided in the bullpen that tomorrow morning Fred Talbot would receive a telegram from Donald Dubois of Gladstone, Oregon, thanking him for his Herculean efforts and telling him that a check for $5,000 was in the mail as a token of esteem and friendship. Since the telegram was my idea, I had to send it. We agreed that my identity would be revealed only under penalty of death.

I checked in with Marvin Milkes tonight and offered to go up to Vancouver and start a game there during the All-star break. I explained about how little I'd been pitching and said I'd like him to see what I could do as a starter, even if it was in the minors.

So Marvin Milkes said, "I don't know if we could guarantee about bringing you back."

I said the first thing that came to my mind. "What?"

"Your coming back would depend on a lot of things; how you did when you were down there and our situation here with this club at the time. We have roster problems. It's not always easy to get rid of a guy, to make room on the roster."

All of a sudden I got the feeling that I was being sent down, was asking to be brought back up and was being told, "Sorry, kid." And here

I was *volunteering* to go to the minors so that I would, in the long run, help the club. I mean, if it worked, they'd have another starting pitcher. And all Milkes could think of was obstacles.

"Have you talked to Joe about starting?" Milkes said.

I was shocked. Milkes was here last year when I had such success starting. You'd think he would have remembered that, talked to Joe about it. Nothing. Nobody talks to anybody around here.

Another example. I went to Sal today and said, "Sal, I've only pitched six innings in fifteen days, and if possible I'd like a little extra time warming up. So if you think we're getting into a situation where you might need me, give me a quick call so I can get a head start."

And Sal said: "What if we need you in a hurry?"

With the Angels in town I took the opportunity to chat with Ed Fisher and Hoyt Wilhelm. I asked Fisher about the curse of inconsistency. "Everyone has the same problem," he said. "Hoyt has it and I have. I'll pitch for three weeks and it'll be going real good for me and then for ten days I can't throw one worth a damn and they hit me all over the place."

And Wilhelm said: "You know you can throw a bad one once in a while if you're throwing a lot of good ones. But you can't throw two or three bad ones in a row. Sometimes when I go out there I throw just about every one of them good. At other times it's just nothing. And I get hit. It takes a lot of work and a lot of concentration. It's that delicate a pitch."

Fisher came in to relieve tonight and got clobbered (in fact Talbot hit the grand-slam off him). And when I came in I pitched two scoreless innings, striking out three. Like Fisher said, that's the way it goes.

JULY

10

Freddy Talbot believes.

The telegram read: "Thank you very much for making our lives so happy, Mr. Talbert. We feel we must share our good fortune with you. A check for $5,000 will be sent to you when the money arrives." (I thought it was a clever touch to misspell his name.)

As soon as he read the telegram, Talbot called over his faithful roommate and asked him to step outside. "You know anything about this, Merritt?" he said. "You think it's a joke?"

"Looks legitimate to me," Ranew said, biting his lip to keep from laughing.

On the bus to the airport for our trip to Minnesota, Talbot showed the telegram to Ray Oyler. "You think it's for real?" Oyler said.

"Yeah, I think so," Talbot said. "If one of the guys had done it he wouldn't have misspelled my name."

"That's right," Oyler said. "And what are you going to do with the money?"

"I think I'll buy that boat I always wanted, one with a 95-horse-power motor. I'll tell my wife I won it in a raffle. Otherwise she'll want me to put the whole $5,000 in the bank. And whatever you do, Ray, don't tell the writers about it. If they put it in the paper I'll have to pay income tax on it."

Ray promised he wouldn't tell.

Because we were rained out in Seattle, Jerry Stephenson did not get his start.

"How do you feel about missing your start tonight?" I asked.

"My one start?" he said. "You mean my one big chance?"

"Right. And how do you feel about the fact that you were going to get this one big chance with only one-third of an inning pitched in the last six weeks?"

"Oh, I've pitched more than that," Stephenson said. "Actually I have a total of two-and-two-thirds innings."

"Only two-and-two-thirds?" I said. "In six weeks? Has anybody said anything to you? Has this situation been discussed?"

"Nope," Stephenson said. "I'm just happy to be here. I'll take whatever they give me. If they took off my hat and shit in it, I'd put it right back on my head and say thanks."

I think he means it. I've felt that way myself.

But it can't be too good for Stephenson that they called up Dick Baney today. He's the righthanded pitcher who almost made the club this spring.

JULY
11

There was a grave meeting before the game in Minnesota tonight. Joe Schultz had a clipping from the Los Angeles *Herald Examiner,* a story by Bud Furillo. The story said that the Seattle ballplayers, upset at the way Marvin Milkes sat in the lobby at around curfew time, checking bodies, had gotten together and had Milkes measured for a suit. Milkes was very pleased at the idea, until the suit arrived. It was a bellhop's uniform, with 38 brass buttons. There were two pictures with the story: one of Milkes, the other of a bellhop.

It was a terrific story in every respect but one. It wasn't true. However, the possibility of fitting Milkes with such a suit *had* been discussed in the bullpen. And something like that gets around.

"Now this kind of thing is bad not only for the general manager," Joe Schultz said, "it's bad for the whole organization. This may sound funny, but things like this can get turned around. If Marvin Milkes has to sit in the lobby and check, the wives might start wondering who's staying out late and what they're doing."

"And that's bad," Ray Oyler said.

"We can all tell our wives it's McNertney he was checking on," Tommy Davis said.

Everyone laughed. McNertney is thirty-two, single, and rumor has it he's never been kissed. He spends all his spare time oiling his fishing rods and thinking about hunting in the winter. He hasn't got time to stay out late.

But Joe Schultz was serious. "Whoever gave out this story is a no-good cocksucker, I'll tell you that," Schultz said. "And I'm going to find out who it is."

At that point I felt a lot of eyes on me. Maybe I'm supersensitive, but it did seem that almost everybody checked me in case I was showing the white feather of guilt. And, of course, after the meeting, Fred

253

Talbot said, loudly, as though he were kidding, "All right, Bouton, what'd you give them the story for?" In this kind of situation I'm always guilty until proven innocent.

That's what happened around the Yankees too. When Johnny Keane was manager and losing control of the ballclub, there was a story in the paper quoting an unnamed player as saying that Keane was a bad manager, that he was handling the club poorly, that none of the players liked him and that there was going to be a mutiny on the club any day now. And this all explained, of course, why the Yankees were losing.

Naturally there was a clubhouse meeting. Keane made a short speech asking who had said those things and what we could do about it? Elston Howard leaped to his feet in a rage, waving his arms and shouting. "How the hell could anyone do such a thing?" he demanded. "When are we going to learn not to talk to these writers? We shouldn't even let them into our clubhouse. And the guy who said those things, we ought to find him and fine him a thousand dollars." And so forth.

During this tirade I once again had that uneasy feeling that there were a lot of eyes on me. This was unfair. I never hid behind anonymous quotes. If I had anything to say to a newspaperman I said it. In fact, newspaper guys who considered themselves my friends sometimes wouldn't print things I said only on the ground that they didn't want to hurt my career with the Yankees. Nevertheless there were the eyes and all I could do was try to look as nonchalant as possible. I probably succeeded only in looking guilty.

The next day I asked the writer of the story to tell me who his source was. He said he'd tell me only if I promised never to reveal it. I promised. And I have never revealed it. Until now. It was Elston Howard.

Sometimes things just run away from a man. Take Pagliaroni. While Joe Schultz was making his speech about what a terrible thing for the ballclub the bellhop-uniform article was, Pag was a vociferous supporter. "Damn right," he said. "Dammit, yes." And like that. But when the idea to do it first came up in the bullpen, Pagliaroni was one of its biggest boosters. I even thought he might run out and do it during the game.

Before the game Dick Baney and I were walking across the outfield grass to the bullpen, and the crowd was buzzing, and the organist was playing, and Baney looked around and said, "Hey, you know something? This is fun, walking across the outfield with all the people looking down at you."

And I thought, "It's true." You forget how much fun it is sometimes just to walk across the outfield. And then I remembered sitting up in the left-field stands in the Polo Grounds as a kid and thinking to myself, "Cheez, if I could only run out on the field and maybe go over and kick second base, or shag a fly ball—God, that would make my year. I'd never forget it as long as I lived if I could just run across that beautiful green outfield grass." And now, sometimes, I forget to tingle.

Baney asked me if I ever got nervous on the mound. I told him no, that you're nervous sometimes until you throw the first pitch, then everything seems to be all right. But I've been nervous. Like the first game I started in Yankee Stadium as a rookie in 1962. My first eight pitches were balls. Then, with two men on, I ran the count on the hitter to 3 and 1. My next pitch was ball four. I saw Houk step out of the dugout to come get me, not only out of the game, but to send me to the minors. Career over. Only the umpire called it a strike. Houk stepped back into the dugout. I got the hitter on a pop-up and went on to pitch the worst shutout in the history of the game. I gave up seven walks and seven hits, stranded fourteen runners and won 8–0.

Then there was my first World Series game, 1963, against the Dodgers. It was the year Maury Wills stole all those bases. He was the first hitter and I stood there looking at him and thinking, "He's going to get on, he's going to steal second, we're going to throw the ball into center field and I'm going to be humiliated on national television." I remember being so nervous I could hardly throw the ball, and on the first pitch, Maury Wills, bless his heart, bunted the ball right back to me. Easy out. I've always been grateful to him for bunting that first pitch.

When Dick Baney went into the game to throw his first major-league pitch everybody in the bullpen moved out to the fence to watch him. We wanted to see how he'd do against the Brew, which is what we call Harmon Killebrew. Inside I still think of him as the Fat Kid, which is what Fritz Peterson over at the Yankees always called him. I'd say, "How'd you do, Fritz?" and he'd answer, "The Fat Kid hit a double with the bases loaded." Well, the first time the Fat Kid faced Dick Baney he hit the second pitch 407 feet into the left-field seats.

255

After the game I was shaving next to Baney. "Welcome to the club," I said. "You lost your virginity tonight."

"The only difference," he said, "is that all you guys will still be here tomorrow."

JULY

12

Today Baney, who's still here, asked me if I was throwing my knuckleball all the time now and I said that indeed I was. "Sal didn't like that pitch this spring," Baney said. "I guess he thought you were throwing it too much. I remember one time you gave up a homer on it and Sal said to Joe, 'Now you see? That's the pitch that's going to get him into trouble.' "

I said that was interesting.

"Well, if Sal didn't want you to throw it, and if you were getting hit, why did you keep throwing the knuckleball?" Baney said.

"My wife told me to," I said.

"And there's something I've always wondered about," Baney said. "When you go to spring training with a club, even a minor-league club, they always tell you to work on something. Then you get hit and they get mad, no matter what you're working on. So I still don't know what to do in the spring—work on something or try to get the hitters out."

Welcome to another club.

I made a terrible mistake today. I was chatting with Fred Talbot and said, "Hey, Fred, by the way, you ever hear from that guy you hit the home run for?"

Fred's eyes narrowed and he looked mean. "Were you the one who sent that telegram?" he said.

"What telegram?" I said, feeling my stupid face breaking up into a giveaway smile.

Now he was clenching his teeth. "I *knew* you sent the damn thing," he said, "and I'm going to get you back for that. I know you sent that paternity suit thing too."

256

"Fred, I did *not* send you the paternity thing," I said, all injured innocence. "I *may* have sent you a telegram. I don't know yet. What did the telegram say?"

And he said: "I'll get you back. I'm going to get you back on something, and when I do it's going to involve your wife, your whole family, your friends back home, everybody in the whole damn country."

After the game Talbot got back at me. It was still so hot that a lot of the guys didn't want to wait for the bus back to the hotel and grabbed air-conditioned cabs instead. We lined up for them, and when I started to get into one as the last man, Talbot, who was behind me in line, leaped in ahead of me and said, "Take the next cab, you Communist."

Got into the ballgame today. Pitched two-and-two-thirds innings and gave up two hits, one of them a tremendous double by a former teammate of mine at Western Michigan, Frank Quilici. We lost this one 11–1 and the Fat Kid hit another. The Seattle staff is impartial in the home-run race between Killebrew and Reggie Jackson. They *both* kill us.

Too bad McNertney didn't make the All-Star team instead of Bill Freehan of the Tigers. Freehan isn't having anywhere near the kind of year McNertney is. This shows that the players are voting on reputation rather than current performance.

Also, I think Mayo Smith should have had a manager from the Western Division as one of his coaches instead of three Eastern managers—Ted Williams, Earl Weaver and Alvin Dark. He could easily have picked Joe Schultz and left off Dark. Take a hike, son.

JULY
13

I've had the feeling for some time now that Wayne Comer and I don't get along. I can tell because every once in a while he says about me, "Get him the fuck out of here." An example. One night we were sitting around in Don Mincher's room waiting to look at some stag movies and Pagliaroni and I got into a conversation about a book we were both reading, *Psycho-cybernetics*. I had just launched into my expert opinion of it when Wayne Comer said, "Get him the fuck out of here." Anyway, we've now lost four straight to the Twins, having dropped a doubleheader, and we're waiting for the bus to leave for the airport. An elderly gentleman walks up to the bus looking for Garry Roggenburk. He wants to thank him for tickets that were left for him. He doesn't actually know Roggenburk, but he's a friend of Bob Locker, who left the tickets, and about fourteen others, in the names of various players. "I was with Locker's group and I just wanted to thank you for leaving the tickets," the old man said to Roggenburk. "I feel bad about how the afternoon went for you boys. It certainly was sad for . . ."

Just then Wayne Comer breaks in with his loud, "Get him the fuck out of here."

Somehow, at this moment, in this place, in front of this nice old gentleman, that seems obscene to me. So I say, "Hey, Wayne, knock it off. That's a friend of Locker's."

"I don't give a fuck," Comer says, with flashing wit.

"Take it easy," I say. "It's only a game, you know."

"Only a game, huh? Well, you want to do something about it?"

"Yeah, I do. I want you to knock it off."

"Why don't you do something about it with your fists then instead of your mouth?"

"Just knock it off. You were wrong and you know it."

"Why don't you crawl all over my ass then? Jump up and crawl all over me."

"Yeah. That will solve it."

And it ends with that.

Except Comer keeps muttering, "Just a game, huh? Just a game."

After the bus left for the airport I was making notes on this brilliant repartee and Ray Oyler looked over my shoulder and tried to read them. "What are you writing?" he said as I covered the notes with my hand.

"None of your business," I answered, sweetly.

"Well, just keep my name out of it," he said.

Can't promise, kid. But it's tempting.

While we were losing the first game of the doubleheader—we were down 5–1 and it was going to be our third straight here—Joe Schultz called to John Gelnar, who was keeping the pitching chart. "C'mere a minute," he said, motioning Gelnar down to the other end of the dug-out. Gelnar was sure he was going to get a big tip on pitching. And Joe Schultz, pointing up into the stands, said, "Up there near the Section 23 sign. Check the rack on that broad."

In the eighth inning, Joe Schultz said, "Well, boys, between games today we have a choice of roast beef, baked ham or tuna salad."

We were winning the second game 4–0 in the eighth when Fred Talbot, who had a beautiful three-hitter going, got tired. He came out with a runner on base and none out. Disaster set in promptly. First Joe Schultz used Locker. Then O'Donoghue, then Segui. Everybody in the Minnesota lineup got a hit. Rod Carew, just off the bus after coming back from his weekend in the army, ran into the stadium, threw on his uniform and, with his fly still unbuttoned, got a hit. I swear they pulled an usher out of the stands and *he* got a hit. We lost 5–4.

JULY
14

Seattle

I called Bud Furillo in Los Angeles today and asked him if he would tell me the name of his source for the bellhop-uniform story. Reporters, he told me, never disclose their sources. Too bad, I told him, because it was a lousy source. The story wasn't true. That shook him up nicely.

I explained to him that it was something we'd kidded about but hadn't actually done, and it turned out he got the story "from a very reliable Los Angeles writer," who got it from one of the Angels, which is about the way I figured it happened.

He said he'd call Milkes and apologize for printing an erroneous story. I also came away with the impression that he'd let Milkes know that no one on our club had given him the story. Not that I think Milkes doesn't know that. I think the whole point of that little meeting was to intimidate us into not telling things to the press in the future. Sneaky.

Jerry Stephenson was outrighted to Vancouver today just as he was moving into his new apartment. I know he lost a deposit and some rent money when he was called up from Vancouver, and I'm sure it will cost him again. Stephenson was here for seventeen days and pitched a total of three innings. He was on the road most of the time, and while he was away his wife had a miscarriage. Stephenson is all shook up. Now wait a minute. Bob Lasko lives in Vancouver and he's spending the summer in Toledo. Mike Marshall had to fight to get sent to Toledo instead of Vancouver. Why couldn't they just have been switched around? Because nobody thought of it. Because nobody cared. I agree with the title of a paper Mike Marshall wrote in college: "Baseball Is an Ass."

JULY
15

We have dropped out of third place into a tie for fifth with Chicago. Kansas City, the other expansion team, is now ahead of us.

When I got to the clubhouse tonight I found that my two pairs of new baseball shoes had been nailed to the clubhouse floor. Used for the operation were square cement nails. They tore huge ugly holes in the soles. Also the buttons were torn off my sweatshirts, my Yoo-Hoo T-shirts were ripped to shreds and several jockstraps were pulled permanently out of stretch. Talbot's revenge, I thought immediately. But he swore it was not him, and he convinced me. Ray Oyler and Gene Brabender admitted they were eyewitnesses, but they wouldn't tell me who did it. They assured me, though, that it wasn't Fred Talbot.

I asked Steve Hovley to find out for me, and he said, "If I can I will, but I doubt if they'll tell me."

The only other guy with a possible motive is Wayne Comer. Somehow I doubt it was him. In fact I can't imagine why anybody would want to do that. I think it was a prank. I think it was funny when I tried to pick up the shoes that were nailed down. I think it was *supposed* to be funny. I think.

Besides, I can still wear the shoes—as long as it doesn't rain.

Made my thirty-seventh appearance of the season tonight against Oakland and my super knuckleball showed up. I struck out the first three guys I faced. The third strike to Rick Monday broke so sharply McNertney never got a glove on it. It rolled between his legs to the backstop and Monday got to first base. Of course, this was after Diego Segui had come into the game at a crucial moment and given up a three-run homer and the game. Pitching in lost causes, my ERA is back down to 3.50. I still can't see how they can keep from starting me.

JULY

16

I should say something about all the injuries we've had. It will explain, at least to some extent, why we've been going so poorly. John Donaldson, our second baseman, has a fractured toe. John Kennedy wrenched his knee and is in a cast. Rich Rollins is having a knee operation that finishes him for the year. Steve Barber is still on the disabled list (his arm doesn't hurt, it's just a little stiff). Tommy Harper has a pulled thigh muscle and a bad sliding strawberry. Ray Oyler has been out with a hamstring pull. So has Mike Hegan.

You will also notice that while our infielders are dropping like flies, our starting pitchers remain disgustingly healthy if not particularly effective.

I was chatting with Fred Talbot about contracts and keeping statistics to use as negotiating arguments and he said, "Aw hell, I don't keep statistics. Whatever they send me, I just sign and send it back. Of course, I call them a few names first."

261

JULY

17

Out for a most pleasant afternoon on my neighbor's boat, cruising through the locks from Lake Washington into Puget Sound with my wife and kids. Also Garry Roggenburk, Gordie Lund, utility infielder, and Steve Hovley, whom I invited along. Hovley wound up stealing my pants.

It was my fault. He was wearing Bermudas, and on the way into the ballpark I suggested he switch, that I'd get less static than he walking into the park in Bermudas. He agreed. But when he got out of the car, running, he had his Bermudas *and* my pants. So I had to walk into the clubhouse, late, wearing my bathing suit. And naturally Hovley was one of the people who said, "A *bathing suit!*"

Tomorrow Diego Segui leaves the bullpen for a start. So I went over to Sal Maglie to chew on his leg for a while.

"Sal, what's the story?"

"About what?"

"About the fact that I'm not starting and Diego Segui is."

"Well, it has nothing to do with personalities."

Never occurred to me that it had. Well, hardly ever.

"You know something, Jim?" Pagliaroni said to me today. "I'm convinced that they think you're a character."

"What kind, Pag?" I said.

"Not your personality or anything," he said. "But that pitch. And the fact that you throw it all the time. As recently as two days ago I heard Sal telling Joe that he's told you time and time again that you're throwing too much in the outfield. I think Joe likes your knuckleball, I really do, but I don't think Sal does, and they think it's a little weird that you do all that throwing."

Jim Pagliaroni is one of the most perceptive Italian catchers in the big leagues.

Joe Schultz called a morale meeting tonight and did a good job of it. He said that we were losing because of injuries and that we shouldn't begin pressing to try to make up for them. He said that if we weren't big-league ballplayers we wouldn't be playing in the big league, and that we were just as good as any other club. "Sometimes things turn around all of a sudden and you start winning a whole lot of games. You can win them just as easy as lose them."

It was a good speech and made us all feel better, and I agreed with all of it. Except one small part. Minnesota is better.

JULY
18

Diego Segui pitched a marvelous ballgame. He was magnificent throughout and won it 2–1. As I watched the game I was torn between wanting him to get bombed and wanting him to do well, because we could use a win and because he's a good fellow. So there I was torn, and warming up in almost every inning. In the second game, same thing. And I never got into either game.

"You know something?" said Pagliaroni. "You looked great warming up."

I told him thanks.

Even winning we didn't do much to stop Rod Carew, who is now leading the league. He's the kind of hitter who puts the ball into a hole someplace, or bloops one, every time. "He can't miss," McNertney said. "If I were him I'd go looking for wallets."

Steve Hovley won the first game for us. It was a 1–1 tie in the last of the ninth, bases loaded, Hovley up and Ron Perranoski, the old pro, pitching. It was a classic confrontation; the graybeard, wily pitcher against the upstart young slugger. In the end, Hovley beat the old man at his own game. He worked the count to 3 and 2 and then fouled off a couple of borderline pitches. It was exciting. Me, I ran all the way down to the dugout so I could be closer to what was happening. And as I watched Hovley struggling out there against the best reliever in the league, I thought, how can a guy with friends like Dostoevski be scared in this kind of situation? He wasn't. He hung in for another foul ball and then got the base on balls, forcing in the run.

As we walked down to the clubhouse I heard John Gelnar say, "You know, one good thing about having Hovley up there, he's too goony to be scared."

In the second game Hovley hit his second home run of the season. I'm the proud owner of the first ball he hit out. I bought it from the kid who caught it. Hovley said he didn't want it. He said he didn't think it was particularly important. The year he hits 62 it may be my most valuable possession.

I think the world should know that a girl one of my teammates goes out with is called "Rotorooter." Around the clubhouse, guys sing, "Tell Rotorooter I love her."

When I came in from the bullpen after we won the second game, Joe was patting everybody on the back, saying "Attaway to go" and "Nice job." When he got to me I said, "Joe, I really had it out there tonight in the bullpen."

"You did?" Joe said.

"Yup. Great knuckleball. Hellacious."

"Did you throw too much?"

"Hell no."

"Good. You're starting tomorrow night. Feel up to it?"

"Hell yes."

Well, what do you know? It's put-up-or-shut-up time for Jim Bouton.

Before I left the ballpark, Sal Maglie said, "Get your sleep, Bouton."

And I said, "Right, Sal. And I want to have a catcher out there five hours before game time so I can start warming up."

Driving home I found myself doing a lot of worrying. Should I take a sleeping pill tonight? Should I sleep late or get up early and take a nap later? What should I eat? At what time? Then I thought, "What the hell am I worried about all this crap for? I've started a lot more important games. World Series games, pennant-race games. And here

I am acting like a kid." Foolishness. I'm just going to be normal. I'm going to sleep tonight and not even think about it. When I start the game I'm going to pretend that I'm in there for relief, that I'm just going to pitch a few innings the way I do almost every day.

Look at it this way. In a couple of days two men are going to land on the moon. How the hell can I be nervous about starting a baseball game? Even if it is against the Fat Kid and his wrecking crew.

Part 6 Shut Up

JULY
19

I went over the hitters with McNertney before the game. For me the only thing this involves is deciding which hitters we're going to throw fastballs to on what particular count. We know we're going to start everyone off with a knuckleball and we're going with it until 3 and 0. On the big hitters, like Killebrew, we decided to throw the knuckleball even on 3 and 0. We'd also throw the 3-and-0 knuckleball to any guy who was hitting in a game-winning situation, even if we walked him. I mean I'd rather give up a base on balls than a three-run homer.

My main concern was that Carew and Tovar would be stealing on my knuckleball, so we went over the pick-off signs carefully and hoped for the best.

It wasn't good enough.

In my first start of the year, on this day of July 19, 1969, A.D., I, James Alan Bouton, was creamed.

Five runs were scored off me before I was mercifully taken out of the game with two out in the fourth. There were two home runs, by Leo Cardenas and Ted Uhlaender. When Joe Schultz came out to get me I could only think of a line Fred Talbot delivered in similar circumstances: "What kept you?"

Not more than one out of every three knuckleballs I threw was doing its proper thing. Besides, my control was way off and I was behind on the hitters.

I started out in trouble and recovered. With two out the Fat Kid got on base because of an error. A single and a walk loaded the bases, but I struck out Bob Allison on a 3-and-2 knuckleball.

After that, oblivion. I blocked it all almost as quickly as I could shower, dress and join my family in the stands. That's the easiest way for me to forget. I crawl back to my family and use them for a crutch. Some guys drink. I talk about the kids needing new shoes.

I was glad to have the chance to start, of course. Yet now that I've fouled everything up so royally I'm thinking of excuses. Why did they have to start me against Minnesota? Maybe if I knew a few days in advance I could have prepared myself better. Maybe I should have taken a greenie. That's just kidding myself, of course. I had a start and I didn't win, and now I can look forward to the All-Star break.

Now that I think of it, I didn't lose either. We were losing 5–0 when I left the game. We tied the game at 7–7 and went sixteen innings before stopping on account of curfew. I think I'll remind Sal and Joe that I'm still undefeated as a starter.

And I just remembered something else. When my boy Mike was still a baby and he cried, I'd say to him, "Harmon Killebrew's little boy doesn't cry." Now I wonder if Harmon Killebrew ever thinks of crying.

JULY
20

Poor John Gelnar. The game was picked up today in the seventeenth inning and he promptly lost it. Then he lost the regular game, which is two in one day and not, under most circumstances, easy to do.

And my record, as we go into the All-Star break, is 1–0. Not much to show for a half-season's work. Still, it's better than 1–1 . . . or 1–2, not to mention 1–3.

JULY
21

Kyong Jo has been with us for almost a year now and the rapidity with which he's learned English is amazing. Today he came to me with a complaint. "Dad, the kids call me John Jo, or King Jo," he said. "Why don't they call me Kyong Jo?"

I explained that Kyong Jo was a Korean name and difficult for American children to pronounce. And I asked him if he would like to have an American name.

This is something Bobbie and I had been talking about for some time. We didn't want to change his name right away. It was difficult enough for him to make the adjustment to a new country and new parents without, at the same time, robbing him of the only familiar thing he had left, his name. So we called him Kyong Jo. But we thought he'd want to change it eventually, and now was the time.

He said yes, he'd like an American name.

"How about David?" I said.

He thought about it for a moment, then said, "Yeah."

"Okay, we'll call you David. You'll be David Kyong Jo Bouton."

"Okay," he said.

And he ran out the front door shouting to the neighborhood kids, "Hey, everybody. I'm David. I'm *David!*"

JULY
22

I take this opportunity to present a lexicon of words and phrases encountered around baseball that are, more or less, unique to the game. There are a great many phrases having to do with a pitcher throwing at a batter. Among them are:

Chin music, as in "Let's hear a little chin music out there," this being a suggestion that the pitcher throw the baseball near the hitter's chin.

Purpose pitch, which is a pitch that knocks a batter down purposely, or perhaps may just

Spin his cap.

Keep him honest, which means, make the batter afraid if you can.

Loosen him up, meaning that if enough baseballs are thrown close to a hitter, he'll fall down easily.

Other phrases that often come up in conversation are:

Tweener, any ball hit not especially hard but directly between two outfielders, neither of whom can reach it in time.

Take him over the wall, hit a home run, as in "Horton took Bouton over the wall in the fifth."

Down the cock is the quintessence of the hitting zone. Any pitch like that is bound to be

Juiced, with some kind of power.

Parts of the body also have special appellations:

Boiler, as in "he's got the bad boiler," or upset stomach.

271

Hose is arm.

Moss is hair.

Shoes are *kicks* and clothes are *vines,* and when the bases are loaded they're *drunk.* A good fielder can really *pick it,* and if you want to tell a guy to go sit down, it's *go grab some bench.* Organized baseball is *O.B.,* and a stupid player has the *worst head in O.B. Wheels* are legs, and an infielder has *the good hands* or *the bad hands* as girls have *the good wheels* or *the bad wheels.* For some reason the definite article is important there. An angry man has the *red ass* or the *R.A.*

Camp-followers, whether they're eleven or sixty-five or somewhere in between, are called *Baseball Annies.* And if a player, coach or manager should bring a girl with him to another city, she's called an *import.* If an import is a *mullion,* she may have to pay her own way.

A pimple or boil is called *a bolt,* as in "get a wrench for that bolt." A hard line drive is a *blue darter, frozen rope,* or an *ungodly shot.* To think is to *have an idea,* so that when a pitcher seems to be losing his cool a coach might shout at him, "Have an idea out there."

And a fellow who talks big but appears to lack courage is said to have an *alligator mouth* and a *hummingbird ass.*

Baseball is not without its charms.

JULY
23

Department of It's Not How You Play the Game, It's Whether You Win or Lose. I was at a pool watching my kids take their swimming lessons today and one of the women said to me, "Why aren't you watching the All-Star game?"

Somewhat abashed, I said, "Well, I'm getting some swimming lessons for my little boys."

And she said, "That's all right. You're really not missing much anyway. The American League's getting slaughtered."

JULY
24

Back to the salt mine. Once again I'm the forgotten man of the bullpen. Used three pitchers in the game, and even Fred Talbot, who's in the starting rotation, was asked to warm up. And I never got a call.

This gave me lots of time to chat with Pagliaroni. He told me about the first talk he had with Marvin Milkes when he came over from the Athletics. The last thing he did in Oakland was break a finger. So when he came to us he had to go on the disabled list. And Milkes said to him: "Now, Pag, I know you were a player representative over there and I know you worked on the salary problems we've had and I know you're going to have to be on the disabled list. But I want you to know you're still going to be receiving your full salary."

This is pretty funny, because they *had* to pay him, even though he was on the disabled list, maybe *especially* because he was on the disabled list.

It's like when the Yankees sent me to Syracuse. I remember Houk saying, "Now, you'll be getting the same salary," and I felt rather grateful until I discovered they *had* to pay me the same salary. It was in the contract.

If you want to know what aspect of the moon landing was discussed most in the bullpen it was the sex life of the astronauts. We thought it a terrible arrangement that they should go three weeks or more without any sex life. Gelnar said that if those scientists were really on the ball they would have provided three germ-free broads for the astronauts.

JULY

25

Word is that Greg Goossen will be up to replace Mike Hegan when he goes into service for two weeks. Goossen is a burly guy with kinky blond hair and looks like a bouncer in an English pub. He also is a flake. And Ranew said to Pagliaroni, "Goossen ought to be assigned to Bouton." Okay, I'll take him.

Pag had a good story about Goossen. He remembered sitting in a bar with him and the Goose was putting them down pretty good. "Don't you have a game tomorrow?" Pag said.

"Yeah, we got a game," Goossen said.

"You're drinking a little heavy, aren't you?"

"You know something?" Goossen said. "I found I can't play if I feel good. I've got to have a little bit of a hangover to get the best out of me."

Got a letter from Jerry Stephenson. Says that God is alive and surfing in Waikiki. He also said that he had a marvelous final conversation with Milkes. He complained that he hadn't had an opportunity to pitch and Milkes said he'd blown two starting opportunities.

"When were those?" Jerry asked.

"You were going to start the night it rained," Milkes said.

"I know," Jerry said. "When was the other one?"

"When your wife had a miscarriage and you had to leave the club for three days."

The next best thing about the way things broke was that on the very day he was sent down Jerry and his wife had moved into a new apartment. That afternoon they had to move out. "We felt groovy moving all that stuff," Jerry wrote. "By the end of the day we were working very well together as a team."

274

O'Donoghue was on the airplane flying east with Don Mincher and Joe Schultz, who were going to the All-Star game, and said Joe was feeling hardly any pain when he left the plane and was mumbling his two favorite words—shit and fuck—in all their possible combinations.

Tony Conigliaro was the subject for discussion at the pregame meeting.

"Curve him away," O'Donoghue said.

"Yeah, he's got a blind spot out there," Brabender said.

And Sal Maglie said, "Don't challenge him."

That's just the kind of thing Tommy Davis loves to pick up on.

"Sal, what do you mean by 'Don't challenge him'?"

And Sal said, "Well, don't throw him a fastball down the middle. You got to spot it."

Like a great work of art, Sal Maglie is priceless.

JULY
26

It's still hard to get used to playing baseball again after the All-Star break. Three days off reminds you how much tension you live under playing baseball every day. During the break Harmon Killebrew can't get you. Reggie Jackson can't get you. It's peaceful. Like looking up at Mt. Rainier. That's the great thing about our ballpark. When a home run hit off you disappears over the fence your eye catches a glimpse of the majesty of Mt. Rainier and some of that bad feeling goes away.

Great thing happened today. Police arrested a twenty-two-year-old blonde who had climbed a tree outside our clubhouse and was peeping in at us in the shower. A female beaver-shooter.

The game was great too, largely because J. Bouton recorded his second win of the season. I started warming up when the score was

3–0 against us. That's still too close to put me in. It was 5–0 with a runner on when I got the big call. I needed one hitter in that inning and got him, mowed them down 1-2-3 in the next inning and, of course, came out for a pinch-hitter. Only this time it was when we were in the process of scoring six runs. The big hit was a three-run homer by McNertney. The final score was 8–5. Locker got the save and I got a pat on the ass from Sal Maglie.

Another infielder got racked up during the game. Ron Clark collided with George Scott of the Red Sox and had thirteen stitches taken in his lip. Ron's a tough, gutty little ballplayer. He has a baby face, two tattoos on his arm (one says "Mother" and the other is of a black panther), smokes big cigars—and when he has thirteen stitches in his lip he drinks beer out of the side of his mouth.

Greg Goossen played his first game and went 3 for 3, including a tremendous line-drive home run into the left-field seats.

I love them, one and all.

We were talking about Bill Valentine, one of the umpires who was fired ostensibly for being incompetent but actually, we all believe, because he was involved in trying to form an umpires' union. What we remembered about him is that he was one of the few umpires who would call Mickey Mantle out on borderline pitches. "Every umpire would give Mickey the benefit of the doubt," O'Donoghue said, "but every time I threw a pitch that nicked the corner on him, Valentine would call it a strike."

The whole Yankee team hated him for that.

The last time Marty Pattin had a bad game—and he's had about eight in a row now—he came charging up the runway to the clubhouse breaking things on the way. He kicked over a couple of garbage cans and crashed the door into the clubhouse. So today Talbot said to him, "Marty, what are your plans if you don't win tomorrow?"

JULY
27

Fred and I hung a hangman's noose in Pattin's locker, but he didn't need it. He pitched well, leaving the game after eight innings with the score 1–1. He didn't break up anything on the way back to the clubhouse.

We went twenty innings before losing it. I pitched two scoreless innings, the tenth and eleventh, which means I had another chance to win. It may also mean that I'll get into more games at crucial points. But if it takes twenty-inning games to do it, I'm still nowhere.

Talbot has finally been able to talk about that fellow Dubois who won that $27,000 on his home run. "Never made a nickel out of it," Talbot said. "They flew me out to Gladstone to go on four different radio shows. I went for the ballclub and they didn't pay anything either."

"Didn't Dubois offer you anything at all?" I said. "What did he say to you?"

"He asked for the bat," Talbot said. "He wanted to have the bat I hit the home run with as a souvenir. And when the whole thing was over it ended up costing me $2.75 for parking."

JULY
29

A bit of clever baseball strategy tonight by Joe Schultz. We're down 4–2 in the ninth against the Senators. Two out, man on second, Frank Howard is the hitter. Howard should be walked. But if

Bob Locker, who's pitching, walks him he will now have to pitch to a lefthanded hitter, Mike Epstein. This won't do. So O'Donoghue, a left-handed pitcher, will be brought in. In which case the Senators will pinch-hit for Epstein, bringing in a righthanded power-hitter, like Brant Alyea, and we're stuck. O'Donoghue will have to pitch against him because the rules say he must pitch to at least one hitter. But Schultz was ahead of everybody. He brought in O'Donoghue just to walk Howard. Sure enough, they brought in Alyea to face O'Donoghue. So Joe took out O'Donoghue and brought me in. I struck Alyea out on three super knuckleballs.

As so often happens in this great game we play, all the strategy went for nothing. We lost 4–2 anyway. At least I was in a position to win a game, though, and Hegan could have tied it up in the ninth with a home run, but just missed.

At the pregame meeting, when Frank Howard's name came up, Joe Schultz said, "Look, whatever you do, don't let him beat you. Don't give him anything good to hit. Throw it outside to him. Christ, I don't mean on the corner, either. He'll hit that pitch right out of here. Throw it a foot outside. Hell, he'll swing at those. *Somebody's* been getting him out. The bastard's only hitting .305."

Joe looked around at the laughing faces, smiled and said. "So whatever you do, don't let him beat you. I'd rather walk him."

And Tommy Davis couldn't resist saying, "Skip, the last time we did that, Mike Epstein beat us."

Which is why I love Tommy Davis.

JULY
30

Dropped by to see Marvin Milkes about the Gatorade. I saw him sitting at his desk, but his secretary said he wasn't in. In that case, I told her, she better call the cops because there was a guy at his desk impersonating him. Not only that, he was wearing one of his sportscoats.

I was rewarded with a dirty look and an audience with himself.

Milkes said he still hadn't made a decision about the Gatorade, hadn't even tasted it yet. But he wanted to talk to me about something else. He got up, closed the door and got very sincere. At first I couldn't imagine what he was getting at. "We've always had a good relationship," he said, turning on his big smile. Milkes has two faces he wears for players. He has this serious face and suddenly, as though he has remembered that he has to show he's your friend, he breaks into this dazzling smile. At first you think it's a real smile, then you realize that it's coming on at the wrong time, out of phase. He's not smiling because he's friendly. He's smiling the way he switches on his toaster. "Sometimes we have different points of view, but we've always gotten along fine and we've done a lot for you," he went on, wearing his sincere look now. "I stuck with you last year. I told Joe Adcock to use you and that I thought you had potential as a major-leaguer, and we paid you a major-league salary last year even though you were a minor-league ballplayer. I had confidence in you and you wouldn't be here now if it hadn't been for me. That's why I'm very upset to find out that you think that I've been a detective with this club, a gumshoe."

He looked so sincere and so sad I could feel a large tear welling up in my eye. How could I be so rotten?

"Now, you have to realize that a general manager's life is a lonely one, particularly when we're on the road," he continued. "I like to stay up at night and be around people. I don't like to sit in my room all night. Today, with the streets the way they are, you can't just walk around anymore. That's why I sit around the lobby and enjoy a cigar.

"But I don't check up on players. I don't fine players. That's not my job. I might tell the manager that somebody's staying out too late and it's making the club look bad, but I wouldn't fine a player myself. That's why I was disappointed to hear what you were saying about me."

"Who said I've been talking about you, Marvin?"

"I hear from people in Los Angeles and various writers. Through the grapevine. This kind of thing upsets me."

"Are you talking about the story in the Los Angeles *Examiner?*"

"Yeah," he said. "Now, that's a funny story. I read it myself and thought it was funny. And if the guy that told the story had come in and said to me, 'Marvin, I just meant that story as a joke,' I would have said, 'I enjoy a joke as much as anybody else,' and I would have forgotten about it. But I understand that you called a writer about it."

"Yes, I called Bud Furillo," I said. "But not to give him the story." I explained the purpose of my call and recounted what Furillo had said.

"Well, that's what he told me," Milkes said. "He called and said he would print a retraction because he knew it didn't happen. I said, 'Hell, don't print a retraction. It's not that important.' And as far as you're concerned in this thing, the only thing I care about is what you do out there between the lines. I know you do imitations and you give speeches and I've heard some of the people on the Yankees say you're kind of crazy and silly and I was told, 'You got stuck with one there.' But I tell them, 'As far as I'm concerned, if he gives me a hundred percent on the field, I'm going to use him. I'm judging him strictly as a ball-player.' You hear all kinds of things through the grapevine. Bouton is this and Bouton is that. Hell, I don't even listen. I just got done reading a story by you in *Sport*. That's the kind of story I'm sure you could call controversial. [It was an account of the work I did in Mexico City during the Olympics. I went there for the American Committee on Africa, which was working to keep South Africa out of the Games.] If that's the way you feel, it's fine with me. That's completely apart from my judgment of you as a ballplayer. If you give me a hundred percent you can write or say anything you want."

I never believed that for a minute. Especially since I had found out that he'd fined Talbot and Oyler, possibly among others, for break- ing curfew. But what I said was, "Well, I'm glad we've cleared it all up. And I hope it's clear to you that I did not call a writer to give him that story and that the only reason I called was so it would be understood that none of our players were responsible."

"Okay," he said. "It's all forgotten."

I didn't believe that either.

Before the game tonight pitchers were taking extra bunting practice because we'd been having trouble moving the runner along. And Joe Schultz said, "Boys, bunting is like jacking off. Once you learn how you never forget."

Garry Roggenburk left the club. Gordie Lund, his roommate, said he woke up this morning, saw him packing and said, "Where you going?"

"I'm going home," Roggenburk said.

He marched in on Marvin Milkes, said that he had no interest in the game anymore, didn't enjoy it, was through with it and was going home. The next thing Gordie knew he was driving him to the airport.

I know Roggenburk has his four years in on the pension and has a college degree and planned to go into teaching this fall. The trouble is, when you're a marginal player and you walk out, you can't come back. No one runs after you. You get marked down as a nut and it's all over. I don't know if Garry fully appreciated that fact when he left. Sometimes it's better not to act. Sometimes it's better just to sit around and grouse.

Greg Goossen hit two home runs and we won 4–3. I thought the outstanding play of the game was made by Wayne Comer, who bunted in a non-sacrifice situation, giving himself up just to move the runner along. He's that kind of player and recently Billy Martin, the Minnesota manager, was quoted as saying that he'd like to have Comer on his team, that he was his kind of ball player. It's true that he's a helluva player. And someday he'll make a pretty good coach.

JULY
31

A ten-year-old lad named Marvin Standifer wandered out of the stands and into the bullpen tonight and I grabbed him, put a warmup jacket and a hat on him and sat him on the bench. All his friends lined the fence and said things like, "Hey, is Marvin going to get into the game?" and "Does Marvin get to keep the hat?" and "How come you let Marvin into the bullpen?" And all the time Marvin had this giant grin on his face.

Of course, Eddie O'Brien said, "We have to get him out of here. We could get in trouble for that."

"Eddie, go sit down," I said. "This kid's got good stuff and we may need him later in the inning." Eddie sat down.

At the end of the inning I hoisted Marvin back into the stands. He'd had a big night.

The conversation turned to freezing people after they die and I said I'd like it to be done to me and then maybe I'd be thawed out in a couple of hundred years when they came up with a cure for whatever I'd died of. O'Donoghue was angry at the idea. "How the hell are they going to thaw you out?" he said. "When you're dead, you should be dead. That's it."

O'Donoghue gets angry easily at what he considers flaky ideas.

Steve Barber pitched five innings of relief the other night and did quite well. I was surprised he went so long and asked him about it. "Joe asked me how I felt," he said, "and I felt all right, so I told him to leave me in there."

That's a tough spot for a ballplayer. What could Steve have said? "My arm doesn't hurt but I don't think it would be a good idea to work anymore." No chance. So he stood out there risking two months of rehabilitation for one stinking ballgame, which we eventually lost anyway.

The Pilots have bought George Brunet from the Angels for something just over the waiver price. He'll fit right in on this ballclub. He's crazy.

I got in for two-thirds of an inning tonight and did well. Struck out Epstein on three pitches, all knuckleballs. I had Bernie Allen just about struck out, but he reached out and tapped one to the second baseman. Oh, Frank Howard got a single off me. He's liable to do that to anybody, isn't he?

I'm glad the knuckleball is in such happy shape. The Yankees arrive here tomorrow.

AUGUST

1

Another example of a general manager generously giving a ballplayer money that he is absolutely entitled to. Greg Goossen told the story. He lost $200 in rent when he was called up and Marvin Milkes put his hand on his shoulder and said, "We're picking up your rent check. [It's a rule that he has to.] And since you've signed a major-league contract, today you start on the pension plan."

"He made it sound like a special gift from him, a pot sweetener," Goossen said. "It was only after I left his office that I realized there was no way he could prevent me from starting on the pension plan today, even if he wanted to."

I talked to Fritz Peterson and Steve Hamilton in the outfield before the game and the pitchers' court fined me $5 for—in the words of Gene Brabender—"flagrantly flouting the rules." The court was in an ugly mood today.

"Before this season's over, Jim," Steve Hovley said, "we've got to steal the money, all $200 of it. We have to take it and keep it for a good long while."

I agreed that it had to be done.

Going over the Yankee hitters we came to Len Boehmer and Ron Plaza said, "Bad curve-ball hitter."

Dick Simpson, who'd played with Boehmer, said, "Hey, he hits the curve. He's a good curve-ball hitter."

"Well, I got it down on the card here," Plaza said. "Bad curve-ball hitter. Somebody must have said it."

And I remembered Gary Bell, and it struck me that somewhere in Plaza's files he's got a bunch of cards that say, "Smoke him inside."

283

Today Joe Schultz said, "Let's keep our minds on the game. And let's remember we're the same as everybody else. Let's go out there, kick the shit out of them and come back in and enjoy that beer."

We went out there, got two hits and lost 4–2. The beer was great.

AUGUST

2

Greg Goossen was doing his Casey Stengel imitation and he remembered the best thing the old man ever said about him. "We got a kid here named Goossen, twenty years old, and in ten years he's got a chance to be thirty."

There was a story in the paper about trades and Milkes saying he was going to make some. He was reminded that the trade deadline was well past and that the only thing he could do was make waiver deals. And Milkes said, "Don't worry, I'll get waivers."

This is a typical attitude toward the rules that baseball itself makes. Waivers are not supposed to be used as trade vehicles. They are, partly at least, supposed to protect the players from front office capriciousness. But that doesn't faze the owners. They make the rules and they break them, and there's not a thing the players can do about it. Not yet anyway.

We got some forms to fill out from the Pilots' publicity department. One of the questions was, "Who is your baseball idol?" Mincher put down Mickey Mantle. Another question was, "What induced a major-league team to sign you to a professional contract?" And Mincher wrote, "Pretty fair country player." Finally there was this: "What's the most difficult thing about playing major-league baseball?" And Mike Hegan said, "Explaining to your wife why *she* needs a penicillin shot for *your* kidney infection."

Sibby Sisti is with us so that he can get in his fifteen years on the pension. And today Tommy Davis said, "I wonder if anybody will ever offer me a job like that?"

"All you'll get is a scouting job in Watts someplace," Tommy Harper said.

So I started doing a general-manager bit, giving scout Tommy Davis his instructions. "Now, Tom, you have to make sure to sign the right kind of colored guy. You know what I mean? None of that rabble-rousing."

"It's not 'colored' now, Marvin, it's 'black,' " Tommy said.

"Yeah, well, you know what I mean. I don't have to tell you. The right kind of kid. Can he laugh? Can he dance? Find out if he knows how to shuffle. We don't want any of that Vic Power shit."

"I know just what you mean," Davis said. "I know just what to look for. I won't give you any trouble."

Steve Hovley says the club wants him to play winter ball and he wanted to know what I thought about it. I said I didn't think it would be a very good idea. If you finish up a season well and leave a good impression you're not going to improve it playing winter ball. All you can do is hurt yourself by playing poorly.

"I know that," Hovley said. "But I've never been to a Spanish-speaking country and I think I'd like that."

It's really just an afterthought to Hovley that he'd have to play baseball while there.

I find myself feeling sorry for Steve Barber. He had to get some shots in his arm today and he's scheduled to pitch against the Yankees tomorrow. He had those five good innings and now he's got trouble again. I asked him about it.

"No, it's nothing," he said. "Just a little tendonitis. It's not the trouble I had before. I'm just taking the shots as a precautionary measure."

Then we went to the outfield, the way we've been doing for the past weeks, and had a catch. He needs somebody to throw to and the price he pays is catching my knuckleball, which means every once in a while I bounce one off his foot. He doesn't complain.

AUGUST

3

"Boys, today it looks like Steve Barber and a cast of thousands." Bob Locker said it before the game and he was right. Steve never got by the first inning. He gave up five runs and we lost, 5–3. That was three in a row to the Yankees.

But it was a good weekend for me. I pitched five innings of relief Friday night and gave up one run, a home run by Pepitone. Saturday I pitched two scoreless innings. So now I've pitched about ten innings against the Yankees and given up only one run.

Ralph Houk has noticed. I was chatting with Fritz Peterson outside the Yankee clubhouse when Houk came out. We shook hands. "I've got to congratulate you," he said. "You're doing a helluva job. It just shows what can be done with a lot of hard work and guts. I knew you'd do it because you don't quit."

I said thanks. Then I said I'd been wanting to talk to him about something and would have called him. But since he was right there . . .

"There's going to come a time in my career, when the kids start going to school, and I have to make a decision about whether I'm going to continue to play baseball," I said. "It will be a lot easier for me to stay if I'm playing with a New York team. And I just wanted you to know that if you ever think you can use me, well, keep it in mind that I'd like to finish up my career near home."

"I'll do that," Houk said. "I'll definitely keep that in mind."

I did it, and I'm glad. I wonder what's going on inside his head, though. I wonder if he said to himself, "If that son of a bitch thinks he'll ever get back to Yankee Stadium while I'm there he's got another think coming." I also wonder if he said to himself, "You know, Bouton could be a help to us." Houk's a good manager and despite what's gone before I can still see myself pitching for him.

After the game I asked Barber how his arm felt and he said, "Oh, my arm felt fine. It was just that my rhythm was off, that's all."

Just then I noticed Fred Talbot packing his arm in ice because every time he pitches his elbow gets sore and I TGFMK—Thank God For My Knuckleball. I can't describe how sweet it is not to have to go through all that.

AUGUST
5

Boston

Started a long road trip in Boston today and we talked in the bullpen about the same kind of thing we talked about in Seattle: Sibby Sisti. We decided that jobs as coaches were really a kind of political patronage. They're dispensed for former favors. There's not much to do. Being a coach requires only showing up at the ballpark, hollering clichés and being able to play false sorrow when you lose. It's a boring job. But people who become coaches are not easily bored. You ever see a baby play with a rattle for two hours?

So it's amusing that these jobs are often held out like a carrot on a stick. Like when a guy is in the middle of his career a general manager will say to him, "Someday we hope to have a place for you in our organization," or "Don't worry, we'll take care of you later on," or "We'll see that you stay in baseball." What he really means is, keep your mouth shut and be a good boy and do what we tell you. Sign a contract for this particular (low) figure and we'll reward you later with a coaching job.

Every once in a while there's a guy that doesn't fit into the coaching mold, a man with an original idea or two who's not afraid to express them, a guy who would like to have some influence on the club. I mean a guy like Johnny Sain. And what happens to him? He moves around a lot. He has to, because as soon as he asserts himself the manager wants to get rid of him, no matter how good a job he's doing.

287

At the start of this trip Joe Schultz called in Steve Hovley and said, "I want you to start dressing like a major-league ballplayer."

Joe only said that because Steve wears Levi's to the park sometimes and thinks nothing of wearing his famous nondescript corduroy jacket seven days in a row (after all, what's a jacket for?). Steve said he thought that was pretty interesting, because when Joe says to dress like a major-league ballplayer he means there's a certain style of dress followed by baseball players and you're supposed to conform. In fact Hovley and I believe the style of the major-league player is not much style at all. Oh, they wear expensive sportscoats and turtleneck sweaters, and a lot of them started wearing Nehru jackets—just as they were going out of style. But the mode is often *nouveau riche* jazzy. I consider it the same kind of taste that features plastic flamingoes on the front lawn or a bullfighter painted on black velvet in the living room.

Started the trip with Steve Hovley assigned to room with Greg Goossen and me with Steve Barber. I told Gabe Paul that Hovley and I wanted to room together and he said, "Marvin Milkes has to approve roommates. Why don't you stay where you are until we hear from Milkes?" I agreed to, reluctantly.

When we met at the hotel desk to pick up our keys, however, Hovley and I decided it was all very silly. It was silly for Milkes to worry about something like roommates and silly for us, as grown men, to care. So we switched, simply by having Steve Barber swap keys with Hovley.

Paul was furious. "I told you to wait until I had a chance to check with Milkes," he said.

I told him we thought it was too unimportant to wait.

"I tell you one thing," Paul said. "Don't ever ask me for any favors."

All right for you too.

Hovley and I were going to see *Midnight Cowboy* here but decided to wait until we got to Baltimore. We figured a good movie might just save Baltimore. On the other hand, probably nothing can.

Clubhouse speech by Joe Schultz. "Boys, I guess you know we're not drawing as well at home as we should. If we don't draw fans, we're not going to be making the old cabbage. I'm in this just as much as you are. We're all in it for the same thing. I'm going to lay it right out on the barrelhead. We got to win some games so we can draw some people.

"Oh yeah, and for you new guys, Brunet, it's two-and-a-half hours after a ballgame. That's curfew."

Tommy Davis started to giggle, and pretty soon everybody was laughing and looking at Brunet, and then he joined in and the whole thing became absurd. I mean, the idea of Brunet, coming in two-and-a-half hours after a game is ridiculous. *Nobody* gets in that fast, except maybe McNertney.

AUGUST

6

Carl Yastrzemski was recently fined $500 for loafing and I've been keeping an eye on him. Sure enough, he hit a ball to second base today and loafed all the way to first. I'm afraid Yastrzemski has a bit of dog in him. Always did, and people around baseball knew it all the time. When things are going good Yastrzemski will go all out. When things aren't going so well he'll give a half-ass effort. But he's got so much ability that the only thing you can do is put up with him.

I asked a few of the Red Sox if they thought he deserved the fine and I thought they would defend him. But they said, "He deserved it all the way."

We took the second-straight game from the Red Sox tonight. We were losing 4–2 when I came in with the bases loaded. I threw one pitch and we were out of the inning with a double play. Then we came from behind to win it. I enjoyed my contribution.

AUGUST

7

Today I didn't make any contribution and I was furious. We had a 4–2 lead going into the ninth and then came the trouble. Before it was over O'Donoghue and Locker were bombed, the game was lost 5–4 and I, the very man who had gotten two out with a single pitch the day before, remained in the bullpen, warming up. *Warming up!* for goodness sakes.

Among the annoyed was Jim Pagliaroni. "If they're not going to use you in a situation like this," Pag said, "why the hell do they warm you up?"

I don't know. I honestly don't know.

Ray Oyler contributed a key ninth-inning error to the loss and spent a long time after the game facing his locker, drinking beer and playing genuine sorrow. The clubhouse was routine morgue and four sportswriters were trying to ask Oyler about the error—in hushed tones, of course. Newspapermen are required to play the sorrow game too, although why they should care, I can't imagine.

O'Donoghue, surveying the scene, said, "Goddam vultures. Hanging around waiting for the meat to dry." And Tommy Harper said, "What the hell do they need quotes for? They all saw the play." And Don Mincher said, "Miserable bastards." And Jim Bouton said, to himself, "Aw shit."

On the bus from the airport to the Shoreham Hotel in Washington we passed a huge government building that had a bronze plaque on the front announcing it had been "erected in 1929." And Greg Goossen said, "That's quite an erection."

Hovley and Goossen were put in the same room again, so I assumed I'd been put in with Barber again and switched keys with Goossen. Then I went to Gabe Paul and told him Hovley and I wanted to room together again. And he said, "Well, I've got you in a room by yourself this trip."

It's interesting that they'd rather pay for a single room than have me room with Hovley. Just like the Yankees. They must think whatever it is I have that they don't like is catching.

I didn't tell Paul about the switch. Let him find out himself.

Hovley, Pagliaroni and I closed out the evening on the roof for a little beaver-shooting. We didn't get many good shots in but we kept trying. And Hovley said, "This is like fishing. All you need is a couple of nibbles to keep you trying."

O'Donoghue wound up his time in Boston screaming at the kids who lean out of the stands and throw things into the bullpen and at the mob of them that collects outside Fenway Park demanding autographs. O'Donoghue has a very low kid threshold.

He'd have hated me as a kid. I remember once at a Giant game in the Polo Grounds I took the top of a Dixie cup and scaled it down onto the field during the game. I couldn't believe how far it went— clear out to the infield. It landed halfway between the mound and home plate. I was scared when I saw it was actually going to drop onto the field and I looked around to see if anybody had noticed me throwing it. Johnny Antonelli, who was pitching for the Giants, walked off the mound, bent down, picked it up and put it in his back pocket. I got a huge kick out of that. Imagine, Johnny Antonelli picking up the cover of my Dixie cup.

One time my brothers and I and a friend decided that the way to catch foul balls in left field at the Polo Grounds was to have a net and stick it out over the stands at the proper moment. We constructed this big net, put a 12-foot pole at the end of it and we were in business. We soon found, though, that we couldn't catch anything smaller than a flying barnyard in it. So we practiced and practiced and after a while we felt confident enough to take the net up to the Polo Grounds. On the train a lady asked us what we were going fishing for. We said baseballs. She gave us a funny look.

At the park we were refused admission. There was a rule they just made up: no nets. So we retreated to plot strategy. We decided to walk in one behind the other, net at our sides (away from the ticket taker, of course) and coats hiding the net and pole. It worked perfectly. Except for one thing. We didn't catch a single baseball.

AUGUST
8

Possibly because we finally all understood thoroughly by now that this club is going nowhere, the guys are very loose. Today, for example, everybody in the clubhouse is listening to Cal Tjader or somebody like him, keeping time by banging clothes hangers on chairs and John Donaldson, who is so skinny we call him Bones, puts two baseballs under his uniform shirt in order to get a set of shoulders, and towels around his middle so he has a belly, and he pulls his pants up so he looks like an old-time ballplayer, and he goes through the silent-film baseball-player routine in time to the music and everybody is having a great time.

"Hey, Mike," I say to Mike Hegan. "I wonder what this club would be like if we were fighting for a pennant."

Mike promptly puckers up his lips, sucks his cheeks in, pulls his legs together, presses his buttocks together with his hands and walks around the room as though he had been dipped in concrete. "Very tight," he says.

Eddie O'Brien continues working at being one of the boys. He didn't even call Marty Pattin for reading a magazine in the bullpen. And when I'm warming up in the bullpen he stands about fifteen feet behind the catcher in order to intercept any wayward knuckleballs. Come to think of it, everybody has been nice to me lately. Well, almost everybody. Plaza lets me take new baseballs out of his ballbag. Sal Maglie actually *smiles* at me. (Shudder. When the friendly undertaker starts smiling he may know more than you do.) I even get the feeling that if I talked to Joe Schultz he'd listen. Maybe (drool) I'll ask for another start.

That's what I say, and sometimes that's what I feel. Then there's a game like we had today. We lost it 10–3, which isn't the point. What is the point is that Brunet, who started, had a 2–0 lead, and as soon as he got into a little trouble the phone rang in the bullpen. I grabbed my glove because I knew it had to be me. It was for Barber and Pattin.

They warmed up and Barber got called. Bang, we're losing 4–2. Then Pattin, and it's 6–2. Again the phone rang, and again I grabbed my glove. This time they wanted O'Donoghue. He got clobbered too. Now the score is 10–3 in the eighth and the phone rings again. This time I don't reach for my glove. But it's for me. So I warm up and pitch the ninth. One guy gets on with a single, another on an error. Nobody hits the ball good and I'm out of the inning. This doesn't change the score, which remains 10–3.

I'm saving up all my statistics for my next year's salary drive. I can just see Marvin Milkes when I whip them out. He'll say the same thing Charlie Brown said to Lucy.

"Charlie, I kept statistics on our ball team last season," Lucy says, "and here they are. There were 57 ballgames played, 57 ballgames lost; 3,000 runs scored by the opposition, two runs scored by our team; 900 walks given up by our team and . . ."

And after a while, Charlie Brown says, "Lucy, tell your statistics to shut up."

Steve Hovley and I spent the afternoon at the National Gallery of Art. Hovley said he had to check to see if Van Gogh's paintings were dry.

AUGUST

9

Took Hovley to my favorite Washington restaurant after the game, El Bodegon. He's been hitting the hell out of the ball and I thought we should celebrate. We had margueritas before dinner and Hovley remarked that before this year he'd *never* had a drink of any kind. But in Louisville he decided to do some testing. So he had a bourbon. Then he tried a Bloody Mary. Then a martini. Then a mint julep. All in the same evening. He said it was very interesting. He also said he had no hangover. I believe most of what Steve Hovley says.

Hovley was particularly interested in the flamenco guitarist at El Bodegon. He says he can't decide whether to play winter ball or stay home and learn to play the guitar.

Perhaps it was the heat. Or maybe just the stage of the season. Or the phase of the moon. No matter the cause, we got into an insane argument in the bullpen. It was a chicken-egg thing and it went like this: Can a pitcher get more strikeouts in a high-scoring game because he faces more hitters?

I said no. I said it didn't matter how many hitters you faced, that you could get only 27 outs in a nine-inning ballgame, and that the ratio between strikeouts and other kinds of outs would not change. Brabender and Pagliaroni thought differently. They said if you faced a hundred hitters you had a lot more chances to strike somebody out than if you faced only 27 or 28. And as he talked, Brabender got hot, and Brabender getting hot is like Old Faithful erupting. So I tried to cool him off. "Gene, you've got to learn that when you argue with somebody it's not a personal thing," I said. "I may disagree with you but I still like you. I just think you're wrong. And that's no reason to get angry."

"I'm angry because you won't accept facts," he said.

"Well, I don't think it's a fact," I said. "I think what I say is a fact and that you won't accept it. But I'm not angry at you because of it."

"You know something?" Brabender said. "You're lucky. Where I come from we just talk for a little while. After that we start to hit."

I felt lucky indeed.

The whole argument seemed to irritate Marty Pattin. "Who wants to listen to all that stuff?" he said. "Why can't we just sit here and watch the ballgame?"

Poor Marty. It's not that he has no soul. It's just that he's been getting bombed lately.

Ran into Jack Mann, who is the author of *The Decline and Fall of the Yankees*. Vic Ziegel of the New York *Post* had asked me to review the book for his column, and when I did he refused to run it. He said I was so hard on the Yankees it would get me into trouble. As things turned out, it couldn't have done me any more harm.

Mann had recently written a piece for the Washington *Daily News* about being mugged by three young men in a park. He said that he believed he understood what motivated the kids and that he felt no hatred toward them. The young men were black, but Mann revealed this only under pressure. His point was that their color was irrelevant—that is, the point of the story was that it would be a better world if indeed it were.

I tell this story because it reminded me of something that happened to Mike Marshall in Cleveland. He was roughed up by a pack of about 15 kids. When it was all over the police had great difficulty dragging out of him the fact that the kids were black. He didn't think it should make any difference either.

There was a difference, though—in Mike's pitching. The injuries he received fighting the kids off seemed superficial. Nevertheless, it was at precisely this point that he went from being our best pitcher to our worst.

Brant Aylea came up to me today and said that Ted Williams was asking about me.

"What was he asking?" I said. "About what kind of person I was?"

"Oh shit no," Alyea said. "What difference does it make what kind of person you are? We're all just merchandise anyway. He wanted to know whether you were in tight with the Pilots and whether they considered you in their plans for the future."

"It's obvious from the way they're using me that they don't consider me in their plans," I said. "So tell Williams I can probably be had right now for a song, maybe a short medley."

Right after that Bob Short, the owner of the Washington club, came by and Alyea introduced me to him. I congratulated him on the fine job he was doing in Washington and he said that I was doing a pretty good job myself. I said I was glad he'd noticed.

What a beautiful day. Imagine playing for Teddy Ballgame. That's what he calls himself, in his autobiography too. What isn't generally known, except around the comfortable confines of the ballpark, is that he thinks of himself as "Teddy Ballgame of the MFL."

That's the Major Fucking Leagues.

Pagliaroni told a story about Joe Brown, the general manager of the Pittsburgh club. Brown called a meeting of the players and said, "Boys, we're fighting for the entertainment dollar. We have to learn to get along with the fans and get along with the writers. And we have to be more colorful as ballplayers."

That very night the Pirates got into an extra-inning game and Pagliaroni scored the winner in the fifteenth. "I come around and I touch home plate," Pag said, "and as I run toward our dugout I take a big slide, feet first, all the way into it."

The next morning there was a call from Joe Brown. "What the hell were you doing out there?" Brown said. "What are you, some kind of clown?"

And Pagliaroni said, "I was just competing for the entertainment dollar, Joe."

AUGUST
10

Talking about Yastrzemski not hustling recalled one of the great non-hustlers of all time, Roger Maris. Rodg always went to first base as though he had sore feet. If he hit a home run it didn't matter, of course. But every time he popped up or hit a routine grounder, it would take him a half-hour to get to first base—if he got there at all. He'd often just peel off halfway down and head for the dugout.

So Houk would call a meeting and he'd say, "Boys, it doesn't look good if we don't run the ball out. I want everybody to show some hustle out there."

And Maris would go out there and damned if he wouldn't do the same thing all over again. I could never believe Ralph's patience. I know Maris was sensitive to what was written about him in the papers, and I don't know why Houk didn't just blast him to the reporters. But he never did. And Maris continued to loaf.

Johnny Sain quit or was fired today. I'm amazed. Also not surprised.

Going into the last of the eighth we're ahead 5–4. O'Donoghue, who has relieved Brabender, has pitched three good innings. Now they get a couple of hits off him and he's lifted for John Gelnar. This isn't too bad a choice. Gelnar was knocked out in his last start, but his relief pitching hasn't been bad. Except he's hit this time and now the score is 5–5 and Gelnar's out.

Who comes in, Bouton? Nope. Steve Barber. We lose 7–5.

Because I have nobody else to talk to I ask Eddie O'Brien, "Eddie, what the hell is going on out there?"

"I don't know," Eddie O'Brien says. "I can't figure it out either."

Well, maybe I can. Maybe I'm about to be traded to the Senators. They can't finish first, but they can finish second. I still think I have a chance to be a hero someplace.

I try, but it remains most difficult to convey the quality of the banter in the back of the bus. There is zaniness to it, and earthiness, and often a quality of *non sequitur* that I find hilarious. Have an example from our trip to the Washington airport.

Greg Goossen: "Hey, does anybody here have any Aqua Velva?"

Fred Talbot: "No, but I gotta take a shit, if that'll help."

I've had some thoughts on what separates a professional athlete from other mortals. In a tight situation the amateur says, "I've failed in this situation many times. I'll probably do so again." In a tight situation the professional says (and means it), "I've failed in this situation and I've succeeded. Since each situation is a separate test of my abilities, there's no reason why I shouldn't succeed this time."

Then there is also the case of the professional player who is not professional enough. He goes on a fifteen-game hitting streak and says, "Nobody can keep this up." And as the streak progresses his belief in his ability to keep it alive decreases to the point where it's almost impossible for him to get a hit.

The *real* professional—and by that I suppose I mean the exceptional professional—can convince himself that each time at bat is an individual performance and that there is no reason he can't go on hitting forever.

Is that clear? If it is, perhaps you ought to check with your doctor.

AUGUST
11

Cleveland

I'm still trying to decide why I haven't been in more ballgames in crucial situations and all I can do is agree with Hovley that it's because they think I'm weird and throw a weird pitch. I need a new image. What I ought to do is take up chewing tobacco and let the dark brown run down the front of my uniform and walk up and down the dugout with a slight, brave limp and tape on my wrist and say things like, "goddammit" and "shit" and "let's get these guys." Then, instead of being weird, I'd be rough and tough.

I think I'd do it, except I can't stand the thought of all that brown down the front of my uniform.

We may not be winning a lot of ballgames, but we've got a lot of spirit. In fact we might have the best "around the horn" in the league. You throw the ball around the horn—catcher to first baseman to short-stop to second baseman to third baseman—after an infield out, and you do it with a lot of élan. We get better at it all the time.

AUGUST
12

Pitched two more innings in another losing cause. We were down three runs when I came in and down three when I came out. The only problem I had was with Home Run Baker, a new Cleveland kid who's been hitting vicious line drives all over the place. This time

298

he hit one right back at me and the only way I was able to avoid certain death was to perform a perfect veronica. Olé.

I also struck out Hawk Harrelson and Duke Simms. Double olé.

Called Mike Marshall. He's alive and well and pitching in Toledo. He's 3–1 and sticking to his no-plan plan, the one Sal Maglie said wouldn't do. Mike said that Bennie Borgmann, the scout, asked him what the problem was, that he had heard there was some personality difficulty. Mike said he didn't know of any. The next day Borgmann talked to Jack Tighe, the manager, and was told "Mike's fine. Gives me 100 percent. You just leave him alone and let him do it his way and he'll be all right."

Borgmann was impressed and asked Marshall if he wanted to go back with Seattle. He said no, not as long as there was no change in the situation there.

We go home after tomorrow night's game. It's commercial all the way with a lay-over in Chicago. Which means we'll get home at four-thirty in the morning local time, but actually about seven-thirty body time. This is done so we can spend all day with our families. It's also done to save a night of hotel expenses. Me, I'll be home with my family, but I'll be in bed all day, sleeping.

Steve Barber suggested to Sal Maglie that he send Brabender home a day early so that he wouldn't miss a night's sleep. Brabender opens for us against Baltimore. And Sal said, "The last time we did that the guy went only two-and-two-thirds innings. So we're not going to do it any-more."

I don't remember what that's called in logic, but the fallacy is: B follows A. Therefore A caused B.

Steve Hovley went down with an inside pitch tonight and took first base. I asked where the ball hit him and he said it didn't hit him at all.

"You sure went down to first like you'd been hit," I said.

"Yeah, that's what you have to do," Steve said. "You have to jump up, throw your bat aside and start down to first as if everybody in the ballpark could see the ball hit you. This intimidates the umpire."

Ray Oyler in the back of the bus: "Boys, I had all the ingredigents for a great piece of ass last night—plenty of time, and a hardon. All I lacked was a broad."

AUGUST
13

Beat Cleveland 5–3 and it was a struggle all the way. Brunet fell three runs behind early but managed to hold on. The reason he was able to hold on is that every time he had a couple of men on base, Fred Talbot yelled at him, "C'mon, fat boy, regroup out there."

There was a lot of grousing about the flight home. We had a three-hour wait after the game was over and then an hour-and-a-half wait in Chicago. If we had a charter flight we could have gotten in to Seattle at about twelve-thirty instead of four-thirty. The ballclub argues that it costs too much money to charter a plane and generally we just shrug and figure, well, it probably does.

There was a United Air Lines man along on the trip, so I said to him, "Just out of curiosity, what does it cost to fly a team like this from Cleveland to Seattle on regularly scheduled flights?"

He said he couldn't give me an exact figure, but if he had to approximate, he'd say $5,200, give or take a few hundred. And what, I asked, would it cost to charter a jet to fly from Cleveland to Seattle?

"I couldn't give you an exact figure," he said. "But I can tell you that it costs $6,200 to charter a plane from New York to Seattle. So if you could get a plane out of Cleveland, it would be a little bit less, probably around $5,900."

Naturally I promptly told Mincher that the only difference between a charter flight and commercial was $700. Just as naturally, Mincher goes to Gabe Paul and says, "What's the story, Gabe? We found out that there's only a $700 difference between charter and commercial. And we don't think the ballclub should be stingy with that kind of money. They should get the guys home at a decent hour."

"I don't know where you got your figures," Paul said.

"Bouton got them from the United Airlines man," Mincher said. Just then the man came along down the aisle, and when Minch told him what we were arguing about, he backed off. "I didn't give any exact figures," he said.

"You tell Mincher that there's a hell of a difference," Paul said. "Tell him."

"Oh yeah," the guy said. "The numbers are real big. I don't know exactly what they are, but there's a hell of a difference."

Mincher stalked off. Later on he came over to me and said, "What the hell are you trying to tell us about $700?"

I told him the way I got my information and said, "Why would I make those numbers up?"

"Well, somebody's lying in this deal," Mincher said.

"It's not me, Minch."

"No, I don't think it's you," Minch said. And he went away mad.

The country western music got a big workout in the clubhouse after the win. There are four or five different tape-players around and they make quite a racket. One of the favorites is "Dirty Old Egg-Sucking Dog." Gene Brabender knows all the words to that one. Another is, "Happy Birthday, Joe Beam." It starts out, "They're hanging Joe Beam today . . ." Seems that Joe Beam killed eleven guys before he was twelve and they said he was an "unruly boy." And right at the end, when they hang him, they break out into "Happy Birthday, Joe Beam."

Breaks us up.

AUGUST
14

Seattle

Today Joe Schultz said to John Kennedy, who just had the cast taken off his knee: "How's your old hinge, John?" Joe Schultz also said, "The starters here will be Brabender, Segui, Talbot and Brunet." When he said Talbot I winced, and Talbot caught it and said, "Eat your heart out, Bouton."

And when we were going over the hitters a lot of the comments consisted of: "He likes the ball over the plate."

Let's see, now. When the ball is over the plate isn't that what the umpires call a strike?

Also, there seemed to be a lot of first-ball hitters in the crowd. Brooks Robinson, Don Buford, Paul Blair, all first-ball hitters. One day I want to hear somebody say, "Good third-ball hitter. Likes to hit that third pitch." Then I'll have learned something.

At the end of the meeting Joe Schultz said, "Anybody got anything else to say about this club?" And in a very low voice, I said, "Pretty good ballclub."

And Joe Schultz said, "Well, hell, let's go beat the shit out of them. Fuck 'em. They ain't no different than anybody else."

He was right. They beat us too. The score was 2–1. Gene Brabender pitched a helluva game.

I was warming up in the bullpen when a fan leaned out and said, "Hey Jim, how do you pitch to Frank Robinson?" I told him the truth. "Reluctantly," I said.

Billy Williams just got called up. He was on the Seattle Angels club with me last year when it was Triple-A. He's played *eighteen* years of minor-league ball. He's a good-hitting outfielder. He should have had a better shot but I think he's one of those Negroes who wasn't quite good enough to be a star and wound up a good minor-leaguer.

The situation of the Negro in baseball is not as equitable as it seems. He still has to be better than his white counterparts to do as well. I recall a story Mike Marshall told about a guy in the Detroit Tiger organization named Ike Brown, who hit .300 for a number of years in Triple-A and was the International League All-Star third baseman for a couple of years. He drove in a lot of runs too, but he was never even invited to spring training by the Tigers. Mike says the fact that he was black must have had a lot to do with it. "How many Negroes on the Detroit club?" Mike said. "Earl Wilson, Gates Brown and Willie Horton. Two stars, and Brown is the best pinch-hitter in the business."

This brings up a point. There are a lot of Negro stars in the game. There aren't too many average Negro players. The obvious conclusion is that there is some kind of quota system. It stands to reason that if 19 of the top 30 hitters in the major leagues are black, as they were in 1968, then almost two thirds of the hitters should be black. Obviously it's not that way at all. In the case of the Tigers the fact that only three of their players are black is no less astonishing.

302

Joe Sparma and Al Kaline have a company that runs baseball clinics around the country. They line up the players to run the clinics and pay a thousand dollars for three mornings of work. It sounded like an unbelievable deal in the letter I got. They wanted me, Ray Oyler, Wayne Comer and two or three other guys. We wanted to know what the next step would be, so we asked Ray Oyler, because he'd played with the Tigers, to call Kaline or Sparma and check. This was about two weeks ago. Tonight I asked Oyler what he'd found out.

"I called Sparma twice," he said. "I wasn't able to get him."

"Oh," I said.

Consider this. There's quite a bit of money involved and Ray Oyler, one of the boys, the man everybody likes, the "in" infielder, makes two phone calls, and gives up. Zero. On the other hand, Mike Marshall arranges to have a railroad car to ship our automobiles from Tempe to Seattle. It takes a lot; phone calls, letters, a lot of organizing. But Oyler is okay and Marshall is a weirdo.

A good word about Sal Maglie. Lately he's been calling down to the bullpen to have me warm up even when I'm not going to get into the game. It makes it easier for me to get a catcher.

AUGUST
16

It's been nippy these last evenings and my fingers have felt a bit wooden. It's not freezing, of course, but the temperature gets down to about 55. So I've been lighting up and using a handwarmer.

Talbot: "What the hell do you need a handwarmer for? Dammit, it's only 60 degrees."

Pattin: "Oh, he's just got to be different. You know him."

Bouton: "Marty, why don't you go feed your gopher?"

I was sorry I said that. Although Marty has been giving up a lot of home runs lately, it's not the kind of thing you mention. He got into the game and gave up two more, which made me feel bad. What made me feel worse was me getting into the game and giving up three runs in two innings. It was a terrible performance. I was wild as hell. I kept telling myself it was because I hadn't been pitching enough and I was angry at Joe, then I got angry because the score was 10–2 against us when he put me in, and when the ball would come back from the catcher I'd slap my glove at it. So instead of thinking about pitching and how to get the ball over the plate I was thinking about being angry. Did I say I loved this game?

AUGUST
18

The Orioles beat us for the fourth-straight time. The score was 15–3. Said Fred Talbot: "We got no business scheduling these guys." Then, "This Baltimore outfit can sure fluff up your ERA."

Sure can. Especially mine. I came into the game in the second inning. George Brunet had had some bad luck; a few bleeders, a few shots, and the game was gone. I knew it was gone because I was in it. Second inning, bases loaded, one out. The first pitch was a good knuckleball that went by McNertney to the screen. A run scored. I walked the hitter, filling the bases again. I got the next guy on a strikeout, but then I got behind and had to come in with a couple of fastballs. Double; two runs. Now all three of poor Brunet's runs have scored and I've got runners on second and third. The pitcher comes up and hits the second pitch into left for a single and Sal Maglie comes out to the mound.

"We're going to have to take you out," Sal says.

"But, Sal," I say, "I need work. We're losing 10–0. What difference does it make now?"

"We brought you in with the bases loaded and you didn't do the job. We have to get you out of there."

So I turned around, walked off the mound and into the dugout. Since I hadn't really thrown much, I then ran out to the bullpen to get some more in. When I got there I picked up a ball and said, "I'd like to do a little throwing now. Who wants to catch?"

"I'm not catching," Ranew said.

"Pag, I'd like to do some throwing," I said.

"Why?" Pagliaroni said.

"Because I didn't get the right feel of the knuckleball and I think I have to do some throwing."

"I don't think you have to do any throwing," Pagliaroni said.

"Well, I think I have to. And I'm the one who decides when I throw and when I don't throw. Right?"

Nobody answered. I glared around the bullpen and no one would look me in the eye. So I sat down and sulked.

Eddie O'Brien had been listening to all of this, of course, but he wasn't going to get involved. He's only the bullpen coach. I decided to involve him. "Eddie, I need to do some throwing," I said. "Do you want to have somebody catch me, or what?"

"You better check with Sal," Eddie said.

"What for? Since I've been back from Vancouver I've had an agreement that I didn't have to check with Sal."

"You better check with Sal anyway," Eddie said. "Especially since you just came out of a ballgame. He might not want you to do any throwing."

So I got up and went down to the dugout. We're still not out of the inning and Pattin is getting pounded. I waited until the inning was over and went up to Maglie. "Sal, I'd like to do a little throwing in the bullpen. Is it all right?"

"No, no. It wouldn't look good. You just came out of a ballgame."

"It'll look okay. It'll look like I was working on something."

"Ah, crissakes. Ask Joe."

"Joe, do you mind if I get some throwing in the bullpen?"

"No. If you want to, go ahead."

Back in the bullpen I said to O'Brien, "Sal and Joe said it was all right if I do some throwing."

O'Brien didn't say a word. He just got up and walked all the way in to the bench. Meanwhile, no one was getting up to catch me. So I stood there, feeling awkward, and mad.

When O'Brien came back he gave Pagliaroni a nod. "It's okay," he said. "Joe said he could throw."

I could feel my neck flame. "I *told* you he said it was all right. What the hell are you going down there for?"

"I just wanted to check," O'Brien said.

"You mean you didn't believe me?" I said. "I have a bad outing or two, Eddie, and now suddenly my word isn't good anymore? Huh, Eddie? I'm not telling the truth, right?"

305

So Pag got up, very slowly put on his glove and mask and crouched down behind the plate. I started to get ready to throw when I heard John Gelnar say, "Come on, Merritt, I'd like to do some throwing myself." Merritt just laughed.

"Don't be a wise guy, Gelnar," I said. "This may be funny to you but it's not funny to me."

"If you're mad at us, don't take it out on John," Pagliaroni said.

"You didn't hear what he said," I told Pag. "He's trying to make fun of the fact that I need to do some throwing. This isn't a popularity contest. If it's between me doing my job or being one of the boys, it's going to be my job that comes first."

I started to throw, but it didn't make me feel any better. After about forty pitches, steaming all the time and thinking how wrong it was for O'Brien to check up on me, how mean it was of Pagliaroni and Ranew to just sit there, how unfair it was of Gelnar to try to make a joke of it, I marched down to the front of the bullpen and made a speech.

"You know something? There are going to be better days for me, but it's going to be hard to forget what people on this bench were like when things were bad. O'Brien, you've been nice to me lately and I thought it was because you were changing. Now I realize it was only because I was pitching well. You're really the same old guy just waiting for the right moment to come out and be yourself."

"You're making an ass out of yourself," Pagliaroni said.

"Well, maybe I'll apologize tomorrow," I said. "But I think I said something that needed to be said."

"Yeah, and how about the night you said, 'The hell with the rest of the guys. They don't pay my salary?' " Pagliaroni said.

I said I didn't know what the hell he was talking about.

"You know, the day we had that extra-inning game," Pagliaroni said. "You left in the ninth inning and when somebody asked you where you were going you said home, and he asked you what about team spirit, and you said, 'The hell with the rest of the guys. They don't pay my salary.' "

"Pag, that actually happened," I said. "But it was meant to be funny. I was smiling when I said it and it was supposed to be a joke. Anyway, it's unfair of you to bring that up now. You're just jumping on a guy when he's down. You're taking something you heard thirdhand and was misinterpreted in the first place and you're trying to tell me you're using that as an excuse not to catch me."

There must have been steam coming out of my ears by now, because Eddie O'Brien said, "Go take a shower."

"Okay, I'll take a shower," I said. "Only I want you guys to think about what I said."

"I'll think about it," Pagliaroni said. "My whole life revolves around Jim Bouton."

"I guess you won't think about it much at that," I said.

In the clubhouse I stomped around for a while and had a few beers, which I seldom do. I watched Brunet getting dressed and I nearly fell off my stool. "George, I got to know something," I said. "This is not a knock. I don't mind guys who do things differently. But I got to know. *Did you forget to put on your undershorts?*"

"No, I never wear undershorts," Brunet said. "Hell, the only time you need them is if you get into a car wreck. Besides, this way I don't have to worry about losing them."

I guess that made me feel better, because I suddenly remembered something Mike Marshall once told me. "It doesn't hurt to say you're sorry," Marshall said, "even if you don't mean it."

All right, all right. I'll apologize. So I sat there eating spicy hot dogs and drinking beer and listening to the radio. When O'Donoghue came in—early, because he'd pitched—I stuck my hand out and said, "I want to apologize for losing my cool in the bullpen tonight."

"Okay, fine," O'Donoghue said.

Later on Gelnar said, "Sure, fine," and Ranew said, "Okay," and Pagliaroni smiled and said, "Likewise."

I didn't apologize to Eddie O'Brien. There are some things I just will not do.

McNertney stopped by my locker to—of all things—apologize. It was for the ball that went back to the screen. "Jesus, it just hit off my glove," he said. "It was a good knuckleball too."

The dear boy.

My wife says I was wrong. She says I blew my cool and that's not something I ought to do, especially if I plan to go into politics some day. She said she thought I was right, but that being right has nothing to do with it. "You won the battle," she said, "and you lost the war."

Maybe she's right. Maybe the only kind of politician I can be is the kind who sits on the sidelines and hollers. Take a guy like Ralph Nader. He's not a politician, I know, but how many politicians have contributed as much to American life as he has? So maybe I can find a way to be heard, to be effective without surrendering my right to pop off when I think I'm right.

In fact, though, I don't really think I did myself any good in the bullpen tonight. I mean what will get around about it is not that I said some tough things, but that I delivered a short speech in front of the bullpen. Nobody delivers short speeches in front of the bullpen. My trouble is I forgot one of baseball's most important axioms: "He's a helluva guy. Wouldn't say shit if he had a mouthful."

AUGUST
19

When I got to the clubhouse I was confronted by Pagliaroni. "Did you send me the check, Bouton?"

"Check? Me? Money?" I said. "How much did I owe you?"

"No. You don't owe me. I got a check for $100 from the guy who won $2700 on Home Run for the Money because I hit one. I just figured it might be a phony from you."

I bit the check and pronounced it genuine. "Nope, I didn't send it," I said.

It was then calculated that if Pagliaroni got $100 for winning his man $2700, Fred Talbot should have gotten a thousand from Donald Dubois. Did he ever get anything? "Nope," Talbot said.

Gee, wonder what old Dubois would do with all that money.

Said Talbot: "I hope he gets drunk on it, wrecks his car and kills himself."

George Brunet (who does not wear undershorts), was talking about the Negro in baseball, Tommy Harper in particular. "You know, for a colored player, he's not a bad hustler. Hell, he wants to play ball."

Before the father-and-son game Sunday, Pagliaroni said to Wayne Comer: "Now, no fair giving your son a greenie."

Greenie or no, the Comer boy stole the show. When he came to bat he took the handle and knocked some imaginary dirt off the bottom of his little sneakers, then he rubbed dirt on his hands, gripped the bat, tapped the plate with it and showed all the mannerisms of the big-league players. Said Fred Talbot: "Comer's kid has a little hot dog in him, doesn't he?"

The kids beat the fathers 40–0, and Sibby Sisti said, "Forty runs, for crissakes, and nobody gets knocked down." And McNertney said that he was standing next to Sal Maglie during the game and swore he heard Sal saying, "He's a first-ball hitter"—"a high-ball hitter"—"a fastball hitter"—and none of the kids was over four feet tall.

For some reason that reminded me of my manager in Amarillo, Sheriff Robinson, who used to say about every hitter, "Jam him." And then later on we talked with some old-timers who'd played with Robinson and they said, "He was a pretty good ballplayer. But we used to jam the hell out of him."

Max Soriano, one of the owners, had a party at his house for the players. It was supposed to be held on an off day except a lot of the players objected that it would ruin their day. So it was switched to Sunday night and, of course, it was a fine party, good food, bar, and the wives enjoyed getting dressed up.

The best line of the evening was delivered by Joe Schultz: "What are you drinking there, honey?" he said to Fred Talbot's wife.

"Coca-Cola," she said.

And Joe Schultz said: "You'll never make it on that, my dear."

This broke everybody up, and Bob Locker said, "You better write that down, Bouton."

My note-taking is beginning to make the natives restless.

A couple of guys have been needling me about it. Tossing fat on the fire, Steve Hovley my roommate, who knows, asks, "Hey, why are you writing down all those notes?"

"Yeah, what's he writing those notes for?" Fred Talbot adds.

So Hovley tells him. "When a guy smells the end of his career coming, he usually starts writing little notes to himself. You'll see. It will happen to you too."

Steve Hovley sauntered over to my locker and asked what was new on the Gatorade front. Not much, friend. Milkes snooped around to find out if I'd actually bought the Gatorade and if it had been drunk by the players. Everybody's checking up on me these days. Then he told Johnny McNamara that he wasn't going to pay for it.

309

What I ought to do about it, of course, is forget it. I never bothered about small things with ballclubs; things like cabfare if I did an appearance, or excess baggage. I'd much rather negotiate them out of $1,000 at contract time than bother about small sums. But things have been so petty around here I'm going to keep the pressure on in the case of the missing Gatorade money. May justice triumph.

Today, with the Orioles gone and the Detroit Tigers coming in, Joe Schultz said, "Well, boys, we got that other outfit out of here with all their bullshit. Fuck it. Let's go get 'em, let's start winning ballgames." We dashed out onto the field cheering. Some of us would run through a cheesecloth curtain for that man.

Bullpen humor:
The attendance at the Baltimore games was respectable, but we're back to not drawing much for the Tigers. It is decided in the bullpen that the people who came to see us play the Orioles are the same kind who went to see the lions eat Christians.

There's going to be a Day soon for Tommy Harper, so John O'Donoghue is reminded of the Day that was given to him in Kansas City. "All my family and friends were there," O'Donoghue says. "And they gave me a Legionnaire's cap, a *used* Legionnaire's cap. They also gave me honorary memberships to all the drinking clubs in town. They gave me two plaques. And then they gave me a wallet, a brand-new wallet. I practically tore that damn thing apart looking for the money. I know there *had* to be something more than a used Legionnaire's cap and a wallet. But there wasn't."

"Hey, Merritt," Fred Talbot says to Merritt Ranew. "Tell Bouton to his face what you said about him last night."

Merritt's face gets red and he says, "I didn't say a thing." And I say, "What'd he say, Fred? You can tell me."

And Fred says: "I didn't get it all. Something about your mother."

I'm telling Talbot and Comer about El Bodeon in Washington and Talbot says, "If Bouton recommends a restaurant, you can be pretty sure they got some good Communist dishes."

Talbot says to Hovley: "Hey Hovley, some of the guys are starting to talk about your hair." He pauses. "And I'm one of them."

Then he turns to me. "You know, writing notes like that, Bouton, it's worse than whispering."

Talbot and Ranew get into a deep discussion about the South.

Ranew is from Georgia and Talbot is from Virginia. Talbot started it because he said that all the guys from the South are dumb.

"Well, where the hell are you from?" Ranew says, because he knows the answer.

"I'm from the north part of the South," Talbot says.

"It's better down where I live than it is where you are," Ranew says.

"Everything but the people," Talbot says. "The people are dumb."

I can't resist. I get into the discussion. "It's true, Merritt," I say. "What other state in the union has a governor that never even finished high school?"

"The reason they got this guy Lester Maddox," says Talbot, "is because he's so dumb. That's what they need to talk to all the dummies they got down there. They'd never understand a guy from Yale or Harvard or one of them colleges."

Ranew scratches his head. "I still think the South is better where I live."

"How can you compare which part of the country is better?" Talbot says. "I say mine, you say yours. How can you compare?"

"Why doesn't Bouton do some research on it tomorrow in the library and come back with some figures for us?" Ranew says.

"Nah, let's do it right here," Talbot says. "All right, let's start. How many dummies you got down there?"

By this time there is a lot of general laughter. I'm not prepared to explain why.

"I tell you one thing," Ranew says. "We got better-looking guys down where I am."

Talbot is shocked. "Better *looking?*" he says. "For crissakes, look at yourself. You've got hair like a sissy."

It's not a felicitous description. Ranew has his hair styled in the modern mode. It is not unattractive. Talbot wears his in an old-fashioned crew cut.

"Look at you," Talbot says, moving in for the kill. "You use hair spray and go to a goddam beauty parlor."

"With that hair *you've* got," Ranew says, "you could use a little beauty parlor yourself."

"I'll tell you one thing," Talbot says. "I don't walk around with hair spray and I don't look like a goddam sissy and I don't squat to piss, either."

Now the laughter has turned against Ranew and he is searching desperately for a counter. One can almost hear the file cards in his head fluttering.

"You know what you look like, Talbot?" Ranew says. "You look like a perch, a goddam perch."

"A *perch?*" Talbot says. "What the hell do you mean, a perch?"

"Well, you look like a perch," Ranew says. "Your head is square, you have hardly any nose at all, your eyes bulge out and you look like some kind of fish."

Now the laughter has turned on Talbot.

"But I don't look like a goddam sissy," he says.

I am afraid he is defeated.

That's not the funniest. The funniest is what happened to Ray Oyler. He was warming up Locker and caught a sinker right on the cup. It didn't even hit the ground first. Ding-dong! He went down on all fours and crawled around that way for a while. Then he limped into the dugout and vomited.

The boys were hysterical. We were getting beat a ballgame and we were *laughing*. Joe Schultz laughed so hard he had to take off his glasses, dry his eyes and hide his head in a warm-up jacket.

AUGUST
20

Big meeting before the game to discuss proposed items for negotiations in the player contract after the season. Mincher started it by saying, "Listen up, everybody." I once had a sergeant who said, "Listen up, everybody."

And Talbot said, "Hey, Bouton, no notes during the player-representative meeting."

I started jotting down some notes anyway in the hope that someone would confiscate them: "One bunch of carrots, loaf of bread, half-a-dozen eggs." No one tried. Foiled again.

The big topic was the reserve clause. There is some thought that we should try to eliminate it, or at least limit it. Joe Schultz led off the discussion by saying: "Boys, the reserve clause is the one thing you can't fool with. It's the foundation of this game. If you get rid of it we're all out of business. And I'm serious."

Contrary to popular belief the reserve clause is not a single paragraph (although its single intent is to bind a player to one club for as long as he lives or until his contract is disposed of). There are a whole set of rules which cover things like options, waivers, severance pay, moving allowance, etc. Many of these rules could be amended without upsetting the structure of the game.

It has been suggested that baseball adopt an option rule like pro football's. Instead I propose that we keep the one-way contract we currently play under and use it as a public relations lever to change some of the more repugnant aspects of the clause.

The football option rule gives only the illusion of freedom. A football player is required to sign a two-year contract, that is, one year plus an option for the next. At the end of the first year of his contract, he may elect to announce that he is playing out his option. In which case he is required to play only one more season and the team may, if it wishes, cut his salary by twenty-five percent. At the end of the option year he theoretically becomes a free agent and can sell his services to the highest bidder. Except that there is a rule which requires his new team to give his old team "equal value." What this amounts to then, is a trade. So the only right a football player has is to demand to be traded. We can do that too. Only it's not a demand, it's a plea.

One rule change I suggested was to have a player receive some kind of bonus when he got traded so that the owners wouldn't feel free to trade guys just to give them a change of scenery. Make it expensive to trade and they'll only do it when they have to.

Another thing that should be done, I said, is to take into consideration the amount of time a man has spent in the minors. If he's had only two years or so in the minors, $10,000 isn't bad to start with. But if a guy has been in the minors for five, seven, ten years or more, a guy who's in his thirties and has a wife and kids, it's unconscionable to start him at $10,000. What made me think of this was talking to Billy Williams the other day. I said he didn't have to tell me if he didn't want to, but I was curious about the kind of money he'd been making in the minors.

"I was making $1,300 a month," he said. That's for a five-month season.

"What did you make last year?"

"Last year I made $1,100 a month, and the year before I was under a thousand."

And this was his eighteenth season in the minors. "Did they sweeten up that $1,300 when they called you up?" I asked.

"Oh yeah, they sweetened it."

"How much?"

"I'm making $10,000." (That's a *rate,* or $1,666 a month.)

"What's so sweet about that? They *have* to pay you that."

"Yeah, that's true. I guess they have to."

It made me sad, and mad.

Finally there was a debate about severance pay. If a player is released in the middle of the season he gets thirty days pay. But if he gets released in spring training, actually at the end of it, he gets nothing. I suggested he get ninety days pay, on the ground that he should get paid for spring training, plus severance. I was voted down. The other guys said we should ask for only thirty days after spring training and sixty days during the season. And what I say is, it doesn't hurt to ask for more than you expect to get. Don't be afraid to climb those golden stairs.

Sitting in the bullpen tonight it seemed as if I'd never given my little bullpen lecture. The guys were coming over to tell me stories and I felt right back in the swing of things. I guess Mike Marshall was right. It doesn't hurt to apologize.

We scored a run in the ninth, which meant we had just enough runs to lose 4–3. I think that's six in a row now and we're in fifth place. Nobody talks about it, except Joe Schultz.

AUGUST
21

Gene Brabender sometimes walks around bellowing "cowabunga!" So I threw some trivia at him. "Bender, who first said 'cowabunga?' "

This upset Marty Pattin. He's never understood the importance of trivia. "Who the hell cares who said 'cowabunga,' for crissakes?" Pattin said.

"This is vital stuff, Marty," I said.

I gave Bender time, but he actually didn't know who said 'cowabunga'—even after I told him the line was "Cowabunga, Buffalo Bob." Poor fellow. It was, as almost everyone knows, Chief Thunder Thud on the "Howdy Doody" show.

It cost me a dollar to the pitchers' fund because I didn't back up third base the other night. The play was at second, so the fine wasn't altogether fair. I think they enjoy taking my money. The play got the talk around to how we backed up plays in high school, and I remembered that when I was a kid I didn't trust anybody else to make a play. I used to run into the outfield for relays and throw the ball home. Sometimes I'd even call the shortstop off a pop fly if I didn't think he was a very good fielder. Which reminded Talbot that high school was great. "In those days I'd pitch, bat fourth and hit .400," he said.

Not me. Even in high school I batted ninth. I knew at an early age I'd never be a hitter. Like I said, pitching's easier.

During the ballgame last night Brunet was watching carefully as Mickey Lolich warmed up. "Hey, you know something?" Brunet announced. "Lolich is fatter than I am." He then proceeded to shout the things that have been used to put him down over the years: "Hey, fatso" and "One man to a pair of pants out there." Fat man's revenge.

It seems awfully late in the season to be learning things about my knuckleball, or rather, my pattern of knuckleball pitching, but the process goes on. Sometimes I'm a little slow.

I got into the game in the eighth inning with the score tied 6–6. *Tied!* I took the count to 3 and 1 on Mickey Stanley, then got a fastball by him for 3 and 2. Full of overconfidence now, I gave him another super Bouton fastball, with smoke on it, and he hit it out of the park with fire on it. *Pow.*

The rest went fairly well. Tresh tried to bunt on me. I made the play myself and when I went to put the tag on him, he decided to knock the ball out of my hand. So I decided to tag him in the face. We both went down and I was left with a good deal of satisfaction and a stiffening leg. Baseball is a strenuous game for men my age. However, I was pleased when Tresh had to leave the game because his back was bothering him.

No hard feelings, understand. If I'd said to him as he was getting up, "How are Cherie and the kids?" he'd have said, "Fine, and how's Bobbie?"

Anyway, after Tresh I struck out Willie Horton and Al Kaline— and what I learned on this late August day was that I should not have thrown Stanley any fastballs. Even if I'd walked him, so what? All season long I've been telling myself, "If you're going to get beat, don't get beat throwing a fastball." And I did it again. My definition of a knucklehead is a man who doesn't learn from experience. So just call me knucklehead. Not only that, my record is now 2 and 1.

AUGUST
22

Pep talk by Joe Schultz before today's game with the Indians. "I know you guys have been reading in the paper that we're supposed to finish third this year. If this is putting pressure on anybody, forget it. I don't want to put any extra pressure on anybody."

He also talked about the possibility of getting fired. "I try to manage the best way I know how. I don't know who's going to be managing this club next year. I don't know if I'll be hired or fired or what. There's been rumors in the papers that I'm not going to be back, and I know one thing—whatever happens I'm going to be boss to the end of this year. Some of you may not like me. It doesn't matter. You're out there to do a job when your name's on that lineup card. You go out there and do the job because you got to do it for yourself. I don't expect you guys to do anything for me. Hell, whoever heard of everybody liking a manager anyway? Think of some of the managers you've known. There's damn few of them that everyone liked, and if they did, sometimes they all go down the drain together. As far as next year goes, I don't know what it's going to hold, but we're all in this together and I'm going to be boss right down to the end of the season."

Actually, I've heard no complaints about Joe. I think he's the kind of manager everybody likes. And we're all going down the drain together.

This was Tommy Harper Night and Joe made him rehearse his speech for us before the game. Tommy got up and said, "'Preciate it. Thanks."

Tommy needs only two more stolen bases to break the American League record and on his Night only 6,000 fans showed up. It's not a good sign for the future of baseball in Seattle. We draw a little better when we're winning, which means the fans have taken this third-place-finish talk seriously. We'd all be better off if they came to see us because we played exciting baseball—like tonight. It was damned exciting, especially for me. We were down 8–4 when I went into the game in the ninth. I throw two knuckleballs to Tony Horton and he misses them both by a foot. The third one spins a bit, so he knocks it out of the park, so it's 9–4 instead of 8–4. I strike out the next two guys on six knuckleballs and get the third on a pop-up, so I'm feeling pretty good about the whole thing. And what happens? So we score four runs in the last of the ninth and have two runners on before losing 9–8. So if I don't give up the home run it's a tie ballgame. And so it goes.

The best gift Tommy Harper got on his Night was from Dewey Soriano: a trip to Hawaii for him and his wife. Greg Goossen said he didn't think that was much. "Soriano sent me to Hawaii, too," he said. "Of course, I had to stop off in Vancouver."

Tommy said they wanted to surprise him by having his mother fly up from Oakland. It would have been a great surprise, except for one thing. United Airlines sent the bill to his house the day before.

"With my luck I'd probably have gotten a season pass to the opera," Fred Talbot said.

We talk a lot about not drawing fans. At the same time most of the players are still telling the fans they'll be fined $50 if they sign any autographs. If some of the guys spent as much time signing autographs as they do shooing kids we'd have a lot more friends around here. Chief kid-shooer is O'Donoghue. He enjoys the work. One of these days he's going to make another Frank Crosetti.

The Cleveland trainer is called Wally (It'll Get Better) Bock. That's because if you come to him with a hangnail or a broken bone, he says the same thing, "It'll get better."

AUGUST

23

Two great putdown lines by Talbot: Before the game the pitchers were running in the outfield and an old, fat guy with two missing front teeth was giving us the business from the stands. "You guys are gonna get murdered in Baltimore," he yelled. Then there was this sudden silence, and Talbot yelled up at him, "Nice teeth ya got there." It put the old guy away for the rest of the night. The other line had to do with John Donaldson's body. Donaldson is the winner of the First Annual Sal Maglie Death Warmed Over Award. Sibby Sisti says he could take a shower in the barrel of a .22. In other words, he's fairly scrawny. And so is Ray Oyler. "Know something about Oyler?" Talbot said. "He's the only guy on the club who's physically afraid of his wife."

Funny thing about the Billy Martin fight with his pitcher Dave Boswell. The guy who sort of caused the whole thing was Art Fowler, the pitching coach. He complained to Martin that Boswell wasn't doing his running. Fowler, when he was a pitcher, was a notorious non-runner (not to mention several other things he was notorious for). In fact Fowler once put it this way: "The only reason I don't like to run is that it makes me tired."

We picnicked with the Steve Hovleys this afternoon but had to leave early because Steve had an audience with Marvin. It turned out that Milkes wanted to know what Hovley's plans were. He said the Pilots didn't want to increase their investment in him if he wasn't going to continue playing baseball. I couldn't think of anything more delicious. Here baseball is shoving around uncounted thousands of human beings who need baseball more than baseball needs them. And here's Hovley, who needs baseball less, and he's got them uptight. Beautiful. Steve told Milkes he wasn't sure, that he'd just have to play it by ear. Which is exactly what baseball tells a player who wants to know what *his* future is.

318

After that, Milkes said, "Steve, how are you doing financially? Is everything all right?"

"Yes, I'm all right financially," Steve said. "Why do you ask?"

"Well, I just wondered if you had enough money to buy the same kind of clothes the other players wear."

"Look, on the road you told me to wear a sportscoat and a tie, and I have been. Are you referring to clothes I wear to the ballpark here?"

"Yes. As you know, one of the problems we're having in this country is a lack of heroes and the improper image that some of our heroes have. We think our players should be clean-cut and well-dressed. It means a lot for the image of baseball, the image of the Seattle Pilots and the image of the country as a whole for the young kids to be able to look up to well-dressed athletes. Don't you agree?"

Steve didn't hesitate. "I consider that nonsense," he said. "The clothing I wear has to do with my preference. I don't see how the Seattle Pilots' image can be threatened in the time it takes to leave my car and enter the clubhouse. Besides, I prefer to have people judge me by what I say and do, not by what I wear."

Hovley hitched up his blue jeans and left.

It's interesting that no one even mentioned his hair. Steve hasn't had a haircut since before spring training and it was six weeks ago that his manager in the minors was getting upset about the length of Steve's hair. But no one says anything here any more. Could it be because Steve is hitting so well? Hitting over hair? Ridiculous.

Joe Schultz threatened Bones Donaldson, an ordinary lefthanded hitter, that he was going to put him in the lineup against super lefthander Sam McDowell. Donaldson sniffed. "Hell, put me in," he said. "I faced him before. The son of a bitch wouldn't throw me a strike."

Joe Schultz was being remarkably cheerful considering that we'd lost eight in a row now. I think he's doing a little in-the-dark whistling, trying to keep us loose. Didn't do any good tonight. Marty Pattin got knocked out in the fourth. Sam McDowell hit a bases-loaded double and we were off again. Number nine.

It doesn't seem to me that there's any complicated formula to building an expansion team. We all know how it's done—the way Kansas City is doing it. You go for young players and understand it's going to take time. Seattle didn't, and it shows. Kansas City, which was getting its brains beat out early in the season, is doing fine now. We're struggling with Chicago to stay out of last. It looks like a losing battle. One question: Who will be blamed for this lack of foresight, Schultz or Milkes? Answer: Can Schultz fire Milkes?

AUGUST
24

"If we get a lead tonight, boys," Fred Talbot said, "let's call time out."

We did get a lead, 3–0. And Fred called time out. Didn't do a bit of good. Pretty soon we were down 4–3. Greg Goossen tied it with a home run, but they got two off Talbot to make it 6–4. In the ninth we scored a run and had two runners on—again—and lost it 6–5. Ten in a row.

One of the reasons the team has been doing so poorly is that we don't make many double plays. And we don't make many because, what with injuries, we've had a lot of different infielders out there. We did manage to work one today and I couldn't resist asking the bullpen a trivia question. "What's it called when you get two out with one ground ball?"

"Wait a minute," Pagliaroni said. "I remember from some of the other clubs I used to be with. I think they called it a double play."

A fan wrote a letter to one of the newspapers the other day about attendance at Sicks' Stadium. He said that the team was playing interesting, exciting baseball, but he thought the blame for low attendance lay with the front office, which priced tickets so high. (Six dollar top.) I think he's partly right. I also don't think this is a town that will ever draw 25, or 30,000 regularly. It's a town that's much more concerned with culture than athletics.

Hy Zimmerman complained in print recently that there was always tax money available for some cultural thing, but there was no money for sports, which is why there was no air-conditioning in the pressbox and the showers in the clubhouse often didn't work.

My feeling is that Seattle is the kind of cosmopolitan city that may never be good for baseball. People *are* interested in cultural events. They're interested in boating. They're interested in a great variety of outdoor sports. I don't think they're very interested in sitting and watching a baseball game. I guess to really like baseball as a fan you've got to have some Richard Nixon in you.

My wife's been having some pains in her stomach and decided it was an ulcer. "Why would you be getting an ulcer?" I said.

"Well, I get nervous when you pitch and you've been getting into so many games this year," she said. "I get nervous every day."

"Why should you get nervous? I don't. Except once in a while."

"I don't know, but I do. And every time they hit a home run off you, I just get sick to my stomach. I worry about how you feel, too, because I want you to be happy."

"Aw, come on," I said. "When they hit a home run off me I have a little switch on the side of my head. I turn it and immediately forget about the home run. Instead I start thinking about the next hitter. Most of the time, anyway. Sometimes I think about Mt. Rainier. Besides, you can't get upset about an individual performance. It's the long view of things that really matters. Hell, even if I got bombed every day, when you take the long view, as far as our life is concerned, why, we've got everything in the world to be happy about. Baseball doesn't really matter that much to us."

"I know," she said. "I know. But I still get upset when they hit those home runs off you."

AUGUST
25

We can now look forward to snapping our losing streak on the road against such weak sisters as Baltimore and Detroit. Maybe something nice will happen in New York.

Part **7** Honey, Meet Me
in Houston

AUGUST
26

Baltimore–St. Louis

Maybe it will. But it won't happen to me. At nine this morning while I was asleep in my room at the Statler Hilton in Baltimore the phone rang. I picked it up and Joe Schultz said: "Jim, you've been traded to the Houston Astros."

There were two things I wanted to know. The first was, where was I? You travel as much as we do and somebody wakes you up in the morning, you don't know where you are. The second thing was, who for? You like to hear a big name on the other end. It's good for your morale.

"Who for?" I said to Schultz.

"Dooley Womack," he said.

Dooley Womack? Holy mackerel. The same Dooley Womack whose great spring I almost matched with the Yankees? Oh Lord! I hope there was a lot of undisclosed cash involved. I hope a hundred thousand, at least. Maybe it's me for a hundred thousand and Dooley Womack is just a throw-in. I'd hate to think that at this stage of my career I was being traded even-up for Dooley Womack.

Joe sounded as down as I felt. I know he's in trouble. All kinds of rumors in the papers about his being fired. So I tried to cheer him up. After all, he wasn't going to the Astros, I was. I told him I thought he was a helluva man and that I was sorry I couldn't do more for him. I told him that even though I disagreed with the way he used me, that looking back I think he did the right thing.

I was only lying a little.

I wouldn't say I was excited, but as soon as I hung up on Schultz I called Gabe Paul to arrange a flight to St. Louis where Houston was playing a twi-night double-header. "Jim Bouton here," I said. "Listen, I've been traded to the Houston Astros and I got to go to . . ." I must have talked for three minutes without pausing. When I finally did, this voice on the other end said, "I think you've got the wrong party. My name is Dave Walker. I'm with Kimberly-Clark. But what you've told me is very interesting. I'll keep it to myself."

"Hey, Steve, wake up, wake up!" I said to Hovley. "Wake up. I've been traded to Houston."

And he sort of rolled over a little and said, "Ah, the dreams, the dreams." Then he said, sitting up, "You can't go to St. Louis today."

"Why not?"

"Because you're supposed to go to the Museum of Art this afternoon. You promised."

We speculated why Milkes would make a deal like that and Hovley said, "He's building a team for the future, and how long can a knuckleball pitcher last?"

It is possible to laugh at nine in the morning in Baltimore.

I thought of calling my wife right away but realized it was only 6 A.M. in Seattle, so I went down to breakfast instead and ran into Mike Hegan, who was just rejoining the club after two weeks in service. Opposite us was Curt Rayer, the trainer. They started talking about how

325

tough it probably was in Houston, since they were only two-and-a-half games out of first place in a five-team race.

"Now you'll be with a real ball-club," Hegan said.

"Think of it, imagine the pressure on those guys," Rayer said.

"Hey, knock it off," I said. "I'm one of them now. I hope they have plenty of Titralac for my stomach."

And I thought, Jesus, the Houston Astros, a pennant race, my first since 1964. Pinocchio, you're a real boy now.

"The end of an era," Mike Hegan said, "and there goes the Seattle dynasty, slowly crumbling."

When I went back to my room to pack I started to feel a knot in my belly. What if I don't have the feel of the knuckleball when I get there? Christ, they'll kill me in that league. Well, I'm just going to have to tell the Astros that I'm still learning the pitch and they'll have to be patient and not expect any miracles. Lord, wouldn't it be awful if I couldn't get the feel of it? If it happened in Seattle, nobody would notice. But here the whole country is watching a pennant race, and I'm in it, and suppose I can't pitch? I took a Titralac and started to pack.

Now about those waivers. I wondered how I happened to be waived out of the American League. I know Williams was interested in me in Washington. What happened? The waiver price is only $25,000. If waivers are supposed to protect players, they're not working. *Somebody* in the American League had to want me. All you can think is that some sort of deal has been made. No wonder Milkes said, "Don't worry, I'll get those waivers." You don't claim my waiver, I won't claim yours. You scratch my back, I scratch yours. One hand washes the other. It takes two to tango. And the player gets the dirty end of the stick.

Not that I mind going to Houston. How much did you say a World Series share would be?

I was supposed to call Spec Richardson, the Houston general manager, first chance I got, so I called him from the room. He seemed pleasant enough for a general manager. I asked him if they had anyone who could catch the knuckleball and he said, "Well, we have Johnny Edwards. He's our catcher. I talked to Johnny and he said he'd give it a battle."

Sudden thought. Could Milkes have traded me because he doesn't want to pay for the Gatorade?

I checked into the Chase Hotel in St. Louis, which brought back memories of staying there with the Yankees for the World Series. I remembered the inside of the hotel very well, because I had spent the night before my first Series game looking at the walls and memorizing the carpet and the potted plants and eating about a dozen times in the coffee shop. It was a good feeling of nervousness, and now I felt it again. I went up to Spec Richardson's room to get a schedule before calling Bobbie. He asked me to sit down. Then he said, "Are you a bad actor? You know what I mean?"

Now, let's see. What's a bad actor? Whose definition should I use? Steve Hovley's? Frank Crosetti's? Jim Turner's? Elston Howard's? The Motion Picture Academy's? So I said, "If I get work, I'll be a happy man here." I thought it was pretty snappy.

He said I'd get plenty of work. Then he began talking about the team, and how it was so young, and that they thought they could win the whole thing, and that I could be a big help because Gladding had 26 saves and needed someone to back him up. "Listen," he said, "if you get your nose out of joint, don't go popping off. You know what I mean? You just come to me first."

Another thing Spec Richardson said was, "Now I want to be honest with you." As soon as a general manager says that, check your wallet. It's like Marvin Milkes telling you, "We've always had a nice relationship." The truth is general managers aren't honest with their players, and they have no relationship with them except a business one.

I called home, but nobody was there. The bus to the ballpark left at three, and when I got there the equipment man told me my number would be 44. I asked if there was any chance I could get 56. He said he didn't think so, that all our pitchers have numbers in the 30's and 40's. He said I'd have to talk to Richardson or manager Harry Walker if I wanted to change the rule. I said I was sure they wouldn't want to be bothered with something so small, and he said, "Oh, you'd be surprised."

Oh no I wouldn't.

I hadn't been on the bus two minutes when the players started warning me about Harry Walker, Harry the Hat. Before the day was over, half the club had whispered into my ear.

"Don't let Harry bother you."

"Harry is really a beauty."

"Harry's going to scream. He screams all the time. He's going to scream at you. Try to keep from laughing if you can."

"Half a dozen guys have wanted to punch him."

"When he starts shouting at you, restrain yourself and be patient. After a while you'll learn to understand him and live with him."

"We've all adjusted to him, and you can too."

After I put my uniform on Harry Walker motioned me to his office, Harry Walker sat me down, and—for the next half-hour, solid—Harry Walker talked.

He said the way you recover from a sore arm is to throw in the outfield as he'd done a long time ago when he used to throw the ball 400 feet and stand at the foul line in Pittsburgh and throw the ball over the roof of the right-field stands. And he said that he came back twice after hurting his arm and now he knew that people have to learn to reach a little bit further back and try harder. And he knew I had a sore arm and there was no reason why I couldn't come back and have a great, whole new career, first getting my slider back, then my fastball.

This reminded him that he was the manager when Jim Owens had a whole new career and that baseball had given him—Harry Walker—everything he's got and baseball can be a wonderful thing and he'd rather be a manager than President of the United States because he doesn't have all the President's worries and he gets to travel first-class just like the President does.

He said he has twenty-five guys to worry about and they have only one guy to worry about. He said that everybody tries to get along and we all have our bad days and we just have to pull together and this team has the best spirit he's ever seen and this is good experience for them to go through a pennant race because next spring they'll all go to spring training together.

Etc.

Etc.

Etc.

All the time I was itching for him to get around to talking about the knuckleball. I know I've got to tell him I'm going to throw it a hundred percent and I figure maybe I'll get an argument. So finally he stops long enough for me to bring it up and I tell him I throw it all the time, no matter what the situation is, unless a pitcher's up and I'm 3 and 0 on him.

"I'd hate to see you throw a knuckleball 3 and 2 to a guy like

328

Maxvill, if the bases are loaded and a walk means your ballgame," he said.

I agreed. "In a situation like that, if the winning run was on third base I'd make him hit the ball. What I want to get across is that I'm not throwing curves and sliders and fastballs and changes, not only because I can't throw them, but because I can't spend time on them and pay proper attention to my knuckleball too."

I told him I was still learning this pitch and that there were going to be some days when it wouldn't be any good. But I had to throw it a lot, before and during games. He said that was fine with him, I could do whatever I wanted.

It looks like I'll be able to get along with Harry the Hat. Even if I'm the only one.

There are rules on this club too. Harry said it's $100 if you're out more than two-and-a-half-hours after the bus gets back to the hotel. Some players say they were hit for $499, a dollar below the figure that is classified as a grievance a player can take to the Commissioner. Also, the word is that Harry doesn't like to see you walking through the lobby with a young woman, even if she's your cousin or aunt or sister. I'll have to check out about good-looking moms. I have one.

Coach Mel McGaha told me first off that as soon as I get on the field I'm to take five windsprints across the outfield, just to loosen up. Everybody does it, not only pitchers. After *that,* the pitchers run. Hoo boy. In Seattle six sprints across the outfield was it for the pitchers. I'm going to have to start building up my legs. Maybe Johnny Sain was wrong. Maybe I *can* run those pitches over the plate.

I asked Harry Walker if I could watch the first inning from the dugout to get a look at the hitters and he said, hell, I didn't have to go down to the bullpen until the fifth. I'm the long man, but they don't plan on needing me until then. In Seattle the long man had to be in the bullpen when the game started.

Larry Dierker, who pitched the first game, has tremendous stuff. I can't believe how young he looks, like a high-school kid. He made me want to look in a mirror for wrinkles. Doug Rader, the third baseman, has an interesting face: curly red hair, big smile, looks half-Jewish, half-Italian. You look at him once and you figure he's your friend. Wade

Blasingame, pitcher, is the mod dresser on the club. He looks like a Latin lover and smokes a long thin cigar. Norm Miller is one of the club characters. He's called Jew, and doesn't mind. Before the game, Miller was doing the radio-broadcaster bit, interviewing Ron Willis, relief pitcher. "How does the team look to you this year, Ron? How about Gary Geiger? He's doing a fine job this year in right field, isn't he?" Geiger is sitting right there. "No," Willis says. "No, no, no. He's doing a brutal job. Just brutal."

"Thank you, Ron. Now tell us about the pitching situation."

"No, I won't tell you about the pitching situation."

"Then to what do you attribute the success of the team this year?"

And Willis says, in a voice loud enough to carry the whole bench, "Oh, of course, Harry Walker. No doubt about it. Harry Walker is the reason for the success of this team."

Harry never turned a hair.

It was exciting to sit out in the bullpen in an Astro uniform in beautiful Busch Stadium with people, real live people, 27,000 of them, in the stands. It was like a goddam World Series. Dierker was losing 1–0 in the eighth when Harry called down and told me to loosen up. Me and Fred Gladding. I guessed Gladding was going in if we tied it or went ahead and I'd go in if we remained behind, which we did. I went in to pitch the last of the eighth. The knuckleball was a doll. An easy one-hopper back to me, a pop fly to first base, then I struck Del Maxvill out on a 3-and-2 knuckleball. Edwards did a fine job catching it. He dropped a few, but none of them got by him to the screen.

When I sat down on the bench, Leon McFadden, the infielder, sat down next to me and said, "A 3-and-2 knuckleball? Man, you were giving those guys some *shit* out there." I told him I'd pay him later.

Jim Owens, the pitching coach, wanted to know how come I threw a 3-and-2 knuckleball. I told him that first time around I want to earn a little respect. I want everyone to know that I'm liable to throw that pitch in *any* situation—3 and 2 or 3 and 0. And I want to do it right off in situations that aren't too crucial. It wouldn't have hurt much to walk Maxvill. But I want them to know that they can't count on getting the fastball.

Still, we lost 1–0.

I still haven't talked to Bobbie. I had tried to call before the game and got the babysitter. She said Bobbie had taken Mike and Dave to see

The Sound of Music. I told the sitter not to tell her I'd been traded, that I'd call between games. And then I thought, "Good grief, she'll put on the Seattle game and hear it on the radio." As it turned out, she didn't. She read it in the paper when she got home. "Oh good," she said to herself. "A picture of Jim." That's how she found out.

She said she was excited and happy for me and we arranged to talk on the phone again and make plans for her to join me. She was happy to hear that I'd already pitched my first successful inning for the pennant-contending Houston Astros.

We won the second game 4–2 with two runs in the ninth. Julio Gotay got a pinch single with the bases loaded. After what I'd been watching and playing with, this looks like a super team, especially the double-play combo—Joe Morgan and Denis Menke are only great.

It was hard for me to feel part of it. It was weird sitting there trying to cheer for guys I didn't know. Hey, come on, let's get a hit, No. 14; you, the tall fellow, what say you get on base for us; lean into one, there No. 7.

I got to learn the names of these guys.

On the bus back to the hotel I was treated to several stanzas of "Proud to Be an Astro." There's a printed songsheet and all rookies get a copy. The song is sung with great gusto—to the tune of Tom Lehrer's "It Makes a Fellow Proud to Be a Soldier"—in the back of the bus and Harry Walker doesn't seem to notice. Sample verses:

Now, the Astros are a team that likes to go out on the town,
We like to drink and fight and fuck till curfew comes around
Then it's time to make the trek,
We better be back to buddy's check,
It makes a fellow proud to be an Astro.

Now, Edwards is our catcher and he's really No. 1,
Dave Bristol said he drinks too much and calls some long
                    home runs,
But we think John will be all right,
If we keep him in his room at night,
It makes a fellow proud to be an Astro.

Now, our pitching staff's composed of guys who think they're
                    'pretty cool,'
With a case of Scotch, a greenie and an old beat-up whirlpool,

331

We'll make the other hitters laugh,
Then calmly break their bats in half,
It makes a fellow proud to be an Astro.

Now, Harry Walker is the one that manages this crew,
He doesn't like it when we drink and fight and smoke and screw,
But when we win our game each day,
Then what the fuck can Harry say?
It makes a fellow proud to be an Astro.

Johnny Edwards says that the most popular verse is the last one.

Back at the hotel I ran into Dooley Womack. He'd sent out his laundry and was waiting for it to come back before he joined the Seattle club. He made me feel a little better about the deal. He said the Astros gave up a minor leaguer in addition to him, and he understood the Pilots were expecting some cash too. He didn't know how much.

Dooley told me he was making $25,000. So here I am making $22,000 and I'm traded for a guy making three thousand more, another player and cash. By rights I should be able to go in and demand at least $3,000 on the spot. Fat chance. But I'm going to think about it.

Curt Blefary invited me up to Jimmy Wynn's room, where some of the guys were sitting around, talking about the games and having a few drinks. Blefary, Wynn, Don Wilson and I. A few of the other guys drifted by and left. At two-fifteen the phone rang and Wynn answered. It was Mel McGaha, the coach, and Wynn said, "Mel, I'll tell you who's here, so you don't have to bother calling their rooms."

And McGaha said, "I don't want to know who's there. Tell them to go back to their rooms right now."

"That's it, men," Wynn said. "Curfew. It's not Mel's fault. He's got a job to do."

AUGUST
27

Plans. Bobbie and the kids are flying to Houston to join me on Sunday, the thirty-first. We'll live in a hotel for the ten-day home stand and then she'll fly to Chicago to go to her brother's wedding in Allegan, Michigan. She'll stay with her folks until the end of the season, except she may be able to join me for a few days in Cincinnati near the end of September. We're having our car driven from Seattle to Michigan by a schoolteacher and his wife who advertised in the paper. It will only cost us about $75 for gas. The air fares are murder, but what the hell, it's only money.

Today Don Blasingame was wearing a blue bellbottom suit, blue shirt, a blue scarf at his throat and was smoking a long thin cigar, brown. "Little boy blue," Fred Gladding said, "come blow my horn." And everybody on the bus went "Oooooh." Blasingame feigned indifference.

Back-of-the-bus story about spring training: A lot of times during the exhibition season you change your clothes in the hotel because there are no clubhouse facilities. So you go down to the lobby in your shower slippers, carrying your spikes in your hand. On this day, we're told Joe Torre of the Cardinals swears, his roommate, already leaving with his spikes in his hand, picked up a girl in the corridor and in a matter of moments, had talked her into his bed. The quote from Torre: "The last thing I remember seeing was my roommate screwing this broad and all he had on was his baseball socks and shower slippers."

The Astro game is mock anger. It's a teasing humor that can be quite funny even if it's directed at you. It goes like this:
Tom Griffin pitched a gutsy game. He'd been having trouble with his arm and at the start of the game he looked like he was just pushing the ball up there. Bob Gibson was firing seeds for the Cards, and I

333

thought, "Forget it. It's all over." The first two Cards got on base and I covered my eyes. But Griffin hung in there and wasn't taken out until the tenth—and then for a pinch-hitter—with the score 1–1. He was sore when Harry took him out. "I'm trying to win a ballgame here," Harry said.

We scored four runs in the tenth and won 5–1. Now the guys gave Griffin the business.

"Who the hell you think you are, Griffin?"

"You know, by getting mad at Harry taking you out, you reflected on Fred Gladding. Whatsamatter, don't you trust Gladding?"

And Gladding said, "That's right. You just showed you have no confidence in me at all."

"Now, wait a minute, Fred," Griffin said. "I've got confidence in you."

"Bullshit," Gladding said. "You don't have any confidence at all. You don't think I can do the job."

On the bus, while Blefary, Dierker, Edwards, Wynn and a few other guys sang a couple of choruses from "Proud to Be an Astro," Gladding apologized to Griffin. "I was just kidding," he said, patting him on the shoulder. "Nice game, bubble ass."

And Blasingame immediately jumped in. "Did you hear what he called you, Tom? Bubble ass? Jesus, that's absolutely uncalled for."

And so on.

There's a different relationship between whites and blacks on this club than there is in Seattle. Although there was no trouble in Seattle, there was a certain distance. Generally Davis and Simpson and Harper went their separate way. Pagliaroni and Segui were quite friendly and had dinner at each other's homes and there were no strained relations. Yet there was not a lot of—what else to call it?—integration. Here it's obviously different. It's as though the blacks go out of their way to join with whites and the whites try extra hard to join in with the blacks. Blefary and Don Wilson room together on the road, and this is probably unique in baseball. In Jimmy Wynn's room the other night the group was thoroughly mixed. Tonight Miller and I were having milkshakes and Joe Morgan and Jimmy Wynn came over and sat down with us. It doesn't seem forced, and I think it's worth a lot to the ballclub.

Of course, the humor sometimes gets self-consciously heavy-handed. Like one time Norm was supposed to play in a game against

334

some tough pitcher, but he had a bad ankle and at the last minute Harry Walker decided to let him rest another night. Naturally the word went right out that Miller had asked out of the lineup, which everybody knew wasn't true. And soon there was a song called "Jew the Jake," sung to the tune of Hava Nagilla.

It just struck me that I'm playing for a team that has beaten the St. Louis Cardinals two out of three and we've got Don Wilson, one of our aces, going tomorrow, and we're in a pennant race, and we won tonight because their shortstop made an error in the tenth and opened the door and we stepped in, just like the old Yankees used to. I think I'm going to cry.

When I got back to the hotel, Harry Walker was standing in the lobby with Jim Owens and a couple of the other coaches. They asked me to join them and Owens asked me what my longest stretch in a game was this season.

"About five innings," I said. "But I could have pitched longer."

"We were just thinking," Harry said.

"I know he likes to run those long sprints," Owens said. "So his legs are in shape."

"Yeah, he just might be able to give them fits," Harry said. "Niekro stopped them 1–0 tonight."

And I think, "What the hell is going on here?"

"We're just thinking about it," Harry said. "There's a possibility we may start you against Pittsburgh on Friday."

"Oh well, hell, sure," I stammered. "I think I can do it." Of course, after facing Niekro's knuckleball they might not think much of mine.

"Well, shit, if you can throw it like you did the other night, that jumps around good enough," Owens said. "You'd give them fits. The knuckleball screws up the mind."

"We're just thinking about it," Harry said again. "We wanted to know how far you'd gone with it."

"I'm ready," I said. "But don't hesitate to use me before in relief if you need me. I can pitch in relief, then start the next night."

I walked away, my head buzzing. Here the Seattle Pilots, fighting to stay out of last place, wouldn't take another chance on starting me and the Houston Astros, in the middle of a pennant race, may just do it. Beautiful.

The Pilots ended their losing streak with a 2–1 win against Balti-more. Brabender pitched. I felt happy for them. I found I wasn't root-ing against them the way I rooted against the Yankees. I guess I'd like Joe Schultz to keep his job. But I wonder what the guys think about getting Dooley Womack. I hope Dooley gets hammered. That way maybe somebody will wise up to Marvin Milkes.

We lost a 2–1 heartbreaker in extra innings. It was tough to take. On the other hand, President Nixon today nominated Judge Hayns-worth for the Supreme Court. I think that will turn out to be a more famous defeat.

AUGUST
29

Houston

I start tonight against Pittsburgh. I decided I wasn't going to be nervous. I wasn't going to let my stomach churn over. It was the Bard or Johnny Sain or somebody who said, "He who would be calm must take on the appearance of being calm." So that's what I did. I tried to look relaxed, and after a while I felt relaxed. Shakespeare or some-body would have been a helluva pitching coach.

I don't think Bobbie would have been very good at it, though.

I called to tell her about the start and she said, "You? Why you?"

Lovely girl.

Why me, at that? I guessed because of Niekro's success against the Pirates. I also guessed because of doubleheaders, which have jammed up the pitching staff. And I guessed because Harry Walker likes to take chances.

The trouble for me in a pressure situation is that the knuckleball isn't like other pitches. Throwing conventional stuff in a tight situation, I'd just throw harder. It didn't take any thinking, just more muscle. Whitey Ford once said to me during a World Series game, "Kid, you're throwing nervous hard out there." But with a knuckleball, if you start cutting loose, it starts spinning and you spend a lot of time watching baseballs fly over fences.

Still, the pressure, I think, is one of the most exciting things about athletics, and it's one of the reasons I have so much fun playing. I remember sitting on the bench before my game in the 1963 Series. I was to pitch against Don Drysdale. Houk was sitting about five feet away from me on the bench and for some reason we were all alone. And I said, "You know something, Ralph? Whether I win today or lose, this sure is a helluva lot of fun, isn't it?"

Houk understood. I could tell because he didn't say, "Whaddaya mean lose? We're gonna win," the way a lot of other managers would have. All he said was, "It sure is. I know just what you mean."

I'm getting a big kick out of Blefary. He's called Buff, short for "Buffalo," because he works so hard. If I had to be in a foxhole I'd like him in there with me. He's the kind who picks up hand grenades and throws them back. He's a perfect marine, yet he doesn't seem to have the marine mentality. One winter he spent his time, not selling mutual funds, but working with retarded children. Blefary on the pick-off play: "Now if you see me reaching for my throat—like this—that means you go into your stretch position, take your set, don't even look over. As soon as you get to your set, turn around and fire over there, hard and low, between the runner and the bag. I'll be there."

"And if you see me going for *my* throat," I said, "it means I'm choking to death."

Which reminds me of Joe Pepitone's pick-off play. In the 1964 World Series with Lou Brock on first base, I gave the pick-off sign to Pepi and when I took my stretch position and looked over toward first, he was standing there shaking his head, tiny shakes because he didn't want anybody to see. It was the first time I ever saw anybody shake off a pick-off sign. It was in the 1963 Series that he lost a throw from third base in the shirts of the crowd and was the goat of the game. Now he didn't want to handle the ball anymore than he had to. Just for the hell of it, I gave him the sign again a few pitches later. I wanted to see if he'd shake me off again. He did.

One day Joe Pepitone inserted a piece of popcorn under his fore-skin and went to the trainer claiming a new venereal disease. "Jesus Christ, Joe, what the hell have you done?" the doctor said. Pepitone didn't start laughing until the doctor had carefully used a forceps to liberate the popcorn.

The Marvin Milkes bellhop story has finally hit the *Sporting News.* It quotes Brabender as saying that Milkes spends more time in the lobby than the bell captain. I wonder if Milkes will call him in for a grilling like I got. Doubt it. Brabender just won his tenth game. Besides, if Brabender gets angry he's liable to crush his spleen.

"Bulldog," said Curt Blefary, "if we get back to the Dome no more than four games out, we're going to win it. We don't get beat in the Dome."

Then Don Wilson came over and said, "When we get back home, we're going to win this thing. We just don't lose in that motherfucking Dome."

The idea is that I'm not supposed to lose there either. I'm willing not to.

Spec Richardson got on the bus to the ballpark last night and there were five Latin players talking Spanish. He stood listening for a while, his eyes shifting back and forth, as if he understood what they were saying. Finally he said, "Abbadabba dabbadabba."

When we got into Houston last night we stopped off at the Astrodome so the players could pick up their cars. I went inside to look at it. I'd been there once, with the Yankees, when it first opened. The only thing I remembered was this huge band that played seven songs during the evening, five of them "Dixie."

Also last night, I was standing in the skin part of the infield before the game and Miller came over and said, "Hey, you're not allowed to stand on the infield dirt." I asked why. "Because Jimmy Wynn was fooling around in the infield and he's an outfielder and he got hit on the finger and couldn't play, so Harry made a rule. Every time something happens, we have a new rule."

It shouldn't matter that much what happens to me tonight. If I win, I'll be all the way back from the basement. On the other hand, if I lose, it will still have been a pretty good season. Still, I've been having all kinds of insane thoughts. On the airplane last night I thought,

338

"Damn, if this plane goes down I hope the newspapers at least have me listed in the probable starting pitchers."

Here it is, my dream. I'm pitching for a pennant contender in August. I really am lucky.

That's what I thought about when I went out to the mound. This is fun, this is kicks. Stay cool. Be calm and try to get the feel of that good knuckleball with the first pitch. Find that tricky abstract thought, the one that makes you feel so competent and smooth. I tried to recall the last few warm-up pitches I threw and I remember thinking, "Why are they playing the National Anthem so slowly?"

I walked the first hitter on four pitches. The first two pitches to the next hitter were balls. Christ, am I ever going to throw one over? Fortunately the runner tried to steal second and Edwards threw him out. Edwards is a great catcher. He catches the knuckleball better than McNertney, and he doesn't have the big glove. Edwards ought to be President.

That enabled me to walk the second hitter. But somehow I got by the inning. I felt a great surge of nervousness, and while I couldn't throw hard, I think I was able to use it, make it work for me.

I just kept throwing the knuckleball, and after a while I looked up at the scoreboard and we were in the fifth inning, leading 1–0. Gravy. After this it's all gravy. I've done it for five innings and nobody could ask for more.

There was a lot of scraping and scrounging after that, hanging tough with men on base, the way it was back in the old days. Each inning I came back to the dugout and I could see a little more respect in the eyes of my teammates. I wasn't with them from the beginning, when they were four and twenty, when they battled back into the pennant race. I'm a newcomer, and I have to prove myself, and I was doing it. I could see new appreciation in their eyes and sense an excitement as they realized how much help I could be.

The game went ten innings. I was ahead 2–1 in the ninth. All I needed was three outs. I got them, but not before a few things happened. Like I bounced a knuckleball off the first batter's kneecap. The next batter conspired with heaven and Astroturf to hit a chopper that took so long coming down it went for a base hit. Two outs later I've got runners on second and third. Now a base hit to center field ends the ball game. I mean it's *over*. Except Jimmy Wynn and Leon McFadden make

339

a blurry fast relay that nails the second runner at the plate and I'm out of it with a 2–2 tie.

Now here I am in the tenth inning, the tenth unbelievable inning, and I swear I expect Joe Schultz or Sal Maglie or Merritt Ranew or somebody to come out and tell me I'm throwing too goddam much. Instead, all I got to do is pitch to Matty Alou. He strikes out. On a passed ball. And reaches first base. It happens.

Then Gene Alley moves him to second on a ground ball and I strike out Willie Stargell. With first base open we walk Roberto Clemente intentionally. Here comes Al Oliver, a lefthanded hitter. I fool him on a knuckleball, outside. Somehow, though, he puts his bat on it and pokes it into left field, on the line. Who'd want to play him there? Nobody. So it goes for a double. Two runs. The ballgame. We lose 4–2.

I could've cried. There wasn't a tear in me, though. Just joy, elation, satisfaction, vindication, a great sense of accomplishment. The knuckleball *worked*. In the National League. For ten innings. I struck out eleven, walked only four. A bounce, a bit of luck, I could have won. No matter. For the first time, for the first time in what seemed eons, I went all the way through a ballgame getting the hitters out on my stuff, my very own personal, natural stuff.

If I cried, it would have been for joy.

I called my wife, and then my mom and dad and brothers. Then I was alone in the Astroworld Hotel, with nobody to talk to but my tape recorder. I was still talking to the machine at 2:30 A.M., knowing it would be hours before I could fall asleep.

AUGUST
30

Norm Miller said he wanted to room with me and I said sure, but wouldn't I be coming between him and somebody else? "Nah," he said, "I've already filed papers on my former roommate."

My note-taking has quickly attracted attention. Dierker got on me pretty good, and since I was going so good I told him flat out I was writing a book. Now he keeps coming around with good stories. "Write this down," he says.

Watching the ballgame today someone broke off a real good curve and I said, "That was a real yellow hammer."

Dierker agreed.

"Hey, Dierk, you ever hear 'yellow hammer' before?" I asked.

Jim Owens jumped to his defense. "Of course he did," Owens said. "You think he came into town on a load of watermelons?"

Then Owens got on me. He insisted I show him my notes. There was nothing much in them, so I did.

"You going to write a book?" he said.

"Yeah," I said. "Someday I might get to be President and want to write a book about my life."

Owens sniffed. "We haven't had any flaky Presidents so far, and I doubt if we'll have any in the future."

Owens may not be much on Presidents, but I think I'll like him as a pitching coach. He thinks rather like Johnny Sain.

"You just can't tell some guy he has to throw a slider," Owens says. "That's what they did to me. I had a helluva overhand curve when I first came up and they told me I had to throw a slider. So I worked on the slider until I lost my overhand curve. That taught me never to take a young pitcher and force him to come up with a new pitch. I give them their own head."

That's just fine with me, Jim baby, especially since every time I try to throw a slider my elbow feels like an alligator is biting it.

Drinking rules: They're different on the Astros. You're allowed to drink at the hotel bar. With the Pilots you were not allowed to. I suppose this goes back to Casey Stengel, who said, "You can't drink at the hotel bar because that's where *I* drink." Billy Martin and Dave Boswell can tell you what happens when managers and players drink in the same bars. Still, it seems more adult to be able to have a beer at the bar of your own hotel.

The other difference is airplanes. With the Astros you're allowed the same two drinks as all the other people aboard. With Seattle you could drink only beer. You could have 143 beers and get sloshed out of your skull, but you were not allowed to enjoy a cocktail before your meal.

AUGUST
31

The football season is almost upon us, so I got to thinking about some basic differences in the two games for the players. Baseball players play so many games it's impossible to get emotionally high for any one of them. Football players get all gung-ho in the locker room. They chant and shout and jump up and down and take pills and hit each other on the helmet and shoulderpads and spit and kick and swear and they're ready to go out and bust some heads. If a baseball player got that emotional, he'd go out swinging hard—and miss. I think baseball is more of a skill sport than any other. Hitting is the single most difficult feat in sports. Second most difficult is preventing hitting. That's why Milkes bugged me when he'd say things like, "If some players don't perform the way they're supposed to, there's going to be some changes." I think we *did* perform the way we were supposed to. It was Milkes who missed. He's the one who chose the ballplayers. Did you ever hear a general manager say, "It looks like I'm not as good at picking talent as I thought I was. I guess I'll take a $10,000 cut"?

Yes, Virginia, baseball players watch the scoreboard. Is Cincinnati changing pitchers? Is Seaver really shutting out San Francisco? Who's No. 37 for St. Louis? It's really exciting. Today Atlanta got beat, San Francisco got beat, Cincinnati won and we could have been no worse than four games out of first and only two behind Los Angeles and San Francisco. But we blew the ballgame. We had a 4–2 lead going into the ninth and we wound up losing 6–4. I can see why this club was desperate for another relief pitcher.

So I play an interesting game. I try to project my performance with Seattle onto this club. Those 24 games I came into without so much as giving up a hit. Not one *hit!* Suppose I'd done it here? Suppose my mother and father had never met?

342

No false sorrow in the clubhouse after that one. Only real sorrow, and a lot of it. Losing a ballgame so suddenly is like being punched in the stomach. You've counted it as a win and you've subtracted a full game from the teams that have lost—then *poof,* it's gone. So there was no food right away in the clubhouse, and when I asked why I was told that once, after a game like that Harry came in and tipped the table over and threw food all over the place. So after tough games, there's a cooling-off period before the food arrives.

Okay, so we're in fifth place and there are four teams that have a better chance. But we're not out of it. That's the way you have to look at it. Especially when it's true.

Trade: Tommy Davis to Houston Astros for Sandy Valdespino. Welcome, Tommy. It makes a fellow proud to be an Astro.

SEPTEMBER
1

Old-Timers Day today and naturally Harry Walker got into the game. For the Astros it was both hilarious and chastening. It was hilarious because the guys gave Harry the business. Everything he'd ever yelled at them, they yelled at him.

While he was at bat:

"Take a shot at left field, Harry."

"Just stroke it up the middle, Harry."

"Go to right field, Harry."

He takes a strike. "Jesus Christ, right down the middle, Harry."

"Just punch at it, Harry."

"Make sure you get your pitch, Harry."

"Step out on him, Harry."

Of course, Harry hung in there, stroked it up the middle and got a base hit, just as he tells everybody else to.

While he was on first base:

"You got to break up two, Harry."

"Make sure you get a good jump, Harry."

"Don't get too far off the bag, Harry."

"Watch out for the pick-off, Harry."

Sure enough, there's a ground ball to the infield and Harry flies into the shortstop and breaks up the double play, a perfect slide.

"Son of a bitch," said Doug Rader, "every time we have an Old-Timers game Harry gets a hit up the middle and breaks up the double play."

We lost again. Jesus Christ, *we lost again*. That's eleven out of seventeen. It doesn't seem possible to have it all slip away so fast.

Harry didn't throw anything. Instead he told Don Wilson what a helluva game he'd pitched. "Go get 'em tomorrow, boys," he said. "We'll be all right."

He sounded just like Joe Schultz.

Norm Miller was doing the broadcast bit in the fourth inning when Joe Morgan came back to the dugout after missing a big curve ball for strike three.

"Joe, Joe Morgan, may I have a word with you?"

"Sure, Norm, how's it going?"

"Fine, Joe, fine. We wanted to ask you about that pitch you missed. What was it?"

"Norm, that was a motherfucking curve."

"Can you tell our listeners, Joe, what's the difference between a regular curve and a motherfucking curve?"

"Well, Norm, your regular curve has a lot of spin on it and you can recognize it real early. It breaks down a little bit, and out. Now, your motherfucker, that's different. It comes in harder, looks like a fastball. Then all of a sudden it rolls off the top of the table and before you know it, it's motherfucking strike three."

"Thank you very much, Joe Morgan."

Tommy Davis says that the day I left, Joe Schultz had a meeting in the clubhouse to discuss the rumors that he would not be back next season and he broke down and cried. "It was a sad and touching scene," Tommy said.

Davis also said that the talk around the club was that I wasn't

344

traded just to get two players, but because Marvin Milkes wanted to get me off the ballclub. The rumor did not explain why.

Gatorade?

Upon a promise from me that I'd never tell, Tommy Davis revealed that the man who had nailed my shoes to the clubhouse floor, tore the buttons off my sweatshirts and pulled my jockstraps out of shape was Gene Brabender. I have kept my word. I have not told a soul. Until now.

My wife watched her first game in the Astrodome and found the fans oddly reserved. They sit there very quietly unless the scoreboard tells them to say something, like "Charge!" or "Go! Go! Go!" So when Mike and Dave started yelling, "We want a hit," people turned around to look at them.

SEPTEMBER

2

I thought I'd climb a few golden stairs today, so I dropped in on Spec Richardson and, speaking over the blare of Billy Graham pouring out of the office radio, I told him my tale of woe. I told him I'd lost a lot of money on the deal—at least $1,000 moving my family, etc.—and that when I signed a contract for $22,000 with Seattle it was on the basis of not knowing whether I'd be able to pitch in the majors. I said I accepted the $22,000 with the thought that if I stayed in the big league for the whole season I would go in and ask for an increase. I was just about to do that, I said, when I was traded and wound up having to *spend* money. I also said I knew that Spec would want to be fair.

Yes, indeed, he said, he wanted to be fair. He said that he certainly would help me with my hotel bill here and that he'd see if anything else could be done. He said if I did the job for him I wouldn't have to worry.

So right away I started worrying.

We're staying in the motel section of the Astroworld Hotel, paying $20 a day for $40 worth of rooms. Both rooms are filled with double-beds, which doesn't give us much running-around room. But there's a swimming pool right outside the door and a nice playground nearby. In order to cut down on the high price of room service we've rented a little refrigerator and have breakfast and lunch in, simple things like cold cereal and sandwiches. I know a lot of the players would laugh at the idea of a refrigerator, but there's a matter of values involved. Like one spring in Ft. Lauderdale I hired a car for a dollar a day. It was a terrible car, with no muffler and a missing door, and I took some abuse because of it. But it's not a matter of being cheap; it's a matter of what you want to spend your money on. In Florida we stayed at a great hotel rather than some crummy apartment. I'd rather pay for that than for a fancy rented car.

Good ballgame tonight. Justice and the Houston Astros triumphed 7–6 in eleven innings. It was a team effort all the way because we were down 5–0 almost before the game started. My own contribution was one scoreless inning followed by one near-disaster. Vic Davalillo led off the inning with a double off a fastball that I shouldn't have thrown. Joe Torre walked. Mike Shannon hit a line drive off a knuckleball that would without doubt have separated me from my head if I hadn't deflected it with my arm, a matter of blind, instinctive self-preservation. It not only raised a big welt on my wrist, it knocked in a run and me out of the game. I told Harry I wanted to stay in, but he said, "No, no. If this was a close game I'd leave you in. But I want to save you for the future."

I think Harry was just trying to be nice.

SEPTEMBER
3

Some more thoughts on getting along with baseball players. The other night after the game we had our usual great spread of food: spaghetti and meatballs, fried chicken, steaks. It really does make a fellow proud to be an Astro. I had a steak in one hand and a glass of milk in the other and Curt Blefary said, "Hey, Bulldog, what's with the milk? Why aren't you drinking beer?"

Rather than tell him the truth—that I'd rather drink milk—I said I had a bad stomach and had to drink milk. Now, why would I do that? Because I want to be one of the boys. I really do, just the way I did in Seattle. I think I failed there, but that doesn't mean I have to fail here. I feel embarrassed at telling a lie. But me drinking milk in the clubhouse is like a guy walking into a western saloon, pounding on the bar and demanding a sarsaparilla.

SEPTEMBER
4

A $37 C.O.D. package arrived today from a photographer in Detroit. In it were 100 color photographs of me in a Seattle Pilots uniform. Just what I needed. Anybody who wrote a letter requesting an autograph prior to my being traded to Houston will get one of those marvelous photos. Also, anyone else who wants one, just send a stamped self-addressed envelope.

Today there was a clubhouse meeting. The guys wanted to get together without Harry and the coaches. Johnny Edwards, one of the team leaders, told us that we had to keep busting ass. Edwards said he was disturbed to hear guys talking about next year. He said that's bad. He said we shouldn't write ourselves off. He said we got to win it this year. The consensus was that we weren't going to let Harry Walker bug us; if necessary we could finish two games ahead of the manager.

Me, I think the reason the club has done as well as it has is Harry Walker. I'm told he can be a pain, but a ballclub like this needs a Harry Walker. It's a club that probably didn't believe in itself, having finished so poorly last year and having started out 4 and 20 this year. So Harry drives and harasses, reminds everyone how to run the bases, how to hit the ball, to watch for this, watch for that, and keeps everybody agitated and playing better baseball.

Right after the meeting I asked Tommy Davis how come he hadn't said anything. "Look, you and I have been through this kind of thing before," he said. "And maybe we could have said something that would have been helpful. But I feel that before I say anything I should do something to help the team."

Interesting that even a Tommy Davis should hesitate to say anything until he's proved himself with a new team. It seems like a nice, modest thing. What it means, really, is that nobody wants to say anything until he's going good. And when he's going good, nobody wants to tell him he's wrong. So we have a tendency to substitute batting average or ERA for brains. The converse is also true. When you're going bad there is no dearth of guys waiting to jump on you with both feet, even if you're right.

On September 1 rosters can be expanded from twenty-five to forty players. This means there are a lot of eager young players around. Mine is named Bob Watson. He's a young catcher who thinks it will help his career if he learns to catch the knuckleball. "Yeah, put that knuckleball on me," he says.

Heh, heh, heh.

348

SEPTEMBER

5

Willie Mays was standing at the batting cage. I stuck my hand out. "I'm Jim Bouton."

"Oh sure," he said. "Jim Bouton. I know you."

"You've always been one of my heroes," I said. "When I was a kid, my brother and I always used to go up to the Polo Grounds to watch you play."

"Now, why'd you have to go and say you came to see me when you were a kid?" Willie Mays said, his voice squeaky with mock anger.

"And you know something, Willie?" Tommy Davis said. "He's only thirty-five years old."

Mays groaned. "Why couldn't you just come over and say 'Hi'?" he said. "Now I feel like an old man."

Funny, he doesn't look like an old man. Especially when he plays baseball.

We beat the Giants 2–0 on a home run by Denis Menke. Larry Dierker pitched a marvelous game. This kid has everything. He's twenty-three years old and he's been in the big leagues five years, having spent only two weeks in the minors. He has a great fastball, great slider, great overhand curve, great control—and he makes me sound like Leo Durocher. Great! He's a smart pitcher too, knows what he's doing out there, and as Jim Owens says, "He has the balls of a burglar."

Watching him pitch I remembered that after pitching a two-hit shutout or something, just completely dominating the game, I'd think, "How in the hell could anybody possibly throw a better ballgame than that?" Dierker showed me how. Just watching him throw his hard slider made my shoulder hurt, and I had to convince my arm, after a short discussion, that we wouldn't go back to that stuff anymore.

Another insight. Between innings of this great ballgame he pitched, Dierker sat on the bench and sang "Rocky Raccoon."

SEPTEMBER

6

There ought to be a third column in the baseball standings: GAT, for games almost tied. Seattle would be leading the American League and Houston would be way up there in the National. We were down 7–1 going into the ninth and lost 7–6. I contributed three scoreless innings and got my hero, Willie Mays, on a pop-up.

What baseball players do to each other is punch each other in the groin and say "cup check." Norm Miller pulled it on me today. Fortunately I was wearing it. When I was in the minors I got caught short a couple of times. The cup is uncomfortable, and on days when I wasn't pitching I wouldn't bother to put it on. This one time the manager said, "Bouton, loosen up. You pitch the next inning."

Now, the last thing you want to tell a manager is that you're not ready. So I warmed up and went in to pitch, scared. I threw every pitch inside, so they'd pull it. The last thing I wanted was any one-bounce comebackers. Ugh.

The clubhouse in the Astrodome is so big you could almost have infield practice in it. I noticed because the Seattle clubhouse was too small for chess.

Niekro pitched a one-hitter against Cincinnati, and that's good, because I'm supposed to pitch against them next time. The idea is that they have a bunch of free-swingers on the club. They also have a lot of .300 hitters. Does that worry me? Yes.

Johnny Edwards was quoted in the paper here today saying that my knuckleball is better than Niekro's. That's progress. When I started out with it last year it was only better than Bob Tiefenauer's.

The Astros have an Exergenie. It's an exercise contraption involving ropes and tension. You lay on your back, put your feet in stirrups and work like hell. Denis Menke says he hadn't had any leg trouble in two years and gives credit to the Exergenie. I haven't had any leg trouble for two years either, and I never even heard of the Exergenie. Still, I'll use it. The word is out that if you do, you make Spec Richardson happy. I like to make general managers happy.

SEPTEMBER
7

Quote from Larry Dierker, whose ERA is so low everybody listens when he talks: "You know a ballclub I can't see? I just can't see Atlanta. They just don't seem to have the depth. You know another club I can't see? Ours."

Fred Gladding, called Fred Flintstone, doesn't look like a baseball player. He doesn't even look like a pitcher. He looks like a grocer who's been eating up a good bit of his profits. The other day Blefary told him, "For crissakes, Fred, put your shirt on. You embarrass the whole ballclub."

Norm Miller is stomping around asking to be traded because he's not playing regularly. He really is too young to be sitting around and he does have a lot of ability. He also has a sense of humor about it all. Today he was watching me squeeze two baseballs with one hand and asked me what for. "To stretch my fingers," I said.

"Yeah, I know what you mean," he said. "I have the same problem. When I wake up in the morning I'm 5–4. I hang on the closet door while my wife makes breakfast and by the time I leave for the ballpark I'm 5–10 again."

Warming up before the game today Wilson didn't seem to have a thing, and it was obvious his arm hurt. But after visiting the clubhouse he came out throwing BB's. "What the hell got into Don?" I said.

"Four greenies," somebody said.

"I'll tell you what makes him throw like that," Blefary said. "Guts. Sheer guts."

He pitched well until the fourth, when he walked four-straight batters and they brought me in with the Giants leading 2–1 and the bases loaded. It wasn't my day. The first hitter bounces one over the first baseman's head for two runs. After an out Ron Hunt hits a 3-and-2 knuckleball into right-center for two more runs. Now I face Willie Mays again. There we are, me and my hero, nose to nose. He hits a single up the middle. Another run. I was glad to escape alive. Still, we came to beat Mike McCormick in the ninth. That's two out of three. If we can beat the contenders two out of three while they play .500 against each other there will be a five-way tie for first place. That's what I'm rooting for. What a playoff!

There was a rumor abroad in the land that the Astros were going to get Richie Allen from the Phillies and some of the Astros were against it. They said he's a bad guy to have on a ballclub. *Humph.* I wonder what the Astros would give to have him come to bat just fifteen times for us this season. It might mean a pennant.

If I could get Allen I'd grab him and tell everybody that he marches to a different drummer and that there are rules for him and different rules for everybody else. I mean what's the good of a .220 hitter who obeys the curfew? Richie Allen doesn't obey the rules, hits 35 home runs and knocks in over 100. I'll take him.

There was a National League questionnaire around asking for our outstanding accomplishments in school and I had a few. I hold the record, as far as I know, for eating two large pizza pies with everything —peppers, onions, anchovies, the works—in an hour. At the time it was for the championship of Western Michigan, and possibly the world. And when I finished there were about ten guys in the dorm who were willing to put up $16.37 that I couldn't follow the two pizzas with 100 sit-ups. Now I knew I could do 650 sit-ups, because I'd practiced. A hundred seemed like child's play. And it was. I picked up the $16.37 and a knack for walking doubled over. It was two days before I could straighten up. I also grew a set of boils on my stomach. But to this day, my name is a legend in the dorm.

352

One of the ways the guys relieve the tensions of the pennant race, and there are some, is by their own version of the Dozens, the insult game. They remind each other of failures on the field of battle.

Blasingame: "That sure was a hell of a performance by you yesterday, Billingham. Three walks in a row. You were so tight you couldn't drive a pin up your ass."

Billingham: "I haven't seen you do anything lately, Blasingame. What's *your* record?"

Blasingame: "I've won some games in the big leagues, sonny. How many have you won in the bigs?"

Billingham: "We can't be talking about ancient history. What have you done this year? Go ahead. Tell me."

Blasingame: "I haven't won a goddam game."

Billingham: "Okay. So you're no one to talk."

Gladding: "Well, maybe not. But he was right about those three walks, Billingham. That was a disgrace."

Billingham: "Oh sure. Listen to you, with your 5.6 earned run average. Some relief pitcher you are."

And like that.

SEPTEMBER

8

We beat San Diego 9–2 tonight and I felt sort of sorry for Mike Corkins, their starting pitcher. It was his first start in the majors and on his very first pitch Joe Morgan hit a triple to right field, and on his second pitch Jesus Alou hit another one to right-center. His third pitch was wild and Alou scored. So on three pitches the kid had given up two runs. And Marty Martinez yelled out to him; "Welcome to the National League, kid."

Before the game one of the clubhouse men asked Fred Gladding, who has the locker next to mine, if he had a spare pair of size-9 spikes. Tom Dukes, a righthanded pitcher who used to be in the Yankee organization and was now with San Diego, had been caught short. Gladding said he didn't have any. So I reached into my bag and pulled out a pair of size 9's. "Only one thing wrong with them," I said. "They have some nail holes in the soles. But it never rains in the Astrodome."

Sure enough, Tom Dukes got into the game. He'll never know what he owes to Gene Brabender.

Some of the guys were on Nate Colbert, the San Diego first baseman, formerly of the Astros. They kept yelling that he was ugly and calling him "Mullion" and other nice things. Blefary said to cut it out, that the last time they got on him Colbert hit a couple of home runs and beat us. Well, we jumped out to a 4–0 lead, but the first time Colbert got up, sure enough he jolted one into the left-field seats. Next time up, Colbert jolts *another* home run. I figured if the game lasts long enough he's bound to beat us. Actually, I think he's rather nice-looking.

I saw Blefary's name on the lineup card and said, "Hey, Buff, go get 'em."

"You know why I'm playing tonight?" he said. "Two reasons. One is that a righthander is pitching. Two is that he's very weak."

Universal beaver-shooting note:
Norm Miller drilled a small hole in the back of the dugout. We can now beaver-shoot any woman who sits in a certain seat in the first row. Not only that, if you blow through the hole you get some interesting reactions. Miller is being acclaimed as a genius.

I have just ordered up a strawberry sundae (for my wife) and three scoops of chocolate ice cream (for me) here at the Astroworld Hotel. The bill came to $3.06, plus tip. Outrageous.

I have this theory that the reason prices are so high in hotels is that no one objects. Thus prices no longer have any relation to reality. We are charged, higgledy-piggledy, whatever number that seems to be wildly high enough.

Example. Checking out of the Sheraton-Cadillac in Detroit not long ago, there was a $9 bill for valet. I was shocked. All I had sent out were three pairs of pants and three Banlon shirts. It was $1.50 each to clean the pants and, get this, $1.50 for each shirt.

"How could that be?" I said to the cashier.

"Well, they classify those shirts as sweaters."

"But they're just shirts," I said. "What's more, I'm not paying."

"Oh, but you have to pay it," she said. "It's on your bill."

"Like hell," I said. "Just because somebody puts a number on a piece of paper that doesn't mean I have to pay it."

She wound up calling the manager and he said, yes, I would have to pay only one dollar per shirt, so I saved a buck and a half. Now if everybody did that, the savings would add up to millions. Millions, I tell you.

Odd thing about being an Astro. When I got to the ballpark one of the coaches told me, "You don't have to be on the field for batting practice tonight. But be ready to run over at Colt Stadium at five-fifteen." I thought he was kidding. Shows what I know. At five-fifteen I was running over at Colt Stadium, which is about ten minutes away from the Astrodome by Astrotram. It's a little-used field, overgrown and dismal. And look out for snakes.

Now hear this. The reason we ran at Colt Stadium—about fifteen of us pitchers—is that just before we go on a road trip Harry Walker likes to have his pitchers run outside the dome so they get used to hot weather.

Harry Walker thinks of everything.

After the ballgame, Buddy Hancken, one of the coaches, sidled up to me and said, "Look, we could be using you almost any night. So would you do me a favor, please. Stay out of the swimming pool there at the Astroworld. You're liable to stay in that pool a couple of hours and there's no telling how much it takes out of you."

"Sure, I'll stay out," I said, wondering all the time how the hell he knew I was swimming. Then I remembered. There's been a helicopter hovering around the Astroworld. I bet Harry Walker was in it.

"I like him," I was saying to Blasingame about Harry Walker. "Maybe it's because I haven't been here long, but I like him."

"I do too," Blasingame said. "You know, he gets on guys and he's always talking and you can't turn him off. But everything he says, he's right. He always makes a point and he's always right."

I agreed. The other night, for example, there was a foul ball hit out near the bullpen and the fielder pulled up well in front of the fence and let it drop. Bang, the phone was ringing in the bullpen. It was Harry telling us not to sit dead-assed out there in the bullpen, to do

355

some yelling, tell the fielder how much room he had. We felt like kids being scolded and didn't like it a bit. In fact, though, Harry was absolutely right.

Jim Owens' famous remark about the Astrodome: "It isn't much, but we call it home."

SEPTEMBER

9

Before the game today Doug Rader was kidding Nate Colbert. "Hey, Nate, I think you're cute," he said. "Not ugly, cute. Cute like an iguana."

Little old star-maker me was at work tonight. I was talking to Tommy Davis about his injured leg and it wasn't hard to tell he wanted to sit down instead of play. "Why don't you tell Harry?" I said.

"I haven't been here that long," Davis said. "I'd feel funny about it."

"But Harry isn't like most managers," I said. "He'd appreciate the information and he wouldn't hold it against you."

"Well, maybe I'll talk to him," Davis said.

Sure enough, he walked into Harry's office and pretty soon he was scratched from the lineup. Harry put Norm Miller in and he went 3 for 4, knocking in four runs. It was a great evening.

After Miller got his third-straight hit, Davis hollered down to Walker, "Hey, Harry, that leg isn't nearly as bad as I thought it was."

Davis is now being called Wally Pipp. That's the fellow who had a minor injury and was replaced by Lou Gehrig. It was ten years before Gehrig missed a game.

I'm in normal weird shape. In the middle of the night I got up, rummaged around until I found that ball I work with and made throwing motions for a half-hour or so, just to get the feel of it. Considering I never released the ball, I did great. My wife never even noticed.

Fantasy time. The Houston Astros are playing the New York Mets for the league championship. I come in to relieve in Shea Stadium with a one-run lead and the bases loaded in the last of the ninth. I get behind 2 and 0 on the first hitter and it looks like we're dead. Of course, I come back and strike him out. I strike out the next guy too, but the ball gets away from Edwards, who goes back to the screen, picks it up and fires it to me at the plate. The throw's a bit late, but I've blocked the plate and I tag him out for the final out. How fabulous are my dreams?

Conversation with Tommy Davis while he's got a hot pad on his leg in the trainer's room:

"Tell me about the attitude toward me on the Pilots," I said. "Don't worry about my feelings. Lay it on the line."

"If you promise not to tell anybody . . ."

"Not a soul. Not a single soul."

"Well, my feeling was that the manager contributed to the guys thinking you were a weirdo. For instance, Joe would watch things that you did out on the field and he'd start laughing and making fun and naturally all the players took the lead from Joe. They laughed at you.

"I didn't see anything funny. I thought, 'Well, here's a guy who's got his own ideas. Some of them are certainly different, but hell, I respect him.' That's what Joe should have said. Joe could have said, 'He's always thinking, anyway. And boy, look at how hard he works.' Instead he sort of smirked and laughed, and you know how players are. They smirked and laughed too."

I suspected as much. Hovley. Marshall. Bouton. And another guy, real early on, Lou Piniella. Joe Schultz would have been a better manager if he understood more. Of course, if he understood more, he might not have been a manager.

I don't want to be that harsh on Joe Schultz. I rather liked him and still do. And I thought he had the most character of anyone on the staff—and in the front office.

Don Wilson was sitting on the other side of Tommy Davis, so Tommy got to saying that it would be great to be young like Wilson, and I said, "Don, did you ever think that someday you'd be sitting on the bench with Tommy Davis? I mean *the* Tommy Davis, just talking

357

to him as though, well as though he were some regular person? Did you ever think that?"

"I thought about it," Wilson said. "I didn't ever think it would be a big deal, though, and I was right."

Turned out Wilson was from Los Angeles too, and he'd once tried to get Tommy Davis' autograph. "He was too good to sign it," Wilson said. "Ever since I never looked forward to sitting with him on a bench."

"You really resent him, huh?" I said, adding eggbeater to troubled waters.

"Well, yeah," Wilson said. "It's been kind of a thing with me. In fact, right now it's no big deal sitting here with him. If he's too good to sign autographs, the hell with him."

"You see how smart these young guys are?" Davis said. "Boy, if I ever said that when I was a kid, that would have been something. Imagine me saying that to Roy Campanella. Boy, for young guys these kids really talk a lot."

And I said, "That's good, too, isn't it Tom? They should be allowed to say whatever they feel, don't you think?"

"Well, that's *your* idea," Davis said. "I know that's what *you* think."

Generation gap revisited. I loved it.

There was a happy, funny clubhouse after the game, which we won 9–2. Nate Colbert was no threat.

Whitey Diskin, the clubhouse man who prepares all that great food every night, an elderly stooped-over gentleman with glasses who looks something like Henry the Chicken Hawk, had this great big pot of chicken à la king. It was fine chicken à la king. It was *great* chicken à la king. But we hadn't been having chicken à la king, so the guys got on it.

"Jesus Christ, Whitey, what the hell *is* this stuff?"

"What have you done here, Whitey?"

And each guy comes over, takes a taste, spits into garbage. Well, not everybody. Me, I had two big plates of it.

"Look at that stuff. Whitey, this is fifth-place food."

"Christ, here we are fighting for a pennant and you serve us this shit."

I couldn't resist calling Jim Ewell, the trainer, in on it. "Doc, you better come in here and examine this stuff," I said. "Maybe you better take its temperature."

So the trainer comes marching in, ceremoniously, with a tongue depressor in one hand, thermometer in the other. He sticks the thermometer into the chicken à la king, reads it, sticks the tongue depressor in, tastes it, shakes his head sadly, says, "No chance," and walks out.

"Holy Budweiser," I yelled, "get the names of the guys who've been pounding that shit into them."

After a while, nobody could think of anything more to say, so Blasingame looked at Whitey with contempt and said, "And that's a horseshit shirt you're wearing, too, Whitey."

When I got back to the hotel, I found the kids had been eating potato chips on my bed. So Bobbie and I took the spread outside to shake it out. And there we were in full view of a patio full of people having a cocktail party. The Beverly Hillbillies eating in their room at a swank hotel.

In the last few weeks little Mike has become more aware that his father has a special occupation. That's because other kids come up to him and say, "Hey, does your dad pitch for the Astros?"

We've tried to get it across to him that what I do is just another job, that it's not special. But it gets a little difficult here, and as his awareness grows, the braggadocio emerges. So now he walks up to people, strangers, and says, "You know something? My dad plays for the Houston Astros." The other day I heard him tell a kid at the swimming pool. "My dad's Jim Bouton of the Houston Astros. I'm not kidding you." And sometimes we'll just be sitting around and he'll say, "Hey, Dad, go over and tell those people who you are."

Pardon me, sir. My name is Jim Bouton. I used to be with the Seattle Pilots. No, not a ferry captain. That's a baseball team. You know, baseball. B-a-s-e-b-a-l-l.

Little David is making a good adjustment. His English is fine, and I think he feels like a part of the family. I believe he's starting to think about the future now and where he fits into the scheme of things. The other day he asked, "Dad, are you going to die?"

"Yes, David. Everybody dies sooner or later."

And he said, "I don't want you to die."

The Mets are beautiful.

Here they are virtually tied with the Cubs and the panic is on in Chicago. Leo Durocher is not talking to the press, and I don't have to be there to know that their clubhouse is like a morgue. And here's the funny thing. The Mets have virtually the same record and they're going crazy with joy. The players are happy, the manager is happy, the fans are happy. Now what's the difference? It's that the Mets won their games at a different stage of the season. The point is that right now they both have an equal chance to win the pennant, yet the Mets are up and the Cubs are down. And the Cubs are down because they think they *should* be down. Why? If they were as happy as the Mets they'd win more games.

SEPTEMBER

10

Up the golden stairs. I'd been itching about it for days.

"Spec, I've been thinking about the conversation we had the other day and I really feel I deserve an increase in salary. Not only do I deserve it, I need it, because of the traveling expenses. What I want you to do is tear up my contract and give me a new one calling for $3,000 more. I wouldn't be asking for this if I didn't think I'd earned it."

"No, Jim. We can't do that."

"I know ballclubs have torn up contracts and given guys more money in the middle of the season when they've done a lot better than expected. So I know it can be done."

"You haven't done anything for me yet."

"I realize that. But you traded for me because you thought I was more valuable than Dooley Womack, and you gave up another player for me besides. So why don't you pay me what Womack was getting?"

"I don't know what Womack was getting."

"He told me he was getting $25,000."

"He was kidding you. He's not getting that much."

"Maybe not. But how many major-leaguers do you know who've been up seven years and have had the kind of year I've had who are getting only $22,000?"

"You signed a contract. If you didn't want to sign it, you shouldn't have."

"I signed as a minor-leaguer. There was a good possibility I'd spend the season in the minors working on my knuckleball. I figured I'd stay in one place and travel wouldn't cost me all that much. Hell, I've had to make three moves."

"Well, I told you I'd help with your hotel bill if you wanted me to."

"I've already made arrangements to send my family to Michigan. Most of our expenses are behind us. And I don't feel it's asking too much if I ask you to give me a $3,000 increase."

"If you want a loan, we can work that out. But we can't give you an increase."

"A loan won't help me any. It would just cut down on my credit possibilities. No, I need the increase."

"You haven't done anything for me yet. As soon as you do something, I'll take care of you."

"But Spec, I can't go back to Seattle and ask *them* for money. And if everybody took your attitude, all you'd have to do is trade a guy toward the end of every season and no one would feel obligated to give him a raise."

"How bad do you need this money?"

"I wanted to get this straightened out before I go on the road trip."

"Well, you're not going to. And if you don't want to go on the road trip, that's your business. If you don't want to suit up for the game tonight, you can pack your stuff and go on home."

"Now wait a minute. I didn't mean I wasn't going to play. I just wanted to get things squared away before my wife left so we'd be able to pay some of our expenses."

"You're not going to get it, and that's all there is to it."

"Well, why not?" They don't call me Bulldog for nothing.

"I don't have to tell you why. I'm the general manager. I'm in charge here. I don't have to give you a reason for anything I do."

"Tell you what. Why can't you give me $3,000 now and we'll just take it out of next year's salary?"

"I can't do that. That would give you a $3,000 head start in the bargaining."

"Well, look. What are we talking about in terms of contract next year? What do you think the kind of season I had is worth? By the time the season is over I'll have been in more than seventy games and say I continue pitching the way I have, which is pretty good, and we finish where we are now, fifth. What would I be worth to you?

"A lot of general managers would tell you $2,000 more, hoping that they could get you at around $5- or $6,000. But I'm going to tell you the truth right out. I think your salary should be increased about $7,000 or $7,500."

"Well, hell, Spec. We're not going to have any problem at all. All we do now is add $7,500 to $22,000. Call it $30,000. I'll tell you what I'll do. I'll sign a contract right now for $27,000 if you give me the other $3,000."

"All right. All right. That's what we'll do. You come in tomorrow and the papers will be ready."

Now that's what I call a fair and reasonable general manager.

Putting my baseball cap on today, I remembered an odd conversation with Mike Marshall. He watched me put on my cap and noticed that I put it on back first, then smoothed the front of it over my forehead. He said that in the minors he had a manager who told him that only colored players put their hats on that way; that white players put their caps on front first and smoothed them in the back. Marshall said that from then on he put his cap on back first and was glad to see I did it that way too.

As I dictated this, my wife said, "How does Joe Pepitone put on *his* cap?"

And I said, "Very carefully."

What a lovely pennant race. Today the Mets beat the Cubs twice, the Pirates lost two to St. Louis, San Diego beat Cincinnati, Atlanta beat San Francisco and we beat Los Angeles. So now we're only two games on the loss side out of first place. It's closer than the Astros have ever been to first place since they were expanded into existence. It is now almost possible to go from first place to fifth in a single afternoon. And vice versa.

SEPTEMBER
11

Claude Osteen, who looks like a white rat, beat us 1–0 tonight. He pitched a great game. Wilson pitched an even better game because his control was off and he had to keep battling out of jams.

In the ninth Tommy Davis came up with two out and two on and Osteen struck him out on three pitches—two fastballs on the outside corner and a curve ball that broke about two feet and bounced on the plate. No one was mad at Tommy. Don Wilson came over and said, "Hang in there. He threw you three bastard pitches."

Road trip starts tomorrow. The family goes to Michigan and I'll have to tell David that I won't be seeing him for four weeks. The other kids don't seem to mind much, but David gets upset. I guess it goes back to when he first arrived from Korea, forlorn and scared, and we developed a special closeness that he still feels. I'll say to him, "Now, David, I won't be seeing you for four weeks. That's this many days." I hold up ten fingers and flash tham three times.

Invariably, he says, "I don't like that many days."

SEPTEMBER
12

Atlanta

Blefary was giving me the business tonight. The first time he played in the big leagues he hit against me. It was after my arm trouble had started, and I must say I wasn't throwing very well. Anyway, it was great for Blefary. "Bulldog," he said, "you made my big-league debut a success. There I was in Yankee Stadium, on national television, with all my friends and relatives looking on, and I hit that blooper pitch of yours into the upper deck with two dudes on base. Thank you, Bulldog."

No scoreboard action tonight because everybody was playing in the West and I had to sit and watch us lose to Atlanta 4–3. But as Harry Walker said on the bench, if we can take two out of three here we'll be in good shape.

It sure has been a long time since I've taken baseball games this seriously.

SEPTEMBER
13

It's been more than two weeks since I was traded and I still haven't received my $900 travel allowance from Seattle. I understand that Valdespino and Dooley Womack both got their money here before they left. It's interesting that when I owed the club $6.48 in incidental expenses at one of the hotels, I got two reminders in four days and then it was taken out of my paycheck.

My joke these days is about Julio Gotay, who scrounges about a dozen passes to every game. His friends are legion all over. The line is that as soon as Joe Schultz hung up in Baltimore after telling me I was traded, the phone rang and it was Gotay. He wanted to know if he could use my passes in St. Louis that night.

Larry Dierker vs. Phil Niekro. Second of this crucial three-game series. My first crucial series in years. It turned into one of those mean, tough ballgames that you try to win even while you're sitting on the bench. At one point I was standing in the dugout when Harry put the pitchout sign on and I thought, damn, if they look over here and see all of us standing up, they'll know there's a play on. So even though I was dying to watch, I turned around and sat down on the bench. It was more neurotic than sensible.

I can't stand the tension of these games. Poor Larry Dierker had a no-hitter going into the ninth inning and hung in there until the top of the thirteenth. We pinch-hit for him, scored two runs and then Gladding came in. They belted him all over the lot, so Blasingame came in and walked in the winning run. Heartbreaker.

I felt terrible for Dierker. Every inning he got up he knew he not only had to get them out in the bottom of the inning, he had to get them out the *next* inning too. It's like climbing a mountain, struggling to the top, then realizing there are two more peaks to climb. And then we go and lose.

It was a tremendous performance by Dierker, and at the end he never said a word. After pitching like that and getting zero for it, he just sat there in the locker room, listened to the game go down the drain and never once so much as flinched. Which is why Paul Richards, when he was with Houston, said of Dierker: "He's a cold-blooded, fish-eyed son of a bitch." He said it with approval.

Me watching Niekro pitch was like a young artist inspecting his first Picasso. I examined him very closely. His knuckleball seems to wobble up there, moving three or four times in a small pattern. Wilhelm's swishes up to the plate in swinging arcs. My knuckleball gets up there in a bigger hurry and breaks more sharply and erratically, but only once. When it's working, I mean.

I think my knuckler has more potential. Nevertheless, I can see why he's more successful than I am. For one thing, he has the knuckleball down to where he can count on it always jumping around. He throws very few that spin on him. This gives him time to concentrate on other aspects of his game. He has a pretty good fastball, and a great pick-off move. Me, I still get real wild with the knuckleball, my fastball isn't that good, and never will be, and I have a lousy pick-off move. I like to think, though, that I'm at a stage where Niekro was two or three years ago. All I need is a little time.

Game was over about eleven-thirty and we got back to the hotel an hour later. There's a day game tomorrow and we were in bed when the phone rang at 2:15 A.M. It was Buddy Hancken, the coach.

"Norm, are you in?" he says to Miller.

Norm, in his pajamas, said, "Yes, but I'm getting ready to go out again."

"You better not. Spec's on a tear."

At 2:45 A.M. the phone rang again. Now we're trying to fall asleep.

"Norm, who's your roommate?" It's Hancken again.

He knows, and Miller knows he knows. But he tells him anyway. "Bouton."

"Is he in?"

"Of course. Do you want to talk to him?"

"No, I'll take your word for it."

Big of him. I mean, a lot of guys would have insisted on talking to me, checking me out, asking me something personal, like my social security number.

"What's going on?" Miller said. "You know you already called me once."

"The shit's hit the fan."

Anyway, because of the two phone calls we decided to stay up an extra fifteen minutes. One small step for freedom.

SEPTEMBER

14

Norm Miller has announced to all the people in our room that he will not play baseball on Jewish holidays. "But Norm," I said, "just last week you were telling me that you look down on organized religion and that you don't observe any of the religious holidays. What makes you suddenly religious?"

"I play on a Jewish holiday and go 0 for 5 against Niekro and the next day I go 0 for 4 and that's it," Miller said. "I'll never play on Jewish holidays again."

The guys were laughing about last night's phone calls. Like when Hancken asked Tommy Davis if he was in, Tommy said, "No. I'm out chasing broads."

Ron Willis was in the coffee shop at two-fifteen. According to club rules he didn't have to be in his room until 2:30, but Richardson walked over to him and said, "What are you doing here?"

"Waiting to order," Willis said alertly.

"Go to your room," Richardson said. "I'm going to call you on the telephone."

He went to his room and sure enough, the phone rings.

"You're suspended," Spec tells him. "Don't suit up. Call Harry in the morning. He'll tell you what to do."

Willis had some trouble sleeping. In the morning he called Harry.

"Don't know anything about it," Harry says. "I'll see you at the ballpark."

So in the clubhouse later, there was Willis, sitting with his baseball shirt on and no pants. "The manager told me to dress," he said, "and the general manager told me I was suspended. I don't know what the hell to do. So I'll stay halfway until I get further instructions."

The other day Wade Blasingame's girlfriend visited him in his room. He's single, of course. Soon Spec called him on the telephone and told him to get that girl out of his room. Fifteen minutes later he was down there in person, telling the girl she ought to be ashamed of herself and to get the hell out of the room.

Later, Blasingame was told he'd been fined $500. I can't believe it. But I do.

I'll tell you why I believe it. Because Blasingame hasn't won any games this year and because he walked in the winning run the other night. And the baseball tradition is if you're going bad on the field you're in trouble all over.

Dierker tells this story. Last year he and Danny Coombs, pitcher, were three hours late for curfew in New York and staggered into the hotel holding each other up. Spec Richardson was in the lobby. As they listed by him, Dierker slurred, "How're you doing, Spec baby?"

The next day Coombs was fined $100 for blowing the curfew and Dierker was fined $200 for being drunk. The premise was that Dierker was the only one who said anything, so he was the only one who could be accused of being drunk.

The payoff is that the $100 was taken out of Coombs' pay, but the $200 was never deducted from Dierker. It must have been that they felt the threat alone was enough punishment for Dierker. It couldn't have had anything to do with the fact that Dierker is a twenty-game winner and Coombs is a marginal relief man. Could it?

Fines and suspensions don't change the score. We lost again today, 3–2, a sweep. Denny Lemaster was the loser. Rico Carty hit two home runs off him. One of them was a two-run job in the last of the eighth and wiped out our 2–1 lead.

Note about Rico Carty. He doesn't trust banks. He also doesn't trust the clubhouse valuables box. So that big lump you see in his back pocket during baseball games is his wallet.

I looked up Niekro before the game tonight and asked if he usually threw so many fastballs. He said he didn't, but that his arm felt too strong when he started pitching and that when his arm is strong he's unable to throw a good knuckleball. So he threw more fastballs to tire his arm out.

They have bedsheet banners in Atlanta too. They say REBEL. Sometimes the bedsheet is a Confederate flag. I wonder how the Negro players feel about them. The worst part is that these things are hung by kids. Why the hell couldn't they let that stuff die with their grandfathers? These are not rebels who want something new. These are rebels who want to bring back the old.

Doug Rader, the third baseman, may be a good-looking cat, but I'm afraid he might be too tight for a pennant race like this. Right after he hit a soft pop-up that sent the second baseman back on the grass, he came into the dugout and said to me, "How far did that last one go?"

"All the way out behind second base," I said.

"It's all in the wrists," he said.

SEPTEMBER

15

San Diego

On our trip from Atlanta to San Diego we had a stopover in Dallas at Love Field. There's a huge statue of a Texas Ranger in the terminal and it's inscribed: "One Riot, One Ranger."

It reminded me of an incident when I was playing baseball in Amarillo. There were about five or six players having a drink at a table in the middle of this large, well-lit bar, all of us over twenty-one. Suddenly, through the swinging doors—Old West fashion—come these four big Texans, ten-gallon hats, boots, spurs, six-shooters holstered at their sides, the works. They stopped and looked around and all of a sudden everybody in the place stopped talking. I wouldn't have been surprised if one of them said, "All right, draw!"

They spotted us ballplayers and sauntered over, all four of them, spurs jangling, boots creaking, all eyes on them.

"Let me see your ID's, boys," one of them says.

I don't know what got into me, but I had to say—I *had* to after that entrance—to these obvious Texas Rangers, "First I'd like to see *your* identification." I said it loud.

He rolled his eyes up into his head in exasperation and very slowly and reluctantly he reached for his wallet, opened it and showed me his badge and identification card. I gave them a good going over. I mean a twenty-second check, looking at the photo and then up at him. Then I said, "He's okay, men."

Then, of course, we all whipped out our ID's, which showed we were all over twenty-one, and the Texas Rangers turned around and walked out, creaking and jangling.

We laughed about that for weeks.

. I find it curious that of all the things Dallas could have chosen to glorify in the airport, it chose law enforcement. The only thing I know about Dallas law enforcement is that its police department allowed a lynching to occur on national television. Maybe the statue should have been of a group of policemen at headquarters, with an inscription that read: "One Police Department, One Lynching."

SEPTEMBER

15

On the bus from the airport to the hotel in San Diego it was a dark and tired time and all you could see was the lighted ends of cigarettes. It was quiet, except for a few mumbled conversations. Then suddenly there was this loud scuffling in the back. A fight between Jimmy Ray, called Stinger (of course), and Blasingame. Foolishness. The Stinger was pretending he was talking a girl into coming up to his room and the Blazer took exception. What he's really upset about is the way he's pitching and that $500 fine and he decided to take the Stinger's monologue personally.

We broke them up quickly enough. What impressed me, though, was the way the guys reacted when a coach tried to get into it. Buddy Hancken started to move toward the back but Curt Blefary, Jimmy Wynn and Joe Morgan stood up and blocked his way and his vision. So the coaches and manager don't know who's involved. "Get the hell up to the front of the bus where you belong," Lemaster said to Hancken. "Stay out of this thing."

Hancken is the kind of coach who enjoys his work. He's always the one who asks on the bus, "What time tonight, Harry? What time?" He's also the guy who checks the Exergenie list and your pockets for baseballs you might be accidentally taking off the field.

A lot of coaches would make very good prison guards.

Jim Owens: "Hey, are you going to use names in that thing you're writing?"

"Once in a while."

"Christ, be careful. I remember the story *Sports Illustrated* did on the Dalton Gang. [This was a group of high-flying Philadelphia Phillies.

370

Owens was a member in good standing.] We thought it was going to be a real nice spread. They took pictures and everything. Then they did a hatchet job on us."

"Weren't you the guys who sued?"

"Yeah, and we'd have gotten a helluva lot more money if one of the guys hadn't attacked a maid a week before the trial."

There was a play in yesterday's game that would have been funny if it weren't so bad. We were leading 2–1 at the time and Jimmy Wynn's on second. With two out Blefary hits a clean single to right, certain to score Wynn—except that Wynn rounds third, gets halfway home, then realizes that he hasn't touched third. So back he goes, tags it and again sets sail for home. Naturally he's thrown out at the plate. All we have on Blefary's perfect scoring single is a third out. So today Blefary was grousing to Joe Morgan about the RBI he lost on the play. "For crissakes, Helen Keller could have scored from second base on that hit. If I was a black man he'd have scored."

"If you were a black, it would've been a home run," Morgan said.

I found the plane ride from Atlanta to San Diego interesting because of a long discussion I got into with Leon McFadden, infielder, black, Doug Rader, infielder, white, and Scipio Spinx (now, there's a name), pitcher, black. McFadden was talking about the first time he ever ran into prejudice. He'd grown up in Los Angeles in a mixed neighborhood and never had a single racial encounter until he was a baseball player in Georgia. The team bus stopped at a restaurant and all the players piled in. The man behind the counter asked McFadden if he'd like to come back and eat in the kitchen.

"I really didn't think anything about it at first," McFadden said. "I thought maybe they had another room in the back, someplace more comfortable. It just didn't register. So I said, 'No thanks, I'll sit here.' "

He was soon enlightened by the manager.

"I was angry. I had a package of crackers in my hand and I just threw them down, walked out and sat in the bus."

After a while his teammates came out, bringing him food, and he got angry at them for that. "I realized later that they were just trying to be nice to me. But when that kind of thing happens, you don't think straight. I was so hurt and so angry I could feel the tears in my eyes. I didn't know whether to cry or punch somebody."

McFadden said that incident marked him. For the first time in his life he began to view white people with anger and suspicion. And as he grew older he saw more and more things. Even on this team. "We'll be riding on the bus and we'll pass a couple of Negro girls in the street and one of the white players will say, 'Hey, Mac, there's a soul sister for you.' Now, why do I have to have any special interest in a black girl? And why can't *he* be just as interested in the black girl? And why can't I be interested in a white girl?"

Another thing he resents is the way ballplayers describe other players. They'll say, "He's that colored first baseman, or the colored catcher." They never say, "He's that *white* first baseman."

My own thinking on that is that black is certainly an identifying characteristic, and that no one should be upset to be identified as black. But McFadden is quite right to be annoyed that no one is ever identified as white.

Then Doug Rader had some interesting comments on Curt Blefary. Curt has a good relationship with at least three of the Negro players. He rooms with Wilson and he's always playing cards with him and Morgan. Because of that, McFadden said, there are guys on the club who are afraid *not* to like him. "It would be healthy if you could say, 'Curt's just not my kind of guy,' without having to be afraid that you'll be considered racist," Rader said.

Nothing works that way, of course. Around baseball you are what people think you are. Like Doug Rader said that white players often call him "nigger-lover" as a result of his friendship with McFadden. Or they say, "You're just like one of them," whatever that means.

McFadden said he frequently runs into players who are friendly, pat-on-the-back types but who, as soon as they're in a group of white players will start throwing "n's" around. "N" is black code for "nigger." "You realize they're only putting up a façade when they're around you," McFadden said. "As soon as they think there are no black guys around they start dropping "n's" all over the place.

Doug Rader said it happened to him all the time. Even though white players know how he feels they drop "n's" on him and all he can do is get up and walk out.

Maybe the best attitude to have is Dick Gregory's. He called his autobiography *Nigger,* dedicated it to his mother and reminded her that when people said "nigger" now they were just promoting his book.

My wife suggested that I might save some money at the Astroworld after she left if I had a roommate. She had noticed that Tommy

Davis was living at the hotel alone and thought maybe he would like to save some money too. So I asked him. He said he'd think about it.

Even though we're friends, there was this moment of awkwardness. Maybe Tommy Davis doesn't want to room with *anybody*. Maybe he doesn't want to room with me but wouldn't mind a different white guy. And he might have wondered if I was trying to prove something. I wondered if he wondered. The tiny tension was there. Too bad.

I think I should explain here that I too have gone through a difficult learning process. When I was in high school I was certain—with all the snobbish certainty of youth—that I would never let my daughter marry a Negro, nor would I like to live next door to a Negro family. What I know now is that life is a lot more complicated than that.

Lost our fifth-straight game today 5–3 to the San Diego Padres. I pitched two scoreless innings, but the game was gone by that time.

If you could disappear from embarrassment I wouldn't have been available.

Coming out to the bullpen just before the game began, in front of thousands of empty seats, I took off my hat, made a deep bow and generally behaved as though I was being acclaimed by millions. Then I looked up and all I could see was San Diego uniforms. "What are you guys doing in our bullpen?" I said. Of course I had it all wrong. I was in *their* bullpen, act and all. I felt like a goddam clown.

SEPTEMBER
16

Doug Rader and I agreed over breakfast that Harry Walker is a good man. One of the things Doug gets a kick out of is when Harry strikes a batting pose in the coffee shop or some other unlikely place to explain how he used to get base hits all the time. He's always giving out useful information. And how many managers are able to go over to a player and say, "Listen, I handled it wrong. I'm sorry"? Harry is.

Another impressive thing about Harry is this blazer he wears. It has his family crest on the breast pocket. Contrary to rumor it's not an open mouth emblazoned on a field of wild verbiage. I know because I checked.

I had a chat with Spec Richardson about how the club came to make a deal for me. He said he'd been talking to Seattle about Tommy Davis and mentioned he could use some pitching. And Milkes said, "How about Bouton?" Spec said he hadn't had any reports on me, but he took a chance.

Anonymity is pitching in 57 ballgames and finding out that no one knows.

Norm Miller says that it has long been his ambition to sit in a laundry bag. He thinks if he did, and pulled the string tight over his head, it would be very quiet and peaceful.

Norm and I came down to the lobby and spotted Ron Willis sitting in a lobby chair. At the same time we noticed a most attractive young girl standing nearby. So naturally we walked over to have a chat with Willis.

"How come the only time someone comes over to talk to me is when there's a pretty girl around?" Willis said.

"Ron, you're getting a complex," Miller said. "You didn't even give us a chance to speak to you."

"No, it's no complex," Willis said. "Bill Henry is the only one who actually sat down here and talked to me. Everybody else is here to check that girl out."

"Listen, Ron," Miller said. "I'm your friend. I'm trying to help you. You're a sick person. You need help."

I couldn't help thinking that Norm would be a sick person too if he were traded from St. Louis in mid-season and did nothing since but pitch batting practice and be threatened with a suspension for sitting in the coffee shop.

Has anybody noticed that we haven't won a game since we ate that chicken à la king?

Jim Owens says he'd like to see me in the starting rotation. He agrees that the knuckleball is far from ideal for short relief. But so far

374

Harry still thinks he needs me more to relieve than to start. "I'm still plugging for you," Owens said. Bless him.

A friend of mine named Lou Kramberg is friendly with a scout in the Chicago Cubs organization. It was still early in the year when Kramberg called this scout and told him about me: that I was getting in a lot of ballgames, pitching effectively, but not accumulating much of a record. He said I was a hard worker, a good battler, that I fielded my position well and could pitch under pressure. Just what the Cubs needed. The scout told him no, that the word on me is that I'm a clubhouse lawyer.

Two losses to San Diego makes it six in a row and Rader decided to do something about it. "Can you drown yourself in the shower?" he asked.

He went up on his toes and put his mouth to the shower nozzle. It looked as though the water was coming out of his ears. Some guys just can't take this pennant pressure.

SEPTEMBER
17

San Francisco

Curt Blefary doesn't like being platooned. So this is him on Harry Walker. "Look, he doesn't drink and he doesn't smoke. He's not my kind of man."

It was great coming back to Candlestick Park. I hadn't been there since the World Series of 1962. The odor of the clubhouse was strangely familiar, and I remembered where all the guys had their lockers and the table in the middle of the room loaded with ten dozen baseballs for us to autograph.

This was my rookie year and I remember Whitey Ford hurt his arm and I was going to have to pitch the seventh game, except that it rained for five days in a row and Ralph Terry was able to come back and win the final game 1–0 when Willie McCovey hit a screaming line drive off him and Bobby Richardson caught it for the final out. And I remember the police escorts we had wherever we went, sirens screaming. Great year for a rookie.

"It was a terrible year," Tommy Davis said. "The Dodgers should have been in that Series, not the Giants."

Except that they lost to them in a playoff. Can't be a great year for everybody, I guess.

Maybe we're not out of this thing yet. We beat the Giants 2–1. Larry Dierker won his twentieth and I saved it with two innings of hitless relief. I shook everybody up by walking a couple of guys right away, but they hit only one ball out of the infield on me, a pop-up that Norm Miller made a nice running catch on. It was a good game because we stopped our losing streak and we beat Gaylord Perry. When I came off the mound, Harry threw his arms around me and said, "Attaboy, this was a real big win."

I felt good about the whole thing until twelve-fifteen, which is when I came into the hotel. Buddy Hancken was in the lobby.

"Go to your room," he said.

"What?" I said, thinking fast.

"Curfew," he said. "Twelve-o'clock curfew."

When I got up to the room Norm Miller said, "They called, they called."

"What time?"

"Well, they called at eleven."

"But the curfew is twelve."

"I know. They called at eleven and asked if you were here. I said you weren't. Then they called again at twelve and I told them you were in the bathroom. I asked if they wanted to talk to you and they said no, they'd take my word."

"Who called?"

"Buddy Hancken."

Poor Norm. I wonder if they'll fine him for lying.

SEPTEMBER
18

The Giants clobbered us 9–3. Denny Lemaster got knocked out in the first inning and that was it. We have only fourteen games left and we'd have to win all of them to accomplish very much. It's not possible. We're out of it now. Ah, shitfuck.

The game depressed me, and coming back to the Astroworld Hotel with Bobbie gone depressed me even further. (Tommy Davis, by the way, has decided against having a roommate. I'm sure it's not because I'm white.) Besides, my stomach has been bothering me and Jim Owens didn't win any fights, so Jimmy Ray, who is called Ultraviolent Ray since his scuffle with Blasingame, is starting against Cincinnati and not me.

Another thing that's depressing. I finally got the traveling-expense check from Seattle and $88.68 was deducted from the $900. That's what Marvin Milkes says is what it cost to repair a clubhouse door I, little old Jim Bouton, pulled off its hinges in a fit of anger. Now, wait a minute. It's true enough that I kicked a door. It was such a minor matter I never even mentioned it in this little diary. All I did was kick it a little bit after one of my frustrating appearances and break loose a bit of molding. Johnny McNamara said not to worry about it, it was a small deal. And now this stupid bill.

As soon as I think up something awful enough to do about it I will.

A group of terrorized pitchers stood around the batting cage watching Willie McCovey belt some tremendous line drives over the right-field fence. Everytime a ball bounced into the seats we'd all make little whimpering animal sounds. "Hey, Willie," I said. "Can you do that whenever you want to?"

He didn't crack a smile.

"Just about," he said, and he hit another one.

More animal sounds.

One of the Houston radio announcers, Loel Passe, interviewed me and a few of the guys were on the earie, so I thought I'd entertain them. "Congratulations are certainly in order for the job you did last night," Loel said.

And I said, "Loel, I couldn't agree with you more. I was absolutely fabulous out there."

Broke the lads up.

I learned that from Mickey Mantle. He'd be interviewed by some announcer about a home run he hit, with the wind blowing from left to right and the ball had been curving into the wind and thus was saved from going foul. "That's right," Mickey said. "When I noticed the wind blowing like that—I always check, you know—I put the proper English on the ball, left or right, up or down, depending upon which way the wind is blowing."

And the poor guy just said, "Uhuh, uhuh, uhuh."

Most interviewers don't listen to the answers; they're too busy thinking of the next question. I've often been tempted, when I notice a guy's eyes all glazed over, when I'm answering a question to say something like, "I believe you know that there were over 20,000 tons of iron ore shipped from Yugoslavia in 1948." And I'm sure he'd say, "Uhuh, uhuh."

Bob Watson's name was on the lineup card but he couldn't play. Seems he was catching some weirdo knuckleball pitcher the other day and the ball took a strange hop in the air and hit him on the finger. He's been taking whirlpool treatments, but the finger is still fat and he can't grip a bat. Sorry about that. I wish it had been Eddie O'Brien instead.

378

SEPTEMBER
19

Houston

Larry Dierker and I much prefer the Beatles to country-western music. As a protest against the amount of country-western we have to listen to, we have composed what we consider a typical song of the genre. It took us about two innings.

> I want my baby back again,
> She done left town with my best friend,
> And now I lie here all alone,
> I'm just awaitin' by the phone.
> Her lips were sweet as summer wine,
> And when I held her hand in mine,
> I thought she'd never be untrue,
> But now she's broke my heart in two.
> The mailman let me down today,
> And so I made that mother pay,
> And now I'm locked in this old jail,
> And my dog died and there's no bail.
> My teardrops fall like pouring rain,
> The bottle doesn't ease my pain,
> And no one gives a hoot for me
> Since Billy Joe took my Marie
> And ran away to Tennessee.
> I wish I had someone to tell
> 'Bout how I'm locked up in this cell,
> And all my kinfolk dead and gone,
> But with the Lord I'll carry on.

Major difference between the National and American leagues. In the American League part of the scouting report on a player is, "Watch out, he takes a big turn at first base and may go to second on you if you're not careful." Maybe one or two players on a team do that. In the National League everybody does it. It's a hustling league.

I pitched two scoreless innings against the Reds, striking out the side in the eighth—Alex Johnson, Tony Perez and Johnny Bench, .300 hitters all. On the second strikeout, the game was stopped to announce that the Astros had broken the league record for strikeouts in a season, 1,123. And there were pictures of me with the ball and me with the manager, and I felt foolish. I mean, here are Dierker, Wilson and Griffin with about 200 strikeouts each, and me with 23, and I happen to be pitching when the record is broken. I feel as awkward about that as I feel about moving in as No. 1 relief man ahead of Fred Gladding. That's why I was pleased that Gladding wound up getting credit for the win tonight, even though if I'd been left in the game I might have picked it up. Gladding has had a helluva year, no matter what's happening right now. Me, all I had was a year with Sal Maglie and Joe Schultz.

Harry Walker was absolutely right. In the ninth inning we were down 2–0 and had a man on base. So he reached down to his bag of tricks and pinch-hit Keith Lampard, a rookie outfielder, for Curt Blefary. A natural move. They're both lefthanded hitters. Lampard won the game for Gladding with a big two-run homer and all the writers crowded around him after the game. And I said to Tommy Davis, "Do you remember the first time you did something big like that in the big leagues?"

He said he did. He said he also remembered when he was a rookie with the Dodgers and made his first trip back to New York to play in front of his home-town fans and friends. "I get a single my first time at bat and I'm going crazy," Tommy said. "The first thing you know, I steal second and I'm out there with a big grin on my face, really having fun. I look up in the stands where my friends are and I shoot them a little bit of a wave and a big smile and I get picked off second base. Boy, did I feel terrible."

He said another big thrill was the 1963 World Series. "Drysdale was the pitcher for us, Willie Davis was on second base, the score was nothing to nothing and I hit a hard smash off Bobby Richardson's knee and we won 1–0. I forget who was pitching for them. Somebody named Button or Bontown or something."

By this time I'd walked away and was in the shower room. I don't have to listen to that stuff. And I yelled back from the shower, "Hard smash, my left clavicle. It was a goddam ground ball that bounced 25 times and took a bad hop off a pebble."

I was happy for Lampard and could see he was having a lot of fun talking to the reporters. And I remembered when that would happen to me with the Yankees, the reporters would be all around me and several of the players would walk by making mouth-moving motions with their hands, meaning I was talking too much. I just don't understand what goes through a man's mind to make him behave that way. Hell, you got to live it up a little when you have a good day.

SEPTEMBER
20

I'm pitching with a runner on third base and Bob Tolan, a lefthanded hitter with a good average, is up. Ted Savage, a right-handed hitter with a batting average of around .220, is the next hitter. Harry Walker motions to Johnny Edwards to see if we want to walk Tolan and pitch to Savage. And I, big thinker that I am, indicate that I want to pitch to Tolan. So Harry gives me an okay wave.

Tolan promptly swats my second pitch into right-center for a triple. Savage I strike out on three pitches. In the dugout, Harry says, "Look, you've got a guy hitting .220 as opposed to a guy hitting .320."

"I was afraid if we walked Tolan he'd steal second base," Edwards said.

"Okay, so Tolan gets on and steals second," Harry said. "Savage gets a hit and drives both of them in. The score is 5–0 instead of 4–0, the way it is now. But as far as I'm concerned I want to hold them at three. Once they get over three that extra run doesn't mean much because we're in the eighth inning. Besides, Tolan's very fast. Even if he tops the ball he can beat it out and you've got a man on third who's going to score. Me, I walk him and pitch to Savage."

Harry was absolutely right. Harry always is. It's why he's considered such a pain.

We were taking physical exams today, and I was glad. I think I need some help. I've lost about seven pounds in the last few weeks and my stomach has been telling me sad stories. Acid indigestion is my constant companion, heartburn keeps me awake. I don't know if it's because of missing my family or pitching every day of this damn pennant race, but I'm suffering.

I was waiting my turn, sitting next to Johnny Edwards, and somehow Jim Turner was mentioned. Maybe it was the talk of heartburn. At any rate, Turner was pitching coach in Cincinnati when Edwards was there. "Boy, that son of a bitch," said Edwards. "I remember when Sammy Ellis won twenty games, Turner was with him every day. He knows how to take a winner and ride him to his next job. But when Ellis started going bad, Turner wouldn't even talk to him. He got a sore arm and Turner didn't say three words to him all season. The funny part was that the guys would kid Turner about being such a frontrunner, but he couldn't stop." Frontrunning was in his blood.

Curt Blefary is a big, rough, physical man. He likes to slap people on the back too hard, jab you in the ribs, squeeze your arm black and blue. He also likes to charge Robert, our twenty-five-year-old clubhouse assistant, throw him to the floor and choke him until he starts to turn blue. Robert laughs about it and pretends he loves every minute of it. But when he sees Blefary, he runs the other way.

On the hospital elevator, Blefary said to Larry Dierker, "C'mon, Rock Pile, get on."

"Curtis, what are you calling him 'Rock Pile' for?" I said. "He's one of the more intelligent guys on this club."

And Blefary said, "When I was in to see that eye doctor today he told me that with my eyes I should be hitting .450."

It's easier to ignore a question, sometimes, than try to answer it.

Johnny Edwards drove some of the players to the hospital, and when we got there he pulled his car into a spot marked "Doctors Only." That's baseball-player all the way. We get used to special privileges and come to expect them. In the minor leagues a baseball player can tear up a bar or impregnate the mayor's daughter and he'll be asked please not to let it happen again. I'm certain that if they'd towed Edwards' car away he wouldn't have had to pay a fine. He'd have said we were with the Houston Astros and somebody would have said, "Oh, the Houston Astros. Okay. Sorry we had to tow you away. Please try to be more careful next time."

I've seen guys get into bar fights and when the cops come the ballplayers are sneaked out the back way. Even if you get stopped for speeding you can usually get away with it if you let the cop know you're a ballplayer. "Jim Bouton of the *Astros?* Hiya Jim, glad to see you. Suppose you can get me a couple of passes to the ballgame?"

SEPTEMBER
21

We have a day off between Cincinnati and our trip to Los Angeles. I'm going to see if I can get permission to stop off and see my family. I need some emotional refueling. So does the family. My wife tells me that when I'm not around for a long time the kids get restless and hard to handle.

I told Tommy Davis about being charged for a broken door and he said that the only man on the club who had strength enough to rip that door off its hinges was Brabender. "I hope you will call the man and get your money back," Davis said.

I said I had, but somehow couldn't get through to him. I also left word for him to call me, but somehow he hasn't. I get the strange feeling he's trying to avoid me. Just for that, it's going to cost him. He's responsible for the expenses of my moving to Vancouver, which I hadn't planned to bill him for. It's a small deal, but if he can take $88 from me, I can bill him for $97. Does he think he's playing with kids?

SEPTEMBER
22

Harry Walker called the pitchers and catchers in for a meeting and made several good points. He thinks that the pitchers should practice their pick-off moves during games. Just keep trying to pick guys off, even if it's not necessary. Then, when you really need it in a close game, maybe you'll have it.

He also suggested we take an Exergenie home over the winter. He says it makes sense to keep your arm stretched. He also thinks we should work on some aspect of our pitching over the winter. We don't have to do any actual pitching, he said, just practice motion or pick-off move. You can do that in your bedroom, he said. (Our wives will love it.)

Finally he reminded us that you're just as strong at thirty-five as you are at twenty-five. He said doctors have proven it. And he said the strongest time of your life is when you're thirty. I hope Harry Walker's right again.

The Houston Astros do not give paychecks to their players. The money is deposited in Judge Roy Hofheinz' bank and the players write personal checks for the money. This does two things. It gives the bank an opportunity to hold onto your money for a while. And it gets you into the habit of banking with the Judge's bank. The Judge never misses a trick.

SEPTEMBER
23

Called Gary Bell just to chat and find out how he was doing. He said he'd just been clipped for $100 by the White Sox for not meeting a curfew and it was the night before an off day. He said about ten guys got caught. But he personally was getting even. "In the last eight days I've taken 25 baseballs home and I'm not going to stop until I have $100 worth."

Then this: "What time is it there, Jim?"

"Two o'clock."

"Don't you have a game today?"

"Yes, but it's a night game."

"Are you sure?"

The rat.

Bell also said that things are going so bad he's working on the knuckleball. He throws it in the outfield and gets pretty good movement on the ball about half the time.

Lots of luck.

I also called Steve Hovley, partly to see if he knew where I could find Marvin Milkes. In this modern time it's impossible not to be able to reach a man by telephone, yet with Marvin Milkes, that seems to be the case. A lesser man than I would become suspicious.

Hovley said the pitchers had their party with the pitchers' fund money (a good deal of it mine) and it was a good one. They had $500, spent it all and did it up brown: posh hotel suite, whiskey, champagne, caviar, the works. He said everybody said to tell me thanks.

Steve asked me how things were over here with Houston. I told him how closely they checked us into our rooms, and he said, "Right now baseball is about twenty years behind the most puritanical of freshman girl dormitories."

Which reminded me of something Tommy Harper once said: "In the winter I have a beard, a mustache and wear my hair long and natural. But before I come to spring training I have to shave off my beard and mustache and cut my hair. I feel like I'm going to boot camp."

With Jimmy Ray pitching, the Braves had runners on first and second and Clete Boyer was the hitter. Ray threw a curve ball and Boyer, attempting to bunt, fouled it back and there was a loud moan in the dugout. "What's it all about, Don?" I said to Don Wilson. "We had our bastard play on," he said. "And you're not supposed to throw a curve ball on the bastard play."

"What's the bastard play?" I said.

"It's where, in a bunt situation, the third baseman and the first baseman charge in for the bunt. The shortstop sneaks over and covers third and the second baseman sneaks over and covers first. Then, whoever fields the ball, fires it to third base. The guy on third fires to first and maybe we get a double play. If we don't, we at least get the lead runner."

"But why is it called the bastard play?"

"Well, if the play works, it's a real bastard for the other team," Don said. "And if the hitter decides to swing away instead of bunt he's

385

got three big targets to hit, pitcher, first baseman and third baseman. All of them are charging in. If he swings it can be a real bastard for them."

And the reason Ray should not have thrown the curve is that when the play is on you *want* the guy to bunt, and it's harder to bunt a curve ball than a fastball. The idea, Harry said, is to just lay it in there and let him bunt. Once again, Harry was right.

My super knuck is gone. And I got racked. No innings pitched; four earned runs on three hits and a walk. Actually the knuckler was fair, but I had no control over it. In fact a couple of balls got away from Marty Martinez and Harry took him out with a count of 2 and 0 and the poor fellow was embarrassed, angry at himself, and angry at Harry for taking him out.

I was embarrassed myself. With the count 3 and 1 on Rico Carty I threw him a fastball that had nothing on it, just trying to get it over for a strike, and he hit a line drive that almost tore my head off. With first base open I should have thrown him a low knuckler and taken my chances of walking him. Harry was pretty good about taking me out of that shambles. He just waved for the new pitcher and said, "Hang in there. Once in a while you have days like that." So I trudged off the mound to a smattering of applause, tipped my cap to show my class and, well, now Jim Owens knows what I mean when I say there are days when I just don't have it. He's been telling me that he doesn't know what I'm talking about.

After the game Marty Martinez came over and apologized for missing so many and I told him to forget it. I'm hell on catchers. Found out tonight that Watson's finger is broken. All those whirlpool treatments and it only got worse. I feel bad about that.

A terrible night. All alone and I just got my ass kicked. To top it all off I was the losing pitcher. What a year. It will go into the books as Jim Bouton: 2–3. It will look like nothing happened. Perhaps there ought to be a suffering quotient (SQ) added to the pitching statistics.

SEPTEMBER
24

Curt Blefary is one of the players who thinks baseball games last too long. I mean, when a pitcher is having control trouble he's yelling over from first base, "C'mon, now, get the ball over. Get it over." The man sounds positively irritated. I do believe he has the potential to be a coach.

Tried to get Marvin Milkes again. No soap. Next time I'm not going to make it a collect call and I'm going to say that Bowie Kuhn is calling.

Well, one more time. And this time his secretary took the call and said she knew all about the problem and that there were two doors involved and I had not been billed for the door that was pulled off its hinges, just the door I'd broken.

So I explained that there was no way I could have caused $88 worth of damage, because all I did was pull a bit of molding away from the door and the clubhouse man said he fixed it and it didn't cost anything.

She said she'd tell Mr. Milkes.

Lost another close one to the Braves tonight 2–1. Tom Griffin was the loser. On the airplane to Cincinnati I asked him what he thinks when he's out there on the mound struggling through a rough inning. "I think to myself, 'If I can just get out of this inning, if I can just get away alive, I'll be all right.'"

Which is about what I do. Particularly this year, when I don't have a good knuckleball and am at their mercy. I think to myself, "I know you're going to nail this next one. Please hit a line drive at somebody. Please." All I want to do is get back into the dugout and get myself together.

Harry gave it to us after this one. He waved all of us into a corner of the clubhouse so he could be sure he had our attention and lit into us. "You guys aren't bearing down," he said. "You *say* you are, but I don't buy that bullshit. You can't be as horseshit as you look out there. You guys look like Tom Thumb."

This fractured us. I had to bite my lip to keep from laughing straight out. We've been called things in the clubhouse before. A lot of managers say their players look like Molly Putz out there. But never Tom Thumb.

"You couldn't knock anybody's hat off," Harry said. "You look like you're going downhill on a scooter." By then it was almost impossible to hold back. Shoulders were shaking, heads were disappearing under sweatshirts, no one could look at anybody else. "And I don't want any bullshit on that airplane tonight. I don't want anybody playing the fool. If you're going to play like you're down, you better act like it."

Then he said, "You used to have some pride in yourselves, but it's gone."

The guys say this was a fairly mild Harry Walker exhibition. He didn't throw any food or kick over any stools and, said Blasingame, "When he's really pissed there are a lot more 'fucks' in there."

Larry Dierker said that when Harry had these meetings at the beginning of the season the guys would huddle together in a corner, really scared. After a while, though, all they could do was giggle.

Dick Williams has been fired as manager of the Red Sox. I think that when a team wins a pennant the tendency is to give too much credit to the manager and when a team loses the tendency is to blame him too much. I don't think Dick Williams was that good a manager when the Red Sox won the pennant. I think there was a right combination—a lot of things falling into place at once. I don't believe that Gil Hodges is as bad as Hawk Harrelson makes him out to be in his book, nor do I think he's as great as he seems to be with the Mets right now. The Mets are putting it all together this year and Hodges just happens to be there at the right moment.

In the dark of the airplane Doug Rader was saying that he feels he's living out of time and out of place. He thinks he would have been much happier as a Tahitian war lord, or even a pirate. And Norm Miller said, "I think I would have made a good pirate too. I wonder if there have ever been any good Jewish pirates?"

388

We also talked about the expressions we used in high school. Things like "Get bent," which was meant to put a guy down. Or if somebody said, "Are you taking Louise to the dance," you had to say, "Fuckin' ay I am." Doug had one I never heard: "You 'bout a cool sucker, Bill." I guess that meant you were cool. But "eat a hodgy" must have been nationwide, because Norm was saying "eat a hodgy" out on the coast while I was saying it in Bloom Township High in Chicago Heights.

John Wilson, the sportswriter, was pretty loose on the plane to-night and we got to talking about Don Wilson.

"What's the matter with Wilson?" he said.

"His arm is bothering him."

"No, no, no," Wilson said. "You've seen him pitch. How can your arm be bothering you if you can go five, six innings? It's only after that that he blows up. How can that be his arm?"

"He's out there on guts," I said. "It hurts him, hurts like hell, but he's doing the best he can."

"No, that's not it," Wilson said.

"Then, what is it?"

Wilson pointed to his head. "Maybe it's all up here," he said. Maybe he's a mental case."

"Are you kidding?" I said. "After all the games Wilson has been in, suddenly he's a mental case? Here's a guy that has over 200 strike-outs, a guy who pitched a no-hitter against the Cincinnati Reds, a proven big-league pitcher, and suddenly he's a mental case? Suddenly he's afraid to pitch against the San Diego Padres?"

That's the same kind of thinking I ran into on the Yankees. This was in '65. My arm hurt and I tried to throw through it. I thought that if I kept throwing it might strengthen and the pain would go away. And people would ask, "If your arm hurts, how can you go out there and throw?" Dammit, you *can* throw. It's just a question of how much it's going to hurt and how effective you're going to be. Granted I shouldn't have been out there. But I didn't realize that until later. I thought I could work it out by pitching. And people began to say after a while that I had a mental problem. Hell, I had a sore arm. It's hard for people to understand how your arm can hurt when it doesn't hurt them to watch you throw.

Baseball player description of Cincinnati: "Horseshit park, horseshit clubhouse, horseshit hotel, lots of movies, nice place to eat after the game, tough town to get laid in."

We had to wait for an hour-and-a-half at the airport because there were no taxis and our bus didn't arrive on time. It was three in the morning, but that's no excuse. And do you know that all you can hear at the Cincinnati airport at three in the morning are crickets? Goddam *crickets?* While we were standing there Larry Dierker said, "This city isn't a completely lost cause. Look, they've got one of those computer IQ games." So we walked over, dropped a couple of quarters in and discovered the machine was broken.

SEPTEMBER
25

Cincinnati

I got into my seventieth ballgame tonight. We were ahead 3–1 in the seventh and I got called in with two out and runners on first and second. Pete Rose up. Real clutch situation. I throw two knuckleballs for balls. Edwards calls for a fastball and I shake him off. Rose is just going to rip my fastball. I know it. So I throw a knuckleball for a strike, another knuckleball for a foul ball, a third for strike three and strut off the mound.

Then we have a long inning and I hate it. I feel like I ought to go down to the bullpen and get some throwing in. I'm not throwing my super knuckler. Sure enough, I go out there and give up three straight singles. They don't splash me against the fences but they hit sharp grounders. So Harry takes me out and says, "Well, you can't get them all the time."

I know, I know.

Fred Gladding came in, stopped them cold, and we won. He's been having his problems for the last month or so, but tonight we all called him "Ace."

After the game Pete Rose told a reporter that he never expected a knuckleball on 2 and 0. I think I'm wising up.

390

SEPTEMBER
26

Persistence is its own reward. I called Marvin Milkes' secretary again. She said the whole thing had been straightened out. Milkes had put a check in the mail for $88. Oh boy. Wonder what caused the change of heart. Could it be that Milkes read Larry Merchant's column in the New York *Post* the other day, which was the first public revelation of the fact that I'm writing a book about this season? Could it?

Norm Miller, who is married to an Italian girl, says he likes the idea of the bar mitzvah. He said he didn't have one. His brother did and Norm was jealous. "A bar mitzvah," he said, "is like signing for a bonus."

I looked like Tom Thumb on my first pitch in the game tonight. Tony Perez hit a knuckleball over Norm Miller's head and Norm could have caught it if he'd climbed over the fence and ran across the street. The fact that I struck out the next two guys didn't ease the pain.

It was a painful evening all around, especially for Jack Billingham. He and Dierker were scheduled to pitch the doubleheader and he asked Jim Owens which game he was pitching. "You pitch against Maloney," Owens told him.

"But he's their best pitcher," Billingham said, figuring that honor should go to Dierker.

"I know, I know," Owens said. "That's why you're pitching against him."

The idea is to win three more games and finish over .500. So you throw Billingham up as a sacrifice to Maloney, a guy you've got to figure on shutting out to beat, and let Dierker win his game. Sure enough, Maloney beat Billingham 3–0 with a one-hitter. We got three runs for Dierker in the second game. Unfortunately they scored four off him and we lost 4–3. Nice doubleheader.

We were kidding in the bullpen about how many greenies the Reds must have been taking during this pennant race and just then there was a ball hit into short right that Pete Rose made a great diving run at and caught on a short hop. "Five more milligrams and he'd have had it," Tom Griffin said.

At this time of year, unless you're in a pennant race, what you really think about most is going home. So the story was told in the bullpen about Umpire Ed Runge and Frank Lary, pitcher. It was the last game of the season, probably 1960, and Frank Lary had booked a three-o'clock flight although it was a two-o'clock game. Of course, he wasn't scheduled to pitch. Right before the game started Lary said to Runge, "Hey, Ed, I've got a three-o'clock plane to catch home. See what you can do about getting me out of this ballgame." Runge said he would.

On the first pitch of the game Runge calls a strike and Lary, standing on the top step of the dugout, yells, "Hey, Runge, what the hell kind of call is that? You trying to make a quick getaway?"

And Runge points a finger at him and says, "You're out of the game."

"Thanks," Lary said. And he left.

The other thing you talk about in the bullpen this time of year is sex. You talk about sex at all other times of the year too. Ballplayers don't exactly admire the sex habits of the human baseball player. They say things like, "If I ever catch my daughter hanging around ballplayers . . ." or, "I'll tell you one thing. I'm never going to let my daughter go to a ballgame."

Anyway, this is about something that happened last year here in Cincinnati. Rader and Miller were out strolling one evening and noticed in the window of a cosmetic shop a vibrating device called, as they recall, a "Personal Vibrator." To their twisted, sex-wracked minds it looked, of course, like nothing but a vibrating phallus.

The next morning they were at the store bright and early, only to discover that Blasingame and Lemaster were already there. "I'll take all of them," Blasingame said, leering evilly at the salesgirl and pointing to the vibrators.

"Now, wait a minute," Rader said. "You can't have them all. Norm and I have got to have at least one each."

Out of the kindness of his heart, Blasingame let them each buy one. And he bought the rest.

That night he called a clubhouse meeting. "Pay attention, men," he said, "especially you married men." And he proceeded to make a speech describing graphically the marvelous uses to which these vibrators could be put. "You married men," he said, "this little device will revitalize your sex life at home."

And he sold every single vibrator, purchased at $4.98, for $10. The demand was greater than the supply.

"Say, Norm," I said. "You happen to remember where that cosmetic shop is?"

SEPTEMBER

27

We had the pleasure today of knocking the Reds out of the race. We beat them 4–3 and they were mathematically eliminated. Tough. A newspaper guy here wrote that Houston always knocks off Cincinnati and then rolls over and plays dead for Atlanta. Silly, of course. We try to win all our games. Against some teams trying isn't enough.

Instead of our usual running in the outfield we were running pass patterns, Jim Owens at quarterback, against pass defenders. The idea was to see who could work the most intricate patterns and who could fake who out of whose jock strap. Harry Walker made us stop. "I hate to spoil your fun, boys," he said. "But we better knock it off. Crissakes, if Dierker gets hurt we're all out of a job."

Harry was probably right. There is a pecking order in the major leagues which goes like this: owner, general manager, super star, manager, established player, coaches, traveling secretary, trainer, clubhouse man, marginal player. That's Harry down there under super-star Dierker. In Seattle that was me down there under the clubhouse man.

I was warming up late in the ballgame when Jim Owens came out and said, "It doesn't look like it's breaking real good."

"No, it isn't," I said.

"Okay," he said. "I'll get Gladding up."

Now this makes sense. I tried to get the idea across in Seattle that there should be some sort of relationship between how a guy looks in the bullpen and how he does on the mound. The conundrum is that often there is *no* relationship. Except that with the knuckleball, if I haven't got it in the bullpen I'm not likely to when I get out on the mound.

I'm reminded of Mike Marshall asking Joe Schultz what to do if he didn't have it in the bullpen and Schultz just walking away.

Bedcheck—with four games left in the season? I suppose that at the end of the season they'll hand out chastity belts for use at home over the winter.

SEPTEMBER
28

Although we'd lost again I was lighthearted as I set off to spend a day with my family in Michigan on the way out to Los Angeles for the final series of the season. No bedcheck tonight.

Sudden thought. Suppose somebody told Johnny Sain to conduct a bedcheck. He'd tell them to take the phone and stick it up their receivers.

SEPTEMBER
30

Los Angeles

When I landed at Los Angeles after flying in from Michigan, I promptly took the limousine for Anaheim. I got out at the Grand Hotel and couldn't figure out why none of the guys were around the lobby. Suddenly there was this little click in my head. The Houston Astros do not play the Los Angeles Angels. They play the Dodgers. So it was into a taxicab to Chavez Ravine, and I barely got there in time for batting practice. The whole thing cost me $17 and some nasty comments from my teammates about the size of my brainpan.

We beat the Dodgers and now have an 81–79 record with two games to go. Can't go below .500, and if we beat them twice we'll tie them for fourth. It could have been worse.

OCTOBER
1

We played bocci with my iron ball in the bullpen during the game, and stickball, and I beat Dierker in a word game, which I consider an accomplishment. The kid has a helluva vocabulary. The most interesting part of the baseball game came when Norm Miller threw his helmet in the dugout and it bounced up and hit Hector Torres in the eye and Harry fined Miller $50 on the spot. Next time up Norm hit a home run.

395

Johnny Edwards asked me if I planned to bring my family to spring training. I said sure, why?

"If you don't you have to stay in the barracks and they padlock the doors at midnight," he said. "If you don't make it in, you have to pound on the door and that's the way they catch you."

OCTOBER

2

The New York *Post* has asked me to cover the World Series for them if the Mets get into it. They said they couldn't pay me for the articles, but might, just might, be able to pay some, only *some,* of my expenses—like, maybe hotel, but not travel. That's very similar to the arrangement that Tom Sawyer had with Huckleberry Finn on painting the fence. The more Huck painted, the more it cost him. I guess they figured I'd enjoy it because I'd get to watch some baseball games for free.

I said no, thanks.

The last day of the season and I'm looking forward to being home again. It's convenient to travel with a ballclub. Your suitcases are picked up at the hotel and your equipment at the ballpark and you never see anything again until you get to the next hotel, the next ballpark. On the last day you carry your own suitcase, and you carry your equipment bag and somehow the weight feels good. On the bus out to the airport I thought about my season; 73 outings, and I graded 52 of them either good or excellent, and for the first time since 1964 I felt no gnawing emptiness at the end of a season. Only quiet fulfillment, the cool of the evening.

It was good that the season was over. And let's see, spring training should start about February 22.

WINTER, 1969/70

In the winter I always find myself remembering more good things than bad. And in many ways 1969 was a great season. I began it as a minor-leaguer trying a new style and a new pitch and finished as a genuine gold-plated, guaranteed-not-to-tarnish major-leaguer again. My 73 appearances for Seattle and Houston were fifth in the majors, and my two wins, three losses and two saves say something—although I'm not sure what.

The pettiness and stupidity were exasperating, sometimes damaging. And it's going to be a long winter before I can enjoy having had my shoes nailed to the clubhouse floor. New levels of noncommunication were reached. Still, there were rewards. There were enough laughs in the bullpen and in the back of the bus to make me eager for a new season. I met a lot of people I'll feel warmly toward for the rest of my life. Observing and recording my experiences for this book taught me a great deal not only about others but about myself. (I'm not sure I liked everything I learned, but learning is often a painful experience.)

I lucked out with five great roommates: Gary Bell, Bob Lasko, Mike Marshall, Steve Hovley and Norm Miller. I went the whole season without an injury. I traveled the country in both leagues. And I saw the look in my son Mike's face when I came back from a road trip and he turned his big eyes up at me and said shyly, "Hey Dad, you're Jim Bouton, aren't you?"

I enjoyed living in the Great Northwest for most of a season and I'm sad that Seattle didn't keep its franchise. A city that seems to care more for its art museums than its ballpark can't be all bad.

The team will play in Milwaukee next season and it will be a new team in every respect. Even before the franchise could be shifted, Marvin Milkes, operating on the theory that when you make a mistake you make a change, made a lot of changes. Joe Schultz was fired and signed on as coach in Kansas City, moving in considerably below Lou Piniella in the team's pecking order. Piniella, groomed for oblivion in the first weeks of spring training with Seattle, became rookie of the year in Kansas City, hitting .282. Sal Maglie, Ron Plaza, Eddie O'Brien and

Frank Crosetti were also fired. As this is written only Crosetti has hooked on—with Minnesota.

Fred Talbot, Diego Segui, Ray Oyler, George Brunet, Don Mincher and Ron Clark were all traded to Oakland for some warm bodies. Dooley Womack was released, Merritt Ranew was sent to the minors and Mike Marshall, sold to Houston, will be back with me this spring. Gary Bell, released by the White Sox, was signed by Hawaii. Hope he can handle *mai tais*.

Houston traded Curt Blefary to the Yankees for Joe Pepitone and we will have all spring to practice Joe's pick-off sign. Wade Blasingame was sent to the minors. Ted Williams of the MFL was Manager of the Year and the Fat Kid won Most Valuable Player.

I did not win Comeback of the Year, but I went to a local sports banquet the other night and took a bow from the audience. As I watched the trophies being handed out, my mind wandered and I saw myself being called up to the dais and accepting the Fireman of the Year award for 1970.

And then I thought of Jim O'Toole and I felt both strange and sad. When I took the cab to the airport in Cincinnati I got into a conversation with the driver and he said he'd played ball that summer against Jim O'Toole. He said O'Toole was pitching for the Ross Eversoles in the Kentucky Industrial League. He said O'Toole is all washed up. He doesn't have his fastball anymore but his control seems better than when he was with Cincinnati. I had to laugh at that. O'Toole won't be trying to sneak one over the corner on Willie Mays in the Kentucky Industrial League.

Jim O'Toole and I started out even in the spring. He wound up with the Ross Eversoles and I with a new lease on life. And as I day-dreamed of being Fireman of the Year in 1970 I wondered what the dreams of Jim O'Toole are like these days. Then I thought, would I do that? When it's over for me, would I be hanging on with the Ross Eversoles? I went down deep and the answer I came up with was yes.

Yes, I would. You see, you spend a good piece of your life gripping a baseball and in the end it turns out that it was the other way around all the time.

398

APPENDIX

TELL YOUR STATISTICS TO SHUT UP

APPEARANCE	HOME OR AWAY	DATE	TEAM	INNINGS PITCHED	HITS	RUNS	EARNED RUNS	WALKS	STRIKEOUTS	RUNNERS ON	RUNNERS SCORED	DECISION	TOTAL INNINGS	TOTAL HITS	TOTAL E. RUNS	TOTAL WALKS	TOTAL STRIKEOUTS	EARNED RUN AVERAGE	EVALUATION
1.	A.	4/9	L.A.	⅓	0	0	0	1	0			—							Good
2.	H.	4/13	Chi.	1	3	3	3	1	0			—	1⅓	3	3	2	0		Bad
SENT TO MINOR LEAGUES																			
	A.	4/19	Tacoma	1	0	0	0	0	2			—							Excellent
	A.	4/20	Tacoma	2⅓	2	1	0	0	0			L							Fair
	A.	4/21	Hawaii	1	0	0	0	0	1			—							Excellent
	A.	4/22	Hawaii	2⅓	1	0	0	1	1			—							Excellent
	A.	4/23	Hawaii	1	0	0	0	1	1			S							Excellent
	A.	4/24	Hawaii	1	0	0	0	2	0			S							Excellent
	A.	4/25	Hawaii	1⅓	0	0	0	1	0			S							Excellent
	A.	4/27	Hawaii	1⅓	1	1	1	2	1			S							Excellent
RECALLED FROM MINORS																			
3.	A.	4/30	Minn.	2	0	0	0	1	1	0	0	—	3⅔	3	3	2	1		Excellent
4.	A.	5/1	Minn.	2⅔	5	1	1	2	2	3	0	—	6⅓	8	4	4	3		Good
5.	A.	5/2	Oak.	3	4	2	2	0	2	0	0	—	9⅓	12	6	4	5		Fair
6.	A.	5/4	Oak.	1⅓	1	3	3	3	0	1	0	—	10⅔	13	9	7	5		Bad
7.	H.	5/6	Bost.	1⅓	0	0	0	0	1	2	0	—	12	13	9	7	6		Excellent
8.	H.	5/10	Wash.	1	1	1	0	1	2	0	0	—	13	14	9	8	8		Good
9.	H.	5/14	N.Y.	1	1	0	0	0	0	0	0	—	14	15	9	8	8		Good
10.	A.	5/16	Bost.	3	0	0	0	1	1	0	0	W	17	15	9	9	9		Excellent
11.	A.	5/22	Wash.	⅓	0	0	0	0	0	2	0	—	17⅓	15	9	9	9		Excellent
12.	A.	5/23	Cleve.	2⅔	3	2	1	0	2	3	0	—	20	18	10	9	11		Good
13.	A.	5/25	Cleve.	⅓	0	0	0	1	0	0	0	—	20⅓	18	10	10	11		Good
14.	H.	5/28	Balt.	1	0	0	0	0	2	0	0	—	21⅓	18	10	10	13		Excellent
15.	H.	6/1	Det.	⅓	0	0	0	0	0	1	0	—	21⅔	18	10	10	13		Excellent
16.	H.	6/2	Cleve.	4	2	1	1	1	3	0	0	S	25⅔	20	11	11	16	3.90	Excellent
17.	H.	6/4	Cleve.	1⅓	5	4	2	1	1	0	0	—	27	25	13	12	17		Bad
18.	A.	6/6	Balt.	⅓	0	0	0	0	0	1	0	—	27⅓	25	13	12	17		Good
19.	A.	6/7	Balt.	1	0	0	0	0	1	0	0	—	28⅓	25	13	12	18		Excellent
20.	A.	6/10	Det.	⅔	2	2	2	3	2	0	0	—	29	27	15	15	20		Bad
21.	A.	6/14	N.Y.	2	0	0	0	0	0	3	1	—	31	27	15	15	20		Excellent
22.	A.	6/15	N.Y.	⅓	0	0	0	0	1	1	0	—	31⅓	27	15	15	21		Excellent
23.	A.	6/16	Chi.	1⅔	1	0	0	0	1	3	3	—	33	28	15	15	22	4.13	Good
24.	A.	6/18	Chi.	1	0	0	0	0	1	0	0	—	34	28	15	15	23		Excellent
25.	A.	6/18	Chi.	1	0	0	0	0	0	0	0	—	35	28	15	15	23	3.89	Excellent
26.	A.	6/19	Chi.	4	3	2	0	2	3	2	2	—	39	31	15	17	26		Excellent
27.	H.	6/20	K.C.	3	3	1	1	0	0	0	0	—	42	34	16	17	26		Good
28.	H.	6/23	Chi.	3⅓	0	0	0	0	1	3	0	—	45⅓	34	16	17	27		Excellent
29.	H.	6/23	Chi.	⅓	0	0	0	0	0	1	0	—	45⅔	34	16	17	27	3.18	Excellent
30.	A.	6/27	L.A.	2⅔	2	0	0	1	2	2	0	—	48⅓	36	16	18	29		Excellent
31.	A.	6/29	L.A.	⅓	0	0	0	0	0	3	0	—	48⅔	36	16	18	29		Excellent
32.	A.	7/3	Oak.	⅓	0	0	0	3	0	3	3	—	49	36	16	21	29	2.93	Bad
33.	A.	7/4	K.C.	1⅓	4	5	5	2	0	2	2	—	50⅓	40	21	23	29	3.78	Bad

APPEARANCE	HOME OR AWAY	DATE	TEAM	INNINGS PITCHED	HITS	RUNS	EARNED RUNS	WALKS	STRIKEOUTS	RUNNERS ON	RUNNERS SCORED	DECISION	TOTAL INNINGS	TOTAL HITS	TOTAL E. RUNS	TOTAL WALKS	TOTAL STRIKEOUTS	EARNED RUN AVERAGE	EVALUATION
34.	A.	7/6	K.C.	2	1	0	0	1	0	0	0	—	52⅓	41	21	24	29		Good
35.	H.	7/9	L.A.	2	2	0	0	0	3	0	0	—	54⅓	43	21	24	32		Excellent
36.	A.	7/12	Minn.	2⅔	5	2	2	0	2	3	2	—	57	48	23	24	34		Fair
37.	H.	7/15	Oak.	2	1	1	0	1	3	0	0	—	59	49	23	25	37	3.51	Excellent
38.	H.	7/17	Oak.	2⅔	2	0	0	0	3	2	0	—	61⅔	51	23	25	40		Excellent
39.	H.	7/19	Minn.	3⅔	6	5	5	2	2	0	0	—	65⅓	57	28	27	42		Bad
40.	H.	7/20	Minn.	⅔	1	1	0	1	0	1	1	—	66	58	28	28	42		Fair
41.	H.	7/25	Bost.	1	0	0	0	1	1	0	0	—	67	58	28	28	43		Good
42.	H.	7/26	Bost.	1⅓	0	0	0	0	0	1	0	W	68⅓	58	28	29	43		Excellent
43.	H.	7/27	Bost.	2	1	0	0	0	3	0	0	—	70⅓	59	28	29	46		Excellent
44.	H.	7/29	Wash.	⅓	0	0	0	0	1	2	0	—	70⅔	59	28	29	47		Excellent
45.	H.	7/31	Wash.	⅔	1	0	0	0	1	2	2	—	71⅓	60	28	29	48		Fair
46.	H.	8/1	N.Y.	5	5	1	1	1	4	0	0	—	76⅓	65	29	30	52	3.41	Excellent
47.	H.	8/2	N.Y.	2	1	0	0	2	1	0	0	—	78⅓	66	29	32	53		Excellent
48.	A.	8/6	Bost.	⅔	0	0	0	0	0	3	0	—	79	66	29	32	53		Excellent
49.	A.	8/8	Wash.	1	0	0	0	1	0	0	0	—	80	66	29	33	52		Excellent
50.	A.	8/9	Wash.	2	1	1	1	0	2	0	0	—	82	67	30	33	55		Good
51.	A.	8/12	Cleve.	2	1	0	0	0	2	0	0	—	85	68	30	33	57		Excellent
52.	H.	8/16	Balt.	2	4	3	3	3	1	0	0	—	86	72	33	36	58	3.45	Bad
53.	H.	8/18	Balt.	⅓	2	2	2	1	1	3	3	—	86⅓	74	35	37	59		Bad
54.	H.	8/19	Det.	1	0	0	0	0	0	0	0	—	87⅓	74	35	37	59		Excellent
55.	H.	8/21	Det.	1	1	1	1	0	2	0	0	L	88⅓	75	36	37	61		Fair
56.	H.	8/22	Cleve.	1	1	1	1	0	2	0	0	—	89⅓	76	37	37	63		Fair
57.	H.	8/23	Cleve.	2⅔	2	1	1	0	4	0	0	—	92	78	38	37	67	3.71	Good

TRADED TO HOUSTON ASTROS   2 Wins, 1 Loss, 1 Save, 43 Good or Excellent, 14 Bad or Fair

APPEARANCE	HOME OR AWAY	DATE	TEAM	INNINGS PITCHED	HITS	RUNS	EARNED RUNS	WALKS	STRIKEOUTS	RUNNERS ON	RUNNERS SCORED	DECISION	TOTAL INNINGS	TOTAL HITS	TOTAL E. RUNS	TOTAL WALKS	TOTAL STRIKEOUTS	EARNED RUN AVERAGE	EVALUATION
58.	A.	8/26	St. L.	1	0	0	0	0	1	0	0	—							Excellent
59.	H.	8/29	Pitt.	10	9	4	2	4	11	0	0	L	11	9	2	4	12		Excellent
60.	H.	9/2	St. L.	1	2	1	1	1	0	3	3	—	12	11	3	5	12		Fair
61.	H.	9/6	S.F.	3	2	0	0	1	1	0	0	—	15	13	3	6	13		Excellent
62.	H.	9/7	S.F.	1⅔	4	1	1	1	1	0	0	—	16⅔	17	4	7	14		Fair
63.	A.	9/14	Atl.	⅓	0	0	0	0	1	2	0	—	17	17	4	7	15		Excellent
64.	A.	9/15	S.D.	2	1	0	0	1	2	0	0	—	19	18	4	8	17		Excellent
65.	A.	9/16	S.D.	2	0	0	0	2	0	0		—	21	18	4	8	19		Excellent
66.	A.	9/17	S.F.	2	0	0	0	2	0	0	0	S	23	20	4	10	19		Excellent
67.	H.	9/19	Cinn.	2	1	0	0	0	4	0	0	—	25	21	4	10	23	1.44	Excellent
68.	H.	9/21	Cinn.	2	3	1	1	0	3	0	0	—	27	24	5	10	26		Good
69.	H.	9/23	Atl.	0	3	4	4	1	0	0	0	L	27	27	9	11	26		Bad
70.	A.	9/25	Cinn.	⅓	3	1	1	0	1	2	0	—	27⅓	30	10	11	27		Fair
71.	A.	9/26	Cinn.	1	1	1	1	0	2	0	0	—	28⅓	31	11	11	29		Fair
72.	A.	9/27	Cinn.	⅓	2	2	2	0	0	0	0	—	28⅔	32	13	11	29		Bad
73.	A.	10/2	L.A.	2	1	1	1	1	2	0	0	—	30⅔	33	14	12	31	4.11	Good

2 Losses, 1 Save, 10 Good or Excellent, 6 Bad or Fair

TOTALS FOR SEATTLE & HOUSTON   122⅔ 111 52 49 98 3.81

2 Wins, 3 Losses, 2 Saves, 53 Good or Excellent, 20 Bad or Fair

ABOUT THE EDITOR

Leonard Shecter, a New Yorker, attended New York University and was with the New York *Post* for nearly twenty years. After covering a variety of sports for the *Post* as a reporter, Shecter went on to write a sports, and then a general, column. He left the *Post* to free-lance and his articles have appeared in all the major magazines—including *Esquire, Life, Sports Illustrated* and the *New York Times Magazine*. He is now the sports editor of *Look*.

Shecter is also the author of *Roger Maris,* a biography; *The Jocks,* an iconoclastic look at sports in America; and *Once Upon the Polo Grounds,* a nostalgic history of the first two years of the New York Mets.

ABOUT THE AUTHOR

James Alan Bouton (pronounced BOW-ton) was born in New Jersey and grew up in the suburbs of New York and Chicago. He attended Western Michigan University and Fairleigh Dickinson. Signed to a bonus contract with the New York Yankees in 1959. Bouton, now 31, spent three years in the minor leagues before making it with the big club on an energetic fast ball and a big, overhand curve. He won 21 games for the Yankees in 1963 and 18 in 1964, when he also won two World Series games. After a spell of arm trouble, Bouton slid all the way back to the minors and is now making a comeback as a knuckleball pitcher with the Houston Astros.

Always outspoken to his teammates and the baseball hierarchy as well as to the press, Bouton has sometimes engendered the enmity of the Neanderthals of the game. He never let that bother him, or stop him. Although he has never considered writing as a career, Bouton did contribute several articles to *Sport* magazine before undertaking this project.

He is married and lives in suburban New Jersey with his wife and three children, one of them an adopted Korean child.